HIGHWAYS AND
BYWAYS IN SUSSEX

PREFACE

Readers who are acquainted with the earlier volumes of this series will not need to be told that they are less guide-books than appreciations of the districts with which they are concerned. In the pages that follow my aim has been to gather a Sussex bouquet rather than to present the facts which the more practical traveller requires.

The order of progress through the country has been determined largely by the lines of railway. I have thought it best to enter Sussex in the west at Midhurst, making that the first centre, and to zig-zag thence across to the east by way of Chichester, Arundel, Petworth, Horsham, Brighton (I name only the chief centres), Cuckfield, East Grinstead, Lewes, Eastbourne, Hailsham, Hastings, Rye, and Tunbridge Wells; leaving the county finally at Withyham, on the borders of Ashdown Forest. For the traveller in a carriage or on a bicycle this route is not the best; but for those who would explore it slowly on foot (and much of the more characteristic scenery of Sussex can be studied only in this way), with occasional assistance from the train, it is, I think, as good a scheme as any.

I do not suggest that it is necessary for the reader who travels through Sussex to take the same route: he would probably prefer to cover the county literally strip by strip—the Forest strip from Tunbridge Wells to Horsham, the Weald strip from Billingshurst to Burwash, the Downs strip from Racton to Beachy Head—rather than follow my course, north to south, and south to north, across the land. But the book is, I think, the gainer by these tangents, and certainly its author is happier, for they bring him again and again back to the Downs.

It is impossible at this date to write about Sussex, in accordance with the plan of the present series, without saying a great many things that others have said before, and without making use of the historians of the county. To the collections of the Sussex Archæological Society I am greatly indebted; also to Mr. J. G. Bishop's *Peep into the Past*, and to Mr. W. D. Parish's *Dictionary of the Sussex Dialect*. Many other works are mentioned in the text.

The history, archæology, and natural history of the county have been thoroughly treated by various writers; but there are, I have noticed, fewer books than there should be upon Sussex men and women. Carlyle's saying that every clergyman should write the history of his parish (which one might amend to the history of his parishioners) has borne too little fruit in our district; nor have lay observers arisen in any number to atone for the shortcoming. And yet Sussex must be as rich in good character, pure, quaint, shrewd, humorous or noble, as any other division of England. In the matter of honouring illustrious Sussex men and women, the late Mark Antony Lower played his part with *The Worthies of Sussex*, and Mr. Fleet with *Glimpses of Our Sussex Ancestors*; but the Sussex "Characters," where are they? Who has set down their "little unremembered acts," their eccentricities, their sterling southern tenacities? The Rev. A. D. Gordon wrote the history of Harting, and quite recently the Rev. C. N. Sutton has published his interesting *Historical Notes of Withyham, Hartfield, and Ashdown Forest*; and there may be other similar parish histories which I am forgetting. But the only books that I have seen which make a patient and sympathetic attempt to understand the people of Sussex are Mr. Parish's *Dictionary*, Mr. Egerton's *Sussex Folk and Sussex Ways*, and "John Halsham's" *Idlehurst*. How many rare qualities of head and heart must go unrecorded in rural England.

I have to thank my friend Mr. C. E. Clayton for his kindness in reading the proofs of this book and in suggesting additions.

E. V. L.
December 12, 1903.

P.S.—The sheets of the one-inch ordnance map of Sussex are fourteen in all, their numbers running thus:

300 Alresford	301 Haslemere	302 Horsham	303 T. Wells	304 Tenterden
316 Fareham	317 Chichester	318 Brighton	319 Lewes	320 Hastings
331 Portsmouth	332 Bognor	333 Worthing	334 Eastbourne	

THE BARBICAN, LEWES CASTLE.

PREFACE TO THE SECOND EDITION

In the present edition a number of small errors have been corrected and a new *chapter* amplifying certain points and supplying a deficit here and there has been added. The passage about Stane Street is reprinted from the *Times Literary Supplement* by kind permission.

E. V. L.
April 20, 1904

CONTENTS

LIST OF ILLUSTRATIONS

CHAPTER I

MIDHURST

The fitting order of a traveller's progress—The Downs the true Sussex—Fashion at bay—Mr. Kipling's topographical creed—Midhurst's advantages—Single railway lines—Queen Elizabeth at Cowdray—Montagus domestic and homicidal—The curse of Cowdray—Dr. Johnson at Midhurst—Cowdray Park.

If it is better, in exploring a county, to begin with its least interesting districts and to end with the best, I have made a mistake in the order of this book: I should rather have begun with the comparatively dull hot inland hilly region of the north-east, and have left it at the cool chalk Downs of the Hampshire border. But if one's first impression of new country cannot be too favourable we have done rightly in starting at Midhurst, even at the risk of a loss of enthusiasm in the concluding chapters. For although historically, socially, and architecturally north Sussex is as interesting as south Sussex, the crown of the county's scenery is the Downs, and its most fascinating districts are those which the Downs dominate. The farther we travel from the Downs and the sea the less unique are our surroundings. Many of the villages in the northern Weald, beautiful as they are, might equally well be in Kent or Surrey: a visitor suddenly alighting in their midst, say from a balloon, would be puzzled to name the county he was in; but the Downs and their dependencies are essential Sussex. Hence a Sussex man in love with the Downs becomes less happy at every step northward.

THE INVIOLATE HILLS

One cause of the unique character of the Sussex Downs is their virginal security, their unassailable independence. They stand, a silent undiscovered country, between the seething pleasure towns of the seaboard plain and the trim estates of the Weald. Londoners, for whom Sussex has a special attraction by reason of its proximity (Brighton's beach is the nearest to the capital in point of time), either pause north of the Downs, or rush through them in trains, on bicycles, or in carriages, to the sea. Houses there are among the Downs, it is true, but they are old-established, the homes of families that can remember no other homes. There is as yet no fashion for residences in these altitudes. Until that fashion sets in (and may it be far distant) the Downs will remain essential Sussex, and those that love them will exclaim with Mr. Kipling,

> God gave all men all earth to love,
>   But since man's heart is small,
> Ordains for each one spot shall prove
>   Beloved over all.

* * * * *

> Each to his choice, and I rejoice
>   The lot has fallen to me
> In a fair ground—in a fair ground—
>   Yea, Sussex by the sea!

MIDHURST

If we are to begin our travels in Sussex with the best, then Midhurst is the starting point, for no other spot has so much to offer: a quiet country town, gabled and venerable, unmodernised and unambitious, with a river, a Tudor ruin, a park of deer, heather commons, immense woods, and the

Downs only three miles distant. Moreover, Midhurst is also the centre of a very useful little railway system, which, having only a single line in each direction, while serving the traveller, never annoys him by disfiguring the country or letting loose upon it crowds of vandals. Single lines always mean thinly populated country. As a pedestrian poet has sung:—

My heart leaps up when I behold
    A single railway line;
For then I know the wood and wold
    Are almost wholly mine.

And Midhurst being on no great high road is nearly always quiet. Nothing ever hurries there. The people live their own lives, passing along their few narrow streets and the one broad one, under the projecting eaves of timbered houses, unrecking of London and the world. Sussex has no more contented town.

The church, which belongs really to St. Mary Magdalen, but is popularly credited to St. Denis, was never very interesting, but is less so now that the Montagu tomb has been moved to Easebourne. Twenty years ago, I remember, an old house opposite the church was rumoured to harbour a pig-faced lady. I never had sight of her, but as to her existence and her cast of feature no one was in the least doubt. Pig-faced ladies (once so common) seem to have gone out, just as the day of Spring-heeled Jack is over. Sussex once had her Spring-heeled Jacks, too, in some profusion.

COWDRAY.

ELIZABETH AT COWDRAY

Cowdray Park is gained from the High Street, just below the Angel Inn, by a causeway through water meadows of the Rother. The house is now but a shell, never having been rebuilt since the fire which ate out its heart in 1793: yet a beautiful shell, heavily draped in rich green ivy that before very long must here and there forget its earlier duty of supporting the walls and thrust them too far from the perpendicular to stand. Cowdray, built in the reign of Henry VIII., did not come to its full glory until Sir Anthony Browne, afterwards first Viscount Montagu, took possession. The seal was put upon its fame by the visit of Queen Elizabeth in 1591 (Edward VI. had been banqueted there by Sir Anthony in 1552, "marvellously, nay, rather excessively," as he wrote), as some return for the loyalty of her host, who, although an old man, in 1588, on the approach of the Armada, had ridden straightway to Tilbury, with his sons and his grandson, the first to lay the service of his house at her Majesty's feet. A rare pamphlet is still preserved describing the festivities during Queen Elizabeth's sojourn. On Saturday, about eight o'clock, her Majesty reached the house, travelling from Farnham, where she had dined. Upon sight of her loud music sounded. It stopped when she set foot upon the bridge, and a real man, standing between two wooden dummies whom he exactly resembled, began to flatter her exceedingly. Until she came, he said, the walls shook and the roof tottered, but one glance from her eyes had steadied the turret for ever. He went on to call her virtue immortal and herself the Miracle of Time, Nature's Glory, Fortune's Empress, and the World's Wonder. Elizabeth, when he had made an end, took the key from him and embraced Lady Montagu and her daughter, the Lady Dormir; whereupon "the mistress of the house (as it were weeping in the bosome) said, 'O happie time! O joyfull daie!'"

A QUEEN'S DIVERSIONS

These preliminaries over, the fun began. At breakfast next morning three oxen and a hundred and forty geese were devoured. On Monday, August 17th, Elizabeth rode to her bower in the park, took a crossbow from a nymph who sang a sweet song, and with it shot "three or four" deer, carefully brought within range. After dinner, standing on one of the turrets she watched sixteen bucks "pulled down with greyhounds" in a lawn. On Tuesday, the Queen was approached by a pilgrim, who first called her "Fairest of all creatures," and expressed the wish that the world might end with her life and then led her to an oak whereon were hanging escutcheons of her Majesty and all the neighbouring noblemen and gentlemen. As she looked, a "wilde man" clad all in ivy appeared and delivered an address on the importance of loyalty. On Wednesday, the Queen was taken to a goodlie fish-pond (now a meadow) where was an angler. After some words from him a band of fishermen approached, drawing their nets after them; whereupon the angler, turning to her Majesty, remarked that her virtue made envy blush and stand amazed. Having thus spoken, the net was drawn and found to be full of fish, which were laid at Elizabeth's feet. The entry for this day ends with the sentence, "That evening she hunted." On Thursday the lords and ladies dined at a table forty-eight yards long, and there was a country dance with tabor and pipe, which drew from her Majesty "gentle applause." On Friday, the Queen knighted six gentlemen and passed on to Chichester.

A DESPERADO POET

A year later the first Lord Montagu died. He was succeeded by another Anthony, the author of the "Book of Orders and Rules" for the use of the family at Cowdray, and the dedicatee of Anthony Copley's *Fig for Fortune*, 1596. Copley has a certain Sussex interest of his own, having astonished not a little the good people of Horsham. A contemporary letter describes him as "the most desperate youth that liveth. He did shoot at a gentleman last summer, and did kill an ox with a musket, and in Horsham church he threw his dagger at the parish clerk, and it stuck in a seat of the church. There liveth not his like in England for sudden attempts." Subsequently the conspirator-poet must have calmed down, for he states in the dedication to my lord that he is "now winnowed by the fan of grace and Zionry." To-day he would say "saved." Copley, after narrowly escaping capital punishment for his share in a Jesuit plot, disappeared.

The instructions given in Lord Montagu's "Booke of Orders and Rules" illustrate very vividly the generous amplitude of the old Cowdray establishment. Thus:—

MY CARVER AND HIS OFFICE.

I will that my carver, when he cometh to the ewerye boorde, doe there washe together with the Sewer, and that done be armed (videlt.) with an armeinge towell cast about his necke, and putt under his girdle on both sides, and one napkyn on his lefte shoulder, and an other on the same arme; and thence beinge broughte by my Gentleman Usher to my table, with two curteseyes thereto, the one about the middest of the chamber, the other when he cometh to ytt, that he doe stande seemely and decently with due reverence and sylence, untill my dyett and fare be brought uppe, and then doe his office; and when any meate is to be broken uppe that he doe carrye itt to a syde table, which shalbe prepared for that purpose and there doe ytt; when he hath taken upp the table, and delivered the voyder to the yeoman Usher, he shall doe reverence and returne to the ewrye boorde there to be unarmed. My will is that for that day he have the precedence and place next to my Gentleman Usher at the wayter's table.

MY GENTLEMEN WAYTERS.

I will that some of my Gentlemen Wayters harken when I or my wiffe att any tyme doe walke abroade, that they may be readye to give their attendance uppon us, some att one tyme and some att another as they shall agree amongst themselves; but when strangeres are in place, then I will that in any sorte they be readye to doe such service for them as the Gentleman Usher shall directe. I will further that they be dayly presente in the greate chamber or other place of my dyett about tenn of the clocke in the forenoone and five in the afternoone without fayle for performance of my service, unles they have license from my Stewarde or Gentleman Usher to the contrarye, which if they exceede, I will that they make knowne the cause thereof to my Stewarde, who shall acquaynte me therewithall. I will that they dyne and suppe att a table appoynted for them, and there take place nexte after the Gentlemen of my Horse and chamber, accordinge to their seniorityes in my service.

THE HOUSE OF MONTAGU

The third Viscount Montagu was not remarkable, but his account books are quaint reading. From July, 1657, to July, 1658, his steward spent £1,945 10s. solely in little personal matters for his master. Among the disbursements were, on September 11th, fourteen pence "for washing Will Stapler"; on November 22nd, 1s. 4d. to the Lewes carrier "for bringing a box of puddings for my mistress and my master"; on January 17th, £4 to "Mr. Fiske the dancing-master for teaching my master to dance, being two months"; and on April 21st, seven shillings "for a Tooth for my Lord."

The fifth Viscount was a man of violent temper. On reaching Mass one day and finding it half done, he drew his pistol and shot the chaplain. The outcry all over the country was loud and vengeful, and my lord lay concealed for fifteen years in a hiding-hole contrived in the masonry of Cowdray for the shelter of persecuted priests. The peer emerged only at night, when he roamed the close walks, repentant and sad. Lady Montagu would then steal out to him, dressing all in white to such good purpose that the desired rumours of a ghost soon flew about the neighbourhood.

The curse of Cowdray, which, if genuinely pronounced, has certainly been wonderfully fulfilled, dates from the gift of Battle Abbey by Henry VIII. to Sir Anthony Browne, the father of Queen Elizabeth's host and friend. Sir Anthony seized his new property, and turned the monks out of the gates, in 1538. Legend says that as the last monk departed, he warned his despoiler that by fire and water his line should perish. By fire and water it perished indeed. A week after Cowdray House was burned, in 1793, the last Viscount Montagu was drowned in the Rhine. His only sister (the wife of Mr. Stephen Poyntz) who inherited, was the mother of two sons both of whom were drowned while bathing at Bognor. When Mr. Poyntz sold the estate to the Earl of Egmont, we may suppose the curse to have been withdrawn.

DR. JOHNSON AT COWDRAY

Among the treasures that were destroyed in the fire were the Roll of Battle Abbey and many paintings. Dr. Johnson visited Cowdray a few years before its demolition; "Sir," he said to Boswell, "I should like to stay here four-and-twenty hours. We see here how our ancestors lived." According to the *Tour of Great Britain*, attributed to Daniel Defoe, but probably by another hand, Cowdray's hall was of Irish oak. In the large parlour were the triumphs of Henry VIII. by Holbein. In the long gallery were the Twelve Apostles "as large as life"; while the marriage of Cupid and Psyche, a tableau that never failed to please our ancestors, was not wanting.

The glory of the Montagus has utterly passed. The present Earl of Egmont is either an absentee or he lives in a cottage near the gates; and the new house, which is hidden in trees, is of no interest. The park, however, is still ranged by its beautiful deer, and still possesses an avenue of chestnut trees and rolling wastes of turf. It is everywhere as free as a heath.

CHAPTER II

MIDHURST'S VILLAGES

Hanging in chains—A wooded paradise—Fernhurst—Shulbrede Priory—Blackdown—Tennyson's Sussex home—Thomas Otway—Kate Hotspur's Grave—A Sussex ornithologist—The friend of owls—William Cobbett looks at the Squire—The charms of South Harting—Lady Mary Caryll's little difficulties—Gilbert White in Sussex—The old field routine—Witchcraft at South Harting—The Rother—Easebourne— West Lavington and Cardinal Manning.

The road from Midhurst to Blackdown ascends steadily to Henley, threading vast woods and preserves. On the left is a great common, on the right North Heath, where the two Drewitts were hanged in chains after being executed at Horsham, in 1799, for the robbery of the Portsmouth mail—probably the last instance of hanging in chains in this country. For those that like wild forest country there was once no better ramble than might be enjoyed here; but now (1903) that the King's new sanatorium is being built in the midst of Great Common, some of the wildness must necessarily be lost. A finer site could not have been found. Above Great Common is a superb open space nearly six hundred feet high, with gorse bushes advantageously placed to give shelter while one studies the Fernhurst valley, the Haslemere heights and, blue in the distance, the North Downs. Sussex has nothing wilder or richer than the country we are now in.

A few minutes' walk to the east from this lofty common, and we are immediately above Henley, clinging to the hill side, an almost Alpine hamlet. Henley, however, no longer sees the travellers that once it did, for the coach road, which of old climbed perilously through it, has been diverted in a curve through the hanger, and now sweeps into Fernhurst by way of Henley Common.

BLACKDOWN.

FERNHURST

Fernhurst, beautifully named, is in an exquisite situation among the minor eminences of the Haslemere range, but the builder has been busy here, and the village is not what it was.

SHULBREDE PRIORY

Two miles to the north-west, on the way to Linchmere, immediately under the green heights of Marley, is the old house which once was Shulbrede Priory. As it is now in private occupation and is not shown to strangers, I have not seen it; but of old many persons journeyed thither, attracted by the quaint mural paintings, in the Prior's room, of domestic animals uttering speech. "Christus natus est," crows the cock. "Quando? Quando?" the duck inquires. "In hac nocte," says the raven. "Ubi? Ubi?" asks the cow, and the lamb satisfies her: "Bethlehem, Bethlehem."

One may return deviously from Shulbrede to Midhurst (passing in the heart of an unpopulated country a hamlet called Milland, where is an old curiosity shop of varied resources) by way of one of the pleasantest and narrowest lanes that I know, rising and falling for miles through silent woods, coming at last to Chithurst church, one of the smallest and simplest and least accessible in the county, and reaching Midhurst again by the hard, dry and irreproachable road that runs between the heather of Trotton Common.

On the eastern side of Fernhurst, to which we may now return, a mile on the way to Lurgashall, was once Verdley Castle; but it is now a castle no more, merely a ruined heap. Utilitarianism was too much for it, and its stones fell to Macadam. After all, if an old castle has to go, there are few better forms of reincarnation for it than a good hard road. While at Fernhurst it is well to walk on to Blackdown, the best way, perhaps, being to take the lane to the right about half a mile beyond the village, and make for the hill across country. Blackdown, whose blackness is from its heather and its firs, frowns before one all the while. The climb to the summit is toilsome, over nine hundred feet, but well worth the effort, for the hill overlooks hundreds of square miles of Sussex and Surrey, between Leith Hill in the north and Chanctonbury in the south.

Aldworth, Tennyson's house, is on the north-east slope, facing Surrey. The poet laid the foundation stone on April 23 (Shakespeare's birthday), 1868: the inscription on the stone running "Prosper thou the work of our hands, O prosper thou our handiwork." Of the site Aubrey de Vere wrote:—"It lifted England's great poet to a height from which he could gaze on a large portion of that English land which he loved so well, see it basking in its most affluent summer beauty, and only bounded by 'the inviolate sea.' Year after year he trod its two stately terraces with men the most noted of their time." Pilgrims from all parts journeyed thither—not too welcome; among them that devout American who had worked his way across the Atlantic in order to recite *Maud* to its author: a recitation from which, says the present Lord Tennyson, his father "suffered." Tennyson has, I think, no poems upon his Sussex home, but I always imagine that the dedication of *The Death of Œnone and other Poems*, in 1894, must belong to Blackdown:—

There on the top of the down,
The wild heather round me and over me June's high blue,
When I look'd at the bracken so bright and the heather so brown,
I thought to myself I would offer this book to you,
This, and my love together,
To you that are seventy-seven,
With a faith as clear as the heights of the June-blue heaven,
And a fancy as summer-new
As the green of the bracken amid the gloom of the heather.

The most interesting village between Midhurst and the western boundary, due west, is Trotton, three miles distant on the superb road to Petersfield, of which I have spoken above. There is no better road in England. Trotton is quiet and modest, but it has two great claims on lovers of the English drama. In the "Ode to Pity" of one of our Sussex poets we read thus of another:—

But wherefore need I wander wide
To old Ilissus' distant side,
  Deserted streams and mute?
Wild Arun, too, has heard thy strains,
And echo, 'midst my native plains,
  Been soothed by pity's lute.

There first the wren thy myrtles shed
On gentlest Otway's infant head,
  To him thy cell was shown;
And while he sung the female heart,
With youth's soft notes unspoiled by art,
  Thy turtles mixed their own.

THOMAS OTWAY

So wrote William Collins, adding in a note that the Arun (more properly the Rother, a tributary of the Arun) runs by the village of Trotton, in Sussex, where Thomas Otway had his birth. The unhappy author of *Venice Preserv'd* and *The Orphan* was born at Trotton in 1652, the son of Humphrey Otway, the curate, who afterwards became rector of Woolbeding close by. Otway died miserably when only thirty-three, partly of starvation, partly of a broken heart at the unresponsiveness of Mrs. Barry, the actress, whom he loved, but who preferred the Earl of Rochester. His two best plays, although they are no longer acted, lived for many years, providing in Belvidera, in *Venice Preserv'd* and Monimia, in *The Orphan* (in which he "sung the female heart") congenial *rôles* for tragic actresses—Mrs. Barry, Mrs. Oldfield, Mrs. Cibber, Mrs. Siddons and Miss O'Neill. Otway was buried in the churchyard of St. Clement Danes, but a tablet to his fame is in Trotton church, which is of unusual plainness, not unlike an ecclesiastical barn. Here also is the earliest known brass to a woman—Margaret de Camoys, who lived about 1300.

HOTSPUR'S LADY

The transition is easy (at Trotton) from Otway to Shakespeare, from *Venice Preserv'd* to *Henry IV*.

Hotspur (to Lady Percy). Come, Kate, thou art perfect in lying down: come quick, quick; that I may lay my head in thy lap.
Lady P. Go, ye giddy goose.
[*The music plays.*

> *Hot.*   Now I perceive, the devil understands Welsh;
> And 't is no marvel' he's so humorous,
> By'r lady, he's a good musician.

Lady P. Then should you be nothing but musical; for you are altogether governed by humours. Lie still, ye thief, and hear the lady sing in Welsh.
Hot. I had rather hear Lady, my brach, howl in Irish.
Lady P. Wouldst have thy head broken?
Hot. No.
Lady P. Then be still.
Hot. Neither: 'tis a woman's fault.
Lady P. Now God help thee!
Hot. To the Welsh lady's bed.
Lady P. What's that?
Hot. Peace! she sings.
[*A Welsh song sung by* Lady Mortimer.
Hot. Come, Kate, I'll have your song too.

Lady P. Not mine, in good sooth.

Hot. Not yours, in good sooth! 'Heart, you swear like a comfit-maker's wife. 'Not you, in good sooth'; and, 'As true as I live'; and,

> 'As God shall mend me'; and, 'As sure as day':
> And giv'st such sarcenet surety for thy oaths,
> As if thou never walk'dst further than Finsbury.
> Swear me, Kate, like a lady as thou art,
> A good mouth-filling oath; and leave 'in sooth,'
> And such protest of pepper-gingerbread,
> To velvet-guards and Sunday-citizens.
> Come, sing.

Lady P. I will not sing.

Hot. 'Tis the next way to turn tailor, or be redbreast teacher. An the indentures be drawn, I'll away within these two hours; and so come in when ye will.

[*Exit.*

My excuse for introducing this little scene is that Kate, whose real name was Elizabeth, lies here. Her tomb is in the chancel, where she reposes beside her second husband Thomas, Lord Camoys, beneath a slab on which are presentments in brass of herself and her lord. It was this Lord Camoys who rebuilt Trotton's church, about 1400, and who also gave the village its beautiful bridge over the Rother at a cost, it used to be said, of only a few pence less than that of the church.

Trotton has still other literary claims. At Trotton Place lived Arthur Edward Knox, whose *Ornithological Rambles in Sussex*, published in 1849, is one of the few books worthy to stand beside White's *Natural History of Selborne*. In Sussex, as elsewhere, the fowler has prevailed, and although rare birds are still occasionally to be seen, they now visit the country only by accident, and leave it as soon as may be, thankful to have a whole skin. Guns were active enough in Knox's time, but to read his book to-day is to be translated to a new land. From time to time I shall borrow from Mr. Knox's pages: here I may quote a short passage which refers at once to his home and to his attitude to those creatures whom he loved to study and studied to love:—"I have the satisfaction of exercising the rites of hospitality towards a pair of barn owls, which have for some time taken up their quarters in one of the attic roofs of the ancient, ivy-covered house in which I reside. I delight in listening to the prolonged snoring of the young when I ascend the old oak stairs to the neighbourhood of their nursery, and in hearing the shriek of the parent birds on the calm summer nights as they pass to and fro near my window; for it assures me that they are still safe; and as I know that at least a qualified protection is afforded them elsewhere, and that even their arch-enemy the gamekeeper is beginning reluctantly, but gradually, to acquiesce in the general belief of their innocence and utility, I cannot help indulging the hope that this bird will eventually meet with that general encouragement and protection to which its eminent services so richly entitle it."

COBBETT LOOKS AT THE SQUIRE

One more literary association: it was at Trotton that William Cobbett looked at the squire. "From Rogate we came on to Trotton, where a Mr. Twyford is the squire, and where there is a very fine and ancient church close by the squire's house. I saw the squire looking at some poor devils who were making 'wauste improvements, ma'am,' on the road which passes by the squire's door. He looked uncommonly hard at me. It was a scrutinising sort of look, mixed, as I thought, with a little surprise, if not of jealousy, as much as to say, 'I wonder who the devil you can be?' My look at the squire was with the head a little on one side, and with the cheek drawn up from the left corner of the mouth, expressive of anything rather than a sense of inferiority to the squire, of whom, however, I had never heard speak before."

HARTING'S RICHES

By passing on to Rogate, whose fine church not long since was restored too freely, and turning due south, we come to what is perhaps the most satisfying village in all Sussex—South Harting. Cool and spacious and retired, it lies under the Downs, with a little subsidiary range of its own to shelter it also from the west. Three inns are ready to refresh the traveller— the Ship, the White Hart (a favourite Sussex sign), and the Coach and Horses (with a new signboard of dazzling freshness); the surrounding country is good; Petersfield and Midhurst are less than an hour's drive distant; while the village has one of the most charming churches in Sussex, both without and within. Unlike most of the county's spires, South Harting's is slate and red shingle, but the slate is of an agreeable green hue, resembling old copper. (Perhaps it is copper.) The roof is of red tiles mellowed by weather, and the south side of the tower is tiled too, imparting an unusual suggestion of warmth—more, of comfort—to the structure; while on the east wall of the chancel is a Virginian creeper, which, as autumn advances, emphasises this effect. Within, the church is winning, too, with its ample arches, perfect proportions, and that æsthetic satisfaction that often attends the cruciform shape. An interesting monument of the Cowper and Coles families is preserved in the south transept—three full-size coloured figures. In the north transept is a spiral staircase leading to the tower, and elsewhere are memorials of the Fords and Featherstonhaughs of Up-Park, a superb domain over the brow of Harting's Down, and of the Carylls of Lady Holt, of whom we shall see more directly. The east window is a peculiarly cheerful one, and the door of South Harting church is kept open, as every church door should be, but as too many in Sussex are not.

In the churchyard, beneath a shed, are the remains of two tombs, with recumbent stone figures, now in a fragmentary state. At the church gates are the old village stocks.

MRS. JONES' MULYGRUBES

Harting has a place in literature, for one of the Carylls was Pope's friend, John (1666-1736), a nephew of the diplomatist and dramatist. Pope's Caryll, who suggested *The Rape of the Lock*, lived at Lady Holt at West Harting (long destroyed) and also at West Grinstead, where, as we shall see, the poem was largely written. Mr. H. D. Gordon, rector of Harting for many years, wrote a history of his parish in 1877: a very interesting, gossipy book; where we may read much of the Caryll family, including passages from their letters—how Lady Mary Caryll had the kind impulse to take one of the parson's nine daughters to France to educate and befriend, but was so thoughtless as to transform into a pretty Papist; how Lady Mary disliked Mrs. Jones, the steward's wife; and many other matters. I quote a passage from a letter of Lady Mary's about Mrs. Jones, showing that human nature was not then greatly different from what it is to-day:—"Mr. Joans and his fine Madam came down two days before your birthday and expected to lye in the house, but as I apprehended the consequence of letting them begin so, I made an excuse for want of roome by expecting company, and sent them to Gould's [Arthur Gould married Kate Caryll, and lived at Harting Place], where they stayed two nights. I invited them the next day to dinner and they came, but the day following Madam huff'd (I believe), for she went away to Barnard's, and wou'd not so much as see the desert [dessert]; however, I don't repent it, he has been here at all the merryment, and I believe you'll find it better to keep them at a civil distance than other ways, for she seems a high dame and not very good humoured, for she has been sick ever since of the mulygrubes." Mrs. Jones soon afterwards succumbed either to the mulygrubes or a worse visitation. Lady Mary thus broke the news:—"Mr. Jones's wife dyed on Sunday, just as she lived, an Independent, and wou'd have no parson with her, because she sayd she cou'd pray as well as they. He is making a great funerall, but I believe not in much affection, for he was all night at a merry bout two days before she died."

On the arrival of the young Squire Caryll at Lady Holt with his bride, in 1739, Paul Kelly, the bailiff, informed Lady Mary that the villagers conducted their lord and lady home "with the upermost satisfaction"—a good phrase.

Mr. Gordon writes elsewhere in his book of a famous writer whom Hampshire claims: "For at least forty years (1754-1792) Gilbert White was an East Harting squire. The bulk of his property was at Woodhouse and Nye woods, on the northern slope of East Harting, and bounded on the west by the road to Harting station. The passenger from Harting to the railway has on his right, immediately opposite the 'Severals' wood, Gilbert White's Farm, extending nearly to the station. White had also other Harting lands. These were upon the Downs, viz.:—a portion of the Park of Uppark on the south side, and a portion of Kildevil Lane, on the North Marden side of Harting Hill. Gilbert White was on his mother's side a Ford, and these lands had been transmitted to him through his great uncle, Oliver Whitby, nephew to Sir Edward Ford."

THE OLD FIELD ROUTINE

A glimpse of the old Sussex field routine, not greatly changed in the remote districts to-day, was given to Mr. Gordon thirty years ago by an aged labourer. This was the day:—"Out in morning at four o'clock. Mouthful of bread and cheese and pint of ale. Then off to the harvest field. Rippin and moen [reaping and mowing] till eight. Then morning brakfast and small beer. Brakfast—a piece of fat pork as thick as your hat [a broad-brimmed wideawake] is wide. Then work till ten o'clock: then a mouthful of bread and cheese and a pint of strong beer ['farnooner,' i.e., forenooner; 'farnooner's-lunch,' we called it]. Work till twelve. Then at dinner in the farm-house; sometimes a leg of mutton, sometimes a piece of ham and plum pudding. Then work till five, then a *nunch* and a quart of ale. Nunch was cheese, 'twas skimmed cheese though. Then work till sunset, then home and have supper and a pint of ale. I never knew a man drunk in the harvest field in my life. Could drink six quarts, and believe that a man might drink two gallons in a day. All of us were in the house [*i.e.*, the usual hired servants, and those specially engaged for the harvest]: the yearly servants used to go with the monthly ones.

"There were two thrashers, and the head thrasher used always to go before the reapers. A man could cut according to the goodness of the job, half-an-acre a day. The terms of wages were £3 10*s.* to 50*s.* for the month.

"When the hay was in cock or the wheat in shock, then the Titheman come; you didn't dare take up a field without you let him know. If the Titheman didn't come at the time, you tithed yourself. He marked his sheaves with a bough or bush. You couldn't get over the Titheman. If you began at a hedge and made the tenth cock smaller than the rest, the Titheman might begin in the middle just where he liked. The Titheman at Harting, old John Blackmore, lived at Mundy's [South Harting Street]. His grandson is blacksmith at Harting now. All the tithing was quiet. You didn't dare even set your eggs till the Titheman had been and ta'en his tithe. The usual day's work was from 7 to 5."

A SUSSEX WITCH

Like all Sussex villages, Harting has had its witches and possessors of the evil eye. Most curious of these was old Mother Digby (*née* Mollen), who, in Mr. Gordon's words, lived at a house in Hog's Lane, East Harting, and had the power of witching herself into a hare, and was continually, like Hecate, attended by dogs. Squire Russell, of Tye Oak, always lost his hare at the sink-hole of a drain near by the old lady's house. One day the dogs caught hold of the hare by its hind quarters, but it escaped down the drain, and Squire Russell, instantly opening the old beldame's door, found her rubbing the part of her body corresponding to that by which the hound had seized the hare. Squire Caryll, however, declined to be hard on the broomstick and its riders, as the following entry in the records of the Court Leet, held for the Hundred of Dumford in 1747, shows:—"Also we present the Honble. John Caryll, Esq., Lord of this Mannor, for not having and keeping a Ducking Stool within the said Hundred of Dumford according to law, for the ducking of scolds and other disorderly persons."

THE BEACON FIRES

The road from South Harting to Elsted runs under the hills, which here rise abruptly from the fields, to great heights, notably Beacon Hill, like a huge green mammoth, 800 feet high, on which, before the days of telegraphy, lived the signaller, who passed on the tidings of danger on the coast to the next beacon hill, above Henley, and so on to London. In the days of Napoleon, when any moment might reveal the French fleet, the Sussex hill tops must often have smouldered under false alarms. The next hill in the east is Treyford Hill, above Treyford village, whose church tower, standing on a little hill of its own nearly three hundred feet high, might take a lesson in beauty from South Harting's, although its spire has a slenderness not to be improved. Next to Treyford Hill is Didling Hill, above Didling, and then Linch Down, highest of all in these parts, being 818 feet.

Elsted, which has no particular interest, possesses an inn, the Three Horse Shoes, on a site superior to that of many a nobleman's house. It stands high above a rocky lane, commanding a superb sidelong view of the Downs and the Weald.

Midhurst's river is the Rother (not to be confounded with the Rother in the east of Sussex), which flows into the Arun near Hardham. It is wide enough at Midhurst for small boats, and is a very graceful stream on which to idle and watch the few kingfishers that man has spared. One may walk by its side for miles and hear no sound save the music of repose—the soft munching of the cows in the meadows, the chuckle of the water as a rat slips in, the sudden yet soothing plash caused by a jumping fish. Around one's head in the evening the stag-beetle buzzes with its multiplicity of wings and fierce lobster-like claws out-stretched.

Following the Rother to the west one comes first to Easebourne, a shady cool village only a few steps from Midhurst, once notable for its Benedictine Priory of nuns. Henry VIII. put an end to its religious life, which, however, if we may believe the rather disgraceful revelations divulged at an episcopal examination, for some years had not been of too sincere a character. In Easebourne church is the handsome tomb of the first Viscount Montagu (the host of Queen Elizabeth), which was brought hither from Midhurst church some forty years ago. Beyond Easebourne, on the banks of the Rother, is Woolbeding, amid lush grass and foliage, as green a spot as any in green England.

MR. LA THANGUE'S HOME

On the eastern side of the town (with a diversion into Queen Elizabeth's sombre wood-walk) one may come by the side of the river part of the way to West Lavington, which stands high on a slope facing the Downs, with pine woods immediately beneath it, perhaps as fair a site as any church can claim. The grave of Richard Cobden, the Free Trader, a native of Heyshott, near by, is in the churchyard. Here, in 1850, Henry Edward Manning, afterwards Cardinal, preached his last sermon for the Church of England. It is, indeed, Manning country, for besides being curate and rector of Woollavington with Graffham (four or five miles to the south-east) from 1833 until his secession, he was for nine years Archdeacon of Chichester; he married Miss Sargent, daughter of the late rector and sister of Mrs. Samuel Wilberforce of Woollavington; and while rector, he rebuilt both churches. Graffham is interesting also as being the present home of one of the most truthful of living painters, Mr. Henry La Thangue, whose scenes of peasants at work (in the manner of Barbizon) and studies of sunlight spattering through the trees are among the triumphs of modern English art.

41

CIDER'S DISAPPEARANCE

One more village and we will make for the hills. A mile beyond the eastern gate of Cowdray Park is Lodsworth, still a paradise of apple orchards, but no longer famous for its cider as once it was. Arthur Young had the pleasure of tasting some Lodsworth cider of a superior quality at Lord Egremont's table at the beginning of the last century, but I doubt if Petworth House honours the beverage to-day. Cider, except in the cider country, becomes less and less common.

COWDRAY.

CHAPTER III

FIRST SIGHT OF THE DOWNS

The Sussex hills—Gilbert White's praise—Britons, Romans, Saxons—
Charles the Second's ride through Sussex.

Between Midhurst and Chichester, our next centre, rise the Downs, to
a height of between seven hundred and eight hundred feet. Although we
shall often be crossing them again before we leave the county, I should
like to speak of them a little in this place.

The Downs are the symbol of Sussex. The sea, the Weald, the heather
hills of her great forest district, she shares with other counties, but the
Downs are her own. Wiltshire, Berkshire, Kent and Hampshire, it is true,
have also their turf-covered chalk hills, but the Sussex Downs are vaster,
more remarkable, and more beautiful than these, with more individuality
and charm. At first they have been known to disappoint the traveller, but
one has only to live among them or near them, within the influence of
their varying moods, and they surely conquer. They are the smoothest
things in England, gigantic, rotund, easy; the eye rests upon their gentle
contours and is at peace. They have no sublimity, no grandeur, only the
most spacious repose. Perhaps it is due to this quality that the Wealden
folk, accustomed to be overshadowed by this unruffled range, are so
deliberate in their mental processes and so averse from speculation or
experiment. There is a hypnotism of form: a rugged peak will alarm the
mind where a billowy green undulation will lull it. The Downs change
their complexion, but are never other than soothing and still: no stress

of weather produces in them any of that sense of fatality that one is conscious of in Westmoreland. Thunder-clouds empurple the turf and blacken the hangers, but they cannot break the imperturbable equanimity of the line; rain throws over the range a gauze veil of added softness; a mist makes them more wonderful, unreal, romantic; snow brings them to one's doors. At sunrise they are magical, a background for Malory; at sunset they are the lovely home of the serenest thoughts, a spectacle for Marcus Aurelius. Their combes, or hollows, are then filled with purple shadow cast by the sinking sun, while the summits and shoulders are gold.

GILBERT WHITE IN SUSSEX

Gilbert White has an often-quoted passage on these hills:—"Though I have now travelled the Sussex downs upwards of thirty years, yet I still investigate that chain of majestic mountains with fresh admiration year by year, and I think I see new beauties every time I traverse it. This range, which runs from Chichester eastward as far as East Bourn, is about sixty miles in length, and is called the South Downs, properly speaking, only round Lewes. As you pass along you command a noble view of the wild, or weald, on one hand, and the broad downs and sea on the other. Mr. Ray used to visit a family [Mr. Courthope, of Danny] just at the foot of these hills, and was so ravished with the prospect from Plumpton Plain, near Lewes, that he mentions those scapes in his *Wisdom of God in the Works of the Creation* with the utmost satisfaction, and thinks them equal to anything he had seen in the finest parts of Europe. For my own part, I think there is somewhat peculiarly sweet and amusing in the shapely-figured aspect of the chalk hills in preference to those of stone, which are rugged, broken, abrupt, and shapeless. Perhaps I may be singular in my opinion, and not so happy as to convey to you the same idea; but I never contemplate these mountains without thinking I perceive somewhat analogous to growth in their gentle swellings and smooth fungus-like protuberances, their fluted sides, and regular hollows and slopes, that carry at once the air of vegetative dilatation and expansion:—Or, was there even a time when these immense masses of calcareous matter were thrown into fermentation by some adventitious moisture, were raised and leavened into such shapes by some plastic power; and so made to swell and heave their broad backs into the sky, so much above the less animated clay of the wild below?"

The Downs have a human and historic as well as scenic interest. On many of their highest points are the barrows or graves of our British ancestors, who, could they revisit the glimpses of the moon, would find little change, for these hills have been less interfered with than any district within twice the distance from London. The English dislike of climbing has saved them. They will probably be the last stronghold of the horse when petrol has ousted him from every other region.

ROMAN AND SAXON

After the Briton came the Roman, to whose orderly military mind such a chain of hills seemed a series of heaven-sent earthworks. Every point in a favourable position was at once fortified by the legionaries. Standing upon these ramparts to-day, identical in general configuration in spite of the intervening centuries, one may imagine one's self a Cæsarian soldier and see in fancy the hinds below running for safety.

After the Romans came the Saxons, who did not, however, use the heights as their predecessors had. Yet they left even more intimate traces, for, as I shall show in a later chapter on *Sussex dialect*, the language of the Sussex labourer is still largely theirs, the farms themselves often follow their original Saxon disposition, the field names are unaltered, and the character of the people is of the yellow-haired parent stock. Sussex, in many respects, is still Saxon. In a poem by Mr. W. G. Hole is a stanza which no one that knows Sussex can read without visualising instantly a Sussex hill-side farm:—

The Saxon lies, too, in his grave where the plough-lands swell;
  And he feels with the joy that is Earth's
  The Spring with its myriad births;
  And he scents as the evening falls
  The rich deep breath of the stalls;
And he says, "Still the seasons bring increase and joy to the world—It
  is well!"

THE ESCAPE OF CHARLES II.

Standing on one of these hills above the Hartings one may remember an event in English history of more recent date than any of the periods that we have been recalling—the escape of Charles II in 1651. It was over these Downs that he passed; and it has been suggested that a traveller wishing for a picturesque route across the Downs might do well to follow his course.

According to the best accounts Charles was met, on the evening of October 13, near Hambledon, in Hampshire (afterwards to be famous as the cradle of first-class cricket), by Thomas and George Gunter of Racton, with a leash of greyhounds as if for coursing. The King slept at the house of Thomas Symonds, Gunter's brother-in-law, in the character of a Roundhead. The next morning at daybreak, the King, Lord Wilmot and the two Gunters crossed Broad Halfpenny Down (celebrated by Nyren), and proceeding by way of Catherington Down, Charlton Down, and Ibsworth Down, reached Compting Down in Sussex. At Stanstead House Thomas Gunter left the King, and hurried on to Brighton to arrange for the crossing to France. The others rode on by way of the hills, with a descent from Duncton Beacon, until they reached what promised to be the security of Houghton Forest. There they were panic-stricken nearly to meet Captain Morley, governor of Arundel Castle, and therefore by no means a King's man. The King, on being told who it was, replied merrily, "I did not much like his starched mouchates." This peril avoided, they descended to Houghton village, where the Arun was crossed, and so to Amberley, where in Sir John Briscoe's castle the King slept.[1]

ROUNDHEADS OUTWITTED

On Amberley Mount the King's horse cast a shoe, necessitating a drop to one of the Burphams, at Lee Farm, to have the mishap put right. Ascending the hills again the fugitives held the high track as far as Steyning. At Bramber they survived a second meeting with Cromwellians, three or four soldiers of Col. Herbert Morley of Glynde suddenly appearing, but being satisfied merely to insult them. At Beeding, George Gunter rode on by way of the lower road to Brighton, while the King and Lord Wilmot climbed the hill at Horton, crossing by way of White Lot to Southwick, where, according to one story, in a cottage at the west of the Green was a hiding-hole in which the King lay until Captain Nicholas Tattersall of Brighton was ready to embark him for Fécamp. George Gunter's own story is, however, that the King rode direct to Brighton. He reached Fécamp on October 16. Two hours after Gunter left Brighton, "soldiers came thither to search for a tall black man, six feet four inches high"—to wit, the Merry Monarch.

Such is the bare narrative of Charles' Sussex ride. If the reader would have it garnished and spiced he should turn to the pages of Ainsworth's *Ovingdean Grange*, where much that never happened is set forth as entertainingly (or so I thought when I read it as a boy) as if it were truth.

FOOTNOTE:

1 That is the story as the Amberley people like to have it, but another version makes him ride from Hambledon to Brighton in one day; in which case he may have avoided Amberley altogether.

CHAPTER IV

CHICHESTER

William Collins—The Smiths of Chichester—Hardham's snuff—C. R. Leslie's reminiscence—The headless Ravenswood—Chichester Cathedral—Roman Chichester—Mr. Spershott's recollections—A warning to swearers—The prettiest alms-house in England.

I have already quoted some lines by Collins on Otway; it is time to come to Collins himself.

> When Music, heavenly maid, was young,
> While yet in early Greece she sung,
> The Passions oft, to hear her shell,
> Throng'd around her magic cell—

The perfect ode which opens with these unforgettable lines belongs to Chichester, for William Collins was born there on Christmas Day, 1721, and educated there, at the Prebendal school, until he went to Winchester. William Collins was the son of the Mayor of Chichester, a hatter, from whom Pope's friend Caryll bought his hats. I have no wish to tell here the sad story of Collins' life; it is better to remember that few as are his odes they are all of gold. He died at Chichester in 1759, and was buried in St. Andrew's Church.

With eyes up-raised, as one inspired,
Pale Melancholy sat retired;
And, from her wild sequester'd seat,
In notes by distance made more sweet,
Pour'd through the mellow horn her pensive soul:
And, dashing soft from rocks around
Bubbling runnels join'd the sound;
Through glades and glooms the mingled measure stole,
Or, o'er some haunted stream, with fond delay,
Round an holy calm diffusing,
Love of peace, and lonely musing,
In hollow murmurs died away.

GEORGE SMITH'S ECLOGUE

Collins is Chichester's great poet. She had a very agreeable minor poet, too, in George Smith, one of the Three Smiths—all artists: William, born in 1707, painter of portraits and of fruit and flower pieces, and George and John, born in 1713 and 1717, who painted landscapes,—known collectively as the Smiths of Chichester. I mention them rather on account of George Smith's poetical experiments than for the brothers' fame as artists; but there is such a pleasant flavour in one at least of his *Pastorals* that I have copied a portion of it. It is called "The Country Lovers; or, Isaac and Marget going to Town on a Summer's Morning." The town is probably Chichester—certainly one in Sussex and near the Downs. Isaac speaks first:—

Come! Marget, come!—the team is at the gate!
Not ready yet!—you always make me wait!

I omit a certain amount of the dialogue which follows, but at last Marget exclaims:—

Well, now I'm ready, long I have not staid.

Isaac.

One kiss before we go, my pretty maid.

Marget.

Go! don't be foolish, Isaac—get away!
Who loiters now?—I thought I could not stay!
There!—that's enough! why, Isaac, sure you're mad!

Isaac.

One more, my dearest girl—

Marget.

Be quiet, lad.
See both my cap and hair are rumpled o'er!
The tying of my beads is got before!

Isaac.

There let it stay, thy brighter blush to show,
Which shames the cherry-colour'd silken bow.
Thy lips, which seem the scarlet's hue to steal,
Are sweeter than the candy'd lemon peel.

Marget.

Pray take these chickens for me to the cart;
Dear little creatures, how it grieves my heart
To see them ty'd, that never knew a crime,
And formed so fine a flock at feeding time!

The pretty poem ends with fervid protestations of devotion from Isaac:—

For thee the press with apple-juice shall foam!
For thee the bees shall quit their honey-comb!
For thee the elder's purple fruit shall grow!
For thee the pails with cream shall overflow!

But see yon teams returning from the town,
Wind in the chalky wheel-ruts o'er the down:
We now must haste; for if we longer stay,
They'll meet us ere we leave the narrow way.

Another of Chichester's illustrious sons is Archbishop Juxon, who stood by the side of Charles I. on the scaffold and bade farewell to him in the words "You are exchanging from a temporal to an eternal crown— a good exchange."

HARDHAM'S SNUFF

Yet another, of a very different type, is John Hardham. "When they talked of their Raphaels, Correggios, and stuff," wrote Goldsmith of Sir Joshua Reynolds,

He shifted his trumpet, and only took snuff.

Had it not been for Chichester the great painter might never have had the second of these consolations, for the only snuff he liked was Hardham's No. 37, and Hardham was a native of Chichester. Before he became famous as a tobacconist, Hardham was, by night, a numberer of the pit for Garrick at Drury Lane. One day he happened to blend Dutch and rappee and poured the mixture into a drawer labelled 37. Garrick so liked the pinch of it which he chanced upon, that he introduced a reference to its merits in some of his comic parts, with the result that Hardham's little shop in Fleet Street soon became a resort, and no nose was properly furnished without No. 37. As Colton wrote, in his *Hypocrisy*:—

A name is all. From Garrick's breath a puff
Of praise gave immortality to snuff;
Since which each connoisseur a transient heaven
Finds in each pinch of Hardham's 37.

The wealth that came to the tobacconist he left to the city of Chichester to relieve it of certain of its poor rates; and the citizens still magnify Hardham's name. He died in 1772 and had the good sense to restrict the expense of his funeral to ten pounds.

WILKIE'S BUMPS

Chichester was the scene of a pleasant incident recorded by Leslie in his *Autobiographical Recollections*. He was staying with Wilkie at Petworth, the guest of their patron, and the patron of so many other painters, Lord Egremont, of whom we shall learn more when Petworth is reached. They all drove over to Chichester after a visit to Goodwood. Lord Egremont, says Leslie, "had some business to transact at Chichester; but one of his objects was to show us a young girl, the daughter of an upholsterer, who was devoted to painting, and considered to be a genius by her friends. She was not at home; but her mother said she could soon be found, 'if his lordship would have the goodness to wait a short time.' The young lady soon appeared, breathless and exhausted with running. Lord Egremont mentioned our names, and she said, looking up to Wilkie with an expression of great respect, 'Oh, sir! it was but yesterday I had your head in my hands.' This puzzled him, as he did not know she was a phrenologist.

"'And what bumps did you find?' said Lord Egremont.

"'The organ of veneration, very large,' was her answer; and Wilkie, making her a profound bow, said:

"'Madam, I have a great veneration for genius.'

"She showed us an unfinished picture from *The Bride of Lammermoor*. The figure of Lucy Ashton was completed, and, she told us, was the portrait of a young friend of hers; but Ravenswood was without a head, and this she explained by saying, 'there are no handsome men in Chichester. But,' she continued, her countenance brightening, 'the Tenth are expected here soon.'" (The Tenth was noted for its handsome officers.)

Leslie does not carry the story farther. Whether poor Ravenswood ever gained his head; whether if he did so it was a military one, or, as a last resource, a Chichester one; and where the picture, if completed, now is, I do not know, nor have I succeeded in discovering any more of the young lady. But passing through the streets of the town I was conscious of the absence of the Tenth.

Chichester is a perfect example of an English rural capital, thronged on market days with tilt carts, each bringing a farmer or farmer's wife, and rich in those well-stored ironmongers' shops that one never sees elsewhere. But it is more than this: it is also a cathedral town, with the ever present sense of domination by the cloth even when the cloth is not visible. Chichester has its roughs and its public houses (Mr. Hudson in his *Nature in Downland* gives them a caustic chapter); it also has its race-week every July, and barracks within hail; yet it is always a cathedral town. Whatever noise may be in the air you know in your heart that quietude is its true characteristic. One might say that above the loudest street cries you are continually conscious of the silence of the close.

CHICHESTER CATHEDRAL.

CHICHESTER CATHEDRAL

Chichester's cathedral is not among the most beautiful or the most interesting, but there is none cooler. It dates from the eleventh century and contains specimens of almost every kind of church architecture; but the spire is comparatively new, having been built in 1866 to take the place of its predecessor, which suddenly dropped like an extinguisher five years before. Seen from the Channel it rises, a friendly landmark (white or gray, according to the clouds), and while walking on the Downs above or on the plain around, one is frequently pleased to catch an unexpected glimpse of its tapering beauty. I have heard it said that Chichester is the only English cathedral that is visible at sea.

Within, the cathedral is disappointing, offering one neither richness on the one hand nor the charm of pure severity on the other. A cathedral must either be plain or coloured, and Chichester comes short of both ideals; it has no colour and no purity. Its proportions are, however, exquisite, and it is impossible to remain here long without passing under the spell of the stone. Yet had it, one feels, only radiance, how much finer it would be.

For the completest contrast to the vastness of the cathedral one may cross into North Street and enter the portal of the toy church of St. Olave, which dates from the 14th century, and is remarkable, not only for its minuteness, but as being one of the churches of Chichester which, in my experience, is not normally locked and barred.

ROMAN CHICHESTER

That Chichester was built by the Romans in the geometrical Roman way you may see as you look down from the Bell Tower upon its four main streets—north, south, east and west—east becoming Stane-street and running direct to London. Chichester then was Regnum. On the departure of the Romans, Cissa, son of Ella, took possession, and the name was changed to Cissa's Ceastre, hence Chichester. Remnants of the old walls still stand; and a path has been made on the portion running from North Street down to West Gate.

A CLERICAL STRONGHOLD

More attractive, because more human, than the cathedral itself are its precincts: the long resounding cloisters, the still, discreet lanes populous with clerics, and most of all that little terrace of ecclesiastical residences parallel with South Street, in the shadow of the mighty fane, covered with creeping greenness, from wistaria to ampelopsis, with minute windows, inviolable front doors and trim front gardens, which (like all similar settlements) remind one of alms-houses carried out to the highest power. Surely the best of places in which to edit Horace afresh or find new meanings in St. Augustine.

CHICHESTER CROSS.

There is a tendency for the cathedral to absorb all the attention of the traveller, but Chichester has other beauties, including the Market Cross, which is a mere child of stone, dating only from the reign of Henry VIII.; St. Mary's Hospital in North Street; and the remains of the monastery of the Grey Friars in the Priory Park. Young Chichester now plays cricket where of old the monks caught fish and performed their duties. It was probably on the mound that their Calvary stood; the last time I climbed it was to watch Bonnor, the Australian giant, practising in the nets below, too many years ago.

Like all cathedral towns Chichester has beautiful gardens, as one may see from the campanile. There are no lawns like the lawns of Bishops, Deans, and Colleges; and few flower beds more luxuriantly stocked. Chichester also has a number of grave, solid houses, such as Miss Austen's characters might have lived in; at least one superb specimen of the art of Sir Christopher Wren, a masterpiece of substantial red brick; and a noble inn, the Dolphin, where one dines in the Assembly room, a relic of the good times before inns became hotels.

SPERSHOTT'S RECOLLECTIONS

We have some glimpses of old Chichester in the reminiscences (about 1720-1730) of James Spershott, a Chichester Baptist Elder, who died in 1789, aged eighty. I quote a passage here and there from his paper of recollections printed in the Sussex Archæological Collections:—

"Spinning of Household Linnen was in use in most Families, also making their own Bread, and likewise their own Household Physick. No Tea, but much Industrey and good Cheer. The Bacon racks were loaded with Bacon, for little Porke was made in these times. The farmers' Wifes and Daughters were plain in Dress, and made no such gay figures in our Market as nowadays. At Christmas, the whole Constellation of Pattypans which adorn'd their Chimney fronts were taken down. The Spit, the Pot, the Oven, were all in use together; the Evenings spent in Jollity, and their Glass Guns smoking Top'd the Tumbler with the froth of Good October, till most of them were slain or wounded, and the Prince of Orange, and Queen Ann's Marlborough, could no longer be resounded . . ."

THE DEATH OF A SWEARER

Here is Mr. Spershott's account of a Chichester calamity:—"Jno. Page, Esq., native of this city, coming from London to Stand Candidate

Here, a great number of voters went on Horseback to meet him. Among the rest Mr. Joshua Lover, a noted School Master, a sober man in the general but of flighty Passions. As he was setting out, one of his Scollers, Patty Smith (afterwards my Spouse) asked him for a Coppy, and in haste he wrote the following:—

Extreames beget Extreames, Extreames avoid
Extreames without Extreames are not Enjoyed.

"He set off in High Carrier, and turning down Rooks's Hill before the Sqr., rideing like a madman To and fro, forward and backward Hallooing among the Company, the Horse at full speed fell with him and kill'd him. A Caution to the flighty and unsteady; and a verification of his Coppy." Again: "Robt. Madlock, a most Prophane Swarer, being Employ'd in Cleaning the outside of the Steeple," fell, owing to a breaking rope, and soon after died. Mr. Spershott adds: "A warning to Swarers." Another entry states: "In my younger years there were many very large corpulent Persons in the City, both of Men and Women. I could now recite by name between twenty and thirty, the great part of that number so Prodigious that like other animals Thoroughly fatted, they could hardly move about."

One of Chichester's epitaphs runs thus:—

Here lies a true soldier, whom all must applaud;
Much hardship he suffer'd at home and abroad;
But the hardest engagement he ever was in,
Was the battle of Self in the conquest of Sin.

THE PERFECT ALMSHOUSE

I have left until the last the prettiest thing in this city of comely streets and houses—St. Mary's Hospital, at the end of Lion Street (out of North

Street): the quaintest almshouse in the world. The building stands back, behind the ordinary houses, and is gained by a passage and a courtyard. You then enter what seems to be a church, for at the far end is an altar beneath an unmistakably ecclesiastical window. But when the first feeling of surprise has passed, you discover that there is only a small chancel at the east end of the building, on either side of which are little dwellings. Each of these is occupied by a nice little old woman, who has two rooms, very minute and cosy, with a little supply of faggots close at hand, and all the dignity of a householder, although the occupant only of an infinitesimal toy house within a house. How do they agree, one wonders, these little old ladies of a touchy age under their great roof?

Different accounts are given of the origin of St. Mary's Hospital. Mr. Lower says that it was founded in 1229 for a chaplain and thirteen bedesmen. In 1562 a warden and five inmates were the prescribed occupants. Now there are eight sets of rooms, each with its demure tenant, all of whom troop into the little chapel at fixed hours. Mrs. Evans, sacristan, who does the honours, would tell me nothing as to the process of selection by which she and the seven other occupants came to be living there; all that she could say was that she was very happy to be a Hospitaller, and that by no possibility could one of the little domiciles ever fall to me.

THE RUINED NAVE OF BOXGROVE.

CHAPTER V

CHICHESTER AND THE HILLS.

Goodwood—The art of being a park—The Cenotaph of Lord Darnley—
Boxgrove—Cowper at Eastham—The Charlton Hunt—A famous
run—Huntsman and Saint—Present day hunting in Sussex—Mr. Knox's
delectable day with his gun—Kingly Bottom—The best white violets—
A demon bowler—Two epitaphs.

Chichester may have a cathedral and a history, but nine out of ten
strangers know of it only as a station for Goodwood race-course; towards
which, in that hot week at the end of July, hundreds of carriages toil by
the steep road that skirts the Duke of Richmond and Gordon's park.

Goodwood Park gives me little pleasure. I miss the deer; and when
the first park that one ever knew was Buxted, with its moving antlers
above the brake fern, one almost is compelled to withhold the word park
from any enclosure without them. It is impossible to lose the feeling that
the right place for cattle—even for Alderneys—is the meadow. Cows in
a park are a poor makeshift; parks are for deer. To my eyes Goodwood
House has a chilling exterior; the road to the hill-top is steep and lengthy;
and when one has climbed it and crossed the summit wood, it is to come
upon the last thing that one wishes to find in the heart of the country,
among rolling Downs, sacred to hawks and solitude—a Grand Stand and
the railings of a race-course! Race-courses are for the outskirts of towns,
as at Brighton and Lewes; or for hills that have no mystery and no magic,

like the heights of Epsom; or for such mockeries of parks as Sandown and Kempton. The good park has many deer and no race-course.

And yet Goodwood is superb, for it has some of the finest trees in Sussex within its walls, including the survivors of a thousand cedars of Lebanon planted a hundred and fifty years ago; and with every step higher one unfolds a wider view of the Channel and the plain. Best of these prospects is, perhaps, that gained from Carne's seat, as the Belvedere to the left of the road to the racecourse is called; its name deriving from an old servant of the family, whose wooden hut was situated here when Carne died, and whose name and fame were thus perpetuated. The stones of the building were in part those of old Hove church, near Brighton, then lately demolished.

THE CENOTAPH OF DARNLEY

In Goodwood House, which is shown on regular days, are fine Vandycks and Lelys, relics of the two Charles', and above all the fascinatingly absorbing "Cenotaph of Lord Darnley," a series of scenes in the life of that ill-fated husband. It may be said that among all the treasures of Sussex there is nothing quite so interesting as this.

BOXGROVE PRIORY CHURCH.

BOXGROVE

Leaving Chichester by East Street (or Stane Street, the old Roman road to London) one comes first to West Hampnett, famous as the birthplace, in 1792, of Frederick William Lillywhite, the "Nonpareil" bowler, whom we shall meet again at Brighton. A mile and a half beyond is Halnaker, midway between two ruins, those of Halnaker House to the north and Boxgrove Priory to the south. Of the remains of Halnaker House, a Tudor mansion, once the home of the De la Warrs, little may now be seen; but Boxgrove is still very beautiful, as Mr. Griggs' drawings prove. The Priory dates from the reign of Henry I., when it was founded very modestly for three Benedictine monks, a number which steadily grew. Seven Henries later came its downfall, and now nothing remains but some exquisite Norman arches and a few less perfect fragments.

Boxgrove church is an object of pilgrimage for antiquaries and architects, the vaulting being peculiarly interesting. At the Halnaker Arms in 1902 was a landlady whom few cooks could teach anything in the matter of pastry.

THE EARTHAM DILLETANTE

The next village on Stane Street, or rather a little south of it, about two miles beyond Halnaker, is Eartham; which brings to mind William Hayley, the friend and biographer of Cowper and the author of *The Triumphs of Temper*, perhaps the least read of any book that once was popular. Hayley succeeded his father as squire of Eartham; here he entertained Cowper and other friends; here Romney painted. When need came for retrenchment, Hayley let Eartham to Huskisson, the statesman, and moved to Felpham, on the coast, where we shall meet with him again. Cowper's occupations upon this charming Sussex hillside are recorded in Hayley's account of the visit: "*Homer* was not the immediate object of our attention while Cowper resided at Eartham. The morning hours that we could bestow on books were chiefly devoted to a complete revisal and correction of all the translations, which my friend had finished, from the Latin and Italian poetry of Milton; and we generally amused ourselves after dinner in forming together a rapid metrical version of Andreini's *Adamo*. But the constant care which the delicate health of Mrs. Unwin required rendered it impossible for us to be very assiduous in study, and perhaps the best of all studies was to promote and share that most singular and most exemplary tenderness of attention with which Cowper incessantly laboured to counteract every infirmity, bodily and mental, with which sickness and age had conspired to load this interesting guardian of his afflicted life . . . The air of the south infused a little portion of fresh strength into her shattered frame, and to give it all possible efficacy, the boy, whom I have mentioned, and a young associate and fellow student of his, employed themselves regularly twice a day in drawing this venerable cripple in a commodious garden-chair round the airy hill of Eartham. To

Cowper and to me it was a very pleasing spectacle to see the benevolent vivacity of blooming youth thus continually labouring for the ease, health, and amusement of disabled age."

COWPER IN SUSSEX

The poet and Mrs. Unwin, after much trepidation and doubt, had left Weston Underwood on August 1, 1792; they slept at Barnet the first night, Ripley the next, and were at Eartham by ten o'clock on the third. They stayed till September. Cowper describes Hayley's estate as one of the most delightful pleasure grounds in the world. "I had no conception that a poet could be the owner of such a paradise, and his house is as elegant as his scenes are charming." The poet, apart from his rapid treatment of *Adamo*, did not succeed independently in attaining to Hayley's fluency among these surroundings. "I am in truth so unaccountably local in the use of my pen," he wrote to Lady Hesketh, "that, like the man in the fable, who could leap well nowhere but at Rhodes, I seem incapable of writing at all except at Weston." Hence the only piece that he composed in our county was the epitaph on Fop, a dog belonging to Lady Throckmorton. But while he was at Eartham Romney drew his portrait in crayons.

BOXGROVE FROM THE SOUTH.

Cowper always looked back upon his visit with pleasure, but, as he remarked, the genius of Weston Underwood suited him better—"It has an air of snug concealment in which a disposition like mine feels itself peculiarly gratified; whereas now I see from every window woods like forests and hills like mountains—a wilderness, in short, that rather increases my natural melancholy . . . Accordingly, I have not looked out for a house in Sussex, nor shall."

The simplest road from Chichester to the Downs is the railway. The little train climbs laboriously to Singleton, and then descends to Cocking and Midhurst. By leaving it at Singleton one is quickly in the heart of this vast district of wooded hills, sometimes wholly forested, sometimes, as in West Dean park, curiously studded with circular clumps of trees.

THE CHARLTON HUNT

The most interesting spot to the east of the line is Charlton, once so famous among sporting men, but now, alas, unknown. For Charlton was of old a southern Melton Mowbray, the very centre of the aristocratic hunting county. The Charlton Hunt had two palmy periods: before the Duke of Monmouth's rebellion, and after the accession of William III. Monmouth and Lord Grey kept two packs, the Master being Squire Roper. With the fall of Monmouth Roper fled to France, to hunt at Chantilly, but on the accession of William III. he returned to Sussex, the hounds resumed their old condition, and the Charlton pack became the most famous in the world. On the death of Mr. Roper—in the hunting field, in 1715, at the age of eighty-four—the Duke of Bolton took the Mastership, which he held until the charms of Miss Fenton the actress (the Polly Peachum of *The Beggars' Opera*) lured him to the tents of the women. Then came the glorious reign of the second Duke of Richmond, when sport with the Charlton was at its height. The Charlton Hunt declined upon his death, in 1750, became known as the Goodwood Hunt, and wholly ceased to be at the beginning of the last century.

The crowning glory of the Charlton Hunt was the run of Friday, January 26, 1738, which is thus described in an old manuscript:—

A FAMOUS RUN

A FULL AND IMPARTIAL ACCOUNT OF THE REMARKABLE CHASE AT CHARLTON, ON FRIDAY, 26TH JANUARY, 1738.

It has long been a matter of controversy in the hunting world to what particular country or set of men the superiority belonged. Prejudices and partiality have the greatest share in their disputes, and every society their proper champion to assert the pre-eminence and bring home the trophy to their own country. Even Richmond Park has the Dymoke. But on Friday, the 26th of January, 1738, there was a decisive engagement on the plains of Sussex, which, after ten hours' struggle, has settled all further debate and given the brush to the gentlemen of Charlton.

PRESENT IN THE MORNING:—

The Duke of Richmond, Duchess of Richmond, Duke of St Alban's, the Lord Viscount Harcourt, the Lord Henry Beauclerk, the Lord Ossulstone, Sir Harry Liddell, Brigadier Henry Hawley, Ralph Jennison, master of His Majesty's Buck Hounds, Edward Pauncefort, Esq., William Farquhar, Esq., Cornet Philip Honywood, Richard Biddulph, Esq., Charles Biddulph, Esq., Mr. St. Paul, Mr. Johnson, Mr. Peerman, of Chichester; Mr. Thomson, Tom Johnson, Billy Ives, Yeoman Pricker to His Majesty's Hounds; David Briggs and Nim Ives, Whippers-in.

At a quarter before eight in the morning the fox was found in Eastdean Wood, and ran an hour in that cover; then into the Forest, up to Puntice Coppice through Heringdean to the Marlows, up to Coney Coppice, back to the Marlows, to the Forest West Gate, over the fields to Nightingale Bottom, to Cobden's at Draught, up his Pine Pit Hanger, where His Grace of St. Alban's got a fall; through My Lady Lewknor's Puttocks, and missed the earth; through Westdean Forest to the corner of Collar Down (where Lord Harcourt blew his first horse), crossed the Hackney-place down the length of Coney Coppice, through the Marlows to Heringdean, into the Forest and Puntice Coppice, Eastdean Wood, through the Lower Teglease across by Cocking Course down between Graffham and Woolavington, through Mr. Orme's Park and Paddock over the Heath to Fielder's Furzes, to the Harlands, Selham, Ambersham, through Todham Furzes, over Todham Heath, almost to Cowdray Park, there turned to the limekiln at the end of Cocking Causeway, through Cocking Park and Furzes; there crossed the road and up the hills between Bepton and Cocking. Here the unfortunate Lord Harcourt's second horse felt the effects of long legs and a sudden steep; the best thing that belonged to him was his saddle, which My Lord had secured; but, by bleeding and Geneva (contrary to Act of Parliament) he recovered, and with some difficulty was got home. Here Mr. Farquhar's humanity claims your regard, who kindly sympathised with My Lord in his misfortunes, and had not power to go beyond him. At the bottom of Cocking Warren the hounds turned to the left across the road by the barn near Heringdean, then took the side near to the north-gate of the Forest (Here General Hawley thought it prudent to change his horse for a true-blue that staid up the hills). Billy Ives likewise took a horse of Sir Harry Liddell's, went quite through the Forest and run the foil through Nightingale Bottom to Cobden at Draught, up his Pine Pit Hanger to My Lady Lewknor's Puttocks, through every mews she went in the morning; went through the Warren above Westdean (where we dropt Sir Harry Liddell) down to Benderton Farm (here Lord Harry sank), through Goodwood Park (here the Duke of Richmond chose to send three lame horses back to Charlton, and took Saucy Face and Sir William, that were luckily at Goodwood; from thence, at a distance, Lord Harry was seen driving his horse before him to Charlton). The hounds went out at the upper end of the Park over Strettington-road by Sealy Coppice (where His Grace of Richmond got a summerset), through Halnaker Park over Halnaker Hill to Seabeach Farm (here the Master of the Stag Hounds, Cornet Honywood, Tom Johnson, and Nim Ives were thoroughly satisfied), up Long Down, through Eartham Common fields and Kemp's High Wood (here Billy Ives tried his second horse and took Sir William, by which the Duke of St. Alban's had no great coat, so returned to Charlton). From Kemp's High Wood the hounds took away through Gunworth Warren, Kemp's Rough Piece, over Slindon Down to Madehurst Parsonage (where Billy came in with them), over Poor Down up to Madehurst, then down to Houghton Forest, where His Grace of Richmond, General Hawley, and Mr. Pauncefort came in (the latter to little purpose, for, beyond the Ruel Hill, neither Mr. Pauncefort nor his horse Tinker cared to go, so wisely returned to his impatient friends), up the Ruel Hill, left Sherwood on the right hand, crossed Ofham Hill to Southwood, from thence to South Stoke to the wall of Arundel River, where the glorious 23 hounds put an end to the campaign, and killed an old bitch fox, ten minutes before six. Billy Ives, His Grace of Richmond, and General Hawley were the only persons in at the death, to the immortal honour of 17 stone, and at least as many campaigns.

JOHNSON THE EXEMPLAR

In Singleton church is a record of the Charlton Hunt in the shape of a memorial to one of the huntsmen, the moral of which seems to be that we must all be huntsmen too:—

"Near this place lies interred
THOMAS JOHNSON,
who departed this life at Charlton,
December 20th, 1774.

"From his early inclination to fox-hounds, he soon became an experienced huntsman. His knowledge in the profession, wherein he had no superior, and hardly an equal, joined to his honesty in every other particular, recommended him to the service, and gained him the approbation, of several of the nobility and gentry. Among these were the Lord CONWAY, Earl of CARDIGAN, the Lord GOWER, the Duke of MARLBOROUGH, the Hon. M. SPENCER. The last master whom he served, and in whose service he died, was CHARLES, Duke of RICHMOND, LENNOX, and AUBIGNY, who erected this monument in memory of a good and faithful servant, as a reward to the deceased, and an incitement to the living.
'GO, and do thou likewise.' (St. Luke, x. 37).

'Here Johnson lies; what human can deny
Old Honest Tom the tribute of a sigh?
Deaf is that ear which caught the opening sound;
Dumb that tongue which cheer'd the hills around.
Unpleasing truth: Death hunts us from our birth
In view, and men, like foxes, take to earth.'"

THE SUSSEX PACKS

A few words on the packs of Sussex at the present time may be interesting in this connection. Chief is the Southdown Fox Hounds, a very fine, fast pack brought to a high state of perfection by the late master, the Hon. Charles Brand. They hunt the open and hill country between the Adur and Cuckmere, between Haywards Heath and the sea. In the north are the Crawley and Horsham Fox Hounds, which have large woodlands, high hedges, and some stiff ploughed soil to their less easy lot. The hounds are bigger and heavier than the South Downers. Smaller packs are Lord Leconfield's Fox Hounds, which have the Charlton country; the Eastbourne Fox Hounds, to which the East Sussex Fox Hounds allotted a share of the western part of their country east of the Cuckmere; and the Burstow and Eridge packs. Of Harriers, the best are the Brighton Harriers, so long hunted by Mr. Hugh Gorringe of Kingston-by-Sea, a very smart pack lately covering the ground between the Adur and Falmer, and now adding the Brookside Harriers' country to their own domain, the two packs having been amalgamated. In the east are the Bexhill Harriers and the Hailsham Harriers; and in the west the South Coast Harriers, for the Chichester country. Sussex, in addition to possessing the Warnham Staghounds, is much raided by the Surrey Staghounds. The Crowhurst Otter Hounds also visit the Sussex streams now and then. Foot Beagles may be numerous but I know only of the Brighton pack.

MR. KNOX'S SETTER

And here let me give Mr. Knox's description of a day's shooting, in the gentlemanly way, on the Sussex Downs, following, in his *Ornithological Rambles*, upon some remarks on the battue. "How different is the pursuit of the pheasant with the aid of spaniels in the thick covers of the weald, or tracking him with a single setter among some of the wilder portions of the forest range!—intently observing your dog and anticipating the wily artifices of some old cock, with spurs as long as a dragon's, who will sometimes lead you for a mile through bog, brake, fern, and heather, before the sudden drop of your staunch companion, and a rigidity in all his limbs, satisfy you that you have at last compelled the bird to squat under that wide holly-bush, from whence you kick him up, and feel some little exultation as you bring him down with a snap-shot, having only caught a glimpse of him through the evergreen boughs, as he endeavoured to escape by a rapid flight at the opposite side of the tree.

A SUSSEX BAG

"And then the woodcock-shooting in November—I must take you back once more to my favourite Downs. With the first full moon during that month, especially if the wind be easterly or the weather calm, arrive flights of woodcocks, which drop in the covers, and are dispersed among the bushy valleys, and even over the heathery summits of the hills. If it should happen to be a propitious year for beech-mast—the great attraction to pheasants on the Downs, as is the acorn in the weald—you may procure partridges, pheasants, hares, and rabbits in perhaps equal proportions, with half a dozen woodcocks to crown the bag.

EAST LAVANT.

"The extensive, undulating commons and heaths dotted with broken patches of Scotch firs and hollies on the ferruginous sand north of the Downs, afford—where the manorial rights are enforced—still greater variety of sport. On this wild ground, accompanied by my spaniels and an old retriever, and attended only by one man, to carry the game, I have enjoyed as good sport as mortal need desire on this side of the Tweed. Here is a rough sketch of a morning's work.

PARTRIDGE AND WOODCOCK

"Commencing operations by walking across a turnip-field, two or three coveys spring wildly from the farther end, and fly, as I expect, to the adjoining common, where they are marked down on a brow thickly clothed with furze. Marching towards them with spaniels at heel, up jumps a hare under my nose, then another, then a rabbit. I reload rapidly, and on reaching the gorse 'put in' the dogs. Whirr! there goes a partridge! The spaniels drop to the report of my gun, but the fluttering wings of the dying bird rouse two of his neighbours before I am ready, and away they fly, screaming loudly. The remainder are flushed in detail and I succeed in securing the greater part of them. Now for the next covey. They were marked down in that little hollow where the heather is longer than usual—a beautiful spot! But before I reach it, up they all spring in an unexpected quarter; that cunning old patriarch at their head had cleverly called them together to a naked part of the hill from whence he could observe my manœuvres, and a random shot sent after him with hearty good will proved totally ineffective.

"Now the spaniels are worming through the thick sedges on either side of the brook which intersects the moor, and by their bustling anxiety it is easy to see that game is afoot. Keeping well in front of them, I am just in time for a satisfactory right and left at two cock pheasants, which they had hunted down to the very edge of the water before they could persuade them to take wing. Now for that little alder coppice at the further end of the marshy swamp. Hark to that whipping sound so different from the rush of the rising pheasant or the drumming flight of the partridge! I cannot see the bird, but I know it is a woodcock. This must be one of his favourite haunts, for I perceive the tracks of his feet and the perforations of his bill in every direction on the black mud around. Mark! again. A second is sprung, and as he flits between the naked alders a snap-shot stops his career. I now emerge at the farther end, just where the trees are thinner than elsewhere. A wisp of snipes utter their well-known cry and scud over the heath; one of these is secured. The rest fly towards a little pool of dark water lying at a considerable distance from the common, a well-known rendezvous for those birds. Cautiously approaching, down wind, I reach the margin. Up springs a snipe; but just as my finger is on the trigger, and when too late to alter my intention, a duck and mallard rise from among the rushes and wheel round my head. One barrel is fortunately left, and the drake comes tumbling to the ground. Three or four pheasants, another couple of woodcocks, a few more snipes, a teal or two, and half a dozen rabbits picked up at various intervals, complete the day's sport, and I return home, better pleased with myself and my dogs than if we had compassed the destruction of all the hares in the county, or assisted at the immolation of a perfect hecatomb of pheasants."

KINGLY BOTTOM

Kingly Bottom is the most interesting spot to the west of Singleton. One may reach it either through Chilgrove, or by walking back towards Chichester as far as Binderton House, turning then to the right and walking due west for a couple of miles. Report says that the yews in Kingly Bottom, or Kingly Vale, mark a victory of Chichester men over a party of marauding Danes in 900, and that the dead were buried beneath the barrows on the hill. The story ought to be true. The vale is remarkable for its grove of yews, some of enormous girth, which extends along the bottom to the foot of the escarpment. The charge that might be brought against Sussex, that it lacks sombre scenery and the elements of dark romance, that its character is too open and transparent, would be urged to no purpose in Kingly Vale, which, always grave and silent, is transformed at dusk into a sinister and fantastic forest, a home for witchcraft and unquiet spirits.

So it seems to me; but among the verses of Bernard Barton, the Quaker poet and the friend of Charles Lamb, I lately chanced upon a sonnet "written on hearing it remarked that the scenery [of Kingly Bottom] was too gloomy to be termed beautiful; and that it was also associated with dolorous recollections of Druidical sacrifices." In this poem Barton takes a surprisingly novel line. "Nay, nay, it is not gloomy" he begins, and the end is thus:—

Nor fancy Druid rites have left a stain
   Upon its gentle beauties:—loiter there
   In a calm summer night, confess how fair
Its moonlight charms, and thou wilt learn how vain
And transitory Superstition's reign
   Over a spot which gladsome thoughts may share.

The ordinary person, not a poet, would, I fear, prefer to think of Kingly Bottom's Druidical past.

THE MARDEN VIOLETS

The last time I was in Kingly Bottom—it was in April—after leaving the barrows on the summit of the Bow Hill, above the Vale, I walked by devious ways to East Marden, between banks thick with the whitest and sweetest of sweet white violets. East Marden, however, has no inn and is therefore not the best friend of the traveller; but it has the most modest and least ecclesiastical-looking church in the world, and by seeking it out I learned two secrets: the finest place for white violets and the finest place to keep a horse. There is no riding country to excel this hill district between Singleton and the Hampshire border.

At the neighbouring village of Stoughton, whither I meant to walk (since an inn is there) was born, in 1783, the terrible George Brown— Brown of Brighton—the fast bowler, whose arm was as thick as an ordinary man's thigh. He had two long stops, one of whom padded his chest with straw. A long stop once held his coat before one of Brown's balls, but the ball went through it and killed a dog on the other side. Brown could throw a 4½ oz. ball 137 yards, and he was the father of seventeen children. He died at Sompting in 1857.

CHURCHYARD POETRY

Of Racton, on the Hampshire border, and its association with Charles II., I have already spoken. Below, it is Westbourne, a small border village in whose churchyard are two pleasing epitaphs. Of Jane, wife of Thomas Curtis, who died in 1719, it is written:—

She was like a lily fresh and green,
Soon cast down and no more seen.

and of John Cook:

Pope said an honest man
Is the noblest work of God.
If Pope's assertion be from error clear,
One of God's noblest works lies buried here.

BOSHAM.

CHAPTER VI

CHICHESTER AND THE PLAIN

Bosham and history—An expensive pun—The Bosham bells—Chidham wheat—The Manhood peninsula—Selsey's adders—Selsey Bill—St. Wilfrid and the Sussex heathen—Pagham Harbour in its palmy days—Bognor—Felpham's great rider—Mr. Hayley and Mrs. Opie—An epitaph and a poem—A fairy's funeral—William Blake in Sussex—The trial of a traitor.

On leaving Chichester West Street becomes the Portsmouth Road and passes through Fishbourne, a pleasant but dusty village. A mile or so beyond, and a little to the south, is Bosham, on one of the several arms of Chichester Harbour, once of some importance but now chiefly mud. Bosham is the most interesting village in what may be called the Selsey peninsula. Yet how has its glory diminished! What is now a quiet abode of fishermen and the tarrying-place of yachtsmen and artists (there are few Royal Academy exhibitions without the spire of Bosham church) has been in its time a very factory of history. Vespasian's camp was hard by, and it is possible that certain Roman remains that have been found here were once part of his palace. Bosham claims to be the scene of Canute's encounter with the encroaching tide; which may be the case, although one has always thought of the king rebuking his flatterers rather by the margin of the ocean itself than inland at an estuary's edge. But beyond question Canute had a palace here, and his daughter was buried in the church.

A COSTLY PUN

Earl Godwin, father of Harold, last of the Saxons, dwelt here also. "Da mihi basium"—give me a kiss—he is fabled to have said to Archbishop Aethelnoth, and on receiving it to have taken the salute as acquiescence in the request—"Da mihi Bosham": probably the earliest and also the most expensive recorded example in England of this particular form of humour.

It was from Bosham that Harold sailed on that visit to the Duke of Normandy which resulted in the battle of Hastings. In the Bayeux tapestry he may be seen riding to Bosham with his company, and also putting up prayers for the success of his mission. Of this success we shall see more when we come to Battle. Bosham furthermore claims Hubert of Bosham, the author of the *Book of Becket's Martyrdom*, who was with Saint Thomas of Canterbury when the assassins stabbed him to the death.

The church is of great age; it is even claimed that the tower is the original Saxon. The circumstance that in the representation of the edifice in the Bayeux tapestry there is no tower has been urged against this theory, although architectural realism in embroidery has never been very noticeable. The bells (it is told) were once carried off in a Danish raid; but they brought their captors no luck—rather the reverse, since they so weighed upon the ship that she sank. When the present bells ring, the ancient submerged peal is said to ring also in sympathy at the bottom of the Channel—a pretty habit, which would suggest that bell metal is happily and wisely superior to changes of religion, were it not explained by the unromantic principles of acoustics.

A heavy pole, known as the staff of Bevis of Southampton (and Arundel), was of old kept in Bosham church.

At high water Bosham is the fair abode of peace. When every straggling arm of the harbour is brimming full, when their still surfaces reflect the sky with a brighter light, and the fishing boats ride erect, Bosham is serenely beautiful and restful. But at low tide she is a slut: the withdrawing floods lay bare vast tracts of mud; the ships heel over into attitudes disreputably oblique; stagnation reigns.

CHIDHAM WHEAT

Chidham, by Bosham, is widely famous for its wheat. Chidham White, or Hedge, wheat was first produced a little more than a century ago by Mr. Woods, a farmer. He noticed one afternoon (probably on a Sunday, when farmers are most noticing) an unfamiliar patch of wheat growing in a hedge. It contained thirty ears, in which were fourteen hundred corns. Mr. Woods carefully saved it and sowed it. The crop was eight pounds and a half. These he sowed, and the crop was forty eight gallons. Thus it multiplied, until the time came to distribute it to other farmers at a high price. The cultivation of Chidham wheat by Mr. Woods at one side of the county, synchronised with the breeding of the best Southdown sheep by John Ellman at the other, as we shall see later.

South of Chichester stretches the Manhood peninsula, of which Selsey is the principal town: the part of Sussex most neglected by the traveller. In a county of hills the stranger is not attracted by a district that might almost have been hewn out of Holland. But the ornithologist knows its value, and in a world increasingly bustling and progressive there is a curious fascination in so remote and deliberate a region, over which, even in the finest weather and during the busiest harvest, a suggestion of desolation broods. Nothing, one feels, can ever introduce Success into this plain, and so thinking, one is at peace.

THE MONOTONY OF MANHOOD

A tramway between Chichester and Selsey has to some extent opened up the east side of the peninsula, but the west is still remote and will probably remain so. The country is, however, not interesting: a dead level of dusty road and grass or arable land, broken only by hedges, dykes, white cottages, and the many homesteads within their ramparts of wind-swept elms. Wheat and oats are the prevailing crops, still for the most part cut and bound by hand. Of the villages in the centre of the peninsula Sidlesham is the most considerable, with its handsome square church tower and its huge red tide-mill, now silent and weather-worn, standing mournfully at the head of the dry harbour of Pagham, whose waters once turned its wheels. On the west, on the shores of the Bosham estuary, or Chichester Harbour, are the sleepy amphibious villages of Appledram, famous once for its salt and its smugglers, Birdham, and Earnley. Let no one be tempted to take a direct line across the fields from Selsey to Earnley, for dykes and canals must effectually stop him. Indeed, cross country walking in this part of the country is practically an impossibility, except by continuous deviations and doublings. In attempting one day to reach Earnley from Selsey in this way (after giving up the beach in despair), I came upon several adders, and I once found one crossing a road absolutely in Selsey.

Selsey is a straggling white village, or town, over populous with visitors in summer, empty, save for its regular inhabitants, in winter. The oldest and truest part of Selsey is a fishing village on the east shore of the Bill, a little settlement of tarred tenements and lobster pots. Selsey church, now on the confines of the town, once stood a mile or more away; whither it was removed (the stones being numbered) and, like Temple Bar, again set up. The chancel was, however, not removed, but left desolate in the fields.

Selsey Bill is a tongue of land projecting into a shallow sea. A lighthouse being useless to warn strange mariners of the sandbanks of this district, a lightship known as the Owers flashes its rays far out in the channel. The sea has played curious pranks on the Selsey coast. Beneath the beach and a large tract of the sea now lies what was once, four hundred years ago, a park of deer, which in its most prosperous day extended for miles. The shallow water covering it is still called the park by the fishermen, who drop their nets where the bucks and does of Selsey were wont to graze.

SUSSEX REPELS ST. WILFRID

But the sea has obliterated more than the pasturage of the deer; a mile distant from the present shore stood the first monastery erected in Sussex after Wilfrid's conversion of the South Saxons to Christianity. Although Saint Wilfrid eventually found a home in Sussex and worked hard among its people, his first attempt to bring Christianity to the county was, according to his friend Edda's *Vita Wilfridi*, ill-starred. I quote the story:—

"A great gale blowing from the South-east, the swelling waves threw them on the unknown coast of the South Saxons. The sea too left the ship and men, and retreating from the land and leaving the shore uncovered, retired into the depths of the abyss.

"And the heathen, coming with a great army, intended to seize the ship, to divide the spoil of money, to take them captives forthwith, and to put to the sword those who resisted. To whom our great bishop spoke gently and peaceably, offering much money, wishing to redeem their souls.

"But they with stern and cruel hearts like Pharaoh would not let the people of the Lord go, saying proudly that, 'All that the sea threw on the land became as much theirs as their own property.'

"And the idolatrous chief priest of the heathen, standing on a lofty mound, strove like Balaam to curse the people of God, and to bind their hands by his magic arts.

"Then one of the bishop's companions hurled, like David, a stone, blessed by all the people of God, which struck the cursing magician in the forehead and pierced his brain, when an unexpected death surprised, as it did Goliath, falling back a corpse in sandy places.

"The heathen therefore preparing to fight, vainly attacked the people of God. But the Lord fought for the few, even as Gideon by the command of the Lord, with 300 warriors slew at one attack 12,000 of the Midianites.

82

"And so the comrades of our holy bishop, well-armed and brave, though few in number (they were 120 men, the number of the years of Moses), determined and agreed that none should turn his back in flight from the other, but would either win death with glory, or life with victory (for both alike are easy to the Lord). So S. Wilfrith with his clerk fell on his knees, and lifting his hands to Heaven again sought help from the Lord. For, as Moses triumphed when Hur and Aaron supported his hands, by frequently imploring the protection of the Lord, when Joshua the son of Nun was fighting with the people of God against Amalek, thus these few Christians after thrice repulsing the fierce and untamed heathen, routed them with great slaughter, with a loss strange to say of only five on their side.

"And their great priest (Wilfrith) prayed to the Lord his God, who immediately ordered the sea to return a full hour before its wont. So that when the heathen, on the arrival of their king, were preparing for a fourth attack with all their forces, the rising sea covered with its waves the whole of the shore, and floated the ship, which sailed into the deep. But, greatly glorified by God, and returning Him thanks, with a South wind they reached Sandwich, a harbour of safety."

JOHN WESLEY'S TESTIMONY

The Sussex people, it would seem, do not take kindly to missionaries, for John Wesley records that he had less success in this county than in all England.

Between Selsey and Bognor lies Pagham, famous in the pages of Knox's *Ornithological Rambles*, but otherwise unknown. Of the lost glories of Pagham, which was once a harbour, but is now dry, let Mr. Knox speak:—"Here in the dead long summer days, when not a breath of air has been stirring, have I frequently remained for hours, stretched on the hot shingle, and gazed at the osprey as he soared aloft, or watched the little islands of mud at the turn of the tide, as each gradually rose from the receding waters, and was successively taken possession of by flocks of sandpipers and ring-dotterels, after various circumvolutions on the part of each detachment, now simultaneously presenting their snowy breasts to the sunshine, now suddenly turning their dusky backs, so that the dazzled eye lost sight of them from the contrast; while the prolonged cry of the titterel,[2] and the melancholy note of the peewit from the distant swamp, have mingled with the scream of the tern and the taunting laugh of the gull.

PAGHAM'S LOST GLORIES

"Here have I watched the oyster-catcher, as he flew from point to point, and cautiously waded into the shallow water; and the patient heron, that pattern of a fisherman, as with retracted neck, and eyes fixed on vacancy, he has stood for hours without a single snap, motionless as a statue. Here, too, have I pursued the guillemot, or craftily endeavoured to cut off the retreat of the diver, by mooring my boat across the narrow passage through which alone he could return to the open sea without having recourse to his reluctant wings. Nor can I forget how often, during the Siberian winter of 1838, when 'a whole gale,' as the sailors have it, has been blowing from the north-east, I used to take up my position on the long and narrow ridge of shingle which separated this paradise from the raging waves without, and sheltered behind a hillock of seaweed, with my long duck-gun and a trusty double, or half buried in a hole in the sand, I used to watch the legions of water-birds as they neared the shore, and dropped distrustfully among the breakers, at a distance from the desired haven, until, gaining confidence from accession of numbers, some of the bolder spirits—the pioneers of the army—would flap their wings, rise from the white waves, and make for the calm water. Here they come! I can see the pied golden-eye pre-eminent among the advancing party; now the pochard, with his copper-coloured head and neck, may be distinguished from the darker scaup-duck; already the finger is on the trigger, when, perhaps, they suddenly veer to the right and left, far beyond the reach of my longest barrel or, it may be, come swishing overhead, and leave a companion or two struggling on the shingle or floating on the shallow waters of the harbour."

Pagham Harbour is now reclaimed, and where once was mud, or, at high tide, shallow water, is rank grass and thistles. One ship that seems to have waited a little too long before making for the open sea again, now lies high and dry, a forlorn hulk. Pagham church is among the airiest that I know, with a shingle spire, the counterpart of Bosham's on the other side of the peninsula.

The walk from Pagham to Bognor, along the sand, is uninspiring and not too easy, for the sand can be very soft. About a mile west of Bognor one is driven inland, just after passing as perfect an example of the simple yet luxurious seaside home as I remember to have seen: all on one floor, thatched, shaded by trees, surrounded by its garden and facing the Channel.

EARLY BOGNOR

Among the unattractive types of town few are more dismal than the watering-place *manqué*. Bognor must, I fear, come under this heading. Its reputation, such as it is, was originally made by Princess Charlotte, daughter of George III., who found the air recuperative, and who was probably not unwilling to lend her prestige to a resort, as her brother George was doing at Brighton, and her sister Amelia had done at Worthing. But before the Princess Charlotte Sir Richard Hotham, the hatter, had come, determined at any cost to make the town popular. One of his methods was to rename it Hothampton. His efforts were, however, only moderately successful, and he died in 1799, leaving to what Horsfield calls "his astonished heirs" only £8,000 out of a great fortune. The name Hothampton soon vanished.

The local authorities of Bognor seem to be keenly alive to the value of enterprise, for their walls are covered with instructions as to what may or may not be done in the interests of cleanliness and popularity; a new sea-wall has been built; receptacles for waste paper continually confront one, and deck chairs at twopence for three hours are practically unavoidable. And yet Bognor remains a dull place, once the visitor has left his beach abode—tent or bathing box, whichever it may be. It seems to be a town without resources. But it has the interest, denied one in more fashionable watering-places, of presenting old and new Bognor at the same moment; not that old Bognor is really old, but it is instructive to see the kind of crescent which was considered the last word in architectural enterprise when our great-grandmothers were young and would take the sea air.

A POET ON HORSEBACK

From Bognor it is a mere step to Felpham, a village less than a mile to the east. Whether or not one goes there to-day is a matter of taste; but a hundred years ago to omit a visit was to confess one's-self a boor, for William Hayley, the poet and friend of genius, lived there, and his castellated stucco house became a shrine. At that day it seems to have been no uncommon sight for the visitor to Bognor to be refreshed by the spectacle of the poet falling from his horse. According to his biographer, Cowper's Johnny of Norfolk, Hayley descended to earth almost as often as Alice's White Knight, partly from the high spirit of his steed, and partly from a habit which he never abandoned of wearing military spurs and carrying an umbrella. The memoir of the poet contains this agreeable passage: "The Editor was once riding gently by his side, on the stony beach of Bognor, when the wind suddenly reversed his umbrella as he unfolded it; his horse, with a single but desperate plunge, pitched him on his head in an instant . . . On another occasion, on the same visit . . . he was tost into the air on the Downs, at the precise moment when an interested friend whom they had just left, being apprehensive of what would happen, was anxiously viewing him from his window, through a telescope." Those who look through telescopes are rarely so fortunate. It is odd that Hayley, a delicate and heavy man suffering from hip-disease, should have taken so little hurt. Although he had a covered passage for horse exercise in the grounds of his villa, no amount of practice seems to have improved his seat. This covered way has been removed, but a mulberry tree planted by Hayley still flourishes.

Whenever Hayley was ill he became an object of intense interest to visitors at Bognor. Binsted's Library in the town exhibited a daily bulletin; and in 1819 the Prince and Princess of Saxe-Coburg called upon him, while the Princess of Hesse Homburg on her return sent a prescription from Germany.

HAYLEY HOUR BY HOUR

Mrs. Opie, the novelist, who stayed with Mr. Hayley every summer, and also served as a magnet to devout sojourners at Bognor, has left an account of the poet's habits which is vastly more entertaining than his poetry. He rose at six or earlier and at once composed some devotional verse. At breakfast, he read to Mrs. Opie; afterwards Mrs. Opie read to him. At eleven they drank coffee, and before he dressed for dinner, a very temperate meal, Mrs. Opie sang. After dinner there was more reading aloud, the matter being either manuscript compositions of Mr. Hayley's, or modern publications. Mr. Hayley took cocoa and Mrs. Opie tea, and afterwards Mrs. Opie read aloud or sang. At nine, the servants came to prayers, which were original compositions of Mr. Hayley's, read by him in a very impressive manner, and before bed, Mrs. Opie sang one of Mr. Hayley's hymns.

Hayley's grave is at Felpham, and his epitaph by Mrs. Opie may be read by the industrious on the wall of the church. Among the many epitaphs on his neighbours by Hayley himself, who had a special knack of mortuary verse, is this on a Felpham blacksmith:—

My sledge and hammer lie reclined;
My bellows too have lost their wind;
My fire's extinct; my forge decay'd,
And in the dust my vice is laid;
My coal is spent, my iron gone;
The nails are driven—my work is done.

The last verses that Hayley wrote have more charm and delicacy than perhaps anything else among his works:

Ye gentle birds that perch aloof,
And smooth your pinions on my roof,
Preparing for departure hence
Ere winter's angry threats commence;
Like you, my soul would smooth her plume
For longer flights beyond the tomb.

May God, by whom is seen and heard
Departing man and wandering bird,
In mercy mark us for his own,
And guide us to the land unknown.

A FAIRY'S FUNERAL

But it is not Hayley that gives its glory to Felpham. The glory of Felpham is that William Blake was happy there for nearly three years. It was at Felpham that he saw the fairy's funeral. "Did you ever see a fairy's funeral, ma'am?" he asked a visitor. "Never, sir!" "I have! . . . I was walking alone in my garden; there was great stillness among the branches and flowers, and more than common sweetness in the air; I heard a low and pleasant sound, and I knew not whence it came. At last I saw the broad leaf of a flower move, and underneath I saw a procession of creatures, of the size and colour of green and grey grasshoppers, bearing a body laid out on a rose-leaf, which they buried with songs, and then disappeared. It was a fairy's funeral!"

Blake settled at Felpham to be near Hayley, for whom he had a number of commissions to execute. He engraved illustrations to Hayley's works, and painted eighteen heads for Hayley's library—among them, Shakespeare, Homer, and Hayley himself; but all have vanished, the present owner knows not where.

In some verses which Blake addressed to Anna Flaxman, the wife of the sculptor, in September, 1800, a few days before moving from London to the Sussex coast, he says:—

This song to the flower of Flaxman's joy;
To the blossom of hope, for a sweet decoy;
Do all that you can and all that you may
To entice him to Felpham and far away.

Away to sweet Felpham, for Heaven is there;
The ladder of Angels descends through the air,
On the turret its spiral does softly descend,
Through the village then winds, at my cot it does end.

THE PROPHETS AT FELPHAM

Blake's house still stands, a retired, thatched cottage, facing the sea, but some distance from it. In a letter to Flaxman a little later, he says, "Felpham is a sweet place for study, because it is more spiritual than London. Heaven opens here on all sides its golden gates; the windows are not obstructed by vapours; voices of celestial inhabitants are more distinctly heard, their forms more distinctly seen; and my cottage is also a shadow of their houses." Beside the sea Blake communed with the spirits of Dante and Homer, Milton and the Hebrew Prophets.

Blake's sojourn at Felpham ended in 1803. A grotesque and annoying incident marred its close, the story of which, as told by the poet in a letter to Mr. Butler, certainly belongs to the history of Sussex. It should, however, first be stated that an ex-soldier in the Royal Dragoons, named John Scholfield, had accused Blake of uttering seditious words. The letter runs:—"His enmity arises from my having turned him out of my garden, into which he was invited as an assistant by a gardener at work therein, without my knowledge that he was so invited. I desired him, as politely as possible, to go out of the garden; he made me an impertinent answer. I insisted on his leaving the garden; he refused. I still persisted in desiring his departure. He then threatened to knock out my eyes, with many abominable imprecations, and with some contempt for my person; it affronted my foolish pride. I therefore took him by the elbows, and pushed him before me until I had got him out. There I intended to have left him; but he, turning about, put himself into a posture of defiance, threatening and swearing at me. I, perhaps foolishly and perhaps not, stepped out at the gate, and, putting aside his blows, took him again by the elbows, and, keeping his back to me, pushed him forward down the road about fifty yards—he all the while endeavouring to turn round and strike me, and raging and cursing, which drew out several neighbours. At length when I had got him to where he was quartered, which was very quickly done, we were met at the gate by the master of the house— the Fox Inn—(who is the proprietor of my cottage) and his wife and daughter, and the man's comrade, and several other people. My landlord compelled the soldiers to go indoors, after many abusive threats against me and my wife from the two soldiers; but not one word of threat on account of sedition was uttered at that time."

WILLIAM BLAKE, TRAITOR

As a result, Blake was haled before the magistrates and committed for trial. The trial was held in the Guildhall at Chichester, on January 11th, 1804. Hayley, in spite of having been thrown from his horse on a flint with, says Gilchrist, Blake's biographer, "more than usual violence" was in attendance to swear to the poet's character, and Cowper's friend Rose, a clever barrister, had been retained. According to the report in the County paper, "William Blake, an engraver at Felpham, was tried on a charge exhibited against him by two soldiers for having uttered seditious and treasonable expressions, such as 'd—n the king, d—n all his subjects, d—n his soldiers, they are all slaves; when Buonaparte comes, it will be cut-throat for cut-throat, and the weakest must go to the wall; I will help him; &c., &c.'" Blake electrified the court by calling out "False!" in the midst of the military evidence, the invented character of which was, however, so obvious that an acquittal resulted. "In defiance of all decency," the spectators cheered, and Hayley carried off the sturdy Republican (as he was at heart) to Mid Lavant, to sup at Mrs. Poole's.

BLAKE'S FLASHING EYE

Mr. Gilchrist found an old fellow who had been present at the trial, drawn thither by the promise of seeing the great man of the neighbourhood, Mr. Hayley. All that he could remember was Blake's flashing eye.

The Fox Inn, by the way, is still as it was, but the custom, I fancy, goes more to the Thatched House, which adds to the charms of refreshment a museum containing such treasures as a petrified cocoanut, the skeleton of a lobster twenty-eight years old, and a representation of Moses in the bulrushes.

A third and fourth great man, of a different type both from Hayley and Blake, met at Felpham in 1819. One was Cyril Jackson, Dean of Christ Church, who, lying on his death-bed in the Manor House, was visited by the other—his old pupil, the First Gentleman in Europe.

FOOTNOTE:

2 The Sussex provincial name for the whimbrel.

ARUNDEL.

CHAPTER VII

ARUNDEL AND NEIGHBOURHOOD

A feudal town—Castles ruined and habitable—The old religion and the new—Bevis of Southampton—Lord Thurlow lays an egg—A noble park—A song in praise of Sussex—The father of cricket.

Seen from the river or from the east side of the Arun valley, Arundel is the most imposing town in Sussex. Many are larger, many are equally old, or older; but none wears so unusual and interesting an air, not even Lewes among her Downs.

Arundel clings to the side of a shaggy hill above the Arun. Castle, cathedral, church—these are Arundel; the town itself is secondary, subordinate, feudal. The castle is what one likes a castle to be—a mass of battlemented stone, with a keep, a gateway, and a history, and yet more habitable than ever. So many of the rich make no effort to live in their ancestral halls; and what might be a home, carrying on the tradition of ages, is so often only a mere show, that to find an historic castle like Arundel still lived in is very gratifying. In Sussex alone are several half-ruined houses that the builders could quickly make habitable once more. Arundel Castle, in spite of time and the sieges of 1102, 1139, and 1643, is both comfortable and modern; Arundel still depends for her life upon the complaisance of her over-lord.

MODERN MEDIEVALISM

I know of no town with so low a pulse as this precipitous little settlement under the shadow of Rome and the Duke. In spite of picnic parties in the park, in spite of anglers from London, in spite of the railway in the valley, Arundel is still medieval and curiously foreign. On a very hot day, as one climbs the hill to the cathedral, one might be in old France, and certainly in the Middle Ages.

Time's revenges have had their play in this town. Although the church is still bravely of the establishment, half of it is closed to the Anglican visitor (the chancel having been adjudged the private property of the Dukes of Norfolk), and the once dominating position of the edifice has been impaired by the proximity of the new Roman Catholic church of St. Philip Neri, which the present Duke has been building these many years. Within, it is finished, a very charming and delicate feat in stone; but the spire has yet to come. The old Irish soldier, humorous and bemedalled, who keeps watch and ward over the fane, is not the least of its merits.

Although the chancel of the parish church has been closed, permission to enter may occasionally be obtained. It is rich in family tombs of great interest and beauty, including that of the nineteenth Earl of Arundel, the patron of William Caxton. In the siege of Arundel Castle in 1643, the soldiers of the parliamentarians, under Sir William Waller, fired their cannon from the church tower. They also turned the church into a barracks, and injured much stone work beyond repair. A fire beacon blazed of old on the spire to serve as a mark for vessels entering Littlehampton harbour.

Bevis of Southampton, the giant who, when he visited the Isle of Wight, waded thither, was a warder at Arundel Castle; where he ate a whole ox every week with bread and mustard, and drank two hogsheads of beer. Hence "Bevis Tower." His sword Morglay is still to be seen in the armoury of the castle; his bones lie beneath a mound in the park; and the town was named after his horse. So runs a pretty story, which is, however, demolished with the ruthlessness that comes so easily to the antiquary and philologist. Bevis Tower, science declares, was named probably after another Bevis—there was one at the Battle of Lewes, who took prisoner Richard, King of the Romans, and was knighted for it—while Arundel is a corruption of "hirondelle," a swallow. Mr. Lower mentions that in recent times in Sussex "Swallow" was a common name in stables, even for heavy dray horses. But before accepting finally the swallow theory, we ought to hear what Fuller has to say:—"Some will have it so named from *Arundel* the *Horse* of *Beavoice*, the great *Champion*. I confess it is not without precedence in *Antiquity* for *Places* to take *names* from *Horses*, meeting with the *Promontory Bucephalus* in Peloponesus, where some report the *Horse* of *Alexander* buried, and Bellonius will have it for the same cause called *Cavalla* at this day. But this *Castle* was so called long before that *Imaginary Horse* was *foled*, who cannot be fancied elder than his Master Beavoice, flourishing after the Conquest, long before which *Arundel* was so called from the river *Arund* running hard by it."

LORD THURLOW LAYS AN EGG

The owls that once multiplied in the keep have now disappeared. They were established there a hundred years or so ago by the eleventh Duke, and certain of them were known by the names of public men. "Please, your Grace, Lord Thurlow has laid an egg," is an historic speech handed down by tradition. Lord Thurlow, the owl in question, died at a great age in 1859.

THE ARUN AT NORTH STOKE.

ARUNDEL PARK

To walk through Arundel Park is to receive a vivid impression of the size and richness of our little isolated England. Two or three great towns could be hidden in it unknown to each other. Valley succeeds to valley; new herds of deer come into sight at almost every turn; as far as the eye can see the grass hills roll away. Those accustomed to parks whose deer are always huddled close and whose wall is never distant, are bewildered by the vastness of this enclosure. Yet one has also the feeling that such magnificence is right: to so lovely a word as Arundel, to the Premier

Duke and Hereditary Earl Marshal of England, should fittingly fall this far-spreading and comely pleasaunce. Had Arundel Park been small and empty of deer what a blunder it would be.

Walking west of Arundel through the vast Rewell Wood, we come suddenly upon Punch-bowl Green, and open a great green valley, dominated by the white façade of Dale Park House, below Madehurst, one of the most remote of Sussex villages.

SLINDON

By keeping due west for another mile Slindon is reached. This village is one of the Sussex backwaters, as one might say. It lies on no road that any one ever travels except for the purpose of going to Slindon or coming from it; and those that perform either of these actions are few. Yet all who have not seen Slindon are by so much the poorer, for Slindon House is nobly Elizabethan, with fine pictures and hiding-places, and Slindon beeches are among the aristocracy of trees. And here I should like to quote a Sussex poem of haunting wistfulness and charm, which was written by Mr. Hilaire Belloc, who once walked to Rome and is an old dweller at Slindon:—

A SOUTH COUNTRY SONG

THE SOUTH COUNTRY.

When I am living in the Midlands,
   That are sodden and unkind,
I light my lamp in the evening:
   My work is left behind;
And the great hills of the South Country
   Come back into my mind.

The great hills of the South Country
   They stand along the sea:
And it's there walking in the high woods
   That I could wish to be,
And the men that were boys when I was a boy
   Walking along with me.

The men that live in North England
   I saw them for a day:
Their hearts are set upon the waste fells,
   Their skies are fast and grey:
From their castle-walls a man may see
   The mountains far away.

The men that live in West England
   They see the Severn strong,
A-rolling on rough water brown
   Light aspen leaves along.
They have the secret of the Rocks,
   And the oldest kind of song.

But the men that live in the South Country
   Are the kindest and most wise,
They get their laughter from the loud surf,
   And the faith in their happy eyes
Comes surely from our Sister the Spring,
   When over the sea she flies;
The violets suddenly bloom at her feet,
   She blesses us with surprise.

I never get between the pines,
   But I smell the Sussex air,

Nor I never come on a belt of sand
   But my home is there;
And along the sky the line of the Downs
   So noble and so bare.

A lost thing could I never find,
   Nor a broken thing mend;
And I fear I shall be all alone
   When I get towards the end.
Who will there be to comfort me,
   Or who will be my friend?

I will gather and carefully make my friends
   Of the men of the Sussex Weald,
They watch the stars from silent folds,
   They stiffly plough the field.
By them and the God of the South Country
   My poor soul shall be healed.

If I ever become a rich man,
   Or if ever I grow to be old,
I will build a house with deep thatch
   To shelter me from the cold,
And there shall the Sussex songs be sung
   And the story of Sussex told.

I will hold my house in the high wood
   Within a walk of the sea,
And the men who were boys when I was a boy
   Shall sit and drink with me.

NEWLAND, NYREN, AND SILVER BILLY

Richard Newland, the father of serious cricket, came from this parish. He was born in 1718, or thereabouts, and in 1745 he made 88 for England against Kent. He was left-handed, and the finest bat ever seen in those days. He taught Richard Nyren, of Hambledon, all the skill and judgment that that noble general possessed; Nyren communicated his knowledge to the Hambledon eleven, and the game was made. An interest in historical veracity compels me to add that William Beldham—Silver Billy—talking to Mr. Pycroft, discounted some of Nyren's praise. "Cricket," he said, "was played in Sussex very early, before my day at least [he was born in 1766]; but that there was no good play I know by this, that Richard Newland, of Slindon in Sussex, as you say, sir, taught old Richard Nyren, and that no Sussex man could be found to play Newland. Now a second-rate man of our parish beat Newland easily; so you may judge what the rest of Sussex then were." But this is disregarding the characteristic uncertainty of the game.

If one would spend a day far from mankind, on high ground, there is no better way than to walk from Arundel through Houghton Forest (where, as we have seen, Charles II. avoided the Governor) to Cocking.

CHAPTER VIII

LITTLEHAMPTON

A children's paradise—Wind-swept villages—Cary and Coleridge—Sussex folklore—Climping—Richard Jefferies and Sussex—John Taylor the Water Poet—Highdown Hill—A miller in love with death—A digression on mills and millers—Treason at Patching—A wife in a thousand—A Sussex truffler—The Palmer triplets.

Littlehampton is favoured in having both sea and river. It also has lawns between the houses and the beach, as at Dieppe, and is as nearly a children's paradise as exists. The sea at low tide recedes almost beyond the reach of the ordinary paddler, which is as it should be except for those that would swim. A harbour, a pier, a lighthouse, a windmill—all these are within a few yards of each other. On the neighbouring beach, springing from the stones, you find the yellow-horned poppy, beautiful both in flower and leaf, and the delicate tamarisk makes a natural hedge parallel with the sea, to Worthing on the one side, and to Bognor on the other.

The little villages in the flats behind the eastern tamarisk hedge—Rustington, Preston, Ferring, are, in summer, veritable sun traps, with their white walls dazzling in radiance. Such trees as grow about here all bow to the north-east, bent to that posture by the prevailing south-west winds. A Sussex man, on the hills or south of them, lost at night, has but to ascertain the outline of a tree, and he may get his bearings. If he cannot see so much as that he has but to feel the bark for lichen, which grows on the north east, or lee, side.

It was at Littlehampton in September, 1817, that Coleridge met Cary, the translator of Dante. Cary was walking on the beach, reciting Homer to his son. Up came a noticeable man with large grey eyes: "Sir, yours is a face I should know. I am Samuel Taylor Coleridge."

A CHURCH DUEL

The county paper for February 27, 1796, has this paragraph: "On Monday last a duel was fought betwixt Mr. R—n and Lieut. B—y, both of Littlehampton, in a field near that place, which, after the discharge of each a pistol, terminated without bloodshed. The dispute, we understand, originated about a pew in the parish church."

A local proverb says that if you eat winkles in March it is as good as a dose of medicine; which reminds me that Sussex has many wise sayings of its own. Here is a piece of Sussex counsel in connection with the roaring month:—

> If from fleas you would be free,
> On the first of March let all your windows closed be.

I quote two other rhymes:—

> If you would wish your bees to thrive
> Gold must be paid for every hive;
> For when they're bought with other money
> There will be neither swarm nor honey.

> The first butterfly you see,
> Cut off his head across your knee,
> Bury the head under a stone
> And a lot of money will be your own.

On Whit Sunday the devout Sussex man eats roast veal and gooseberry pudding. A Sussex child born on Sunday can neither be hanged nor drowned.

"CLIMPING FOR PERFECTION"

West of Littlehampton is an architectural treasure, in the shape of Climping church, which no one should miss. The way is over the ferry and along the road to the first signboard, when one strikes northward towards Ford, and comes suddenly upon this squat and solid fane. A Saxon church stood here, built by the Prioress of Leominster, before the Conquest: to Roger de Montgomerie was the manor given by the Conqueror, as part of the earldom of Arundel and Chichester, together with Atherington manor, much of which is now, like Selsey's park, under the Channel. De Montgomerie gave Climping manor to the nuns of Almanesches, by whom the present Norman fortress-tower (with walls 4¼ feet thick) was added, and in 1253 John de Climping, the vicar, rebuilt the remainder. The church is thus six and a half centuries old, and parts of it are older. "Bosham, for antiquity; Boxgrove, for beauty; and Climping, for perfection" is the dictum of an antiquary quoted by the present vicar in a little pamphlet-history of his parish. As regards the Norman doorway, at any rate, he is right: there is nothing in Sussex to excel that; while in general architectural attraction the building is of the richest. It is also a curiously homely and ingratiating church.

One of the new windows, representing St. Paul, has a peculiar interest, as the vicar tells us:—"St. Paul was a prisoner at Rome shortly after Caractacus, the British Chief, whose daughter, Claudia, married Pudens, both friends of the Apostle (2 Tim. iv. 21). Pudens afterwards commanded the Roman soldiers stationed at Regnum (Chichester), and if St. Paul came to Britain, at Claudia's request (as ancient writers testify), he certainly would visit Sussex. How close this brings us here in Sussex to the Bible story!"

At Baylies Court, now a farmhouse, the Benedictine monks of Seez, also protégés of Robert de Montgomerie, had their chapel, remains of which are still to be seen.

Climping, which otherwise lives its own life, is the resort of golfers (who to the vicar's regret play all Sunday and turn Easter Day into "a Heathen Festival") and of the sportsmen of the Sussex Coursing Club, who find that the terrified Climping hare gives satisfaction beyond most in the county.

Of Ford, north of Climping, there is nothing to say, except that popular rumour has it that its minute and uninteresting church (the antithesis of Climping) was found one day by accident in a bed of nettles.

JEFFERIES IN SUSSEX

A good eastern walk from Littlehampton takes one by the sea to Goring, and then inland over Highdown Hill to Angmering, and so to Littlehampton again or to Arundel, our present centre. Goring touches literature in two places. The great house was built by Sir Bysshe Shelley, grandfather of the poet; and in the village died, in 1887, Richard Jefferies, author of *The Story of My Heart*, after a life of ill-health spent in the service of nature. Many beautiful and sympathetic descriptions of Sussex are scattered about in Jefferies' books of essays, notably, "To Brighton," "The South Down Shepherd," and "The Breeze on Beachy Head" in *Nature near London*; "Clematis Lane," "Nature near Brighton," "Sea, Sky and Down," and "January in the Sussex Woods" in *The Life of the Fields*; "Sunny Brighton" in *The Open Air*, and "The Country-Side, Sussex" and "Buckhurst Park" in *Field and Hedgerow*. Jefferies had a way of blending experiences and concealing the names of places, which makes it difficult to know exactly what part of Sussex he is describing; but I think I could lead anyone to Clematis Lane. I might, by the way, have remarked of South Harting that the luxuriance of the clematis in its hedges is unsurpassed.

John Taylor, the water poet, has a doggerel narrative entitled "A New Discovery by Sea with a Wherry from London to Salisbury," 1623, wherein he mentions a woful night with fleas at Goring, and pens a couplet worthy to take a place with the famous description of a similar visitation in *Eothen*:—

Who in their fury nip'd and skip'd so hotly,
That all our skins were almost turned to motley.

JOHN TAYLOR AND THE CONSTABLE

Taylor gives us in the same record a pleasant picture of the Sussex constable in 1623:—

The night before a Constable there came,
Who asked my trade, my dwelling, and my name,
My businesse, and a troupe of questions more,
And wherefore we did land vpon that shore?
To whom I fram'd my answers true and fit,
(According to his plenteous want of wit)
But were my words all true or if I ly'd
With neither I could get him satisfi'd.
He ask'd if we were Pyrats? We said No,
(*As if we had we would haue told him so*)
He said that Lords sometimes would enterprise
T' escape and leaue the Kingdome in disguise:
But I assur'd him on my honest word
That I was no disguisèd Knight or Lord.
He told me then that I must goe six miles
T' a Justice there, Sir John or else Sir Giles:
I told him I was lothe to goe so farre,
And he told me he would my journey barre.

Thus what with Fleas and with the seuerall prates
Of th' officer, and his *Ass*-sociats
We arose to goe, but Fortune bade us stay:
The Constable had stolne our oares away,
And borne them thence a quarter of a mile
Quite through a Lane beyond a gate and stile;
And hid them there to hinder my depart,
For which I wish'd him hang'd with all my heart.
A plowman (for us) found our Oares againe,
Within a field well fil'd with Barley Graine.
Then madly, gladly, out to sea we thrust,
'Gainst windes and stormes, and many a churlish Gust,
By *Kingston* Chappelle and by *Rushington*,
By *Little-Hampton* and by *Middleton*.

THE MILLER AND SWEET DEATH

Highdown, above Goring, is a good hill in itself, conical in shape, as a hill should be according to the exacting ideas of childhood, with a sweeping view of the coast and the Channel; but its fame as a resort of holiday makers comes less from its position and height than from the circumstance that John Oliver is buried upon it. John Oliver was the miller of Highdown Hill. When not grinding corn he seems to have busied himself with thoughts upon the necessary end of all things, to such an extent that his meditations on the subject gradually became a mania. His coffin was made while he was still a young man, and it remained under his bed until its time was ripe, fitted—to bring it to a point of preparedness unusual even with the Chinese, those masters of anticipatory obsequies— with wheels, which the miller, I doubt not, regularly oiled. John Oliver did not stop there. Having his coffin comfortably at hand, he proceeded to erect his tomb. This was built in 1766, with tedious verses upon it from the miller's pen; while in an alcove near the tomb was a mechanical arrangement of death's-heads which might keep the miller's thoughts from straying, when, as with Dr. Johnson's philosopher, cheerfulness would creep in.

The miller lived in the company of his coffin, his tomb, and his *mementi mori*, until 1793, when at the age of eighty-four his hopes were realised. Those who love death die old.

Between two and three thousand persons attended the funeral; no one was permitted to wear any but gay clothes; and the funeral sermon was read by a little girl of twelve, from the text, Micah vii. 8, 9.

A DIGRESSION ON MILLS

The mill of John Oliver has vanished, nothing but a depression in the turf now indicating where its foundations stood. Too many Sussex windmills have disappeared. Clayton still has her twain, landmarks for many miles—I have seen them on exceptionally clear days from the Kentish hills—and other windmills are scattered over the county; but many more than now exist have ceased to be, victims of the power of steam. There is probably no contrast æsthetically more to the disadvantage of the modern substitute than that of the steam mill of to-day with the windmill of yesterday. The steam mill is always ugly, always dusty, always noisy, usually in a town. The windmill stands high and white, a thing of life and radiance and delicate beauty, surrounded by grass, in communion with the heavens. Such noise as it has is elemental, justifiable, like a ship's cordage in a gale. No one would paint a steam mill; a picture with a windmill can hardly be a failure. Constable, who knew everything about the magic of windmills, painted several in Sussex—one even at Brighton.

Brighton now has but one mill. There used to be many: one in the West Hill road, a comelier landmark than the stucco Congregational tower that has taken its place close by and serves as the town's sentinel from almost every point of approach. In 1797 a miller near Brighton anticipated American enterprise by moving his mill bodily to a place two miles distant by the help of eighty oxen.

Another weakness of steam mills is that they are apparently without millers—at least there is no unmistakable dominating presence in a white hat, to whom one can confidently apply the definite article, as in the mill on the hill. Millers' men there are in plenty, but the miller is lacking. This is because steam mills belong to companies. Thus, with the passing of the windmill we lose also the miller, that notable figure in English life and tradition; always jolly, if the old songs are true; often eccentric, as the story of John Oliver has shown; and usually a character, as becomes one who lives by the four winds, or by water—for the miller of tradition was often found in a water-mill too. The water-miller's empire has been threatened less than that of the windmill, for there is no sudden cessation of water power as of wind power. Sussex still has many water-mills—cool and splashing homes of peaceful bustle. Long may they endure.

Highdown Hill has other associations. In 1812 the Gentlemen of the Weald met the Gentlemen of the Sea-coast at cricket on its dividing summit. The game, which was for one hundred guineas, was a very close thing, the Gentlemen of the Weald winning by only seven runs. Among the Gentlemen of the Sea-coast was Mr. Osbaldeston, while the principal Gentleman of the Weald was Mr. E. H. Budd.

A mile north of Highdown Hill, in a thickly wooded country, are Patching and Clapham; Patching celebrated for its pond, which washes the high-road to Arundel, and Clapham for its woods. Three hundred and more years ago Patching Copse was the scene of a treasonable meeting between William Shelley, an ancestor of the poet, one branch of whose family long held Michelgrove (where Henry VIII. was entertained by our plotter's grandfather), and Charles Paget: sturdy Roman Catholics both, who thus sought each other out, on the night of September 16, 1583, to confer as to the possibility of invading England, deposing Elizabeth, and setting Mary Queen of Scots upon the throne. Nothing came of the plot save the imprisonment of Shelley (who was condemned to death but escaped the sentence) and the flight of Paget, to hatch further treason abroad.

THE PERFECT WIFE

The last Shelley to hold Michelgrove, now no more, was Sir John, who, after it had been in the family for three hundred and fifty years, sold it in 1800. This was the Sir John Shelley who composed the following epitaph in Clapham church (one of Sir Gilbert Scott's restorations) to commemorate the very remarkable virtues of his lady—untimely snatched from his side:—

Here Lyeth the Body of Wilhelmina Shelley
who departed this Life the 21st of March 1772y
Aged Twenty three years.
She was a pattern for the World to follow:y
Such a being both in form and mind perhaps never
existed before.y
A most dutiful, affectionate, and Virtuous Wife,y
A most tender and Anxious parent,y
A most sincere and constant Friend,
A most amiable and elegant companion;
Universally Benevolent, generous, and humane;
The Pride of her own Sex,
The admiration of ours.
She lived universally belov'd, and admir'd
She died as generally rever'd, and regretted,
A loss felt by all who had the happiness of knowing Her,
By none to be compar'd to *that* of her disconsolate, affectionate,
Loving,
& in this World everlastingly Miserable Husband,
Sir JOHN SHELLEY,
Who has caused this inscription to be Engrav'd.

Horsfield tells us that "the beechwoods in this parish [Patching] and its immediate neighbourhood are very productive of the Truffle (*Lycoperdon tuber*). About forty years ago William Leach came from the West Indies, with some hogs accustomed to hunt for truffles, and proceeding along the coast from the Land's End, in Cornwall, to the mouth of the River Thames, determined to fix on that spot where he found them most abundant. He took four years to try the experiment, and at length settled in this parish, where he carried on the business of truffle-hunter till his death."

Angmering, which we may take on our return to Arundel, is a typically dusty Sussex village, with white houses and thatched roofs, and a rather finer church than most. On our way back to Arundel, in the middle of a wood, a little more than a mile from Angmering, to the west, we come upon an interesting relic of a day when tables bore nobler loads than now they do: a decoy pond formed originally to supply wild duck to the kitchen of Arundel Castle, but now no longer used. The long tapering tunnels of wire netting, into which the tame ducks of the decoy lured their wild cousins, are still in place, although the wire has largely perished.

THE PALMER TRIPLETS

At an old house near the Decoy (now converted into cottages), which any native will gladly and amusedly point out, lived, in the reign of Henry VIII., Lady Palmer, the famous mother of the Palmer triplets, who were distinguished from other triplets, not only by being born each on a successive Sunday but by receiving each the honour of knighthood. The curious circumstances of their birth seem to be well attested.

GATEWAY, AMBERLEY CASTLE.

CHAPTER IX

AMBERLEY AND PARHAM

Sussex fish—A straw-blown village—A painter of Sussex light—A castle only in name—Parham's treasures—The Parham heronry—Storrington and the sagacious Jack Pudding—A Sussex audience.

SUSSEX FISH

Five miles to the north of Arundel by road (over the Arun at Houghton's ancient bridge, restored by the bishops of Chichester in the fifteenth century), and a few minutes by rail, is Amberley, the fishing metropolis of Sussex, where, every Sunday in the season, London anglers meet to drop their lines in friendly rivalry. "Amerley trout" (as Walton calls them) and Arundel mullet are the best of the Arun's treasures; and this reminds me of Fuller's tribute to Sussex fish, which may well be quoted in this watery neighbourhood: "Now, as this County is eminent for both *Sea* and *River*-fish, namely, an *Arundel Mullet*, a *Chichester Lobster*, a *Shelsey Cockle*, and an *Amerly Trout*; so *Sussex* aboundeth with more *Carpes* than any other of this Nation. And though not so great as *Jovius* reporteth to be found in the *Lurian Lake* in *Italy*, weighing more than fifty pounds, yet those generally of great and goodly proportion. I need not adde, that *Physicians* account the galls of *Carpes*, as also a stone in their heads, to be *Medicinable*; only I will observe that, because *Jews* will not eat *Caviare* made of *Sturgeon* (because coming from a fish wanting Scales, and therefore forbidden in

112

the *Levitical Law*); therefore the *Italians* make greater profit of the *Spaun* of *Carps*, whereof they make a *Red Caviare*, well pleasing the *Jews* both in *Palate* and *Conscience*. All I will adde of *Carps* is this, that *Ramus* himself doth not so much redound in *Dichotomies* as they do; seeing no one bone is to be found in their body, which is not *forked* or divided into two parts at the end thereof."

Amberley proper, as distinguished from Amberley of the anglers, is a mile from the station and is built on a ridge. The castle is the extreme western end of this ridge, the north side of which descends precipitously to the marshy plain that extends as far as Pulborough. Standing on the castle one sees Pulborough church due north—height calling unto height. The castle is now a farm; indeed, all Amberley is a huge stockyard, smelling of straw and cattle. It is sheer Sussex—chalky soil, whitewashed cottages, huge waggons; and one of the best of Sussex painters, and, in his exquisite modest way, of all painters living, dwells in the heart of it—Edward Stott, who year after year shows London connoisseurs how the clear skin of the Sussex boy takes the evening light; and how the Southdown sheep drink at hill ponds beneath a violet sky; and that there is nothing more beautiful under the stars than a whitewashed cottage just when the lamp is lit.

AMBERLEY AND PARHAM

Amberley has no right to lay claim to a castle, for the old ruins are not truly, as they seem, the remains of a castellated stronghold, but of a crenellated mansion. John Langton, Bishop of Chichester in the fourteenth century, was the first builder. Previously the Church lands here had been held very jealously, and in 1200 we find Bishop Gilbert de Leofard twice excommunicating, and as often absolving, the Earl of Arundel for poaching (as he termed it) in Houghton Forest. The Church lost Amberley in the sixteenth century. William Rede, who succeeded Langton to both house and see, wishing to feel secure in his home, craved permission to dig a moat around it and to render it both hostile and defensive. Hence its lion-like mien; but it has known no warfare, and the castle's mouldering walls now give what assistance they can in harbouring live stock. Twentieth-century sheds lean against fourteenth-century masonry; faggots are stored in the moat; lawn tennis is played in the courtyard; and black pigeons peep from the slits cut for arquebusiers.

AMBERLEY CASTLE.

Amberley Castle only once intrudes itself in history: Charles II., during his flight in 1651, spent a night there under the protection of Sir John Briscoe, as we saw in *Chapter III.*

In winter, if you ask an Amberley man where he dwells, he says, "Amberley, God help us." In summer he says, "Amberley—where *would* you live?"

114

From Amberley to Parham one keeps upon the narrow ridge for a mile or so, branching off then to the left. Parham's advance guard is seen all the way—a clump of fir trees, indicating that the soil there changes to sand.

A NOBLE DAME

For two possessions is Parham noted: a heronry in the park, and in the house a copy of Montaigne with Shakespeare's autograph in it. The house, a spreading Tudor mansion, is the seat of Lord Zouche, a descendant of the traveller, Robert Curzon, who wrote *The Monasteries of the Levant*, that long, leisurely, and fascinating narrative of travel. In addition to Montaigne, it enshrines a priceless collection of armour, of incunabula and Eastern MSS. Among the pictures are full lengths of Sir Philip Sidney and Lady Sidney, and that Penelope D'Arcy—one of Mr. Hardy's "Noble Dames"—who promised to marry three suitors in turn and did so. We see her again at Firle Place.

A hiding hole for priests and other refugees is in the long gallery, access to it being gained through a window seat. There was hidden Charles Paget after the Babington conspiracy.

THE PARHAM HERONS

Parham Park has deer and a lake and an enchanted forest of sombre trees. On the highest ground in this forest is the clump of firs in which the famous herons build. The most interesting time to visit the heronry is in the breeding season, for then one sees the lank birds continually homing from the Amberley Wild Brooks with fishes in their bills and long legs streaming behind. The noise is tremendous, beyond all rookeries. Mr. Knox's *Ornithological Rambles*, from which I have already quoted freely, has this passage: "The herons at Parham assemble early in February, and then set about repairing their nests, but the trees are never entirely deserted during the winter months; a few birds, probably some of the more backward of the preceding season, roosting among their boughs every night. They commence laying early in March, and the greater part of the young birds are hatched during the early days of April. About the end of May they may be seen to flap out of their nests to the adjacent boughs, and bask for hours in the warm sunshine; but although now comparatively quiet during the day, they become clamorous for food as the evening approaches, and indeed for a long time appear to be more difficult to wean, and less able to shift for themselves, than most birds of a similar age. They may be observed, as late as August, still on the trees, screaming for food, and occasionally fed by their parents, who forage for them assiduously; indeed, these exertions, so far from being relaxed after the setting of the sun, appear to be redoubled during the night; for I have frequently disturbed herons when riding by moonlight among the low grounds near the river, where I have seldom seen them during the day, and several cottagers in the neighbourhood of Parham have assured me that their shrill cry may be heard at all hours of the night, during the summer season, as they fly to and fro overhead, on their passage between the heronry and the open country.

AMBERLEY CASTLE, ENTRANCE TO CHURCHYARD.

MANY MIGRATIONS

"The history or genealogy of the progenitors of this colony is remarkable. They were originally brought from Coity Castle, in Wales, by Lord Leicester's steward, in James the First's time, to Penshurst, in Kent, the seat of Lord de Lisle, where their descendants continued for more than two hundred years; from thence they migrated to Michelgrove, about seventy miles from Penshurst and eight from Parham; here they remained for nearly twenty years, until the proprietor of the estate disposed of it to the late Duke of Norfolk, who, having purchased it, not as a residence, but with the view of increasing the local property in the neighbourhood of Arundel, pulled down the house, and felled one or two of the trees on

117

which the herons had constructed their nests. The migration commenced immediately, but appears to have been gradual; for three seasons elapsed before all the members of the heronry had found their way over the Downs to their new quarters in the fir-woods of Parham. This occurred about seventeen years ago [written c. 1848]."

Sussex, says Mr. Borrer, author of *The Birds of Sussex*, has two other large heronries—at Windmill Hill Place, near Hailsham, and Brede, near Winchelsea—and some smaller ones, one being at Molecomb, above Goodwood.

Betsy's Oak in Parham Park is said to be so called because Queen Elizabeth sat beneath it. But another and more probable legend calls it Bates's Oak, after Bates, an archer at Agincourt in the retinue of the Earl of Arundel (and in *Henry V.*). Good Queen Bess, however, dined in the hall of Parham House in 1592. At Northiam, in East Sussex, we shall come (not to be utterly baulked) to a tree under which she truly did sit and dine too.

JACK PUDDING'S WISDOM

Beyond Parham, less than two miles to the east, is Storrington, a quiet Sussex village far from the rail and the noise of the world, with the Downs within hail, and fine sparsely-inhabited country between them and it to wander in. The church is largely modern. I find the following sententious paragraph in the county paper for 1792:—"This is an age of *Sights* and *polite entertainment* in the country as well as in the city.—The little town of *Storrington* has lately been visited by a *Company of Comedians,—a Mountebank Doctor,*—and a *Puppet Show*. One day the Doctor's *Jack Pudding* finding the shillings come in but slowly, exclaimed to his Master, 'Gad, Sir, it is not worth *our* while to stay here any longer, *players* have got all the *gold, we* all the *silver*, and *Punch* all the *copper*, so, like sagacious locusts, let us migrate from the place we helped to impoverish."

AMBERLEY CHURCH.

A TRAVELLING CIRCUS

A TIME-HONOURED JOKE

This reminds me that I saw recently at Petworth, whither we are now moving, a travelling circus whose programme included a comic interlude that cannot have received the slightest modification since it was first planned, perhaps hundreds of years ago. It was sheer essential elemental horse-play straight from Bartholomew Fair, and the audience received it with rapture that was vouchsafed to nothing else. The story would be too long to tell; but briefly, it was a dumb show representation of the visit of a guest (the clown) to a wife, unknown to her husband. The scenery consisted of a table, a large chest, a heap of straw and a huge barrel. The fun consisted in the clown, armed with a bladder on a string, hiding in the barrel, from which he would spring up and deliver a sounding drub upon the head of whatever other character—husband or policeman—might be passing, to their complete perplexity. They were, of course, incapable of learning anything from experience. At other times he hid himself or others in the straw, in the chest, or under the table. When, in a country district such as this, one hears the laughter that greets so venerable a piece of pantomime, one is surprised that circus owners think it worth while to secure novelties at all. The primitive taste of West Sussex, at any rate, cannot require them.

PULBOROUGH CHURCH.

CHAPTER X

PETWORTH

Pulborough and its past—Stopham—Fittleworth—The natural advantages of the Swan—Petworth's feudal air—An historical digression naming many Percies—The third Earl of Egremont—The Petworth pictures—Petworth Park—Cobbett's opinion—The vicissitudes of the Petworth ravens—Tillington's use to business men—A charming epitaph—Noah Mann of the Hambledon Club.

Petworth is not on the direct road to Horsham, which is our next centre, but it is easily gained from Arundel by rail (changing at Pulborough), or by road through Bury, Fittleworth, and Egdean.

AN ANCIENT FORTRESS

Pulborough is now nothing: once it was a Gibraltar, guarding Stane Street for Rome. The fort was on a mound west of the railway, corresponding with the church mound on the east. Here probably was a catapulta and certainly a vigilant garrison. Pulborough has no invader now but the floods, which every winter transform the green waste at her feet into a silver sea, of which Pulborough is the northern shore and Amberley the southern. The Dutch *polder* are not flatter or greener than are these intervening meadows. The village stands high and dry above the water level, extended in long line quite like a seaside town. Excursionists come too, as to a watering place, but they bring rods and creels and return at night with fish for the pan.

121

Between Pulborough and Petworth lie Stopham and Fittleworth, both on the Rother, which joins the Arun a little to the west of Pulborough. Stopham has the most beautiful bridge in Sussex, dating from the fourteenth century, and a little church filled with memorials of the Bartelott family. One of Stopham's rectors was Thomas Newcombe, a descendant of the author of *The Faerie Queene*, the friend of the author of *Night Thoughts*, and the author himself of a formidable poem in twelve books, after Milton, called *The Last Judgment*.

Fittleworth has of late become an artists' Mecca, partly because of its pretty woods and quaint architecture, and partly because of the warm welcome that is offered by the "Swan," which is probably the most ingeniously placed inn in the world. Approaching it from the north it seems to be the end of all things; the miles of road that one has travelled apparently have been leading nowhere but to the "Swan." Runaway horses or unsettled chauffeurs must project their passengers literally into the open door. Coming from the south, one finds that the road narrows by this inn almost to a lane, and the "Swan's" hospitable sign, barring the way, exerts such a spell that to enter is a far simpler matter than to pass.

AT PULBOROUGH.

AN IRRESISTIBLE INN

The "Swan" is a venerable and rambling building, stretching itself lazily with outspread arms; one of those inns (long may they be preserved from the rebuilders!) in which one stumbles up or down into every room, and where eggs and bacon have an appropriateness that make them a more desirable food than ambrosia. The little parlour is wainscoted with the votive paintings—a village Diploma Gallery—of artists who have made the "Swan" their home.

Fittleworth has a dual existence. In the south it is riparian and low, much given to anglers and visitors. In the north it is high and sandy, with clumps of firs, living its own life and spreading gorse-covered commons

123

at the feet of the walker. Between its southern border and Bignor Park is a superb common of sand and heather, an inland paradise for children.

Petworth station and Petworth town are far from being the same thing, and there are few more fatiguing miles than that which separates them. A 'bus, it is true, plies between, but it is one of those long, close prisons with windows that annihilate thought by their shattering unfixedness. Petworth's spire is before one all the way, Petworth itself clustering on the side of the hill, a little town with several streets rather than a great village all on one artery. I say several streets, but this is dead in the face of tradition, which has a joke to the effect that a long timber waggon once entered Petworth's single, circular street, and has never yet succeeded in emerging. I certainly met it.

THE SHADOW OF THE PEER

The town seems to be beneath the shadow of its lord even more than Arundel: it is like Pompeii, with Vesuvius emitting glory far above. One must, of course, live under the same conditions if one is to feel the authentic thrill; the mere sojourner cannot know it. One wonders, in these feudal towns, what it would be like to leave democratic London or the independence of one's country fastness, and pass for a while beneath the spell of a Duke of Norfolk, or a Baron Leconfield—a spell possibly not consciously cast by them at all, but existing none the less, largely through the fostering care of the townspeople on the rent-roll, largely through the officers controlling the estates; at any rate unmistakable, as present in the very air of the streets as is the presage of a thunderstorm. Surely, to be so dominated, without actual influence, must be very restful. Petworth must be the very home of low-pulsed peace; and yet a little oppressive too, with the great house and its traditions at the top of the town—like a weight on the forehead. I should not like to make Petworth my home, but as a place of pilgrimage, and a stronghold of architectural taste, it is almost unique.

STOPHAM BRIDGE.

PETWORTH'S HISTORY

HOTSPUR'S DESCENDANTS

In the Domesday Book Petworth is called Peteorde. It was rated at 1,080 acres, and possessed a church, a mill worth a sovereign, a river containing 1,620 eels, and pannage for 80 hogs. In the time of the Confessor the manor was worth £18; a few years later the price went down to ten shillings. Robert de Montgomerie held Petworth till 1102, when he defied the king and lost it. Adeliza, widow of Henry I., having a brother Josceline de Louvaine whom she wished to benefit, Petworth was given to him. Josceline married Agnes, daughter of William de Percy, the descendant of one of the Conqueror's chief friends, and, doing so, took his name. In course of time came Harry Hotspur, whose sword, which he swung at the Battle of Shrewsbury, is kept at Petworth House. The second

Earl was his son, also Henry, who fought at Chevy Chase; he was not, however, slain there, as the balladmonger says, but at St. Albans. Henry, the third Earl, fell at Towton; Henry, the fourth Earl, was assassinated at Cock Lodge, Thirsk; Henry, the fifth Earl, led a regiment at the Battle of the Spurs; Henry, the sixth Earl, fell in love with Anne Boleyn, but had the good sense not to let Henry the Eighth see it. Thomas, his brother, was beheaded for treason; Thomas, the seventh Earl, took arms against Queen Elizabeth, and was beheaded in Scotland; Henry, the eighth Earl, attempted to liberate Mary Queen of Scots, and was imprisoned in the Tower, where he slew himself; Henry, the ninth Earl, was accused of assisting Guy Fawkes and locked up for fifteen years. He was set at liberty only after paying £30,000, and promising never to go more than thirty miles from Petworth House. This kept him out of London.

The last two noble Earls of Northumberland were Algernon, Lord High Admiral of England, who married Lady Anna Cecil, and planted an oak in the Park (it is still there) to commemorate the union; and Josceline, eleventh Earl, who died in 1670, leaving no son. He left, however, a daughter, a little Elizabeth, Baroness Percy, who had countless suitors and was married three times before she was sixteen. Her third husband was Charles Seymour, sixth Duke of Somerset, who became in time the father of thirteen children. Of these all died save three girls, and a boy, Algernon, who became seventh Duke of Somerset. Through one of the daughters, Catherine, who married Sir William Wyndham, the estates fell to the present family. The next important Lord of Petworth was George O'Brien Wyndham, third Earl of Egremont, the friend of art and agriculture, who collected most of the pictures. The present owner is the third Baron Leconfield.

THE ROTHER AT FITTLEWORTH.

THE EARL AND THE HOUSEMAID

C. R. Leslie, who painted more than one picture in the Petworth gallery, has much to say in his *Autobiographical Recollections* of its noble founder the third Earl, his generosity, courtesy, kindly thoughtfulness, and extreme modesty of bearing. One story contains half his biography. I give it in Leslie's words. After referring to his Lordship's men-servants and their importance in the house, the painter continues: "His own dress, in the morning, being very plain, he was sometimes by strangers mistaken for one of them. This happened with a maid of one of his lady guests, who had not been at Petworth before. She met him, crossing the hall, as the bell was ringing for the servants' dinner, and said: 'Come, old gentleman, you and I will go to dinner together, for I can't find my way in this great house.' He gave her his arm, and led her to the room where the other maids were assembled at their table, and said: 'You dine here, I don't dine till seven o'clock.'"

THE PETWORTH PICTURES

On certain days in the week visitors are allowed to walk through the galleries of Petworth House. The parties are shown by a venerable servitor into the audit room, a long bare apartment furnished with a statue and the heads of stags; and at the stroke of the hour a commissionaire appears at the far door and leads the way to the office, where a visitors' book is signed. Then the real work of the day begins, and for fifty-five minutes one passes from Dutch painters to Italian, from English to French: amid boors by Teniers, beauties by Lely, landscapes by Turner, carvings by Grinling Gibbons. The commissionaire knows them all. The collection is a fine one, but the lighting is bad, and the conditions under which it is seen are not favourable to the intimate appreciation of good art. One finds one's attention wandering too often from the soldier with his little index rattan to the deer on the vast lawn that extends from the windows to the lake—the lake that Turner painted and fished in. Hobbemas, Vandycks, Murillos—what are these when the sun shines and the ceaseless mutations of a herd of deer render the middle distance fascinating? Among the more famous pictures is a Peg Woffington by Hogarth, not here "dallying and dangerous," but demure as a nun; also the "Modern Midnight Conversation" from the same hand; three or four bewitching Romneys; a room full of beauties of the Court of Queen Anne; Henry VIII by Holbein; a wonderful Claude Lorraine; a head of Cervantes attributed to Velasquez; and four views of the Thames by Turner. Hazlitt, in his *Sketches of the Picture Galleries of England*, says of this collection:—"We wish our readers to go to Petworth . . . where they will find the coolest grottoes and the finest Vandykes in the world."

A PICTORAL PARK

Lord Leconfield's park has not the remarkable natural formation of the Duke of Norfolk's, nor the superb situation of the Duke of Richmond and Gordon's, with its Channel prospects, but it is immense and imposing.

Also it is unreal: it is like a park in a picture. This effect may be largely due to the circumstance that *fêtes* in Petworth Park have been more than once painted; but it is due also, I think, to the shape and colour of the house, to the lake, to the extent of the lawn, to the disposition of the knolls, and to the deer. A scene-painter, bidden to depict an English park, would produce (though he had never been out of the Strand) something very like Petworth. It is the normal park of the average imagination on a large scale.

ALMSHOUSE AT PETWORTH.

Cobbett wrote thus of Petworth:—"The park is very fine, and consists of a parcel of those hills and dells which nature formed here when she was in one of her most sportive moods. I have never seen the earth flung about in such a wild way as round about Hindhead and Blackdown, and this park forms a part of this ground. From an elevated part of it, and, indeed, from each of many parts of it, you see all around the country to the distance of many miles. From the south-east to the north-west the hills are so lofty and so near that they cut the view rather short; but for the rest of the circle you can see to a very great distance. It is, upon the whole, a most magnificent seat, and the Jews will not be able to get it from the *present* owner, though if he live many years they will give even him a *twist*."

THE YOUNG RAVENS

On an eminence in the west is a tower (near a clump where ravens build), from which the other parks of this wonderful park-district of Sussex may be seen: Cowdray to the west, the highest points of Goodwood to the south-west, the highest points of Arundel to the south-east, and Parham's dark forest more easterly still. Mr. Knox's account of the vicissitudes of the Petworth ravens sixty years ago is as interesting as any history of equal length on the misfortunes of man. Their sufferings at the hands of keepers and schoolboys read like a page of Foxe. The final disaster was the spoliation of their nest by a boy, who removed all four of the children, or "squabs" as he called them. Mr. Knox, who used to come every day to examine them through his glass, was in despair, until after much meditation he thought of an expedient. Seeking out the boy he persuaded him to give up the one "squab" whose wings had not yet been clipped, and this the ornithologist carried to the clump and deposited in the ruined nest. The next morning the old birds were to be seen, just as of old, and that was their last molestation.

Just under the park on the road to Midhurst is Tillington, a little village with a rather ornamental church, which dates from 1807. There is nothing to say of Tillington, but I should like to quote a pretty sentence from Horsfield's *History of Sussex* concerning the monuments in the church, in a kind of writing of which we have little to-day:—"And as the volume, for which this has been written, is likely to fall chiefly into the hands of men who are occupied almost solely with the cares and business of this life, this slight reference is made to the monuments of the dead in order that, should the reader of this book find, in the present dearth of honesty, of faithfulness, of disinterested valour and of loyalty, an aching want in his spirit for such high qualities, let him hence be taught where to go—let him learn that, though they are rarely found in the busy haunts of men, they are still preserved and have their home around the sanctuary of the altar of his God."

A TREASURY OF ARCHITECTURE

Petworth should be visited by all young architects; not for the mansion (except as an object-lesson, for it is like a London terrace), but for the ordinary buildings in the town. It is a paradise of old-fashioned architecture. The church is hideous; the new hotel, the "Swan," might be at Balham; but the old part of the town is perfect. There is an almshouse (which Mr. Griggs has drawn), in which in its palmy days a Lady Bountiful might have lived; even the workhouse has charms—it is the only pretty workhouse I remember: with the exception, perhaps, of Battle, but that is, however, self-conscious.

Petworth has known, at any rate, one poet. In the churchyard was once this epitaph, now perhaps obliterated, from a husband's hand:—

"She was! She was! She was, what?
She was all that a woman should be, she was that."

NOAH MANN

In a book which takes account of Sussex men and women of the past, it is hard to keep long from cricket. To the north of Petworth, whither we now turn, is Northchapel, where was born and died one of the great men of the Hambledon Club, Noah Mann, who once made ten runs from one hit, and whose son was named Horace, after the cricketing baronet of the same name, by special permission. "Sir Horace, by this simple act of graceful humanity, hooked for life the heart of poor Noah Mann," says Nyren; "and in this world of hatred and contention, the love even of a dog is worth living for."

PETWORTH CHURCHYARD.

This is Nyren's account of Noah Mann:

GEORGE LEAR'S STRATEGY

"He was from Sussex, and lived at Northchapel, not far from Petworth. He kept an inn there, and used to come a distance of at least twenty miles every Tuesday to practise. He was a fellow of extraordinary activity, and could perform clever feats of agility on horseback. For instance, when he has been seen in the distance coming up the ground, one or more of his companions would throw down handkerchiefs, and these he would collect, stooping from his horse while it was going at full speed. He was a fine batter, a fine field, and the swiftest runner I ever remember:

indeed, such was his fame for speed, that whenever there was a match going forward, we were sure to hear of one being made for Mann to run against some noted competitor; and such would come from the whole country round. Upon these occasions he used to tell his friends, 'If, when we are half-way, you see me alongside of my man, you may always bet your money upon me, for I am sure to win.' And I never saw him beaten. He was a most valuable fellow in the field; for besides being very sure of the ball, his activity was so extraordinary that he would dart all over the ground like lightning. In those days of fast bowling, they would put a man behind the long-stop, that he might cover both long-stop and slip; the man always selected for this post was Noah. Now and then little George Lear (whom I have already described as being so fine a long-stop), would give Noah the wink to be on his guard, who would gather close behind him: then George would make a slip on purpose, and let the ball go by, when, in an instant, Noah would have it up, and into the wicket-keeper's hands, and the man was put out. This I have seen done many times, and this nothing but the most accomplished skill in fielding could have achieved . . .

"At a match of the Hambledon Club against All England, the club had to go in to get the runs, and there was a long number of them. It became quite apparent that the game would be closely fought. Mann kept on worrying old Nyren to let him go in, and although he became quite indignant at his constant refusal, our General knew what he was about in keeping him back. At length, when the last but one was out, he sent Mann in, and there were then ten runs to get. The sensation now all over the ground was greater than anything of the kind I ever witnessed before or since. All knew the state of the game, and many thousands were hanging upon this narrow point. There was Sir Horace Mann, walking about outside the ground, cutting down the daisies with his stick—a habit with him when he was agitated; the old farmers leaning forward upon their tall old staves, and the whole multitude perfectly still. After Noah had had one or two balls, Lumpy tossed one a little too far, when our fellow got in, and hit it out in his grand style. Six of the ten were gained. Never shall I forget the roar that followed this hit. Then there was a dead stand for some time, and no runs were made; ultimately, however, he gained them all, and won the game. After he was out, he upbraided Nyren for not putting him in earlier. 'If you had let me go in an hour ago' (said he), 'I would have served them in the same way.' But the old tactician was right, for he knew Noah to be a man of such nerve and self-possession, that the thought of so much depending upon him would not have the paralysing effect that it would upon many others. He was sure of him, and Noah afterwards felt the compliment. Mann was short in stature, and, when stripped, as swarthy as a gipsy. He was all muscle, with no incumbrance whatever of flesh; remarkably broad in the chest, with large hips and spider legs; he had not an ounce of flesh about him, but it was where it ought to be. He always played without his hat (the sun could not affect *his* complexion), and he took a liking to me as a boy, because I did the same."

A LURGASHALL SATIRIST

Lurgashall, on the road to Northchapel, is a pleasant village, with a green, and a church unique among Sussex churches by virtue of a curious wooden gallery or cloister, said to have been built as a shelter for parishioners from a distance, who would eat their nuncheon there. The church, which has distinct Saxon remains, once had for rector the satirical James Bramston, author of "The Art of Politics" and "The Man of Taste," two admirable poems in the manner of Pope. This is his unimpeachable advice to public speakers:—

Those who would captivate the well-bred throng,
Should not too often speak, nor speak too long:
Church, nor Church Matters ever turn to Sport,
Nor make *St. Stephen's Chappell, Dover-Court.*

CHAPTER XI

BIGNOR

Burton and the sparrowhawk—James Broadbridge—The quaintest of grocer's shops—A transformation scene—The Roman pavement—Charlotte Smith the sonneteer—Parson Dorset's advice—Humility at West Burton—Bury's Amazons.

Two miles due south from Petworth is Burton Park, a modest sandy pleasaunce, with some beautiful deer, an ugly house, and a church for the waistcoat pocket, which some American relic hunter will assuredly carry off unless it is properly chained.

Mr. Knox has an interesting anecdote of a sparrowhawk at Burton. "In May, 1844," he writes, "I received from Burton Park an adult male sparrowhawk in full breeding plumage, which had killed itself, or rather met its death, in a singular manner. The gardener was watering plants in the greenhouse, the door being open, when a blackbird dashed in suddenly, taking refuge between his legs, and at the same moment the glass roof above his head was broken with a loud crash, and a hawk fell dead at his feet. The force of the swoop was so great that for a moment he imagined a stone hurled from a distance to have been the cause of the fracture."

At Duncton, the neighbouring village, under the hill, James Broadbridge was born in 1796—James Broadbridge, who was considered the best all-round cricketer in England in his day. He had a curious hit to square-leg between the wicket and himself, and he was the first of whom it was said that he could do anything with the ball except make it speak. In order to get practice with worthy players he would walk from Duncton to Brighton, just as Lambert would walk from Reigate to London, or Noah Mann ride to Hambledon from Petworth. Jim Broadbridge's first great match was in 1815, for Sussex against the Epsom Club, including Lambert and Lord Frederick Beauclerk, for a Thousand Guineas. Broadbridge, after his wont, walked from Duncton to Brighton in the morning, and he looked so much like a farmer and so little like a cricketer that there was some opposition to his playing. But he bowled out three and caught one and Sussex won the money.

Above Duncton rises Duncton Down, which is eight hundred and thirty-seven feet high, one of our mountains. But we are not to climb it just now, having business in the weald some four miles away to the east, past Barlavington and Sutton, at Bignor.

THE OLDEST GROCER'S SHOP

Admirers of yew trees should make a point of visiting Bignor churchyard. The village has also what is probably the quaintest grocer's shop in England; certainly the completest contrast that imagination could devise to the modern grocer's shop of the town, plate-glassed, illumined and stored to repletion. It is close to the yew-shadowed church, and is gained by a flight of steps. I should not have noticed it as a shop at all, but rather as a very curious survival of a kindly and attractive form of architecture, had not a boy, when asked the way to the Roman pavement, which is Bignor's glory, mentioned "the grocer's" as one of the landmarks. One's connotation of "grocer" excluding diamond panes, oak timbers, difficult steps, and reverend antiquity, I was like to lose the way in earnest, had not a customer emerged opportunely from the crazy doorway with a basket of goods. It was natural for the boy, whose pennies had gone in oranges and sweets, to lay the emphasis on the grocery; but the house externally is the only one of its kind within miles.

A ROMAN VILLA

In some respects there is no more interesting spot in Sussex than the mangold field on Mr. Tupper's farm that contains the Roman pavements. Approaching this scene of alien treasure one observes nothing but the mangolds; here and there a rough shed as if for cattle; and Mr. Tupper, the grandson of the discoverer of the mosaics, at work with his hoe. This he lays on one side on the arrival of a visitor, taking in his hand instead a large key. So far, we are in Sussex pure and simple; mangolds all around, cattle sheds in front, a Sussex farmer for a companion, the sky of Sussex over all, and the twentieth century in her nonage. Mr. Tupper turns the key, throws open the creaking door—and nearly two thousand years roll away. We are no longer in Sussex but in the province of the Regni; no longer at Bignor but Ad Decimum, or ten miles from Regnum (or Chichester) on Stane Street, the direct road to Londinum, in the residence of a Roman Colonial governor of immense wealth, probably supreme in command of the province.

The fragments of pavement that have been preserved are mere indications of the splendour and extent of the building, which must have covered some acres—a welcome and imposing sight as one descended Bignor Hill by Stane Street, with its white walls and columns rising from the dark weald. The pavement in the first shed which Mr. Tupper unlocks has the figure of Ganymede in one of its circular compartments; and here the hot-air pipes, by which the villa was heated, may be seen where the floor has given way. A head of Winter in another of the sheds is very fine; but it is rather for what these relics stand for, than any intrinsic beauty, that they are interesting. They are perfect symbols of a power that has passed away. Nothing else so brings back the Roman occupation of Sussex, when on still nights the clanking of armour in the camp on the hill-top could be heard by the trembling Briton in the Weald beneath; or by day the ordered sounds of marching would smite upon his ears, and, looking fearfully upwards, he would see a steady file of warriors descending the slope. I never see a Sussex hill crowned by a camp, as at Wolstonbury, without seeing also in imagination a flash of steel. Perhaps one never realises the new terror which the Romans must have brought into the life of the Sussex peasant—a terror which utterly changed the Downs from ramparts of peace into coigns of minatory advantage, and transformed the gaze of security, with which their grassy contours had once been contemplated, into anxious glances of dismay and trepidation—one never so realises this terror as when one descends Ditchling Beacon by the sunken path which the Romans dug to allow a string of soldiers to drop unperceived into the Weald below. That semi-subterranean passage and the Bignor pavements are to me the most vivid tokens of the Roman rule that England possesses.

PARSON DORSET

Charlotte Smith, the sonneteer and novelist, was the daughter of Nicholas Turner, of Bignor Park, which contains, I think, the plainest house I ever saw in the country. Charlotte Smith, who was all her life very true to Sussex both in her work and in her homes—she was at school at Chichester, and lived at Woolbeding and Brighton—was born in 1749. A century ago her name was as well known as that of Mrs. Hemans was later. To-day it is unknown, and her poems and novels are unread, nor will they, I fear, be re-discovered. Her sister, Catherine Turner, afterwards Mrs. Dorset, was the author of *The Peacock at Home*, a very popular book for children at the beginning of the last century, suggested by Roscoe's *Butterfly's Ball*. Mrs. Dorset, by the way, married a son of the vicar of Walberton and Burlington, whose curious head-dress gave to an odd-looking tree on Bury hill the name of Parson Dorset's wig—for the parson was known by his eccentricities far from home. The old story of advice to a flock: "Do as I say, not as I do," is told also of him.

VILLAGE HUMILITY

The little village of West Burton, east of Bignor, is associated in my mind with an expression of the truest humility. A kindly villager had given me a glass of water, and I unfolded my map and spread it on her garden wall to consult while I drank. "Why," she said, "you don't mean to say a little place like West Burton is marked on a map." This is the very antipodes of the ordinary provincial pride, which would have the world's axis project from the ground hard by the village pump. But pride of place is not, I think, a Sussex characteristic.

Bury, the next hamlet in the east, under the hills, has curious cricket traditions. In June, 1796, the married women of Bury beat the single women by 80 runs, and thereupon, uniting forces, challenged any team of women in the county. Not only did the women of Bury shine at cricket, but in a Sussex paper for 1791 I find an account of two of Bury's daughters assuming the names of Big Ben and Mendoza and engaging in a hardly contested prize fight before a large gathering. Big Ben won.

THE CAUSEWAY, HORSHAM.

CHAPTER XII

HORSHAM

Horsham stone—Horsham and history—- Pressing to death—Juvenile hostility to statues—Horsham's love of pleasure—Percy Bysshe Shelley's boyhood—a letter of invitation—Sedition in Sussex—a Slinfold epitaph—Rudgwick's cricket poet—Warnham pond—Stane Street—Cobbett at Billingshurst—The new Christ's Hospital.

Horsham is the capital of West Sussex: a busy agricultural town with horse dealers in its streets, a core of old houses, and too many that are new. There is in England no more peaceful and prosperous row of venerable homes than the Causeway, joining Carfax and the church, with its pollarded limes and chestnuts in line on the pavement's edge, its graceful gables, jutting eaves, and glimpses of green gardens through the doors and windows. The sweetest part of Horsham is there. Elsewhere the town bustles. (I should, however, mention the very picturesque house—now cottages—on the left of the road as one leaves the station: as fine a mass of timbers, gables, and oblique lines as one could wish, making an effect such as time alone can give. The days of such relics are numbered.)

HORSHAM STONE

Horsham not only has beautiful old houses of its own, but it has been the cause of beautiful old houses all over the county; since nothing so adds to the charm of a building as a roof of Horsham stone, those large grey flat slabs on which the weather works like a great artist in harmonies of moss, lichen, and stain. No roofing so combines dignity and homeliness, and no roofing except possibly thatch (which, however, is short-lived) so surely passes into the landscape. But Horsham stone is no longer used. It is to be obtained for a new house only by the demolition of an old; and few new houses have rafters sufficiently stable to bear so great a weight. Our ancestors built for posterity: we build for ourselves. Our ancestors used Sussex oak where we use fir.

Not only is Horsham stone on the roofs of the neighbourhood: it is also on the paths, so that one may step from flag to flag for miles, dryshod, or at least without mud.

Horsham's place in history is unimportant: but indirectly it played its part in the fourteenth century, by supplying the War Office of that era with bolts for cross bows, excellent for slaying Scots and Frenchmen. The town was famous also for its horseshoes. In the days of Cromwell we find Horsham to have been principally Royalist; one engagement with Parliamentarians is recorded in which it lost three warriors to Cromwell's one. In the reign of William III. a young man claiming to be the Duke of Monmouth, and travelling with a little court who addressed him as "Your Grace," turned the heads of the women in many an English town— his good looks convincing them at once, as the chronicler says, that he was the true prince. Justices sitting at Horsham, however, having less susceptibility to the testimony of handsome features, found him to be the son of an innkeeper named Savage, and imprisoned him as a vagrant and swindler.

PRESSING TO DEATH

Horsham was the last place in which pressing to death was practised. The year was 1735, and the victim a man unknown, who on being charged with murder and robbery refused to speak. Witnesses having been called to prove him no mute, this old and horrible sentence, proper (as the law considered) to his offence and obstinacy, was passed upon him. The executioner, the story goes, while conveying the body in a wheelbarrow to burial, turned it out in the roadway at the place where the King's Head now stands, and then putting it in again, passed on. Not long afterwards he fell dead at this spot.

The church of St. Mary, which rises majestically at the end of the Causeway, has a slender shingled spire that reaches a great height—not altogether, however, without indecision. There is probably an altitude beyond which shingles are a mistake: they are better suited to the more modest spire of the small village. The church is remarkable also for length of roof (well covered with Horsham stone), and it is altogether a singularly commanding structure. Within is an imposing plainness. The stone effigy of a knight in armour reclines just to the south of the altar: son of a branch of the Braose family—of Chesworth, hard by, now in ruins—of whose parent stock we shall hear more when we reach Bramber. The knight, Thomas, Lord Braose, died in 1395. The youth of Horsham, hostile invincibly, like all boys, to the stone nose, have reduced that feature to the level of the face; or was it the work of the Puritans, who are known to have shared in the nasal objection? South of the churchyard is the river, from the banks of which the church would seem to be all Horsham, so effectually is the town behind it blotted out by its broad back. On the edge of the churchyard is perhaps the smallest house in Sussex: certainly the smallest to combine Gothic windows with the sale of ginger-beer.

A SCHOOL OF CHAMPIONS

Horsham seems always to have been fond of pleasure. Within iron railings in the Carfax, in a trim little enclosure of turf and geraniums, is the ancient iron ring used in the bull-baiting which the inhabitants indulged in and loved until as recently as 1814. That the town is still disposed to entertainment, although of a quieter kind, its walls testify; for the hoardings are covered with the promise of circus or conjuror, minstrels or athletic sports, drama or lecture. In July, when I was there last, Horsham was anticipating a *fête*, in which a mock bull-fight and a battle of confetti were mere details; while it was actually in the throes of a fair. The booths filled an open space to the west of the town known as the Jew's Meadow, and among the attractions was Professor Adams with his "school of undefeated champions." The plural is in the grand manner, giving the lie to Cashel Byron's pathetic plaint:—

It is a lonely thing to be a champion.

Avoiding Professor Adams, and walking due west, one comes after a couple of miles to Broadbridge Heath, where is Field Place, the birthplace of the greatest of Sussex poets, and perhaps the greatest of the county's sons—Percy Bysshe Shelley. The author of *Adonais* was born in a little bedroom with a south aspect on August 4, 1792. His father's mother, *née* Michell, was the daughter of a late vicar of Horsham and member of an old Sussex family; another Horsham cleric, the Rev. Thomas Edwards, gave the boy his first lessons. Field Place is still very much what it was in Shelley's early days—the only days it was a home to him. It stands low, in a situation darkened by the surrounding trees, a rambling house neither as old as one would wish for æsthetic reasons nor as new as comfort might dictate. There is no view. In the garden one may in fancy see again the little boy, like all poetic children, "deep in his unknown day's employ." Indeed, like all children, might be said, for is not every child a poet for a little while? In the *Life of Shelley* by his cousin Thomas Medwin is printed the following letter to a friend at Horsham, written when he was nine, which I quote not for any particular intrinsic merit, but because it helps to bring him before us in his Field Place days, of which too little is known:—

"*Monday, July 18, 1803.*

"Miss Kate,
"Horsham,
"Sussex.

"Dear Kate,—We have proposed a day at the pond next Wednesday, and if you will come to-morrow morning I would be much obliged to you, and if you could any how bring Tom over to stay all the night, I would thank you. We are to have a cold dinner over at the pond, and come home to eat a bit of roast chicken and peas at about nine o'clock. Mama depends upon your bringing Tom over to-morrow, and if you don't we shall be very much disappointed. Tell the bearer not to forget to bring me a fairing, which is some ginger-bread, sweetmeat, hunting-nuts, and a pocket-book. Now I end.

"I am not
"Your obedient servant,
"P. B. Shelley."

SHELLEY IN SUSSEX

We are proud to call Shelley the Sussex poet, but he wrote no Sussex poems, and a singularly uncongenial father (for the cursing of whom and the King the boy was famous at Eton) made him glad to avoid the county when he was older. It was, however, to a Sussex lady, Miss Hitchener of Hurstpierpoint, that Shelley, when in Ireland in 1812, forwarded the box of inflammatory matter which the Custom House officers confiscated—copies of his pamphlet on Ireland and his "Declaration of Rights"

144

broadside, which Miss Hitchener was to distribute among Sussex farmers who would display them on their walls. These were the same documents that Shelley used to put in bottles and throw out to sea, greatly to the perplexity of the spectators and not a little to the annoyance of the Government. Miss Hitchener, as well as the revolutionary, was kept under surveillance, as we learn from the letter from the Postmaster-General of the day, Lord Chichester:—"I return the pamphlet declaration. The writer of the first is son of Mr. Shelley, member for the Rape of Bramber, and is by all accounts a most extraordinary man. I hear he has married a servant, or some person of very low birth; he has been in Ireland for some time, and I heard of his speaking at the Catholic Convention. Miss Hitchener, of Hurstpierpoint, keeps a School there, and is well spoken of; her Father keeps a Publick House in the Neighbourhood, he was originally a Smuggler and changed his name from Yorke to Hitchener before he took the Public House. I shall have a watch upon the daughter and discover whether there is any Connection between her and Shelley."

"THE SUSSEX MUSE"

There Shelley's connection with Sussex may be said to end. Yet a poet, whether he will or no, is shaped by his early surroundings. In some verses by Mr. C. W. Dalmon called "The Sussex Muse," I find the influence of Shelley's surroundings on his mind happily recorded:—

"When Shelley's soul was carried through the air
Toward the manor house where he was born,
    I danced along the avenue at Denne,
And praised the grace of Heaven, and the morn
    Which numbered with the sons of Sussex men
        A genius so rare!
So high an honour and so dear a birth,
    That, though the Horsham folk may little care

To laud the favour of his birthplace there,
My name is bless'd for it throughout the earth.

I taught the child to love, and dream, and sing
Of witch, hobgoblin, folk and flower lore;
   And often led him by the hand away
Into St. Leonard's Forest, where of yore
    The hermit fought the dragon—to this day,
      The children, ev'ry Spring,
Find lilies of the valley blowing where
   The fights took place. Alas! they quickly drove
   My darling from my bosom and my love,
And snatched my crown of laurel from his hair."

COTTAGES AT SLINFOLD.

SLINFOLD

Two miles south-west of Field Place, by a footpath which takes us beside the Arun, here a narrow stream, and a deserted water mill, we come to the churchyard of Slinfold, a little quiet village with a church of almost suburban solidity and complete want of Sussex feeling. James Dallaway, the historian of Western Sussex, was rector here from 1803 to 1834. He lived, however, at Leatherhead, Slinfold being a sinecure. A Slinfold epitaph on an infant views bereavement with more philosophy than is usual: in conclusion calling upon Patience thus to comfort the parents:

Teach them to praise that God with grateful mind
For babes that yet may come, for one still left behind.

A quarter of a mile west is Stane Street, striking London-wards from Billingshurst, and we may follow it for a while on our way to Rudgwick, near the county's border. We leave the Roman road (which once ran as straight as might be as far as Billingsgate, but is now diverted and lost in many spots) at the drive to Dedisham, on the left, and thus save a considerable corner. Dedisham, in its hollow, is an ancient agricultural settlement: a farm and feudatory cottages in perfect completeness, an isolated self-sufficing community, lacking nothing—not even the yellow ferret in the cage. The footpath beyond the homestead crosses a field where we find the Arun once again—here a stream winding between steep banks, sure home of kingfisher and water-rats.

RUDGWICK

Rudgwick, which is three miles farther west along the hard high road, is a small village on a hill, with the most comfortable looking church-tower in Sussex hiding behind the inn and the general shop. In the churchyard lies a Frusannah—a name new to me.

Rudgwick was the birthplace, in 1717, of Reynell Cotton, destined to be the author of the best song in praise of cricket. He entered Winchester College in 1730, took orders and became master of Hyde Abbey school in the same city, and died in 1779. Nyren prints his song in full. This is the heart of it:—

The wickets are pitch'd now, and measur'd the ground,
Then they form a large ring, and stand gazing around,
Since AJAX fought HECTOR, in sight of all TROY,
No contest was seen with such fear and such joy.

Ye bowlers, take heed, to my precepts attend,
On you the whole fate of the game must depend;
Spare your vigour at first, nor exert all your strength,
But measure each step, and be sure pitch a length.

Ye fieldsmen, look sharp, lest your pains ye beguile;
Move close, like an army, in rank and in file,
When the ball is return'd, back it sure, for I trow
Whole states have been ruin'd by one overthrow.

Ye strikers, observe when the foe shall draw nigh,
Mark the bowler advancing with vigilant eye:
Your skill all depends upon distance and sight,
Stand firm to your scratch, let your bat be upright.

Further west is Loxwood, on the edge of a little-known tract of country, untroubled by railways, the most unfamiliar village in which is perhaps Plaistow. Plaistow is on the road to nowhere and has not its equal for quietude in England. It is a dependency of Kirdford, whence comes the Petworth marble which we see in many Sussex churches. Shillinglee Park, the seat of the Earl of Winterton, is hard by.

From these remote parts one may return to Horsham by way of Warnham, on whose pond Shelley as a boy used to sail his little boat, and where perhaps he gained that love of navigation which never left him and brought about his death. Warnham, always a cricketing village, until lately supplied the Sussex eleven with dashing Lucases; but it does so no more.

STANE STREET

Before passing to the east of Horsham, something ought to be said of one at least of the villages of the south-west, namely, Billingshurst, on Stane Street, once an important station between Regnum and Londinum, or Chichester and London, as we should now say. It has been conjectured that Stane Street (which we first saw at Chichester under the name of East Street, and again as it descended Bignor hill in the guise of a bostel) was constructed by Belinus, a Roman engineer, who gave to the woods through which he had to cut his way in this part of Sussex the name, Billingshurst, and to the gate by which London was entered, Billingsgate.

Billingshurst's place in literature was made by William Cobbett, for it was here that he met the boy in a smock frock who recalled to his mind so many of his deeds of Quixotry. The incident is described in the *Rural Rides*:—

COBBETT AND THE LITTLE CHAP

"This village is seven miles from Horsham, and I got here to breakfast about seven o'clock. A very pretty village, and a very nice breakfast, in a very neat little parlour of a very decent public-house. The landlady sent her son to get me some cream, and he was just such a chap as I was at his age, and dressed just in the same sort of way, his main garment being a blue smock-frock, faded from wear, and mended with pieces of *new* stuff, and, of course, not faded. The sight of this smock-frock brought to my recollection many things very dear to me. This boy will, I daresay, perform his part at Billingshurst, or at some place not far from it. If accident had not taken me from a similar scene, how many villains and fools, who have been well teased and tormented, would have slept in peace at night, and have fearlessly swaggered about by day!

RUDGWICK.

"When I look at this little chap—at his smock-frock, his nailed shoes, and his clean, plain, coarse shirt, I ask myself, will anything, I wonder, ever send this chap across the ocean to tackle the base, corrupt, perjured Republican Judges of Pennsylvania? Will this little lively, but, at the same time, simple boy, ever become the terror of villains and hypocrites across the Atlantic? What a chain of strange circumstances there must be to lead this boy to thwart a miscreant tyrant like M'keen, the Chief Justice, and afterwards Governor, of Pennsylvania, and to expose the corruptions of the band of rascals, called a 'Senate and a House of Representatives,' at Harrisburgh, in that state!"

A VILLAGE DISPUTE

Billingshurst church has an interesting ceiling, an early brass (to Thomas and Elizabeth Bartlet), and the record of one of those disputes over pews which add salt to village life and now and then, as we saw at Littlehampton, lead to real trouble. The verger (if he be the same) will tell the story, the best part of which describes the race which was held every Sunday for certain seats in the chancel, and the tactical "packing" of the same by the winning party. In the not very remote past a noble carved chair used to be placed in one of the galleries for the schoolmaster, and there would he sit during service surrounded by his boys.

One returns to Horsham from Billingshurst through Itchingfield, where the new Christ's Hospital has been built in the midst of green fields: a glaring red-brick settlement which the fastidiously urban ghost of Charles Lamb can now surely never visit. "Lamb's House," however, is the name of one of the buildings; and Time the Healer, who can do all things, may mellow the new school into Elian congeniality.

CHAPTER XIII

ST. LEONARD'S FOREST

Recollections of the Forest—Leonardslee—Michael Drayton and the iron country—Thomas Fuller on great guns—The serpent of St. Leonard's Forest—The Headless Horseman—Sussex and nightingales.

To the east of Horsham spreads St. Leonard's Forest, that vast tract of moor and preserve which, merging into Tilgate Forest, Balcombe Forest, and Worth Forest, extends a large part of the way to East Grinstead.

Only on foot can we really explore this territory; and a compass as well as a good map is needed if one is to walk with any decision, for there are many conflicting tracks, and many points whence no broad outlook is possible. Remembering old days in St. Leonard's Forest, I recall, in general, the odoriferous damp open spaces of long grass, suddenly lighted upon, over which silver-washed fritillaries flutter; and, in particular, a deserted farm, in whose orchard (it must have been late June) was a spreading tree of white-heart cherries in full bearing. One may easily, even a countryman, I take it, live to a great age and never have the chance of climbing into a white-heart cherry tree and eating one's fill. Certainly I have never done it since; but that day gave me an understanding of blackbirds' temptations that is still stronger than the desire to pull a trigger. The reader must not imagine that St. Leonard's Forest is rich in deserted farms with attractive orchards. I have found no other, and indeed it is notably a place in which the explorer should be accompanied by provisions.

LEONARDSLEE

To take train to Faygate and walk from that spot is the simplest way, although more interesting is it perhaps to come to Faygate at the end of the day, and, gaining permission to climb the Beacon Tower on the hill, in the Holmbush estate, retrace one's steps in vision from its summit. In this case one would walk from Horsham to Lower Beeding, then strike north over Plummer's Plain. This route leads by Coolhurst and through Manning Heath, just beyond which, by following the south, that runs for a mile, one could see Nuthurst. Lower Beeding is not in itself interesting; but close at hand is Leonardslee, the seat of Sir Edmund Loder, which is one of the most satisfying estates in the county. North and south runs a deep ravine, on the one side richly wooded, and on the other, the west, planted with all acclimatisable varieties of Alpine plants and flowering shrubs. The chain of ponds at the bottom of the ravine forms one of the principal sources of the Adur. In an enclosure among the woods the kangaroo has been acclimatised; and beavers are given all law.

North of Plummer's Plain, in a hollow, are two immense ponds, Hammer Pond and Hawkin's Pond, our first reminder that we are in the old iron country. St. Leonard's Forest, and all the forests on this the forest ridge of Sussex, were of course maintained to supply wood with which to feed the furnaces of the iron masters—just as the overflow of these ponds was trained to move the machinery of the hammers for the breaking of the iron stone. The enormous consumption of wood in the iron foundries was a calamity seriously viewed by many observers, among them Michael Drayton, of the *Poly Olbion*, who was, however, distressed less as a political economist than as the friend of the wood nymphs driven by the encroaching and devastating foundrymen from their native sanctuaries to the inhospitable Downs. Thus he writes, illustrating Lamb's criticism of him that in this work he "has animated hills and streams with life and passion above the dreams of old mythology":—

The daughters of the Weald
(That in their heavy breasts had long their griefs concealed),
Foreseeing their decay each hour so fast come on,
Under the axe's stroke, fetched many a grievous groan.
When as the anvil's weight, and hammer's dreadful sound,
Even rent the hollow woods and shook the queachy ground;
So that the trembling nymphs, oppressed through ghastly fear,
Ran madding to the downs, with loose dishevelled hair.
The Sylvans that about the neighbouring woods did dwell,
Both in the tufty frith and in the mossy fell,
Forsook their gloomy bowers, and wandered far abroad,
Expelled their quiet seats, and place of their abode,
When labouring carts they saw to hold their daily trade,
Where they in summer wont to sport them in the shade.
"Could we," say they, "suppose that any would us cherish
Which suffer every day the holiest things to perish?
Or to our daily want to minister supply?
These iron times breed none that mind posterity.
'Tis but in vain to tell what we before have been,
Or changes of the world that we in time have seen;
When, now devising how to spend our wealth with waste,
We to the savage swine let fall our larding mast,
But now, alas! ourselves we have not to sustain,
Nor can our tops suffice to shield our roots from rain.
Jove's oak, the warlike ash, veined elm, the softer beech,
Short hazel, maple plain, light asp, the bending wych,
Tough holly, and smooth birch, must altogether burn;
What should the builder serve, supplies the forger's turn,
When under public good, base private gain takes hold,
And we, poor woful woods, to ruin lastly sold."

GREAT GUNS

We shall learn later more of this old Sussex industry, but here, in the heart of St. Leonard's Forest, I might quote also what another old author, with less invention, says of it. Under the heading of Sussex manufactures, Thomas Fuller writes, in the *Worthies*, of great guns:—

"It is almost incredible how many are made of the Iron in this County. Count *Gondomer* well knew their goodness, when of King James he so often begg'd the boon to transport them. A Monke of Mentz (some three hundred years since) is generally reputed the first Founder of them. Surely *ingenuity* may seem *transpos'd*, and to have *cross'd her hands*, when about the same time a Souldier found out Printing; and it is questionable which of the two Inventions hath done more good, or more harm. As for Guns, it cannot be denied, that though most behold them as *Instruments of cruelty*; partly, because subjecting *valour* to *chance*; partly, because *Guns give no quarter* (which the Sword sometimes doth); yet it will appear that, since their invention, Victory hath not stood so long a Neuter, and hath been determined with the loss of fewer lives. Yet do I not believe what Souldiers commonly say, 'that *he was curs'd in his Mother's belly, who is kill'd with a Cannon*,' seeing many prime persons have been slain thereby."

SUSSEX IRON WORKS

Cannon were not, of course, the only articles which the old Sussex ironmasters contrived. The old railings around St. Paul's were cast in Sussex; and iron fire-backs were turned out in great numbers. These are still to be seen in a few of the older Sussex cottages in their original position. Most curiosity dealers in the country have a few fire-backs on sale. Iron tombstones one meets with too in a few of the churches and churchyards in the iron district. There are several at Wadhurst, for example.

THE "LAND SERPENT"

I have seen grass snakes in plenty in St. Leonard's Forest, and was once there with a botanist who, the day being fine, killed a particularly beautiful one; but the Forest is no longer famous, as once it was, for really alarming reptiles. The year 1614 was the time. A rambler in the neighbourhood, in August of that year, ran the risk of meeting something worth running away from; just as John Steel, Christopher Holder, and a widow woman did. Their story may be read in the Harleian Miscellany. *True and Wonderful* is the title of the narrative, *A Discourse relating a strange and monstrous Serpent (or Dragon) lately discovered, and yet living, to the great Annoyance and divers Slaughters both of Men and Cattell, by his strong and violent Poyson: In Sussex, two Miles from Horsam, in a Woode called St. Leonard's Forrest, and thirtie Miles from London, this present Month of August, 1614. With the true Generation of Serpents.* The discourse runs thus:—"In Sussex, there is a pretty market-towne, called Horsam, neare unto it a forrest, called St. Leonard's Forrest, and there, in a vast and unfrequented place, heathie, vaultie, full of unwholesome shades, and over-growne hollowes, where this serpent is thought to be bred; but, wheresoever bred, certaine and too true it is, that there it yet lives. Within three or four miles compasse, are its usual haunts, oftentimes at a place called Faygate, and it hath been seene within halfe a mile of Horsam; a wonder, no doubt, most terrible and noisome to the inhabitants thereabouts. There is always in his tracke or path left a glutinous and slimie matter (as by a small similitude we may perceive in a snaile's) which is very corrupt and offensive to the scent; insomuch that they perceive the air to be putrified withall, which must needes be very dangerous. For though the corruption of it cannot strike the outward part of a man, unless heated into his blood; yet by receiving it in at any of our breathing organs (the mouth or nose) it is by authoritie of all authors, writing in that kinde, mortall and deadlie, as one thus saith:

"*Noxia serpentum est admixto sanguine pestis.*—LUCAN.

"This serpent (or dragon, as some call it) is reputed to be nine feete, or rather more, in length, and shaped almost in the forme of an axeltree of a cart; a quantitie of thickness in the middest, and somewhat smaller at both endes. The former part, which he shootes forth as a necke, is supposed to be an elle long; with a white ring, as it were, of scales about it. The scales along his backe seem to be blackish, and so much as is discovered under his bellie, appeareth to be red; for I speak of no nearer description than of a reasonable ocular distance. For coming too neare it, hath already beene too dearely payd for, as you shall heare hereafter.

"It is likewise discovered to have large feete, but the eye may be there deceived; for some suppose that serpents have no feete, but glide upon certain ribbes and scales, which both defend them from the upper part of their throat unto the lower part of their bellie, and also cause them to move much the faster. For so this doth, and rids way (as we call it) as fast as a man can run. He is of countenance very proud, and at the sight or hearing of men or cattel, will raise his necke upright, and seem to listen and looke about, with great arrogancy. There are likewise on either side of him discovered, two great bunches so big as a large foote-ball, and (as some thinke) will in time grow to wings; but God, I hope, will (to defend the poor people in the neighbourhood) that he shall be destroyed before he grow so fledge.

"He will cast his venome about four rodde from him, as by woefull experience it was proved on the bodies of a man and a woman comming that way, who afterwards were found dead, being poysoned and very much swelled, but not prayed upon. Likewise a man going to chase it, and as he imagined, to destroy it with two mastive dogs, as yet not knowing the great danger of it, his dogs were both killed, and he himselfe glad to

157

returne with hast to preserve his own life. Yet this is to be noted, that the dogs were not prayed upon, but slaine and left whole: for his food is thought to be, for the most part, in a conie-warren, which he much frequents; and it is found much scanted and impaired in the encrease it had woont to afford.

SIGNED AND WITNESSED

"These persons, whose names are hereunder printed, have seene this serpent, beside divers others, as the carrier of Horsam, who lieth at the White Horse in Southwarke, and who can certifie the truth of all that has been here related.

John Steele.
Christopher Holder.
And a Widow Woman
dwelling nere Faygate."

It would be very interesting to know what John Steele, Christopher Holder, and the widow woman really saw. Such a story must have had a basis of some kind. A printed narrative such as this would hardly have proceeded from a clear sky.

St. Leonard's Forest has another familiar; for there the headless horseman rides, not on his own horse, but on yours, seated on the crupper with his ghostly arms encircling your waist. His name is Powlett, but I know no more, except that his presence is an additional reason why one should explore the forest on foot.

SUSSEX NIGHTINGALES

Sussex, especially near the coast, is naturally a good nightingale country. Many of the birds, pausing there after their long journey at the end of April, do not fly farther, but make their home where they first alight. I know of one meadow and copse under the north escarpment of the Downs where three nightingales singing in rivalry in a triangle (the perfect condition) can be counted upon in May, by night, and often by day too, as surely as the rising and setting of the sun. But in St. Leonard's Forest the nightingale never sings. American visitors who, as Mr. John Burroughs once did, come to England in the spring to hear the nightingale, must remember this.

CHAPTER XIV

WEST GRINSTEAD, COWFOLD
AND HENFIELD

"The Rape of the Lock"—Knepp castle—The Cowfold brass—Carthusians in Sussex—The Oakendene cricketers—Fourteen Golden Orioles on Henfield common—A Henfield botanist—Dr. Thomas Stapleton's merits—A good epitaph—Sussex humour.

West Grinstead is perhaps the most remarkable of the villages on the line from Horsham to Steyning, by reason of its association with literature, *The Rape of the Lock* having been to a large extent composed beneath a tree in the park. Yet as one walks through this broad expanse of brake-fern, among which the deer are grazing, with the line of the Downs, culminating in Chanctonbury Ring, in view, it requires a severe effort to bring the mind to the consideration of Belinda's loss and all the surrounding drama of the toilet and the card table. If there is one thing that would not come naturally to the memory in West Grinstead park, it is the poetry of Pope.

The present house, the seat of the Burrells, was built in 1806. It was in the preceding mansion that John Caryll, Pope's friend, made his home, moving hither from West Harting, as we have seen. Caryll suggested to Pope the subject of *The Rape of the Lock*, the hero of which was his cousin, Lord Petre. The line:—

This verse to Caryll, Muse, is due,

is the poet's testimony and thanks. John Gay, who found life a jest, has also walked amid the West Grinstead bracken.

West Grinstead church is isolated in the fields, a curiously pretty and cheerful building, with a very charming porch and a modest shingled spire rising from its midst. Brasses to members of the Halsham family are within, and a monument to Captain Powlett, whose unquiet ghost, hunting without a head, we have just met. Hard by the church is one of the most attractive and substantial of the smaller manor houses of Sussex, square and venerable and well-roofed with Horsham stone.

A mile to the west, in a meadow by the Worthing road, stands the forlorn fragment of the keep which is all that remains of the Norman stronghold of Knepp. For its other stones you must seek the highways, the road-menders having claimed them a hundred years ago. William de Braose, whom we shall meet at Bramber, built it; King John more than once was entertained in it; and now it is a ruin. Yet if Knepp no longer has its castle, it has its lake—the largest in the county, a hundred acres in extent, a beautiful sheet of water the overflow of which feeds the Adur.

Within a quarter of a mile of the ruin is the new Knepp Castle, which was built by Sir Charles Merrik Burrell, son of Sir William Burrell, the antiquary, whose materials for a history of Sussex on a grand scale, collected by him for many years, are now in the British Museum. But Knepp Castle, the new, with all its Holbeins, was destroyed by fire this 1904.

THE NELOND BRASS

THE COWL IN SUSSEX

To the east of the line lies Cowfold, balancing West Grinstead, a village ranged on either side of a broad road. It is famous chiefly for possessing, in its very pretty church, the Nelond brass, being the effigy of Thomas Nelond, Prior of Lewes, who died in 1433. Few brasses are finer or larger; in length it is nearly ten feet, its state is practically perfect, and pilgrims come from all quarters to rub it. John Nelond, in the dress of a Cluniac monk, stands with folded hands beneath an arch, protected by the Virgin and Child, St. Pancras, and St. Thomas à Becket. This splendid relic would, perhaps, were ours an ideal community, be handed over to the keeping of the Carthusian monks near by, in the Monastery of St. Hugh, the commanding building to the south of Cowfold, whose spire is to the Weald what that of Chichester Cathedral is to the plain between the Downs and the sea, and whose Angelus may be heard, on favourable evenings, for many miles. The Carthusian monks of St. Hugh's lend a very foreign air to the village when they walk through it. Visitors are encouraged to call at the porter's gate and explore this huge settlement— often in the very competent care of an Irish brother; while to suffer an accident anywhere in the neighbourhood is to be certain of a cordial glass of the monastery's own Chartreuse.

It was at Brook Hill, just to the north of Cowfold, that William Borrer, the ornithologist and the author of *The Birds of Sussex*, lived and made many of his interesting observations.

Near Cowfold is Oakendene, a stronghold of cricket at the beginning of the last century. William Wood was the greatest of the Oakendene men. He was the best bowler in Sussex, the art having been acquired as he walked about his farm with his dog, when he would bowl at whatever he saw and the dog would retrieve the ball. Borrer of Ditchling, Marchant of Hurst, Voice of Hand Cross, and Vallance of Brighton, also belonged to the Oakendene club. Borrer and Vallance played for Brighton against Marylebone, at Lord's, in 1792, and, when all the betting was against them, including gold rings and watches, won the match in the second innings by making respectively 60 and 68 not out. Another player in that match was Jutten, the fast bowler, who when things were going against him bowled at his man and so won by fear what he could not compass by skill. There are too many Juttens on village greens.

Five miles south of Cowfold is Henfield, separated from Steyning, in the south-west, by the low-lying meadows through which the Adur runs and which in winter are too often a sheet of water.

Henfield consists of the usual street, and a quiet, retired common, flat and marshy, with a flock of geese, some Scotch firs, and a fine view of Wolstonbury rising in the east. It was on Henfield common that Mr. Borrer once saw fourteen Golden Orioles on a thorn bush. Adventures are to the adventurous, birds to the ornithologist; most of us have never succeeded in seeing even one Oriole.

STAPLETON'S MERITS

William Borrer, the botanist, uncle of the ornithologist, was born in Henfield and is buried there. In his Henfield garden, in 1860, as many as 6,600 varieties of plants were growing. Beyond a small memoir on Lichens, written in conjunction with Dawson Turner, he left no book. Another illustrious son of Henfield was Dr. Thomas Stapleton, once Canon of Chichester and one of the founders of the Catholic College of Douay, of whom it was written, somewhat ambiguously, that he "was a man of mild demeanour and unsuspected integrity." Fuller has him characteristically touched off in the *Worthies*:—"He was bred in New Colledge in Oxford, and then by the Bishop (Christopherson, as I take it) made Cannon of Chichester, which he quickly quitted in the first of Queen *Elizabeth*. Flying beyond the Seas, he first fixed at *Douay*, and there commendably performed the office of *Catechist*, which he discharged to his commendation.

"Reader, pardon an Excursion caused by just *Grief* and *Anger*. Many, counting themselves Protestants in England, do slight and neglect that *Ordinance* of *God*, by which their Religion was *set up*, and *gave Credit* to it in the first *Reformation*; I mean, CATECHISING. Did not our *Saviour* say even to Saint *Peter* himself, 'Feed my Lambs, feed my Sheep'? And why *Lambs* first? 1. Because they were *Lambs* before they were *Sheep.* 2. Because, if they be not fed whilst *Lambs* they could never be *Sheep.* 3. Because *Sheep* can in some sort feed themselves; but *Lambs* (such their tenderness) must either be *fed* or *famished.* Our Stapleton was excellent at this *Lamb-feeding.*"

An epitaph in Henfield Church is worth copying for its quaint mixture of mythology and theology. It bears upon the death of a lad, Meneleb Raynsford, aged nine, who died in 1627:—

Great Jove hath lost his Gannymede, I know,
Which made him seek another here below—
And finding none—not one—like unto this,
Hath ta'en him hence into eternal bliss.
Cease, then, for thy dear Meneleb to weep,
God's darling was too good for thee to keep:
But rather joy in this great favour given,
A child on earth is made a saint in heaven.

Three miles east of Henfield, and a little to the north, is a farm the present tenant of which has made an interesting experiment. He found in the house an old map of the county, and identifying his own estate, discovered a large sheet of water marked on it. On examining the site he saw distinct traces of this ancient lake, and at once set about building a dam to restore it. Water now, once again, fills the hollow, completely transforming this part of the country, and bringing into it wild duck and herons as of old. The lake is completely hidden from the neighbouring roads and is accessible only by field paths, but it is well worth finding.

A WOODCOCK ON AN OAK

There once hung in the parlour of Henfield's chief inn—I wonder if it is there still—a rude etching of local origin, rather in the manner of Buss's plates to *Pickwick*, representing an inn kitchen filled with a jolly company listening uproariously to a fat farmer by the fire, who, with arm raised, told his tale. Underneath was written, "Mr. West describing how he saw a woodcock settle on an oak"—a perfect specimen of the Sussex joke.

CHURCH STREET, STEYNING.

CHAPTER XV

STEYNING AND BRAMBER

Saint Cuthman and his mother—Steyning's architecture—Steyning's wise passiveness—Bramber castle—A corrupt pocket borough—A Taxidermist-humorist—Joseph Poorgrass in Sussex—The widow of Beeding and the Romney—A digression on curio-hunting.

Of great interest and antiquity is Steyning, the little grey and red town which huddles under the hill four miles to Henfield's south-west.

THE ADVENTURES OF CUTHMAN

The beginnings of Steyning are lost in the distance. Its church was founded, probably in the eighth century, by St. Cuthman, an early Christian whose adventures were more than usually quaint. He began by tending his father's sheep, with which occupation his first miracle was associated. Being called one day to dinner, and having no one to take his place as shepherd, he drew a circle round the flock with his crook, and bade the sheep, in the name of the Lord, not to stray beyond it. The sheep obeyed, and thenceforward on repeating the same manœuvre he left them with an easy mind. In course of time his father died, and Cuthman determined to travel; intense filial piety determined him to take his aged mother with him. In order to do this he constructed a wheelbarrow couch, which he partly supported by a cord over his shoulders. Thus united, mother and son fared forth into the cold world; which was, however, warmed for

166

them by the watchful interest taken in Cuthman by a vigilant Providence. One day, for example, the cord of the barrow broke in a hayfield, where Cuthman, who supplied its place by elder twigs, was the subject of much ridicule among the haymakers. Immediately a heavy storm broke over the field, destroying the crop; and not only then, but ever afterwards in the same field—possibly to this day—has haymaking been imperilled by a similar storm. So runs the legend.

The second occasion on which the cord broke and let down Cuthman's mother was at Steyning. Cuthman took the incident as a divine intimation that the time had come to settle, and he thereupon first built for his mother and himself a hut and afterwards a church. The present church stands on its site. Cuthman was buried there. So, also, was Ethelwulf, father of Alfred the Great, whose body afterwards was moved to Winchester. Alfred the Great had estates at Steyning, as elsewhere in Sussex.

While Cuthman was building his church a beam shifted, making a vast amount of new labour necessary. But as the Saint sorrowfully was preparing to begin again, a stranger appeared, who pointed out how the mischief could be repaired in a more speedy manner and with less toil. Cuthman and his men followed his instructions, and all was quickly well again. Cuthman thereupon fell on his knees and asked the stranger who he was. "I am He in whose name thou buildest this temple," he replied, and vanished.

STEYNING CHURCH.

The present church, which stands on the site of St. Cuthman's, is only a reminder of what it must have been in its best days. When one faces the curiously chequered square tower, an impression of quiet dignity is imparted; but a broadside view is disappointing by reason of the high deforming roof, giving an impression as of a hunched back. (One sees the same effect at Udimore, in the east of Sussex.) Within are two rows of superb circular arches, with zigzag mouldings, on massive columns.

STEYNING AND HISTORY

Steyning has an importance in English history that is not generally credited to it. Edward the Confessor gave a great part of the land to the Abbey at Fécamp, whose church is, or was, the counterpart of Steyning's. These possessions Harold took away, an act that, among others, decided William, Duke of Normandy, upon his assailing, and conquering, course. Steyning should be proud. To have brought the Conqueror over is at least as worthy as to have come over with him, and far more uncommon.

In Church Street stands Brotherhood Hall, a very charming ancient building, long used as a Grammar School, flanked by overhanging houses, which, though less imposing, are often more quaint and ingratiating. Most of Steyning, indeed, is of the past, and the spirit of antiquity is visibly present in its streets.

The late Louis Jennings, in his *Rambles among the Hills*, was fascinated by the placid air of this unambitious town—as an American might be expected to be in the uncongenial atmosphere of age and serenity. "One almost expects," he wrote, "to see a fine green moss all over an inhabitant of Steyning. One day as I passed through the town I saw a man painting a new sign over a shop, a proceeding that so aroused my curiosity that I stood for a minute or two to look on. The painter filled in one letter, gave a huge yawn, looked up and down two or three times as if he had lost something, and finally descended from his perch and disappeared. Five weeks later I passed that way again, and it is a fact that the same man was at work on the same sign. Perhaps when the reader takes the walk I am about to recommend to his attention—a walk which comprises some of the finest scenery in Sussex—that sign will be finished, and the accomplished artist will have begun another; but I doubt it. There is plenty of time for everything in Steyning." I am told that Steyning was incensed when this criticism was printed (there was even talk of an action for libel); but it seems to me that whatever may have been intended, the words contain more of compliment than censure. In this hurrying age, it is surely high praise to have one's "wise passiveness" (as Wordsworth called it) so emphasised. The passage calls to mind Diogenes requesting, as the greatest of possible boons, that Alexander the Great would stand aside and not interrupt the sunshine; only at Steyning would one seek for Diogenes to-day. No commendation of Steyning in the direction of its enterprise, briskness, smartness, or any of the other qualities which are now most in fashion, would so speedily decide a wise man to pitch his tent there as Mr. Jennings' certificate of inertia.

STEYNING HARBOUR

Steyning, if still disposed to stand on its defence, might plead external influence, beyond the control of man, as an excuse for some of its interesting placidity. For this curiously inland town was once a port. In Saxon times (when Steyning was more important than Birmingham), the Adur was practically an estuary of the sea, and ships came into Steyning Harbour, or St. Cuthman's Port, as it was otherwise called. There is notoriously no such quiet spot as a dry harbour town. In those days, Steyning also had a mint.

Bramber, a little roadside village less than a mile south-east of Steyning, also a mere relic of its great days, was once practically on the coast, for the arm of the sea which narrowed down at Steyning was here of great breadth, and washed the sides of the castle mound. The last time I came into Steyning was by way of the bostel down Steyning Round Hill. The old place seems more than ever medieval as one descends upon it from the height (the best way to approach a town); and sitting among the wild thyme on the turf I tried to reconstruct in imagination the scene a thousand years ago, with the sea flowing over the meadows of the Adur valley, and the masts of ships clustered beyond Steyning church. Once one had the old prospect well in the mind's eye, the landscape became curiously in need of water.

BRAMBER.

BRAMBER

After rain, Bramber is a pleasant village, but when the dust flies it is good neither for man nor beast. All that remains of the castle is crumbling battlement and a wall of the keep, survivals of the renovation of the old Saxon stronghold by William de Braose, the friend of the Conqueror and the Sussex founder of the Duke of Norfolk's family. Picnic parties now frolic among the ruins, and enterprising boys explore the rank overgrowth in the moat below.

The castle played no part in history, its demolition being due probably to gunpowder pacifically fired with a view to obtaining building materials. But during the Civil War the village was the scene of an encounter between Royalists and Roundheads. A letter from John Coulton to Samuel Jeake of Rye, dated January 8, 1643-4, thus describes the event:—"The enemy attempted Bramber bridge, but our brave Carleton and Evernden with his Dragoons and our Coll.'s horse welcomed them with drakes and musketts, sending some 8 or 9 men to hell (I feare) and one trooper to Arundel Castle prisoner, and one of Capt. Evernden's Dragoons to heaven." A few years later, as we have seen, Charles II. ran a grave risk at Bramber while on his way to Brighton and safety.

A POCKET BOROUGH

Bramber was, for many years, a pocket borough of the worst type. George Spencer, writing to Algernon Sidney after the Bramber election in 1679, says:—"You would have laughed to see how pleased I seemed to be in kissing of old women; and drinking wine with handfuls of sugar, and great glasses of burnt brandy; three things much against the stomach." In 1768, eighteen votes were polled for one candidate and sixteen for his rival. One of the tenants, in a cottage valued at about three shillings a week, refused £1000 for his vote. Bramber remained a pocket borough until the Reform Bill. William Wilberforce, the abolitionist, sat for it for some years; there is a story that on passing one day through the village he stopped his carriage to inquire the name. "Bramber? Why, that's the place I'm Member for."

Bramber possesses a humorist in taxidermy, whose efforts win more attention than the castle. They are to be seen in a small museum in its single street, the price of admission being for children one penny, for adults twopence, and for ladies and gentlemen "what they please" (indicating that the naturalist also knows human nature). In one case, guinea-pigs strive in cricket's manly toil; in another, rats read the paper and play dominoes; in a third, rabbits learn their lessons in school; in a fourth, the last scene in the tragedy of the *Babes of the Wood* is represented, Bramber Castle in the distance strictly localising the event, although Norfolk usually claims it.

Isolated in the fields south of Bramber are two of the quaintest churches in the county—Coombes and Botolphs. Neither has an attendant village.

COOMBES CHURCH.

JOSEPH POORGRASS IN FACT

The owl story, which crops up all over the country and is found in literature in Mr. Hardy's novel *Far from the Madding Crowd*, the scene whereof is a hundred miles west of Sussex, has a home also at Upper Beeding, the little dusty village beyond Bramber across the river. Mr. Hardy gives the adventure to Joseph Poorgrass; at Beeding, the hero is one Kiddy Wee. His rightful name was Kidd; but being very small the village had invented this double diminutive. Lost in the wood he cried for help, just as Poorgrass did. "Who? who?" asked the owl. "Kiddy Wee o' Beedin'," was the reply.

A DEALER OUTWITTED

It was not long ago that a masterpiece was discovered at Beeding, in one of those unlikely places in which with ironical humour fine pictures so often hide themselves. It hung in a little general shop kept by an elderly widow. After passing unnoticed or undetected for many years, it was silently identified by a dealer who happened to be buying some biscuits. He made a casual remark about it, learned that any value that might be set upon it was sentimental rather than monetary, and returned home. He laid the matter before one or two friends, with the result that they visited Beeding in a party a day or so later in order to bear away the prize. Outside the shop they held a council of war. One was for bidding at the outset a small but sufficient sum for the picture, another for affecting to want something else and leading round to the picture, and so forth; but in the discussion of tactics they raised their voices too high, so that a visitor of the widow, sitting in the room over the shop, heard something of the matter. Suspecting danger, but wholly unconscious of its nature, she hurried downstairs and warned her friend of a predatory gang outside who were not to be supplied on any account with anything they asked for. The widow obeyed blindly. They asked for tea—she refused to sell it; they asked for biscuits—she set her hand firmly on the lid; they mentioned the picture—she was a rock. Baffled, they withdrew; and the widow, now on the right scent, took the next train to Brighton to lay the whole matter before her landlord. He took it up, consulted an expert, and the picture was found to be a portrait of Mrs. Jordan, the work either of Romney or Lawrence.

THE FURNITURE SWINDLE

Furniture is the usual prey of the dealer who lounges casually through old villages in the guise of a tourist, asking for food or water at old cottages and farmhouses, and using his eyes to some purpose the while. Pictures are rare. The search for chests, turned bed-posts, fire-backs, Chippendale chairs, warming pans, grandfather's clocks, and other indigenous articles of the old simple homestead which are thought so decorative in the sophisticated villa and establish the artistic credit and taste of their new owner, has been prosecuted in Sussex with as much energy as elsewhere—not only by the professional dealer, but by amateurs no less unwilling to give an ignorant peasant fifteen shillings for an article which they know to be worth as many pounds. But suspicion of the plausible furniture collector has, I am glad to say, begun to spread, and the palmiest days of the spoliation of the country are probably over. It must not, however, be thought that the peasant is always the under dog, the amateur the upper. A London dealer informs me that the planting of spurious antiques in old cottages has become a recognised form of fraud among less scrupulous members of the trade. An oak chest bearing every superficial mark of age that a clever workman can give it (and the profession of wormholer, is now, I believe, recognised) is deposited in a tumble-down, half-timbered home in a country village, whose occupant is willing to take a share in the game; a ticket marked "Ginger-beer; sold Here" is placed in the window, and the trap is ready. It is almost beyond question that everyone who bids for this chest, which has, of course, been in the family for generations, is hoping to get it at a figure much lower than is just; it is quite certain that whatever is paid for it will be too much. Ugly as the situation is, I like to think of this biting of the biter.

174

CHANCTONBURY RING.

CHAPTER XVI

CHANCTONBURY,
WASHINGTON, AND WORTHING

Chanctonbury Ring—The planter of the beeches—The Gorings—Thomas
Fuller on the Three Shirleys—Ashington's chief—Warminghurst and
the phantasm—Washington—An expensive mug of beer—Findon—A
champion pluralist—Cissbury—John Selden's wit and wisdom—Thomas
à Becket's figs—Worthing's precious climate—Sompting church.

For nothing within its confines is Steyning so famous as for the hill
which rises to the south-west of it—Chanctonbury Ring. Other of the
South Downs are higher, other are more commanding: Wolstonbury, for
example, standing forward from the line, makes a bolder show, and Firle
Beacon daunts the sky with a braver point; but when one thinks of the
South Downs as a whole it is Chanctonbury that leaps first to the inward
eye. Chanctonbury, when all is said, is the monarch of the range.

The words of the Sussex enthusiast, refusing an invitation to spend a
summer abroad, express the feeling of many of his countrymen:—

For howsoever fair the land,
   The time would surely be
That brought our Wealden blackbird's note
   Across the waves to me.

And howsoever strong the door,
   'Twould never keep at bay
The thought of Fulking's violets,
   The scent of Holmbush hay.

And ever when the day was done,
   And all the sky was still,
How I should miss the climbing moon
   O'er Chanctonbury's hill!

CHANCTONBURY RING

It is Chanctonbury's crown of beeches that lifts it above the other hills. Uncrowned it would be no more noticeable than Fulking Beacon or a score of others; but its dark grove can be seen for many miles. In Wiston House, under the hill, the seat of the Goring family, to whom belong the hill and a large part of the country that it dominates, is an old painting of Chanctonbury before the woods were made, bare as the barest, without either beech or juniper, and the eye does not notice it until all else in the picture has been examined. The planter of Chanctonbury's Ring, in 1760, was Mr. Charles Goring of Wiston, who wrote in extreme old age in 1828 the following lines:—

How oft around thy Ring, sweet Hill,
   A Boy, I used to play,
And form my plans to plant thy top
   On some auspicious day.
How oft among thy broken turf
   With what delight I trod,
With what delight I placed those twigs
   Beneath thy maiden sod.
And then an almost hopeless wish

Would creep within my breast,
Oh! could I live to see thy top
　In all its beauty dress'd.
That time's arrived; I've had my wish,
　And lived to eighty-five;
I'll thank my God who gave such grace
　As long as e'er I live.
Still when the morning Sun in Spring,
　Whilst I enjoy my sight,
Shall gild thy new-clothed Beech and sides,
　I'll view thee with delight.

Most of the trees on the side of Chanctonbury and its neighbours were self-sown, children of the clumps which Mr. Goring planted. I might add that Mr. Charles Goring was born in 1743, and his son, the present Rev. John Goring, in 1823, when his father was eighty; so that the two lives cover a period of one hundred and sixty years—true Sussex longevity.

Wiston House (pronounced Wisson) is a grey Tudor building in the midst of a wide park, immediately under the hill. The lofty hall, dating from Elizabeth's reign, is as it was; much of the remainder of the house was restored in the last century. The park has deer and a lake. The Goring family acquired Wiston by marriage with the Faggs, and a superb portrait of Sir John Fagg, in the manner of Vandyck with a fine flavour of Velasquez, is one of the treasures of the house.

Before the Faggs came the Shirleys, a family chiefly famous for the three wonderful brothers, Anthony, Robert, and Thomas.

SIR ANTHONY SHIRLEY

Fuller, in the *Worthies*, gives them full space indeed considering that none was interested in the Church. I cannot do better than quote him:—

"SIR ANTHONY SHIRLEY, second Son to Sir *Thomas*, set forth from *Plimouth*, *May* the 21st, 1596, in a Ship called the *Bevis of Southampton*, attended with six lesser vessels. His design for *Saint Thome* was violently diverted by the contagion they found on the South Coast of Africa, where the rain did stink as it fell down from the heavens, and within six hours did turn into magots. This made him turn his course to *America*, where he took and kept the city of *St. Jago* two days and nights, with two hundred and eighty men (whereof eighty were wounded in the service), against three thousand *Portugalls*.

"Hence he made for the Isle of *Fuego*, in the midst whereof a Mountaine, Ætna-like, always burning; and the wind did drive such a shower of ashes upon them, that one might have wrote his name with his finger on the upper deck. However, in this fiery Island, they furnished themselves with good water, which they much wanted.

"Hence he sailed to the Island of *Margarita*, which to him did not answer its name, not finding here the *Perl Dredgers* which he expected. Nor was his gaine considerable in taking the Town of *Saint Martha*, the Isle and chief town of *Jamaica*, whence he sailed more than *thirty* leagues up the river *Rio-dolci*, where he met with great extremity.

"At last, being diseased in person, distressed for victuals, and deserted by all his other ships, he made by *New-found-land* to *England*, where he arrived June 15, 1597. Now although some behold his voyage, begun with more courage then counsel, carried on with more valour then advice, and coming off with more honour than profit to himself or the nation (the Spaniard being rather frighted then harmed, rather braved then frighted therewith); yet unpartial judgments, who measure not worth by success, justly allow it a prime place amongst the probable (though not prosperous) English Adventures.

SIR ROBERT SHIRLEY

"SIR ROBERT SHIRLEY, youngest Son to Sir *Thomas*, was, by his Brother *Anthony*, entred in the *Persian* Court. Here he performed great Service against the *Turkes*, and shewed the difference betwixt *Persian* and *English* Valour; the latter having therein as much Courage, and more Mercy, giving Quarter to Captives who craved it, and performing Life to those to whom he promised it. These his Actions drew the Envie of the *Persian* Lords, and Love of the Ladies, amongst whom one (reputed a Kins-man to the great *Sophy*) after some Opposition, was married unto him. She had more of *Ebony* than *Ivory* in her Complexion; yet amiable enough, and very valiant, a quality considerable in that Sex in those Countries. With her he came over to *England*, and lived many years therein. He much affected to appear in *forreign Vestes*; and, as if his *Clothes* were his limbs, accounted himself never ready till he had something of the Persian Habit about him.

"At last a Contest happening betwixt him and the Persian Ambassadour (to whom some reported Sir Robert gave a Box on the Ear) the King sent them both into *Persia*, there mutually to impeach one another, and joyned Doctor *Gough* (a Senior Fellow of *Trinity colledge* in *Cambridge*) in commission with Sir Robert. In this Voyage (as I am informed) both died on the Seas, before the controverted difference was ever heard in the Court of *Persia*, about the beginning of the Reign of King *Charles*.

SIR THOMAS SHIRLEY

"Sir THOMAS SHIRLEY, I name him the last (though the eldest Son of his Father) because last appearing in the world, men's *Activity* not always observing the method of their *Register*. As the Trophies of *Miltiades* would not suffer *Themistocles* to sleep; so the Atchievements of his two younger brethren gave an Alarum unto his spirit. He was ashamed to see them worne like Flowers 'in the *Breasts* and *Bosomes* of forreign Princes, whilst he himself withered upon the stalk he grew on'.

This made him leave his aged Father and fair Inheritance in this *County*, and to undertake *Sea Voyages* into forreign parts, to the great *honour* of his *Nation*, but small *inriching* of *himself*; so that he might say to his Son, as *Æneas* to *Æscanius*:—

'Disce, puer, Virtutem ex me verumque Laborem,
Fortunam ex aliis.'

'Virtue and Labour learn from me thy Father,
As for Success, Child, learn from others rather.'

"As to the generall performance of these *three brethren*, I know the *Affidavit* of a Poet carrieth but a small credit in the *court of History*; and the *Comedy* made of them is but a *friendly foe* to their Memory, as suspected more accomodated to please the present spectators, then inform posterity. However, as the belief of Mitio (when an *Inventory* of his adopted *Sons misdemeanours* was brought unto him) embraced a middle and moderate way, *nec omnia credere nec nihil*, neither to *believe all things nor nothing* of what was told him: so in the *list of their Atchievements* we may safely pitch on the same proportion, and, when abatement is made for *poeticall embellishments*, the remainder will speak them Worthies in their generations."—Such were the three Shirleys.

Wiston church, which shelters under the eastern wall of the house, almost leaning against it, has some interesting tombs.

BIOHCHANDOUNE

Walking west from Wiston we come to the tiny hamlet of Buncton, one of the oldest settlements in Sussex, a happy hunting ground for excavators in search of Roman remains, and possessing in Buncton chapel a quaint little Norman edifice. The word Buncton is a sign of modern carelessness for beautiful words: the original Saxon form was "Biohchandoune," which is charming.

Buncton belongs to Ashington, two miles to the north-west on the Worthing road, a quiet village with a fifteenth-century church (a mere child compared with Buncton Chapel) and a famous loss. The loss is tragic, being no less than that of the parish register containing a full and complete account, by Ashington's best scribe, of a visit of Good Queen Bess to the village in 1591. A destroyed church may be built again, but who shall restore the parish register? The book, however, is perhaps still in existence, for it was deliberately stolen, early in the eighteenth century, by a thief who laid his plans as carefully as did Colonel Blood in his attack on the regalia, abstracting the volume from a cupboard in the rectory, through a hole which he made in the outside wall. No interest in the progress of Queen Elizabeth prompted him: the register was taken during the hearing of a law suit in order that its damning evidence might not be forthcoming.

WILLIAM PENN IN SUSSEX

While at Ashington we ought to see Warminghurst, only a mile distant, once the abode of the Shelleys, and later of William Penn, who bought the great house in 1676. One of his infant children is buried at Coolham, close by, where he attended the Quakers' meeting and where services are still held. The meeting-house was built of timber from one of Penn's ships.

A later owner than Penn, James Butler, rebuilt Warminghurst and converted a large portion of the estate into a deer park; but it was thrown back into farm land by one of the Dukes of Norfolk, while the house was destroyed, the deer exiled, and the lake drained. Perhaps it was time that the house came down, for in the interim it had been haunted; the ghost being that of the owner of the property, who one day, although far distant, was seen at Warminghurst by two persons and afterwards was found to have died at the time of his appearance. Warminghurst in those days of park and deer, lake and timber (it had a chestnut two hundred and seventy years old), might well be the first spot to which an enfranchised spirit winged its way.

From Warminghurst is a road due south, over high sandy heaths, to Washington, which, unassuming as it is, may be called the capital of a large district of West Sussex that is unprovided with a railway. Steyning, five miles to the east, Amberley, seven miles to the west, and West Worthing, eight miles to the south, on the other side of the Downs, are the nearest stations. In the midst of this thinly populated area stands Washington, at the foot of the mountain pass that leads to Findon, Worthing and the sea. It was once a Saxon settlement (Wasa inga tun, town of the sons of Wasa); it is now derelict, memorable only as a baiting place for man and beast. But there are few better spots in the country for a modest contented man to live and keep a horse. Rents are low, turfed hills are near, and there is good hunting.

A COSTLY QUART

The church, which was restored about fifty years ago, but retains its Tudor tower, stands above the village. In 1866 three thousand pennies of the reign of Edward the Confessor and Harold were turned up by a plough in this parish, and, says Mr. Lower, were held so cheaply by their finders that half a pint measure of them was offered at the inn by one man in exchange for a quart of beer. Possibly Mr. Hilaire Belloc would not think the price excessive, for I find him writing, in a "Sussex Drinking Song":

They sell good beer at Haslemere
   And under Guildford Hill;
At little Cowfold, as I've been told,
   A beggar may drink his fill.
There is a good brew in Amberley too,
   And by the Bridge also;

But the swipes they take in at the Washington Inn
   Is the very best beer I know.

The white road to Worthing from Washington first climbs the hills and then descends steadily to the sea. The first village is Findon, three miles distant, but one passes on the way two large houses, Highden and Muntham. Muntham, which was originally a shooting box of Viscount Montagu, lord of Cowdray, was rebuilt in the nineteenth century by an eccentric traveller in the East, named Frankland, a descendant of Oliver Cromwell, who, settling at home again, gave up his time to collecting mechanical appliances.

Findon is a pleasant little village at the bottom of the valley, the home of the principal Sussex training stable, which has its galloping course under Cissbury. Training stables may be found in many parts of the Downs, but the Sussex turf has not played the same part in the making of race horses as that of Hampshire and Berkshire.

Lady Butler painted the background of her picture of Balaclava at Findon, the neighbourhood of which curiously resembles in configuration the Russian battlefield.

A FINISHED PLURALIST

The rector of Findon in 1276, Galfridus de Aspall, seems to have brought the art of pluralising to a finer point than most. In addition to being rector of Findon, he had, Mr. Lower tells us, a benefice in London, two in the diocese of Lincoln, one in Rochester, one in Hereford, one in Coventry, one in Salisbury, and seven in Norwich. He was also Canon of St. Paul's and Master of St. Leonard's Hospital at York.

Above Findon on the south-east rises Cissbury, one of the finest of the South Downs, but, by reason of its inland position, less noticeable than the hills on the line. There have been many conjectures as to its history. The Romans may have used it for military purposes, as certainly they did for the pacific cultivation of the grape, distinct terraces as of a vineyard being still visible; traces of a factory of flint arrow heads have been found (giving it the ugly name of the "Flint Sheffield"); while Cissa, lord of Chichester, may have had a bury or fort there. Mr. Lower's theory is that the earthworks on the summit, whatever their later function, were originally religious, and probably druidical.

Salvington (a little village which is gained by leaving the main road two miles beyond Cissbury and bearing to the west) is distinguished as the birthplace, in 1584, of one who was considered by Hugo Grotius to be the glory of the English nation—John Selden. Nowadays, when we choose our glories among other classes of men than jurists and wits, it is more than possible for even cultured persons who are interested in books to go through life very happily without knowledge at all of this great man, the friend of great men and the writer best endowed with common sense of any of his day. From Selden's *Table Talk* I take a few passages on the homelier side, to be read at Salvington:—

JOHN SELDEN'S WISDOM

FRIENDS.

Old Friends are best. King James used to call for his old Shoes; they were easiest for his Feet.

CONSCIENCE.

Some men make it a Case of Conscience, whether a Man may have a Pigeon-house, because his Pigeons eat other Folks' Corn. But there is no such thing as Conscience in the Business; the Matter is, whether he be a Man of such Quality, that the State allows him to have a Dove-house; if so, there's an end of the business; his Pigeons have a right to eat where they please themselves.

CHARITY.

Charity to Strangers is enjoin'd in the Text. By Strangers is there understood those that are not of our own Kin, Strangers to your Blood; not those you cannot tell whence they come; that is, be charitable to your Neighbours whom you know to be honest poor People.

CEREMONY.

Ceremony keeps up all things: 'Tis like a Penny-Glass to a rich Spirit, or some excellent Water; without it the Water were spilt, the Spirit lost.

Of all people Ladies have no reason to cry down Ceremony, for they take themselves slighted without it. And were they not used with Ceremony, with Compliments and Addresses, with Legs and Kissing of Hands, they were the pitifullest Creatures in the World. But yet methinks to kiss their Hands after their Lips, as some do, is like little Boys, that after they eat the apple, fall to the Paring, out of a Love they have to the Apple.

RELIGION.

Religion is like the Fashion: one Man wears his Doublet slashed, another laced, another plain; but every Man has a Doublet. So every man has his Religion. We differ about Trimming.

Alteration of Religion is dangerous, because we know not where it will stay: 'tis like a *Millstone* that lies upon the top of a pair of Stairs; 'tis hard to remove it, but if once it be thrust off the first Stair, it never stays till it comes to the bottom.

We look after Religion as the Butcher did after his Knife, when he had it in his Mouth.

WIT.

Nature must be the ground-work of Wit and Art; otherwise whatever is done will prove but Jack-pudding's work.

WIFE.

You shall see a Monkey sometime, that has been playing up and down the Garden, at length leap up to the top of the Wall, but his Clog hangs a great way below on this side: the Bishop's Wife is like that Monkey's Clog; himself is got up very high, takes place of the Temporal Barons, but his Wife comes a great way behind.

Selden's father was a small farmer who played the fiddle well. The boy is said at the age of ten to have carved over the door a Latin distich, which, being translated, runs:—

Walk in and welcome, honest friend; repose.
Thief, get thee gone! to thee I'll not unclose.

SAINT THOMAS'S FIGS

Between Salvington and Worthing lies Tarring, noted for its fig gardens. It is a fond belief that Thomas à Becket planted the original trees from which the present Tarring figs are descended; and there is one tree still in existence which tradition asserts was set in the earth by his own hand. Whether this is possible I am not sufficiently an arboriculturist to say; but Becket certainly sojourned often in the Archbishop of Canterbury's palace in the village. The larger part of the present fig garden dates from 1745. I have seen it stated that during the season a little band of *becca ficos* fly over from Italy to taste the fruit, disappearing when it is gathered; but a Sussex ornithologist tells me that this is only a pretty story.

The fig gardens are perhaps sufficient indication that the climate of this part of the country is very gentle. It is indeed unique in mildness. There is a little strip of land between the sea and the hills whose climatic conditions approximate to those of the Riviera: hence, in addition to the success of the Tarring fig gardens, Worthing's fame for tomatoes and other fruit. I cannot say when the tomato first came to the English table, but the first that I ever saw was at Worthing, and Worthing is now the centre of the tomato-growing industry. Miles of glass houses stretch on either side of the town.

Worthing (like Brighton and Bognor) owed its beginning as a health resort to the house of Guelph, the visit of the Princess Amelia in 1799 having added a *cachet*, previously lacking, to its invigorating character. But, unlike Brighton, neither Worthing nor Bognor has succeeded in becoming quite indispensable. Brighton has the advantage not only of being nearer London but also nearer the hills. One must walk for some distance from Worthing before the lonely highland district between Cissbury and Lancing Clump is gained, whereas Brighton is partly built upon the Downs and has her little Dyke Railway to boot. But the visitor to Worthing who, surfeited of sea and parade, makes for the hill country, knows a solitude as profound as anything that Brighton's heights can give him.

"HAWTHORN AND LAVENDER"

Worthing has at least two literary associations. It was there that that most agreeable comedy *The Importance of Being Earnest* was written: the town even gave its name to the principal character—John Worthing; and it was there that Mr. Henley lived while the lyrics in *Hawthorn and Lavender* were coming to him. The beautiful dedication to the book is dated "Worthing, July 31, 1901."

> Ask me not how they came,
> These songs of love and death,
> These dreams of a futile stage,
> These thumb-nails seen in the street:
> Ask me not how nor why,

But take them for your own,
Dear Wife of twenty years,
Knowing—O, who so well?—
You it was made the man
That made these songs of love,
Death, and the trivial rest:
So that, your love elsewhere,
These songs, or bad or good—
How should they ever have been?

SOMPTING.

SOMPTING

Of the villages to the west we have caught glimpses in an earlier *chapter*—Goring, Angmering, Ferring, and so forth; to the north and east are Broadwater, Sompting and Lancing. Broadwater is perhaps a shade too near Worthing to be interesting, but Sompting, lying under the Downs, is unspoiled, with its fascinating church among the elms and rocks. The church (of which Mr. Griggs has made an exquisite drawing) was built nearly eight hundred years ago. Within are some curious fragments of sculpture, and a tomb which Mr. Lower considered to belong to Richard Bury, Bishop of Chichester in the reign of Henry VIII. East of Sompting lie the two Lancings, North Lancing on the hill, South Lancing on the coast. East of North Lancing, the true village, stands Lancing College, high above the river, with its imposing chapel, a landmark in the valley of the Adur and far out to sea.

LANCING.

CHAPTER XVII

BRIGHTON

A decline in interest—The storied past of Brighton—Dr. Russell's discovery—The First Gentleman in Europe—The resources of the Steyne—Promenade Grove—A loyal journalist—The Brighton bathers—Smoaker and Martha Gunn—The Prince and cricket—The Nonpareil at work—Byron at Brighton—Hazlitt's observation—Horace Smith's verses—Sidney Smith on the M.C.—Captain Tattersall—Pitt and the heckler—Dr. Johnson in the sea—Mrs. Pipchin and Dr. Blimber—The Brighton fishermen—Richard Jefferies on the town—The Cavalier—Mr. Booth's birds—Old Pottery.

Brighton is interesting only in its past. To-day it is a suburb, a lung, of London; the rapid recuperator of Londoners with whom the pace has been too severe; the Mecca of day-excursionists, the steady friend of invalids and half-pay officers. It is vast, glittering, gay; but it is not interesting.

To persons who care little for new towns the value of Brighton lies in its position as the key to good country. In a few minutes one can travel by train to the Dyke, and leaving booths and swings behind, be free of miles of turfed Down or cultivated Weald; in a few minutes one can reach Hassocks, the station for Wolstonbury and Ditchling Beacon; in a few minutes one can gain Falmer and plunge into Stanmer Park; or, travelling to the next station, correct the effect of Brighton's hard brilliance amid the soothing sleepinesses of Lewes; in a few minutes on the western line one can be at Shoreham, amid ship-builders and sail-makers, or on the ramparts of Bramber Castle, or among the distractions of Steyning cattle market, with Chanctonbury Ring rising solemnly beyond. Brighton, however, knows little of these homes of peace, for she looks only out to sea or towards London.

BRIGHTON'S STORIED PAST

Brighton was, however, interesting a hundred years ago; when the Pavilion was the favourite resort of the First Gentleman in Europe (whose opulent charms, preserved in the permanency of mosaic, may be seen in the Museum); when the Steyne was a centre of fashion and folly; coaches dashed out of Castle Square every morning and into Castle Square every evening; Munden and Mrs. Siddons were to be seen at one or other of the theatres; Martha Gunn dipped ladies in the sea; Lord Frederick Beauclerck played long innings on the Level; and Mr. Barrymore took a pair of horses up Mrs. Fitzherbert's staircase and could not get them down again without the assistance of a posse of blacksmiths.

Brighton was interesting then, reposing in the smiles of the Prince of Wales and his friends. But it is interesting no more,—with the Pavilion a show place, the Dome a concert hall, the Steyne an enclosure, Martha Gunn in her grave, the Chain Pier a memory, Mrs. Fitzherbert's house the headquarters of the Young Men's Christian Association, and the Brighton road a racing track for cyclists, motor cars and walking stockbrokers. Brighton is entertaining, salubrious, fashionable, what you will. Its interest has gone.

The town's rise from Brighthelmstone (pronounced Brighton) a fishing village, to Brighton, the marine resort of all that was most dashing in English society, was brought about by a Lewes doctor in the days when Lewes was to Brighton what Brighton now is to Lewes. This doctor was Richard Russell, born in 1687, who, having published in 1750 a book on the remedial effects of sea water, in 1754 removed to Brighton to be able to attend to the many patients that were flocking thither. That book was the beginning of Brighton's greatness. The seal was set upon it in 1783, when the Prince of Wales, then a young man just one and twenty, first visited the town.

LE PRINCE S'AMUSE

The Prince's second visit to Brighton was in July 1784. He then stayed at the house engaged for him by his cook, Louis Weltje, which, when he decided to build, became the nucleus of the Pavilion. The Prince at this time (he was now twenty-two) was full of spirit and enterprise, and in the company of Colonel Hanger, Sir John Lade of Etchingham, and other bloods, was ready for anything: even hard work, for in July 1784 he rode from Brighton to London and back again, on horse-back, in ten hours. One of his diversions in 1785 is thus described in the Press: "On Monday, June 27, His Royal Highness amused himself on the Steyne for some time in attempting to *shoot doves with single balls*; but with what result we have not heard, though the Prince is esteemed a most excellent shot, and seldom presents his piece without doing some execution. The Prince, in the course of his diversion, either by design or accident, *lowered the tops of several of the chimneys of the Hon. Mr. Windham's house.*" The Prince seemed to live for the Steyne. When the first scheme of the Pavilion was completed, in 1787, his bedroom in it was so designed that he could recline at his ease and by means of mirrors watch everything that was happening on his favourite promenade.

The Prince was probably as bad as history states, but he had the quality of his defects, and Brighton was the livelier for the presence of his friends. Lyme Regis, Margate, Worthing, Lymington, Bognor—these had nothing to offer beyond the sea. Brighton could lay before her guests a thousand odd diversions, in addition to concerts, balls, masquerades, theatres, races. The Steyne, under the ingenious direction of Colonel

Hanger, the Earl of Barrymore, and their associates, became an arena for curious contests. Officers and gentlemen, ridden by other officers and gentlemen, competed in races with octogenarians. Strapping young women were induced to run against each other for a new smock or hat. Every kind of race was devised, even to walking backwards; while a tame stag was occasionally liberated and hunted to refuge.

AN EARTHLY PARADISE

To the theatre came in turn all the London players; and once the mysterious Chevalier D'Eon was exhibited on its stage in a fencing bout with a military swordsman. The Promenade Grove, which covered part of the ground between New Road, the Pavilion, North Street and Church Street, was also an evening resort in fine weather (and to read about Brighton in its heyday is to receive an impression of continual fine weather, tempered only by storms of wind, such as never failed to blow when Rowlandson and his pencil were in the town, to supply that robust humorist with the contours on which his reputation was based). The Grove was a marine Ranelagh. Masquers moved among the trees, orchestras discoursed the latest airs, rockets soared into the sky. In the county paper for October 1st, 1798, I find the following florid reference to a coming event in the Grove:—"The glittering Azure and the noble Or of the peacock's wings, under the meridian sun, cannot afford greater exultation to that bird, than some of our beautiful belles of fashion promise themselves, from a display of their captivating charms at the intended masquerade at Brighton to-morrow se'nnight."

In another issue of the paper for the same year are some extempore lines on Brighton, dated from East Street, which end thus ecstatically:—

Nature's ever bounteous hand
Sure has bless'd this happy land.
'Tis here no brow appears with care,
What would we be, but what we are?

Before leaving this genial county organ I must quote from a paragraph in 1796 on the Prince himself:—"The following couplet of Pope may be fitly applied to his Royal Highness:—

If to his share some manly errors fall,
Look on his face and you'll forget them all."

What could be kinder? A little earlier, in a description of these anodyne features, the journalist had said of his Royal Highness's "arch eyes," that they "seem to look more ways than one at a time, and especially when they are directed towards the fair sex."

Quieter and more normal pastimes were gossip at the libraries, riding and driving, and bathing in the sea. Bathing seems to have been taken very seriously, with none of the present matter-of-course haphazardness. In an old Guide to Brighton, dated 1794, I find the following description of the intrepid dippers of that day:—"It may not be improper here to introduce a short account of the manner of bathing in the sea at Brighthelmston. By means of a hook-ladder the bather ascends the machine, which is formed of wood, and raised on high wheels; he is drawn to a proper distance from the shore, and then plunges into the sea, the guides attending on each side to assist him in recovering the machine, which being accomplished, he is drawn back to shore. The guides are strong, active, and careful; and, in every respect, adapted to their employments."

"SMOAKER"

MARTHA GUNN

Chief of the bathing women for many years was Martha Gunn, whose descendants still sell fish in the town; chief among the men was the famous Smoaker (his real name, John Miles) the Prince of Wales's swimming tutor. There is a story of his pulling the Prince back by the

195

ear, when he had swum out too far against the old man's instructions; while on another occasion, when the sea was too rough for safety, he placed himself in front of his obstinate pupil in a fighting attitude, with the words, "What do you think your father would say to me if you were drowned? He would say, 'This is all owing to you, Smoaker. If you'd taken proper care of him, Smoaker, poor George would still be alive.'" Another of the pleasant stories of the Prince refers to Smoaker's feminine correlative—Martha Gunn. One day, being in the act of receiving an illicit gift of butter in the pavilion kitchen just as the Prince entered the room, she slipped the pat into her pocket. But not quite in time. Talking with the utmost affability, the Prince proceeded to edge her closer and closer to the great fire, pocket side nearest, and there he kept her until her sin had found her out and dress and butter were both ruined. Doubtless his Royal Highness made both good, for he had all the minor generosities.

An old book, quoted in Mr. Bishop's interesting volume *A Peep into the Past*, gives the following scrap of typical conversation between Martha and a visitor:—"'What, my old friend, Martha,' said I, 'still queen of the ocean, still industrious, and busy as ever; and how do you find yourself'? 'Well and hearty, thank God, sir,' replied she, 'but rather hobbling. I don't bathe, because I a'nt so strong as I used to be, so I superintend on the beach, for I'm up before any of 'em; you may always find me and my pitcher at one exact spot, every morning by six o'clock.' 'You wear vastly well, my old friend, pray what age may you be'? 'Only eighty-eight, sir; in fact, eighty-nine come next Christmas pudding; aye, and though I've lost my teeth I can mumble it with as good relish and hearty appetite as anybody.' 'I'm glad to hear it; Brighton would not look like itself without you, Martha,' said I. 'Oh, I don't know, it's like to do without me, some day,' answered she, 'but while I've health and life, I must be bustling amongst my old friends and benefactors; I think I ought to be proud, for I've as many bows from man, woman, and child, as the Prince hisself; aye, I do believe, the very dogs in the town know me.' 'And your son, how is he'? said I. 'Brave and charming; he lives in East Street; if your honour wants any prime pickled salmon, or oysters, there you have 'em.'"

On the Prince's birthday, and on the birthday of his royal brothers, Brighton went mad with excitement. Oxen were roasted whole, strong beer ran like water, and among the amusements single-wicket matches were played. One of the good deeds of the Prince was the making of a cricket ground. Before 1791, when the Prince's ground was laid out, matches had been played on the neighbouring hills, or on the Level. The Prince's ground stood partly on the Level as it now is, and partly on Park Crescent. In 1823, it became Ireland's Gardens, upon whose turf the most famous cricketers of England played until 1847. In 1848 the Brunswick ground at Hove was opened, close to the sea, into which the ball was occasionally hit by Mr. C. I. Thornton. The present Hove ground dates from 1871. I like to think that George IV., though no great cricketer himself (he played now and then when young "with great condescension and affability"), is the true father of Sussex cricket. He may deserve all that Lamb, Leigh Hunt, and Thackeray said of him, but without his influence and patronage the history of cricket would be the poorer by many bright pages.

THE NONPAREIL

Where Montpellier Crescent now stands, was, eighty years ago, the ground on which Frederick William Lillywhite, the Nonpareil, used to bowl to gentlemen young or old who were prepared to put down five shillings for the privilege. Little Wisden acted as a long stop. Lillywhite was the real creator of round-arm bowling, although Tom Walker of the Hambledon Club was the pioneer and James Broadbridge an earlier exponent. It was not until 1828 that round-arm was legalised. "Me bowling, Pilch batting, and Box keeping wicket—that's cricket," was the old man's dictum; or "When I bowls and Fuller bats," a variant has it, bowl being pronounced to rhyme with owl, "then you'll see cricket." He was thirty-five before he began his first-class career, he bowled fewer than a dozen wides in twenty-seven years, and his myriad wickets cost only seven runs a-piece.

Brighton in its palmiest days was practically contained within the streets that bear boundary names, North Street, East Street, West Street, and the sea, with the parish church high on the hill. On the other side of the Steyne were the naked Downs, while the Lewes road and the London Road were mere thoroughfares between equally bare hills, with a few houses here and there.

During the town's most fashionable period, which continued for nearly fifty years—say from 1785 to 1835—everyone journeyed thither; and indeed everyone goes to Brighton to-day, although its visitors are now anonymous where of old they were notorious. I believe that Robert Browning is the only eminent Englishman that never visited the town. Perhaps it does little for poets; yet Byron was there as a young man, much in the company of a charming youth with whom he often sailed in the Channel, and who afterwards was discovered to be a girl.

HORACE SMITH

A minor poet, Horace Smith, gives us, in *Horace in London*, a sprightly picture of the town in 1813, from which we see that the changes between now and then are only in externals:—

BRIGHTON.

Solvitur acris hyems gratâ vice veris.

Now fruitful autumn lifts his sunburnt head,
   The slighted Park few cambric muslins whiten,
The dry machines revisit Ocean's bed,
   And Horace quits awhile the town for *Brighton*.

The cit foregoes his box at Turnham Green,
   To pick up health and shells with Amphitrite,
Pleasure's frail daughters trip along the Steyne,
   Led by the dame the Greeks call Aphrodite.

Phœbus, the tanner, plies his fiery trade,
   The graceful nymphs ascend Judea's ponies,
Scale the west cliff, or visit the parade,
   While poor papa in town a patient drone is.

Loose trowsers snatch the wreath from pantaloons;
   Nankeen of late were worn the sultry weather in;
But now, (so will the Prince's light dragoons,)
   White jean have triumph'd o'er their Indian brethren.

Here with choice food earth smiles and ocean yawns,
   Intent alike to please the London glutton;
This, for our breakfast proffers shrimps and prawns,
   That, for our dinner, South-down lamb and mutton.

Yet here, as elsewhere, death impartial reigns,
   Visits alike the cot and the *Pavilion*,
And for a bribe with equal scorn disdains
   My half a crown, and *Baring's* half a million.

Alas! how short the span of human pride!
   Time flies, and hope's romantic schemes, are undone;
Cosweller's coach, that carries four inside,
   Waits to take back the unwilling bard to London.

Ye circulating novelists, adieu!
   Long envious cords my black portmanteau tighten;

Billiards, begone! avaunt, illegal loo!
　Farewell old Ocean's bauble, glittering Brighton.

Long shalt thou laugh thine enemies to scorn,
　Proud as Phœnicia, queen of watering places!
Boys yet unbreech'd, and virgins yet unborn,
　On thy bleak downs shall tan their blooming faces.

I believe that the phrase "Queen of Watering Places" was first used in this poem.

EXTINCT COURTESY

An odd glimpse of a kind of manners (now extinct) in Brighton visitors in its palmy days is given in Hazlitt's *Notes of a Journey through France and Italy*. Hazlitt, like his friends the Lambs, when they visited Versailles in 1822, embarked at Brighton. That was in 1824. He reached the town by coach in the evening, in the height of the season, and it was then that the incident occurred to which I have referred. In Hazlitt's words:—"A lad offered to conduct us to an inn. 'Did he think there was room?' He was sure of it. 'Did he belong to the inn?' 'No,' he was from London. In fact, he was a young gentleman from town, who had been stopping some time at the White-horse Hotel, and who wished to employ his spare time (when he was not riding out on a blood-horse) in serving the house, and relieving the perplexities of his fellow-travellers. No one but a Londoner would volunteer his assistance in this way. Amiable land of *Cockayne*, happy in itself, and in making others happy! Blest exuberance of self-satisfaction, that overflows upon others! Delightful impertinence, that is forward to oblige them!"

THE LORD OF THE TIDES

Brighton's decline as a fashionable resort came with the railway. Coaches were expensive and few, and the number of visitors which they brought to the town was negotiable; but when trains began to pour crowds upon the platforms the distinction of Brighton was lost. Society retreated, and the last Master of Ceremonies, Lieut. Col. Eld, died. It was of this admirable aristocrat that Sydney Smith wrote so happily in one of his letters from Brighton: "A gentleman attired *point device*, walking down the Parade, like Agag, 'delicately.' He pointed out his toes like a dancing-master; but carried his head like a potentate. As he passed the stand of flys, he nodded approval, as if he owned them all. As he approached the little goat carriages, he looked askance over the edge of his starched neckcloth and blandly smiled encouragement. Sure that in following him, I was treading in the steps of greatness, I went on to the Pier, and there I was confirmed in my conviction of his eminence; for I observed him look first over the right side and then over the left, with an expression of serene satisfaction spreading over his countenance, which said, as plainly as if he had spoken to the sea aloud, 'That is right. You are low-tide at present; but never mind, in a couple of hours I shall make you high-tide again.'"

Beyond its connection with George IV. Brighton has played but a small part in history, her only other monarch being Charles II., who merely tarried in the town for awhile on his way to France, in 1651, as we have seen. The King's Head, in West Street, claims to be the scene of the merry monarch's bargain with Captain Nicholas Tattersall, who conveyed him across the Channel; but there is good reason to believe that the inn was the George in Middle Street, now demolished, but situated on the site of No. 44. The epitaph on Tattersall in Brighton old parish church contains the following lines:—

When Charles ye great was nothing but a breath
This valiant soul stept betweene him and death . . .

Which glorious act of his for church and state
Eight princes in one day did gratulate.

The episode of the captain's cautious bargaining with the King, of which Colonel Gunter tells in the narrative from which I have quoted in an earlier *chapter*, is carefully suppressed on the memorial tablet.

PHEBE HESSEL

Another famous Brighton character and friend of George IV. was Phebe Hessel, who died at the age of 106, and whose tombstone may be seen in the old churchyard. Phebe had a varied career, for having fallen in love when only fifteen with Samuel Golding, a private in Kirk's Lambs, she dressed herself as a man, enlisted in the 5th Regiment of Foot, and followed him to the West Indies. She served there for five years, and afterwards at Gibraltar, never disclosing her sex until her lover was wounded and sent to Plymouth, when she told the General's wife, and was allowed to follow and nurse him. On leaving hospital Golding married her, and they lived, I hope happily, together for twenty years. When Golding died Phebe married Hessel.

In her old age she became an important Brighton character, and attracting the notice of the Prince was provided by him with a pension of eighteen pounds a year, and the epithet "a jolly good fellow." It was also the Prince's money which paid the stone cutter. When visited by a curious student of human nature as she lay on her death-bed, Phebe talked much of the past, he records, and seemed proud of having kept her secret when in the army. "But I told it to the ground," she added; "I dug a hole that would hold a gallon and whispered it there." Phebe kept her faculties to the last, and to the last sold her apples to the Quality by the sea, returned repartees with extraordinary verve and contempt for false delicacy, and knew as much of the quality of Brighton liquor as if she were a soldier in earnest.

One ought to mention Pitt's visit to Brighton, in 1785, as an historical event, if only for the proof which it offers that Sussex folk have an effective if not nimble wit. I use Mr. Bishop's words: "Pitt during his journey to Brighton, in the previous week, had some experience of popular feeling in respect of the obnoxious Window Tax. Whilst horses were being changed at Horsham, he ordered *lights* for his carriage; and the persons assembled, learning who was within, indulged pretty freely in ironical remarks on *light* and *darkness*. The only effect upon the Minister was, that he often laughed heartily. Whilst in Brighton, a country glove-maker hung about the door of his house on the Steyne; and when the Minister came out, showed him a *hedger's cuff*, which he held in one hand, and a *bush* in the other, to explain the use of it, and asked him if the former, being an article he made and sold, was subject to a *Stamp Duty?* Mr. Pitt appeared rather struck with the oddity and bluntness of the man's question, and, mounting his horse, waived a satisfactory answer by referring him to the *Stamp Office* for information."

DR. JOHNSON IN THE SEA

Brighton's place in literature makes up for her historical poverty. Dr. Johnson was the first great man of letters to visit the town. He stayed in West Street with the Thrales, rode on the Downs and, after his wont, abused their bareness, making a joke about our dearth of trees similar to one on the same topic in Scotland. The Doctor also bathed. Mrs. Piozzi relates that one of the bathing men, seeing him swim, remarked, "Why, sir, you must have been a stout-hearted gentleman forty years ago!"—much to the Doctor's satisfaction.

MRS. PIPCHIN'S CASTLE

It was, I always think, in Hampton Place that Mrs. Pipchin, whose husband broke his heart in the Peruvian mines, kept her establishment for children and did her best to discourage Paul Dombey. How does the description run?

> This celebrated Mrs. Pipchin was a marvellous ill-favoured, ill-conditioned old lady, of a stooping figure, with a mottled face, like bad marble, a hook nose, and a hard grey eye, that looked as if it might have been hammered at on an anvil without sustaining any injury. Forty years at least had elapsed since the Peruvian mines had been the death of Mr. Pipchin; but his relict still wore black bombazeen, of such a lustreless, deep, dead, sombre shade, that gas itself couldn't light her up after dark, and her presence was a quencher to any number of candles. She was generally spoken of as "a great manager" of children; and the secret of her management was, to give them everything that they didn't like, and nothing that they did—which was found to sweeten their dispositions very much. She was such a bitter old lady, that one was tempted to believe there had been some mistake in the application of the Peruvian machinery, and that all her waters of gladness and milk of human kindness had been pumped out dry, instead of the mines.
>
> The Castle of this ogress and child-queller was in a steep bye-street at Brighton; where the soil was more than unusually chalky, flinty, and sterile, and the houses were more than usually brittle and thin; where the small front-gardens had the unaccountable property of producing nothing but marigolds, whatever was sown in them; and where snails were constantly discovered holding on to the street doors, and other public places they were not expected to ornament, with the tenacity of cupping-glasses. In the winter-time the air couldn't be got out of the Castle, and in the summer-time it couldn't be got in. There was such a continual reverberation of wind in it, that it sounded like a great shell, which the inhabitants were obliged to hold to their ears night and day, whether they

liked it or no. It was not, naturally, a fresh-smelling house; and in the window of the front parlour, which was never opened, Mrs. Pipchin kept a collection of plants in pots, which imparted an earthy flavour of their own to the establishment. However choice examples of their kind, too, these plants were of a kind peculiarly adapted to the embowerment of Mrs. Pipchin. There were half-a-dozen specimens of the cactus, writhing round bits of a lath, like hairy serpents; another specimen shooting out broad claws, like a green lobster; several creeping vegetables, possessed of sticky and adhesive leaves; and one uncomfortable flower-pot hanging to the ceiling, which appeared to have boiled over, and tickling people underneath with its long green ends, reminded them of spiders—in which Mrs. Pipchin's dwelling was uncommonly prolific, though perhaps it challenged competition still more proudly, in the season, in point of earwigs.

From Mrs. Pipchin's Paul Dombey passed to the forcing-house of Dr. Blimber, Mrs. Blimber, Miss Blimber and Mr. Feeder, B.A., also at Brighton, where he met Mr. Toots. "The Doctor's," says Dickens, "was a mighty fine house, fronting the sea. Not a joyful style of house within, but quite the contrary. Sad-coloured curtains, whose proportions were spare and lean, hid themselves despondently behind the windows. The tables and chairs were put away in rows, like figures in a sum; fires were so rarely lighted in the rooms of ceremony, that they felt like wells, and a visitor represented the bucket; the dining-room seemed the last place in the world where any eating or drinking was likely to occur; there was no sound through all the house but the ticking of a great clock in the hall, which made itself audible in the very garrets; and sometimes a dull cooing of young gentlemen at their lessons, like the murmurings of an assemblage of melancholy pigeons."—Dr. Blimber's must have been, I think, somewhere in the neighbourhood of the Bedford Hotel.

THACKERAY'S PRAISE

Among other writers who have found Brighton good to work in I might name the authors of *The Strange Adventures of a Phaeton* and *A System of Synthetic Philosophy*. Mr. William Black was for many years a familiar figure on the Kemp Town parade, and Brighton plays a part in at least two of his charming tales—*The Beautiful Wretch*, and an early and very sprightly novel called *Kilmeny*. Brighton should be proud to think that Mr. Herbert Spencer chose her as a retreat in which to come to his conclusions; but I doubt if she is. Thackeray's affection is, however, cherished by the town, his historic praise of "merry cheerful Dr. Brighton" having a commercial value hardly to be over-estimated. Brighton in return gave Thackeray Lord Steyne's immortal name and served as a background for many of his scenes.

Although Brighton has still a fishing industry, the spectacle of its fishermen refraining from work is not an uncommon one. It was once the custom, I read, and perhaps still is, for these men, when casting their nets for mackerel or herring, to stand with bare heads repeating in unison these words: "There they goes then. God Almighty send us a blessing it is to be hoped." As each barrel (which is attached to every two nets out of the fleet, or 120 nets) was cast overboard they would cry:—

Watch, barrel, watch! Mackerel for to catch,
White may they be, like a blossom on a tree.
God send thousands, one, two, and three,
Some by their heads, some by their tails,
God sends thousands, and never fails.

When the last net was overboard the master said, "Seas all!" and then lowered the foremast and laid to the wind. If he were to say, "Last net," he would expect never to see his nets again.

BRIGHTON'S FAIR DAUGHTERS

"There are more handsome women in Brighton than anywhere else in the world," wrote Richard Jefferies some twenty years ago. "They are so common that gradually the standard of taste in the mind rises, and good-looking women who would be admired in other places pass by without notice. Where all the flowers are roses you do not see a rose." (Shirley Brooks must have visited Brighton on a curiously bad day, for seeing no pretty face he wrote of it as "The City of the Plain.") Richard Jefferies, who lived for a while at Hove, blessed also the treelessness of Brighton. Therein he saw much of its healing virtue. "Let nothing," he wrote, "cloud the descent of those glorious beams of sunlight which fall at Brighton. Watch the pebbles on the beach; the foam runs up and wets them, almost before it can slip back, the sunshine has dried them again. So they are alternately wetted and dried. Bitter sea and glowing light, bright clear air, dry as dry—that describes the place. Spain is the country of sunlight, burning sunlight; Brighton is a Spanish town in England, a Seville."

THE PAVILION

The principal inland attraction of Brighton is still the Pavilion, which is indeed the town's symbol. On passing through its very numerous and fantastic rooms one is struck by their incredible smallness. Sidney Smith's jest (if it were his; I find Wilberforce, the Abolitionist, saying something similar) is still unimproved: "One would think that St. Paul's Cathedral had come to Brighton and pupped." Cobbett in his rough and homely way also said something to the point about the Prince's pleasure-house: "Take a square box, the sides of which are three feet and a half, and the height a foot and a half. Take a large Norfolk turnip, cut off the green of the leaves, leave the stalks nine inches long, tie these round with a string three inches from the top, and put the turnip on the middle of the top of the box. Then take four turnips of half the size, treat them in the same way, and put them on the corners of the box. Then take a considerable number of bulbs of the crown-imperial, the narcissus, the hyacinth, the tulip, the crocus, and others; let the leaves of each have sprouted to about an inch, more or less according to the size of the bulb; put all these, pretty promiscuously, but pretty thickly, on the top of the box. Then stand off and look at your architecture."

To its ordinary museum in the town Brighton has added the collection of stuffed birds made by the late Mr. E. T. Booth, which he housed in a long gallery in the road that leads to the Dyke. Mr. Booth, when he shot a bird in its native haunts, carried away some of its surroundings in order that the taxidermist might reproduce as far as possible its natural environment. Hence every case has a value that is missing when one sees merely the isolated stuffed bird. In one instance realism has dictated the addition of a clutch of pipit's eggs found on the Bass Rock, in a nest invisible to the spectator. The collection in the Natural History Museum at South Kensington is of course more considerable, and finer, but some of Mr. Booth's cases are certainly superior, and his collection has the special interest of having been made by one man.

CRITICISM BY JUG

Brighton has another very interesting possession in the collection of old domestic pottery in the museum: an assemblage (the most entertaining and varied that I know) of jugs and mugs, plates and ornaments, all English, all quaint and characteristic too, and mostly inscribed with mottoes or decorated with designs in celebration of such events as the battle of Waterloo, or the discomfiture of Mr. Pitt, or a victory of Tom Cribb. Others are ceramic satires on the drunkard's folly or the inconstancy of women. Why are the potters of our own day so dull? History is still being made, human nature is not less frail; but I see no genial commentary on jug or dish. Is it the march of Taste?

CHAPTER XVIII

ROTTINGDEAN AND WHEATEARS

Ovingdean—Charles II.—The introduction of Mangel Wurzel—
Rottingdean as a shrine—Mr. Kipling's Sussex poem—Thomas Fuller
on the Wheatear—Mr. Hudson's description of the traps—The old
prosperous days for shepherds—Luring larks—A fight on the beach—
The town that failed.

Beyond Kemp Town's serene and silent line of massive houses is the
new road that leads to Rottingdean. The old road fell into the sea some
few years ago—the fourth or fifth to share that fate. But the pleasantest
way thither is on foot over the turf that tops the white cliffs.

By diverging inland between Brighton and Rottingdean, just beyond
the most imposing girls' school in the kingdom, Ovingdean is reached,
one of the nestling homesteads of the Downs. It is chiefly known as
providing Harrison Ainsworth with the very pretty title of one of his
stories, *Ovingdean Grange*. The gallant novelist, however, was a poor
historian in this book, for Charles the Second, as we have seen, never set
foot east of Brighton on the occasion of his journey of escape over the
Sussex Downs. The legend that lodges him at Ovingdean, although one
can understand how Ovingdean must cherish it, cannot stand. (Mock
Beggars' Hall, in the same romance, is Southover Grange at Lewes.)

Peace hath her victories no less renowned than war. Ovingdean is
famous not only for its false association with Charles the Second but as

the burial place of Thomas Pelling, an old-time Vicar, "the first person who introduced Mangul Wurzel into England."

ROTTINGDEAN

Rottingdean to-day must be very much of the size of Brighton two centuries ago, before fashion came upon it; but the little village is hardly likely ever to creep over its surrounding hills in the same way. The past few years, however, have seen its growth from an obscure and inaccessible settlement to a shrine. It is only of quite recent date that a glimpse of Rottingdean has become almost as necessary to the Brighton visitor as the journey to the Dyke. Had the Legend of the Briar Rose never been painted; had Mulvaney, Ortheris and Learoyd remained unchronicled and the British soldier escaped the label "Absent-minded Beggar," Rottingdean might still be invaded only occasionally; for it was when, following Sir Edward Burne-Jones, Mr. Rudyard Kipling found the little white village good to make a home in, that its public life began. Although Mr. Kipling has now gone farther into the depths of the county, and the great draughtsman, some of whose stained glass designs are in the church, is no more, the habit of riding to Rottingdean is likely, however, to persist in Brighton. The village is quaint and simple (particularly so after the last 'bus is stabled), but it is valuable rather as the key to some of the finest solitudes of the Downs, in the great uninhabited hill district between the Race Course at Brighton and Newhaven, between Lewes and the sea, than for any merits of its own. One other claim has it, however, on the notice of the pilgrim: William Black lies in the churchyard.

"BLUE GOODNESS OF THE WEALD"

Mr. Kipling, as I have said, has now removed his household gods farther inland, to Burwash, but his heart and mind must be still among the Downs. The Burwash country, good as it is, can (I think) never inspire

him to such verse as he wrote in *The Five Nations* on the turf hills about
his old home:—

No tender-hearted garden crowns,
  No bosomed woods adorn
Our blunt, bow-headed, whale-backed Downs,
  But gnarled and writhen thorn—
Bare slopes where chasing shadows skim,
  And through the gaps revealed
Belt upon belt, the wooded, dim
  Blue goodness of the Weald.

Clean of officious fence or hedge,
  Half-wild and wholly tame,
The wise turf cloaks the white cliff edge
  As when the Romans came.
What sign of those that fought and died
  At shift of sword and sword?
The barrow and the camp abide,
  The sunlight and the sward.

Here leaps ashore the full Sou'west
  All heavy-winged with brine,
Here lies above the folded crest
  The Channel's leaden line;
And here the sea-fogs lap and cling,
  And here, each warning each,
The sheep-bells and the ship-bells ring
  Along the hidden beach.

We have no waters to delight
  Our broad and brookless vales—

Only the dewpond on the height
　　Unfed, that never fails,
Whereby no tattered herbage tells
　　Which way the season flies—
Only our close-bit thyme that smells
　　Like dawn in Paradise.

Here through the strong and salty days
　　The unshaded silence thrills;
Or little, lost, Down churches praise
　　The Lord who made the Hills:
But here the Old Gods guard their round,
　　And, in her secret heart,
The heathen kingdom Wilfrid found
　　Dreams, as she dwells, apart.

WHEATEARS

Of old the best wheatear country was above Rottingdean; but the South Down shepherds no longer have the wheatear money that used to add so appreciably to their wages in the summer months. A combination of circumstances has brought about this loss. One is the decrease in wheatears, another the protection of the bird by law, and a third the refusal of the farmers to allow their men any longer to neglect the flocks by setting and tending snares. But in the seventeenth, eighteenth and early part of the nineteenth centuries, wheatears were taken on the Downs in enormous quantities and formed a part of every south county banquet in their season. People visited Brighton solely to eat them, as they now go to Greenwich for whitebait and to Colchester for oysters.

This is how Fuller describes the little creature in the *Worthies*— "*Wheatears* is a bird peculiar to this County, hardly found out of it. It is so called, because fattest when Wheat is ripe, whereon it feeds; being no bigger than a Lark, which it equalleth in *fineness* of the flesh, far exceedeth in the *fatness* thereof. The worst is, that being onely seasonable in the heat of summer, and naturally larded with lumps of fat, it is soon subject to corrupt, so that (though abounding within *fourty* miles) *London Poulterers* have no mind to meddle with them, which no care in carriage can keep from Putrefaction. That *Palate-man* shall pass in silence, who, being seriously demanded his judgment concerning the abilities of a great *Lord*, concluded him a man of very weak parts, '*because once he saw him, at a great Feast, feed on* CHICKENS *when there were* WHEATEARS *on the Table.*' I will adde no more in praise of this *Bird*, for fear some *female Reader* may fall in *longing* for it, and unhappily be disappointed of her desire." A contemporary of Fuller, John Taylor, from whom I have already quoted, and shall quote again, thus unscientifically dismisses the wheatear in one of his doggerel narratives:—

Six weeks or thereabouts they are catch'd there,
And are well-nigh 11 months God knows where.

As a matter of fact, the winter home of the wheatear is Africa.

THE SHEPHERDS' TRAPS

The capture of wheatears—mostly illegally by nets—still continues in a very small way to meet a languid demand, but the Sussex ortolan, as the little bird was sometimes called, has passed from the bill of fare. Wheatears (which, despite Fuller, have no connection with ears of wheat, the word signifying white tail) still abound, skimming over the turf in little groups; but they no longer fly towards the dinner table. The best and most interesting description that I know of the old manner of taking them, is to be found in Mr. W. H. Hudson's *Nature in Downland*. The season began in July, when the little fat birds rest on the Downs on their way from Scotland and northern England to their winter home, and lasted through September. In July, says Mr. Hudson, the "Shepherds made their 'coops,' as their traps were called—a **T**-shaped trench about fourteen inches long, over which the two long narrow sods cut neatly out of the turf were adjusted, grass downwards. A small opening was left at the end for ingress, and there was room in the passage for the bird to pass through towards the chinks of light coming from the two ends of the cross passage. At the inner end of the passage a horse-hair springe was set, by which the bird was caught by the neck as it passed in, but the noose did not as a rule strangle the bird. On some of the high downs near the coast, notably at Beachy Head, at Birling Gap, at Seaford, and in the neighbourhood of Rottingdean, the shepherds made so many coops, placed at small distances apart, that the Downs in some places looked as if they had been ploughed. In September, when the season was over, the sods were carefully put back, roots down, in the places, and the smooth green surface was restored to the hills."

On bright clear days few birds would be caught, but in showery weather the traps would all be full; this is because when the sun is obscured wheatears are afraid and take refuge under stones or in whatever hole may offer. The price of each wheatear was a penny, and it was the custom of the persons in the neighbourhood who wanted them for dinner to visit the traps, take out the birds and leave the money in their place. The shepherd on returning would collect his gains and reset the traps. Near Brighton, however, most of the shepherds caught only for dealers; and one firm, until some twenty years ago, maintained the practice of giving an annual supper at the end of the season, at which the shepherds would be paid in the mass for their spoil.

A RECORD BAG

An old shepherd, who had been for years on Westside Farm near Brighton, spoke thus, in 1882, as Mr. Borrer relates in his *Birds of Sussex*:— "The most I ever caught in one day was thirteen dozen, but we thought it a good day if we caught three or four dozen. We sold them to a poulterer at Brighton, who took all we could catch in a season at 18*d*. a dozen. From what I have heard from old shepherds, it cannot be doubted that they were caught in much greater numbers a century ago than of late. I have heard them speak of an immense number being taken in one day by a shepherd at East Dean, near Beachy Head. I think they said he took nearly a hundred dozen, so many that they could not thread them on crow-quills in the usual manner, but he took off his round frock and made a sack of it to put them into, and his wife did the same with her petticoat. This must have happened when there was a great flight. Their numbers now are so decreased that some shepherds do not set up any coops, as it does not pay for the trouble."

THE LARK-GLASS

Although wheatears are no longer caught, the Brighton bird-catcher is a very busy man. Goldfinches fall in extraordinary plenty to his nets. A bird-catcher told Mr. Borrer that he once caught eleven dozen of them at one haul, and in 1860 the annual take at Worthing was 1,154 dozen. Larks are also caught in great numbers, also with nets, the old system still practised in France, of luring them with glasses, having become obsolete. Knox has an interesting description of the lark-glass and its uses:—"A piece of wood about a foot and a half long, four inches deep, and three inches wide, is planed off on two sides so as to resemble the roof of a well-known toy, yclept a Noah's ark, but, more than twice as long. In the sloping sides are set several bits of looking-glass. A long iron spindle, the lower end of which is sharp and fixed in the ground, passes freely through the centre; on this the instrument turns, and even spins rapidly when a string has been attached and is pulled by the performer, who generally stands at a distance of fifteen or twenty yards from the decoy. The reflection of the sun's rays from these little revolving mirrors seems to possess a mysterious attraction for the larks, for they descend in great numbers from a considerable height in the air, hover over the spot, and suffer themselves to be shot at repeatedly without attempting to leave the field or to continue their course."

To return to Rottingdean, it was above the village, seven hundred years ago, that a "sore scrymmysche" occurred between the French and the Cluniac prior of Lewes. The prior was defeated and captured, but the nature of his resistance decided the enemy that it was better perhaps to retreat to their boats. The holy man, although worsted, thus had the satisfaction of having proved to the King that a Cluniac monk in this country, was not, as was supposed at court, necessarily on the side of England's foes, even though they were of his own race.

According to the scheme of this book, we should now return to Brighton; but, as I have said, the right use to which to put Rottingdean is as the starting point for a day among the hills. Once out and above the village, the world is your own. A conspiracy to populate a part of the Downs near the sea, a mile or so to the east of Rottingdean, seems gloriously to have failed, but what was intended may be learned from the skeleton roads that, duly fenced in, disfigure the turf. They even have names, these unlovely parallelograms: one is Chatsworth Avenue, and Ambleside Avenue another.

CHAPTER XIX

SHOREHAM

Hove the impeccable—The Aldrington of the past—A digression on seaports—Old Shoreham and history—Mr. Swinburne's poem—A baby saint—Successful bribery—The Adur—Old Shoreham church and bridge.

The cliffs that make the coast between Newhaven and Brighton so attractive slope gradually to level ground at the Aquarium and never reappear in Sussex on the Channel's edge again, although in the east they rise whiter and higher, with a few long gaps, all the way to Dover. It is partly for this reason that the walk from Brighton to Shoreham has no beauty save of the sea. Hove, which used to be a disreputable little smuggling village sufficiently far from Brighton for risks to be run with safety, is now the well-ordered home of wealthy rectitude. Mrs. Grundy's sea-side home is here. Hove is, perhaps, the genteelest town in the world, although once, only a poor hundred years ago, there was no service in the church on a certain Sunday, because, as the clerk informed the complaisant vicar, "The pews is full of tubs and the pulpit full of tea"—a pleasant fact to reflect upon during Church Parade amid the gay yet discreet prosperity of the Brunswick Lawns.

NEW SHOREHAM CHURCH.

West of Hove, and between that town and Portslade-by-Sea, is Aldrington. Aldrington is now new houses and brickfields. Thirty years ago it was naught. But five hundred years ago it was the principal township in these parts, and Brighthelmstone a mere insignificant cluster of hovels. Centuries earlier it was more important still, for, according to some authorities, it was the Portus Adurni of the Romans. The river Adur, which now enters the sea between Shoreham and Southwick, once flowed along the line of the present canal and the Wish Pond, and so out into the sea. I have seen it stated that the mouth of the river was even more easterly still—somewhere opposite the Norfolk Hotel at Brighton; but this may be fanciful and can now hardly be proven. The suggestion, however, adds interest to a walk on the otherwise unromantic Brunswick Lawns. In those days the Roman ships, entering the river here, would sail up as far as Bramber. Between the river and the sea were then some two miles—possibly more—of flat meadow land, on which Aldrington was largely built. Over the ruins of that Aldrington the Channel now washes.

THE LIFE OF A HARBOUR

Beyond Aldrington is Portslade, with a pretty inland village on the hill; beyond Portslade is Southwick, notable for its green; and beyond Southwick is Shoreham. Southwick and Shoreham both have that interest which can never be wanting to the seaport that has seen better days. The life of a harbour, whatever its state of decay, is eternally absorbing; and in Shoreham harbour one gets such life at its laziest. The smell of tar; the sound of hammers; the laughter and whistling of the loafers; the continuous changing of the tide; the opening of the lock gates; the departure of the tug; its triumphant return, leading in custody a timber-laden barque from the Baltic, a little self-conscious and ashamed, as if caught red-handed in iniquity by this fussy little officer; the independent sailing of a grimy steamer bound for Sunderland and more coal; the elaborate wharfing of the barque:—all these things on a hot still day can exercise an hypnotic influence more real and strange than the open sea. The romance and mystery of the sea may indeed be more intimately near one on a harbour wharf than on the deck of a liner in mid-ocean.

Shoreham has its place in history. Thence as we have seen, sailed Charles II. in Captain Tattersall's *Enterprise*. Four hundred and fifty years earlier King John landed here with his army, when he came to succeed to the English throne. In the reign of Edward III. Shoreham supplied twenty-six ships to the Navy: but in the fifteenth century the sea began an encroachment on the bar which disclassed the harbour. It is now unimportant, most of the trade having passed to Newhaven; but in its days of prosperity great cargoes of corn and wine were landed here from the Continent.

When people now say Shoreham they mean New Shoreham, but Old Shoreham is the parent. Old Shoreham, however, declined to village state when the present harbour was made.

MR. SWINBURNE'S POEM

New Shoreham church, quite the noblest in the county, dates probably from about 1100. It was originally the property of the Abbey of Saumur, to whom it was presented, together with Old Shoreham church, by William de Braose, the lord of Bramber Castle. It is New Shoreham Church which Mr. Swinburne had in mind (or so I imagine) in his noble poem "On the South Coast":—

Strong as time, and as faith sublime,—clothed round with shadows of
    hopes and fears,
Nights and morrows, and joys and sorrows, alive with passion of prayers
    and tears,—
Stands the shrine that has seen decline eight hundred waxing and waning
    years.

Tower set square to the storms of air and change of season that glooms
    and glows,
Wall and roof of it tempest-proof, and equal ever to suns and snows,
Bright with riches of radiant niches and pillars smooth as a straight stem
    grows.

* * * * *

Stately stands it, the work of hands unknown of: statelier, afar and near,
Rise around it the heights that bound our landward gaze from the seaboard
    here;
Downs that swerve and aspire, in curve and change of heights that the
    dawn holds dear.

Dawn falls fair on the grey walls there confronting dawn, on the low
    green lea,
Lone and sweet as for fairies' feet held sacred, silent and strange and
    free,
Wild and wet with its rills; but yet more fair falls dawn on the fairer sea.

* * * * *

Rose-red eve on the seas that heave sinks fair as dawn when the first ray
    peers;
Winds are glancing from sunbright Lancing to Shoreham, crowned with
    the grace of years;
Shoreham, clad with the sunset, glad and grave with glory that death
    reveres.

OLD SHOREHAM BRIDGE.

A SHOREHAM EPITAPH

In the churchyard there was once (and may be still, but I did not find it) an epitaph on a child of eight months, in the form of a dialogue between the deceased and its parents. It contained these lines:—

"'I trust in Christ,' the blessed babe replied,
Then smil'd, then sigh'd, then clos'd its eyes and died."

OLD SHOREHAM CHURCH.

Shoreham's notoriety as a pocket borough—it returned two members to Parliament, who were elected in the north transept of the church—came to a head in 1701, when the naïve means by which Mr. Gould had proved his fitness were revealed. It seemed that Mr. Gould, who had never been to Shoreham before, directed the crier to give notice with his bell that every voter who came to the King's Arms would receive a guinea in which to drink Mr. Gould's good health. This fact being made public by the defeated candidate, Mr. Gould was unseated. At the following election, such was the enduring power of the original guinea, he was elected again.

After the life of the harbour, the chief interest of Shoreham is its river, the Adur, a yellow, sluggish, shallow stream, of great width near the town, which at low tide dwindles into a streamlet trickling through a desert of mud, but at the full has the beauty of a lake. Mr. Swinburne, in the same poem from which I have been quoting, thus describes the river at evening:—

Skies fulfilled with the sundown, stilled and splendid, spread as a flower
    that spreads,
Pave with rarer device and fairer than heaven's the luminous oyster-
    beds,
Grass-embanked, and in square plots ranked, inlaid with gems that the
    sundown sheds.

MR. HENLEY'S POEM

To the Adur belongs also another lyric. It is printed in *Hawthorn and Lavender*, to which I have already referred, and is one of Mr. Henley's most characteristic and remarkable poems:—

In Shoreham River, hurrying down
To the live sea,
By working, marrying, breeding, Shoreham Town,
Breaking the sunset's wistful and solemn dream,
An old, black rotter of a boat
Past service to the labouring, tumbling flote,
Lay stranded in mid-stream;
With a horrid list, a frightening lapse from the line,
That made me think of legs and a broken spine;
Soon, all too soon,

Ungainly and forlorn to lie
Full in the eye
Of the cynical, discomfortable moon
That, as I looked, stared from the fading sky,
A clown's face flour'd for work. And by and by
The wide-winged sunset wanned and waned;
The lean night-wind crept westward, chilling and sighing;
The poor old hulk remained,
Stuck helpless in mid-ebb. And I knew why—
Why, as I looked, my heart felt crying.
For, as I looked, the good green earth seemed dying—
Dying or dead;
And, as I looked on the old boat, I said:—
"Dear God, it's I!"

The Adur is no longer the home of birds that once it was, but in the early morning one may still see there many of the less common water fowl. The road to Portsmouth is carried across the Adur by the Norfolk Suspension Bridge, to cross which one must pay a toll,—not an unpleasant reminder of earlier days.

Old Shoreham, a mile up the river, is notable for its wooden bridge across the Adur to the Old Sussex Pad, at one time a famous inn for smugglers. Few Royal Academy exhibitions are without a picture of Old Shoreham Bridge and the quiet cruciform church at its eastward end.

THE LOYAL CLERK

A pleasant story tells how, in some Sussex journey, William IV. and his queen chanced to be passing through Shoreham, coming from Chichester to Lewes, one Sunday morning. The clerk of Old Shoreham church caught sight through the window of the approaching cavalcade, and leaping to his feet, stopped the sermon by announcing: "It is my solemn duty to inform you that their Majesties the King and Queen are just now crossing the bridge." Thereupon the whole congregation jumped up and ran out to show their loyalty.

CHAPTER XX

THE DEVIL'S DYKE AND HURSTPIERPOINT

Sussex and Leith Hill—The Dyke hill—Two recollections—Bustard hunting on the Downs—The Queen of the gipsies—The Devil in Sussex—The feeble legend of the Dyke—Poynings—Newtimber—Pyecombe and shepherds' crooks—A Patcham smuggler—Wolstonbury—Danny—An old Sussex diary—Fish-culture in the past—Thomas Marchant's Sunday head-aches—Albourne and Bishop Juxon—Twineham and Squire Stapley—Zoological remedies—How to make oatmeal pudding.

POYNINGS, FROM THE DEVIL'S DYKE.

Had the hill above the Devil's Dyke—for the Dyke itself wins only a passing glance—been never popularised, thousands of Londoners, and many of the people of Brighton, would probably never have seen the Weald from any eminence at all. The view is bounded north and west only by hills: on the north by the North Downs, with Leith Hill standing forward, as if advancing to meet a southern champion, and in the west, Blackdown, Hind Head and the Hog's Back. The patchwork of the Weald is between. The view from the Dyke Hill, looking north, is comparable to that from Leith Hill, looking south; and every day in fine weather there are tourists on both of these altitudes gazing towards each other. The worst slight that Sussex ever had to endure, so far as my reading goes, is in Hughson's *London . . . and its Neighbourhood*, 1808, where the view from Leith Hill is described. After stating that the curious stranger on the summit "feels sensations as we may suppose Adam to have felt when he instantaneously burst into existence and the beauties of Eden struck his all-wondering eyes," Mr. Hughson describes the prospect. "It commands a view of the county of Surrey, part of Hampshire, Berkshire, Nettlebed in Oxfordshire, some parts of Bucks, Hertfordshire, Middlesex, Kent and Essex; and, by the help of a glass, Wiltshire." Not a word of Sussex.

A SEA OF MIST

The wisest course for the non-gregarious traveller is to leave the Dyke on the right, and, crossing the Ladies' Golf Links, gain Fulking Hill, from which the view is equally fine (save for lacking a little in the east) and where there is peace and isolation. I remember sitting one Sunday morning on Fulking Hill when a white mist like a sea filled the Weald, washing the turf slopes twenty feet or so below me. In the depths of this ocean, as it were, could be heard faintly the noises of the farms and the chime of submerged bells. Suddenly a hawk shot up and disappeared again, like a leaping fish.

The same spot was on another occasion the scene of a superb effort of courageous tenacity. I met a large hare steadily breasting the hill. Turning neither to the right nor left it was soon out of sight over the crest. Five or more minutes later there appeared in view, on the hare's trail, a very tired little fox terrier not much more than half the size of the hare. He also turned aside neither to the right nor the left, but panted wearily yet bravely past me, and so on, over the crest, after his prey. I waited for some time but the terrier never came back. Such was the purpose depicted on his countenance that I can believe he is following still.

On these Downs, near the Dyke, less than a century ago the Great Bustard used to be hunted with greyhounds. Mr. Borrer tells us in the *Birds of Sussex* that his grandfather (who died in 1844) sometimes would take five or six in a morning. They fought savagely and more than once injured the hounds.

Enterprise has of late been at work at the Dyke. A cable railway crosses the gully at a dizzy height, a lift brings travellers from the Weald, a wooden cannon of exceptional calibre threatens the landscape, and pictorial advertisements of the Devil and his domain may be seen at most of the Sussex stations. Ladies also play golf where, when first I knew it, one could walk unharmed. A change that is to be regretted is the exile to the unromantic neighbourhood of the Dyke Station of the Queen of the Gipsies, a swarthy ringletted lady of peculiarly comfortable exterior who, splendid (yet a little sinister) in a scarlet shawl and ponderous gold jewels, used once to emerge from a tent beside the Dyke inn and allot husbands fair or dark. She was an astute reader of her fellows, with an eye too searching to be deceived by the removal of tell-tale rings. A lucky shot in respect to a future ducal husband of a young lady now a duchess, of the accuracy of which she was careful to remind you, increased her reputation tenfold in recent years. Her name is Lee, and of her title of Queen of the Gipsies there is, I believe, some justification.

"HE"

Sussex abounds in evidences of the Devil's whimsical handiwork, although in ordinary conversation Sussex rustics are careful not to speak his name. They say "he." Mr. Parish, in his *Dictionary of the Sussex Dialect*, gives an example of the avoidance of the dread name: "'In the Down there's a golden calf buried; people know very well where it is—I could show you the place any day.' 'Then why don't they dig it up?' 'Oh, it's not allowed: *he* wouldn't let them.' 'Has any one ever tried?' 'Oh yes, but it's never there when you look; *he* moves it away.'" His punchbowl may be seen here, his footprints there; but the greatest of his enterprises was certainly the Dyke. His purpose was to submerge or silence the irritating churches of the Weald, by digging a ditch that should let in the sea. He began one night from the North side, at Saddlescombe, and was working very well until he caught sight of the beams of a candle which an old woman had placed in her window. Being a Devil of Sussex rather than of Miltonic invention, he was not clever, and taking the candle light for the break of dawn, he fled and never resumed the labour. That is the very infirm legend that is told and sold at the Dyke.

HANGLETON

I might just mention that the little church which one sees from the Dyke railway, standing alone on the hill side, is Hangleton. Dr. Kenealy, who defended the Claimant, is buried there. The hamlet of Hangleton, which may be seen in the distance below, once possessed a hunting lodge of the Coverts of Slaugham, which, after being used as labourers' cottages, has now disappeared. The fine Tudor mansion of the Bellinghams', now transformed into a farm house, although it has been much altered, still retains many original features. In the kitchen, no doubt once the hall, on an oak screen, are carved the Commandments, followed by this ingenious motto, an exercise on the letter E:

Persevere, ye perfect men,
Ever keep these precepts ten.

HANGLETON HOUSE.

From the Dyke hill one is within easy walking distance of many Wealden villages. Immediately at the north end of the Dyke itself is Poynings, with its fine grey cruciform church raising an embattled tower among the trees on its mound. It has been conjectured from the similarity of this beautiful church to that of Alfriston that they may have had the same architect. Poynings (now called Punnings) was of importance in Norman times, and was the seat of William FitzRainalt, whose descendants afterwards took the name of de Ponyngs and one of whom was ennobled as Baron de Ponyngs. In the fifteenth century the direct line was merged into that of Percy. The ruins of Ponyngs Place, the baronial mansion, are still traceable.

Following the road to the west, under the hills, we come first to Fulking (where one may drink at a fountain raised by a brewer to the glory of God and in honour of John Ruskin), then to Edburton (where the leaden font, one of three in Sussex, should be noted), then to Truleigh, all little farming hamlets shadowed by the Downs, and so to Beeding and Bramber, or, striking south, to Shoreham.

NEWTIMBER

If, instead of turning into Poynings, one ascends the hill on the other side of the stream, a climb of some minutes, with a natural amphitheatre on the right, brings one to the wooded northern escarpment of Saddlescombe North Hill, or Newtimber Hill, which offers a view little inferior to that of the Dyke. At Saddlescombe, by the way, lives one of the most learned Sussex ornithologists of the day, and a writer upon the natural history of the county (so cavalierly treated in this book!), for whose quick eye and descriptive hand the readers of *Blackwood* have reason to be grateful. Immediately beneath Newtimber Hill lies Newtimber, consisting of a house or two, a moated grange, and a little church, which, though only a few yards from the London road, is so hidden that it might be miles from everywhere. On the grass bank of the bostel descending through the hanger to Newtimber, I counted on one spring afternoon as many as a dozen adders basking in the sun. We are here, though so near Brighton, in country where the badger is still found, while the Newtimber woods are famous among collectors of moths.

PYECOMBE CROOKS

If you are for the Weald it is by this bostel that you should descend, but if still for the Downs turn to the east along the summit, and you will come to Pyecombe, a straggling village on each side of the London road just at the head of Dale Hill. Pyecombe has lost its ancient fame as the home of the best shepherds' crooks, but the Pyecombe crook for many years was unapproached. The industry has left Sussex: crooks are now made in the north of England and sold over shop counters. I say "industry" wrongly, for what was truly an industry for a Pyecombe blacksmith is a mere detail in an iron factory, since the number of shepherds does not increase and one crook will serve a lifetime and more. An old shepherd at Pyecombe, talking confidentially on the subject of crooks, complained that the new weapon as sold at Lewes, although nominally on the Pyecombe pattern, is a "numb thing." The chief reason which he gave was that the maker was out of touch with the man who was to use it. His own crook (like that of Richard Jefferies' shepherd friend) had been fashioned from the barrel of an old muzzle-loader. The present generation, he added, is forgetting how to make everything: why, he had neighbours, smart young fellows, too, who could not even make their own clothes.

Pyecombe is but a few miles from Brighton, which may easily be reached from it. A short distance south of the village is the Plough Inn, the point at which the two roads to London—that by way of Clayton Hill, Friar's Oak, Cuckfield, Balcombe and Redhill, and the other (on which we are now standing) by way of Dale Hill, Bolney, Hand Cross, Crawley and Reigate—become one.

On the way to Brighton from the Plough one passes through Patcham, a dusty village that for many years has seen too many bicycles, and now is in the way of seeing too many motor cars. In the churchyard is, or was, a tomb bearing the following inscription, which may be quoted both as a reminder of the more stirring experiences to which the Patcham people were subject a hundred years ago, and also as an example of the truth which is only half a truth:

SMUGGLER AND EXEMPLAR

Sacred to the memory of Daniel Scales, who was unfortunately shot on Thursday Evening, Nov. 7, 1796.

Alas! swift flew the fatal lead
Which pierced through the young man's head,
He instant fell, resigned his breath,

And closed his languid eyes in death.
All ye who do this stone draw near,
Oh! pray let fall the pitying tear.
From the sad instance may we all
Prepare to meet Jehovah's call.

The facts of the case bear some likeness to the death of Mr. Bardell and Serjeant Buzfuz's reference to that catastrophe. Daniel Scales was a desperate smuggler who, when the fatal lead pierced him, was heavily laden with booty. He was shot through the head only as a means of preventing a similar fate befalling his slayer.

Just beyond Patcham, as we approach Brighton, is the narrow chalk lane on the left which leads to the Lady's Mile, the beginning of a superb stretch of turf around an amphitheatre in the hills by which one may gallop all the way to the Clayton mills. The grass ride extends to Lewes.

Preston, once a village with an independent life, is now Brighton; but nothing can harm its little English church, noticeable for a fresco of the murder of Thomas à Becket, a representation dating probably from the reign of Edward I.

This, however, is a digression, and we must return to Pyecombe in order to climb Wolstonbury—the most mountainous of the hills in this part, and indeed, although far from the highest, perhaps the noblest in mien of the whole range, by virtue of its isolation and its conical shape. The earthworks on Wolstonbury, although supposed to be of Celtic origin, were probably utilised by the Romans for military purposes. More than any of the Downs does Wolstonbury bring before one the Roman occupation of our country.

DANNY

Immediately below Wolstonbury, on the edge of the Weald, is Danny, an Elizabethan house, to-day the seat of the Campions, but two hundred and more years ago the seat of Peter Courthope, to whom John Ray dedicated his *Collection of English Words not generally used*, and before then the property of Sir Simon de Pierpoint. The park is small and without deer, but the house has a façade of which one can never tire. I once saw *Twelfth Night* performed in its gardens, and it was difficult to believe that Shakespeare had not the spot in mind when he wrote that play.

MALTHOUSE FARM, HURSTPIERPOINT.

The Danny drive brings us to Hurstpierpoint, or Hurst as it is generally called, which is now becoming a suburb of Brighton and thus somewhat losing its character, but which the hills will probably long keep sweet. James Hannington, Bishop of Equatorial East Africa, who was murdered by natives in 1885, was born here; here lived Richard Weeks, the antiquary; and here to-day is the home of Mr. Mitten, most learned of Sussex botanists.

To Hurst belongs one of the little Sussex squires to whose diligence as a diarist we are indebted for much entertaining knowledge of the past. Little Park, now the property of the Hannington family, where Thomas Marchant, the diarist in question, lived, and kept his journal between 1714 and 1728, is to the north of the main street, lying low. The original document I have not seen, but from passages printed by the Sussex

Archæological Society I borrow a few extracts for the light they throw on old customs and social life.

FISH-BREEDING

"October 8th, 1714. Paid 4s. at Lewes for ¼ lb., of tea; 5d. for a quire of paper; and 6d. for two mousetraps.

"October 29th, 1714. Went to North Barnes near Homewood Gate to see the pond fisht. I bought all the fish of a foot long and upwards at 50s. per C. I am to give Mrs. Dabson 200 store fish, over and above the aforesaid bargain; but she is to send to me for them.

"October 30th, 1714. We fetched 244 Carps in three Dung Carts from a stew of Parson Citizen at Street; being brought thither last night out of the above pond.

"October 31st, 1714 (Sunday). I could not go to Church, being forced to stay at home to look after, and let down fresh water to, the fish; they being—as I supposed—sick, because they lay on the surface of the pond and were easily taken out. But towards night they sunk."

The Little Park ponds still exist, but the practice of breeding fish has passed. In Arthur Young's *General View of the Agriculture of the County of Sussex*, 1808, quoted elsewhere in this book, is a chapter on fish, wherein he writes: "A Mr. Fenn of London, has long rented, and is the sole monopolizer of, all the fish that are sold in Sussex. Carp is the chief stock; but tench and perch, eels and pike are raised. A stream should always flow through the pond; and a marley soil is the best. Mr. Milward has drawn carp from his marl-pits 25lb. a brace, and two inches of fat upon them, but then he feeds with pease. When the waters are drawn off and re-stocked, it is done with stores of a year old, which remain four years: the carp will then be 12 or 13 inches long, and if the water is good,

14 or 15. The usual season for drawing the water is either Autumn or Spring: the sale is regulated by measure, from the eye to the fork of the tail. At twelve inches, carp are worth 50*s.* and 3*l.* per hundred; at fifteen inches, 6*l.*; at eighteen inches, 8*l.* and 9*l.* A hundred stores will stock an acre; or 35 brace, 10 or 12 inches long, are fully sufficient for a breeding pond. The first year they will be three inches long; second year, seven; third year, eleven or twelve; fourth year, fourteen or fifteen. This year they breed."

THOMAS MARCHANT'S HEADACHES

Although fish-breeding is not what it was, many of the Sussex ponds are still regularly dragged, and the proceeds sold in advance to a London firm. Sometimes the purchaser wins in the gamble, sometimes the seller. The fish are removed alive, in large tanks, and sold as they are wanted, chiefly for Jewish tables. But we must return to Thomas Marchant:—

"January 16th (Sunday) 1715. I was not at church having a bad headache.

"January 25th, 1715. We had a trout for supper, two feet two inches long from eye to fork, and six inches broad; it weighed ten-and-a-half pounds. It was caught in the Albourne Brook, near Trussell House . . . We staid very late and drank enough.

"April 15th, 1715. Paid my uncle Courtness 15*d.* for a small bottle of Daffey's Elixir.

"July 18th, 1715. I went to Bolney and agreed with Edw. Jenner to dig sandstone for setting up my father's tombstone, at 5*s.* I gave him 6*d.* to spend in drink that he might be more careful.

"August 7th, (Sunday) 1715. I was not at church as my head ached very much.

"November 22nd, 1716. Fisht the great pond and put 220 of the biggest carp into the new pond, and 18 of the biggest tench.

Put also 358 store carp into the flat stew, and 36 tench; and also 550 very small carp into a hole in the low field.

"November 24th, 1716. Fisht the middle pond. Put 66 large carp into the new pond, and 380 store tench into the flat stew, and 12 large carp, 10 large tench, and 57 middle sized tench into the hovel field stew.

"June 12th, 1717. I was at the cricket match at Dungton Gate towards night.

"January 24th, 1718. A mountebank came to our towne to-day. He calls himself Dr. Richard Harness. Mr. Scutt and I drank tea with the tumbler. Of his tricks I am no judge: but he appears to me to play well on the fiddle.

"January 30th (Friday), 1719. King Charles' Martyrdom. I was not at church, as my head ached very much.

"February 28th, 1719. We had news of the Chevalier de St. George, the Pretender, being taken and carried into the Castle of Milan.

"September 19th, 1719. John Parsons began his year last Tuesday. He is to shave my face twice a week, and my head once a fortnight, and I am to give him 100 faggots per annum.

"September 30th, 1719. Talked to Mrs. Beard, for Allan Savage, about her horse that was seized by the officers at Brighton running brandy.

"December 5th, 1719. My Lord Treep put a ferral and pick to my stick. [My Lord Treep was a tinker named Treep who lived in Treep's Lane. My Lord Burt, who is also mentioned in the diary, was a farrier.]

"July 28th, 1721. Paid Harry Wolvin of Twineham, for killing an otter in our parish. [An otter, of course, was a serious enemy to the owner of stews and ponds.]

"February 7th, 1722. Will and Jack went to Lewes to see a prize fight between Harris and another.

"September 18th, 1727. Dined at Mr. Hazelgrove's and cheapened
a tombstone."

Thomas Marchant was buried September 17, 1728.

Less than two miles west of Hurstpierpoint is Albourne, so hidden
away that one might know this part of the country well and yet be
continually overlooking it. The western high road between Brighton
and London passes within a stone's throw of Albourne, but one never
suspects the existence, close by, of this retired village, so compact and
virginal and exquisitely old fashioned. It is said that after the execution
of Charles I Bishop Juxon lived for a while at Albourne Place during
the Civil War, and once escaped the Parliamentary soldiers by disguising
himself as a bricklayer. There is a priest's hiding hole in the house.

A GIANT TROUT

Some three miles north of Albourne is Twineham, another village
which, situated only on a by-road midway between two lines of railway,
has also preserved its bloom. Here, at the end of the seventeenth and
beginning of the eighteenth centuries, at Hickstead Place, a beautiful
Tudor mansion that still stands, lived Richard Stapley, another of the
Sussex diarists whose MSS. have been selected for publication by the
Sussex Archæological Society. I quote a few passages:—

"In ye month of November, 1692, there was a trout found in
ye Poyningswish, in Twineham, which was 29 inches long from ye
top of ye nose to ye tip of ye taile; and John fflint had him and eat
him. He was left in a low slank after a fflood, and ye water fell away
from him, and he died. The fish I saw at John fflint's house ye Sunday
after they had him: and at night they boiled him for supper, but could
not eat one halfe of him; and there was six of them at supper; John
fflint and his wife Jane, and four of their children; and ye next day
they all fell on him again, and compassed him."

Here we have the spectacle of a good man struggling with accuracy:—"August 19th, 1698. Paid Mr. Stheward for Dr. Comber's paraphrase on ye Common Prayer, 20*s.* and 6*d.* for carriage. I paid it at ye end of ye kitchen table next ye chamber stairs door, and nobody in ye room but he and I. No, it was ye end of ye table next ye parlour.

"April 26th, 1709. I bought a salmon-trout of William Lindfield of Grubbs, in Bolney, which he caught ye night before in his net, by his old orchard, which was wounded by an otter. The trout weighed 11 lbs. and ½; and was 3 foot 2 inches long from end to end, and but 2 foot 9 inches between ye eye and ye forke." There is also a record of a salmon trout being caught at Bolney early in the last century, which weighed 22lbs. and was sent to King George IV. at Brighton.

I must quote a prescription from the diary:—"To cure the hoopingcough:—get 3 field mice, flaw them, draw them, and roast one of them, and let the party afflicted eat it; dry the other two in the oven until they crumble to a powder, and put a little of this powder in what the patient drinks at night and in the morning." Mice played, and still play in remote districts, a large part in the rural pharmacopeia. A Sussex doctor once told me that he had directed the mother of a boy at Portslade to put some ice in a bag and tie it on the boy's forehead. When, the next day, the doctor asked after his patient, the mother replied briskly:—"Oh, Tommy's better, but the mice are dead."

OATMEAL PUDDING

The Stapley family ate an oatmeal pudding made in the following manner:—

Of oats decorticated take two pound,
And of new milk enough the same to dround;
Of raisins of the sun, ston'd, ounces eight;
Of currants, cleanly picked, an equal weight;

Of suet, finely sliced, an ounce at least;
And six eggs newly taken from the nest;
Season this mixture well with salt and spice;
Twill make a pudding far exceeding nice;
And you may safely feed on it like farmers.
For the receipt is learned Dr. Harmer's.

THE GOOD HORSE'S REWARD

Richard Stapley's diary was continued by his son Anthony and grandson John. The most pleasing among the printed extracts is this:—"1736, May the 21st. The white horse was buried in the saw-pit in the Laine's wood. He was aged about thirty-five years, as far as I could find of people that knew him foaled. He had been in his time as good a horse as ever man was owner of, and he was buried in his skin being a good old horse."

DITCHLING.

CHAPTER XXI

DITCHLING

Stanmer Park and Dr. Johnson—The Roman way down Ditchling Beacon—Sussex folk in London—Jacob's Post—The virtues of gibbets—Mr. John Burgess's diary.

Another good walk from Brighton begins with a short railway journey to Falmer on the Lewes line. Then strike into Stanmer Park, the seat of the Earl of Chichester, a descendant of the famous Sussex Pelhams, with the church and the little village of Stanmer on the far edge of it, and so up through the hollows and valleys to Ditchling Beacon. Dr. Johnson's saying of the Downs about Brighton, that "it was a country so truly desolate that if one had a mind to hang oneself for desperation at being obliged to live there, it would be difficult to find a tree on which to fasten a rope," proves beyond question that his horse never took him Stanmer way, for the park is richly wooded.

On Ditchling Beacon, one of the noblest of the Sussex hills and the second if not the first in height of all the range (the surveys differ, one giving the palm to Duncton) the Romans had a camp, and the village of Ditchling may still be gained by the half-subterranean path that our conquerors dug, so devised that a regiment might descend into the Weald unseen.

Ditchling is a quiet little village on high ground, where Alfred the Great once had a park. The church is a very interesting and graceful specimen of early English architecture, dating from the 13th century. A hundred and more years ago water from a chalybeate spring on the common was drunk by Sussex people for rheumatism and other ills; but the spring has lost its fame. The village could not well be more out of the movement, yet an old lady living in the neighbourhood who, when about to visit London for the first time, was asked what she expected to find, replied, "Well, I can't exactly tell, but I suppose something like the more bustling part of Ditchling." A kindred story is told of a Sussex man who, finding himself in London for the first time, exclaimed with astonishment—"What a queer large place! Why, it ain't like Newick and it ain't like Chailey."

OLD HOUSE AT DITCHLING.

On Ditchling Common are the protected remains of a stake known as Jacob's Post. A stranger requested to supply this piece of wood with the origin of its label would probably adventure long before hitting upon the right tack; for Jacob, whose name has in this familiar connection a popular and almost an endearing sound, was Jacob Harris, a Jew pedlar of astonishing turpitude, who, after murdering three persons at an inn on Ditchling Common and plundering their house, was hanged at Horsham in the year 1734, and afterwards suspended, as a lesson, to the gibbet, of which this post—Jacob's Post—is the surviving relic.

A CURE FOR TOOTHACHE

All gibbets, it is said, are "good" for something, and a piece of Jacob's Post carried on the person is sovran against toothache. A Sussex archæologist tells of an old lady, a resident on Ditchling Common for more than eighty years, whose belief in the Post was so sound that her pocket contained a splinter of it long after all her teeth had departed.

JOHN BURGESS'S DIARY

From extracts from the diary of Mr. John Burgess, tailor, sexton and Particular Baptist, of Ditchling, which are given in the Sussex Archæological Collections, I quote here and there:—

"August 1st, 1785. There was a cricket match at Lingfield Common between Lingfield in Surrey and all the county of Sussex, supposed to be upwards of 2,000 people.

"June 29th, 1786. Went to Lewes with some wool to Mr. Chatfield, fine wool at 8-5-0 per pack. Went to dinner with Mr. Chatfield. Had boiled Beef, Leg of Lamb and plum Pudden. Stopped there all the afternoon. Mr. Pullin was there; Mr. Trimby and the Curyer, &c., was there. We had a good deal of religious conversation, particularly Mr. Trimby.

"June 11th, 1787. Spent 3 or 4 hours with some friends in Conversation upon Moral and religious Subjects; the inquiry was the most easy and natural evedences of ye existence and attributes of ye supream Being—in discussing upon the Subject we was nearly agreed and propose meeting again every first monday after the fool Moon to meet at 4 and break-up at 8.

"March 14th, 1788. Went to Fryersoake to a Bull Bait to Sell My dog. I seld him for 1 guineay upon condition he was Hurt, but as he received no Hurt I took him back again at the same price. We had a good dinner; a round of Beef Boiled, a good piece roasted, a Lag of Mutton and Ham of Pork and plum pudden, plenty of wine and punch.

"At Brightelmstone:—washed in ye sea."

CHAPTER XXII

CUCKFIELD

Hayward's Heath—Rookwood and the fatal tree—Timothy Burrell and his account books—Old Sussex appetites—Plum-porridge—A luckless lover—The original Merry Andrew—Ancient testators—Bolney's bells—The splendour of the Slaugham Coverts—Hand Cross—Crawley and the new discovery of walking—Lindfield—*Idlehurst*—Richard Turner's epitaph—Ardingly.

Hayward's Heath, on the London line, would be our next centre were it not so new and suburban. Fortunately Cuckfield, which has two coaching inns and many of the signs of the leisurely past, is close by, in the midst of very interesting country, with a church standing high on the ridge to the south of the town, broadside to the Weald, its spire a landmark for miles. Cuckfield Place (a house and park, according to Shelley, which abounded in "bits of Mrs. Radcliffe") is described in Harrison Ainsworth's *Rookwood*. It was in the avenue leading from the gates to the house that that fatal tree stood, a limb of which fell as the presage of the death of a member of the family. So runs the legend. Knowledge of the tree is, however, disclaimed by the gatekeeper.

CUCKFIELD CHURCH.

THE COACHMAN'S PLANS

Ockenden House, in Cuckfield, has been for many years in the possession of the Burrell family, one of whom, Timothy Burrell, an ancestor of the antiquary, left some interesting account books, which contain in addition to figures many curious and sardonic entries and some ingenious hieroglyphics. I quote here and there, from the Sussex Archæological Society's extracts, by way of illustrating the life of a Sussex squire in those days, 1683-1714:—

1705. "Pay'd Gosmark for making cyder 1 day, whilst John
    Coachman was to be drunk with the carrier's money, by

agreement; and I pay'd 2*d.* to the glasier for mending John's casement broken at night by him when he was drunk.

"1706. 25th March. Pd. John Coachman by Ned Virgo, that he may be drunk all the Easter week, in part of his wages due, £1."

ANCIENT APPETITES

This was the fare provided on January 1, 1707, for thirteen guests:—

Plumm pottage.	Plumm pottage.
Calves' head and bacon.	Boiled beef, a clod.
	Two baked
Goose.	
	puddings.
	Three dishes of
Pig.	minced
	pies.
Plumm pottage.	
Roast beef, sirloin.	Two capons.
Veale, a loin.	Two dishes of tarts.
Goose.	Two pullets.

Plum porridge, it may interest some to know, was made thus: "Take of beef-soup made of legs of beef, 12 quarts; if you wish it to be particularly good, add a couple of tongues to be boiled therein. Put fine bread, sliced, soaked, and crumbled; raisins of the sun, currants and pruants two lbs. of each; lemons, nutmegs, mace and cloves are to be boiled with it in a muslin bag; add a quart of red wine and let this be followed, after half an hour's boiling, by a pint of sack. Put it into a cool place and it will keep through Christmas."

Mr. Burrell giving a small dinner to four friends, offered them

Pease pottage.

2 carps. 2 tench.	Roast leg of mutton.
Capon. Pullet.	Apple pudding.
Fried oysters.	Goos.
Baked pudding.	Tarts. Minced pies.

It is perhaps not surprising that the host had occasionally to take the waters of Ditchling, which are no longer drunk medicinally, or to dose himself with hieræ picræ.

One more dinner, this time for four guests, who presumably were more worthy of attention:—

A soup take off.
Two large carps at the upper end.
Pidgeon pie, salad, veal ollaves,
Leg of mutton, and cutlets at the lower end.
Three rosed chickens.
Scotch pancakes, tarts, asparagus.
Three green gees at the lower end.
In the room of the chickens removed,
Four-souced Mackerel.
Rasins in cream at the upper end.
Calves' foot jelly, dried sweetmeats, calves' foot jelly.
Flummery, Savoy cakes.
Imperial cream at the lower end.

In October, 1709, Mr. Burrell writes in Latin: "From this time I have resolved, as long as the dearth of provisions continues, to give to the poor who apply for it at the door on Sundays, twelve pounds of beef every week, on the 11th of February 4lbs. more, in all 16lbs., and a bushel of wheat and half a bushel of barley in 4 weeks."

MERRY ANDREW

From Borde Hill to the north-east of Cuckfield, is supposed to have come Andrew Boord, the original Merry Andrew. Among the later Boords who lived there was George Boord, in whose copy of *Natura*

Brevium and *Tenores Novelli*, bound together (given him by John Sackville of Chiddingly Park) is written:—

> Sidera non tot habet Celum, nec flumina pisces,
> Quot scelera gerit femina mente dolos.
> Dixit Boordus;

which Mr. Lower translates:

> Quoth Boord, with stars the skies abound,
>   With fish the flowing waters;
> But far more numerous I have found
>   The tricks of Eve's fair daughters.

This Boord would be a relative of the famous Andrew, priest, doctor and satirist (1490-1549) who may indeed have been the author of the distich above. It is certainly in his vein.

Andrew Boord gave up his vows as a Carthusian on account of their "rugorosite," and became a doctor, travelling much on the Continent. Several books are known to be his, chief among them the *Dyetary* and *Brevyary of Health*. He wrote also an *Itinerary of England* and is credited by some with the *Merrie Tales of the Mad Men of Gotham*. Lower and Horsfield indeed hold that the Gotham intended was not the Nottinghamshire village but Gotham near Pevensey, where Boord had property. That he knew something of Sussex is shown by *Boord's Boke of Knowledge*, where he mentions the old story, then a new one, that no nightingale will sing in St. Leonard's Forest. It is the *Boke of Knowledge* that has for frontispiece the picture of a naked Englishman with a pair of shears in one hand and a piece of cloth over the other arm, saying:

> I am an English man and naked I stand here,
> Musing in my mund what rayment I shall were;

For now I wyll were this, and now I wyl were that;

Now I wyl were I cannot tel what.

We shall see Andrew again when we come to Pevensey.

OLD WILLS

A glimpse of the orderly mind of a pre-Reformation Cuckfield yeoman is given in a will quoted recently in the *Sussex Daily News*, in an interesting series of articles on the county under the title of "Old-time Sussex":

"In the yere of our lorde god 1545. the 26 day of June, I, Thomas Gaston, of the pish of Cukefelde, syke in body, hole, and of ppt [perfect] memorie, ordene and make this my last will and test, in manr. and forme folling.

Fyrst I bequethe my sowle to Almyghty god or [our] lady St. Mary and all the holy company of heyvyng, my bodie to be buried in the church yarde of Cukefeld.

It. (item) to the Mother Church of Chichester 4*d*.

It. to the hye alter of Cuckfeld 4*d*.

It. I will have at my buryall 5 masses. In lykewise at my monthes mynd and also at my yerely mynd all the charge of the church set apart I will have in meate and drynke and to pore people 10*s*. at every tyme."

The high altar was frequently mentioned favourably in these old wills. Another Cuckfield testator, in 1539, left to the high altar, "for tythes and oblacions negligently forgotten, sixpence." The same student of the *Calendar of Sussex Wills in the District Probate Registry at Lewes, between 1541 and 1652*, which the British Record Society have just published, copies the following passage from the will of Gerard Onstye, in 1568: "To mary my daughter £20, the ffeatherbed that I lye upon the bolsters and coverlete of tapestaye work with a blankett, 4 payres of shetts that is to say four pares of the best flaxon and other 2 payre of the best hempen the greate brasse potte that hir mother brought, the best bord-clothe (table cloth?) a lynnen whelle (*i.e.*, spinning-wheel) that was hir mothers, the chaffing dish that hangeth in the parlor."

In those simple days everything was prized. In one of these Sussex wills, in 1594, Richard Phearndeane, a labourer, left to his brother Stephen his best dublett, his best jerkin and his best shoes, and to Bernard Rosse his white dublett, his leathern dublett and his worst breeches.

THE BELLS OF BOLNEY

Three miles west of Cuckfield is Bolney, just off the London road, a village in the southern boundary of St. Leonard's Forest, the key to some very rich country. Before the days of bicycles Bolney was practically unknown, so retired is it. The church, which has a curious pinnacled tower nearly 300 years old, is famous for its bells, concerning whose melody Horsfield gives the following piece of counsel: "Those who are fond of the silvery tones of bells, may enjoy them to perfection, by placing themselves on the margin of a large pond, the property of Mr. W. Marshall; the reverberation of the sound, coming off the water, is peculiarly striking."

Sixty years ago this sheet of water had an additional attraction. Says Mr. Knox, "During the months of May and June, 1843, an osprey was observed to haunt the large ponds near Bolney. After securing a fish he used to retire to an old tree on the more exposed bank to devour it, and about the close of evening was in the habit of flying off towards the north-west, sometimes carrying away a prize in his talons if his sport had been unusually successful, as if he dreaded being disturbed at his repast during the dangerous hours of twilight. Having been shot at several times without effect, his visits to these ponds became gradually less frequent, but the surrounding covers being unpreserved, and the bird itself too wary to suffer a near approach, he escaped the fate of many of his congeners, and even re-appeared with a companion early in the following September, to whom he seemed to have imparted his salutary dread of man—his mortal enemy—for during the short time they remained there it was impossible to approach within gunshot of either of them."

The indirect road from Bolney to Hand Cross, through Warninglid and Slaugham (parallel with the coaching road), is superb, taking us again into the iron country and very near to Leonardslee, which we have already seen.

THE MAGNIFICENT COVERTS

The glory of Slaugham Place is no more; but one visible sign of it is preserved in Lewes, in the Town Hall, in the shape of its old staircase. Slaugham Place was the seat of the Covert family, whose estates extended, says tradition, "from Southwark to the Sea," and, says the more exact Horsfield, from Crawley to Hangleton, above Brighton. Slaugham Park used to cover 1200 acres, the church being within it. Perhaps nowhere in Sussex is the change so complete as here, and within recent times too, for Horsfield quotes, in 1835, the testimony of "an aged person, whom the present rector buried about twenty-five years back, who used to relate, that he remembered when the family at Slaugham Park, or Place, consisted of seventy persons." Horsfield continues, in a footnote (the natural receptacle of many of his most interesting statements):—"The name of the aged person alluded to was Harding, who died at nearly 100. According to his statement, the family were so numerous, they kept constantly employed mechanics of every description, who resided on the premises. A conduit, which supplied the mansion with water, is now used by the inhabitants of the village. The kitchen fireplace still remains, of immense size, with the irons that supported the cooking apparatus. The arms of the Coverts, with many impalements and quarterings, yet remain on the ruins. The principal entrance was from the east, and the grand front to the north. The pillars at the entrance, fluted, with seats on each side, are still there. According to the statement of the above person, there was a chapel attached to the mansion at the west part. The mill-pond flowed over nearly 40 acres, according to a person's statement who occupied the mill many years." The ruins, little changed since Horsfield wrote, stand in a beautiful old-world garden, which the traveller must certainly endeavour to enter.

THE BRIGHTON ROAD

A mile north of Slaugham is Hand Cross, a Clapham Junction of highways, whence Crawley is easily reached. Crawley, however, beyond a noble church, has no interest, its distinction being that it is halfway between London and Brighton on the high road—its distinction and its misfortune. One would be hard put to it to think of a less desirable existence than that of dwelling on a dusty road and continually seeing people hurrying either from Brighton to London or from London to Brighton. Coaches, phaetons, motor cars, bicycles, pass through Crawley so numerously as almost to constitute one elongated vehicle, like the moving platform at the last Paris Exhibition.

And not only travellers on wheels; for since the fashion for walking came in, Crawley has had new excitements, or monotonies, in the shape of walking stockbrokers, walking butchers, walking auctioneers' clerks, walking Austrians pushing their families in wheelbarrows, walking bricklayers carrying hods of bricks, walking acrobats on stilts—all striving to get to Brighton within a certain time, and all accompanied by judges, referees, and friends. At Hand Cross, lower on the road, the numbers diminish; but every competitor seems to be able to reach Crawley, perhaps because the railway station adjoins the high road. It was not, for example, until he reached Crawley that the Austrian's wheelbarrow broke down.

LINDFIELD

On the other side of the line, two miles north-east of Hayward's Heath, is Lindfield, with its fine common of geese, its generous duck-pond, and wide straggling street of old houses and new (too many new, to my mind), rising easily to the graceful Early English church with its slender shingled spire. Just beyond the church is one of the most beautiful of timbered houses in Sussex, or indeed in England. When I first knew this house it was a farm in the hands of a careless farmer; it has been restored by its present owner with the most perfect understanding and taste. For too long no one attempted to do as much for East Mascalls, a timbered ruin lying low among the fields to the east of the village; but quite recently it has been taken in hand.

EAST MASCALLS—BEFORE RENOVATION.

A quaint Lindfield epitaph may be mentioned: that of Richard Turner, who died in 1768, aged twenty-one:—

Long was my pain, great was my grief,
Surgeons I'd many but no relief.
I trust through Christ to rise with the just:
My leg and thigh was buried first.

"IDLEHURST"

I must not betray secrets, but it might be remarked that that kindly yet melancholy study of Wealden people and Wealden scenery, called *Idlehurst*—the best book, I think, that has come out of Sussex in recent years—may be read with some special appropriateness in this neighbourhood.

North of Lindfield is Ardingly, now known chiefly in connection with the large school which travellers on the line to Brighton see from the carriage windows as they cross the viaduct over the Ouse. The village, a mile north of the college, is famous as the birthplace of Thomas Box, the first of the great wicket-keepers, who disdained gloves even to the fastest bowling. The church has some very interesting brasses to members of the Wakehurst and Culpeper families, who long held Wakehurst Place, the Elizabethan mansion to the north of the village. Nicholas Culpeper of the *Herbal* was of the stock; but he must not be confounded with the Nicholas Culpeper whose brass, together with that of his wife, ten sons and eight daughters, is in the church, possibly the largest family on record depicted in that metal. The church also has a handsome canopied tomb, the occupant of which is unknown.

From Ardingly superb walks in the Sussex forest country may be taken.

CHAPTER XXIII

FOREST COUNTRY AGAIN

Balcombe—The iron furnace and the iron horse—Leonard Gale of Tinsloe Forge—Mr. Wilfred Scawen Blunt of Crabbet—"The Old Squire"—Frederick Locker-Lampson of Rowfant—The Rowfant books—"To F. L."—The Rowfant titmice.

On leaving the train at Balcombe, one is quickly on the densely wooded Forest Ridge of Sussex, here fenced and preserved, but farther east, when it becomes Ashdown Forest, consisting of vast tracts of open moorland and heather. Balcombe has a simple church, protected by a screen of Scotch firs; its great merit is its position as the key to a paradise for all who like woodland travel. From Balcombe to Worth is one vast pheasant run, with here and there a keeper's cottage or a farm: originally, of course, a series of plantations growing furnace wood for the ironmasters. In Tilgate Forest, to the west of Balcombe Forest, are two large sheets of water, once hammer-ponds, walking west from which, towards Horsham, one may be said to traverse the Lake Country of Sussex. A strange transformation, from Iron Black Country to Lake Country!—but nature quickly recovers herself, and were the true Black Country's furnaces extinguished, she would soon make even that grimy tract a haunt of loveliness once more.

No longer are heard the sounds of the hammers, but Balcombe Forest, Tilgate Forest, and Worth Forest have still a constant reminder of machinery, for very few minutes pass from morning to night without the rumble of a train on the main line to Brighton, which passes through the very midst of this wild game region, and plunges into the earth under the high ground of Balcombe Forest. I know of no place where the trains emit such a volume of sound as in the valley of the Stanford brook, just north of the tunnel.

The noise makes it impossible ever quite to lose the sense of modernity in these woods, as one may on Shelley Plain, a few miles west, or at Gill's Lap, in Ashdown Forest; unless, of course, one's imagination is so complaisant as to believe it to proceed from the old iron furnaces. This reminds me that Crabbet, just to the north of Worth (where church and vicarage stand isolated on a sandy ridge on the edge of the Forest), was the home of one of the most considerable of the Sussex ironmasters, Leonard Gale of Tinsloe Forge, who bought Crabbet, park and house, in 1698—since "building," in his own words, is a "sweet impoverishing."

WORTH CHURCH

But we must pause for a moment at Worth, because its church is remarkable as being the largest in England to preserve its Saxon foundations. Sussex, as we have seen, is rich in Saxon relics, but the county has nothing more interesting than this. The church is cruciform, as all churches should be, and there is a little east window in the north transept through which, it is conjectured, arrows were intended to be shot at marauding Danes; for an Englishman's church was once his castle. Archæologists familiar with Worth church have been known to pass with disdain cathedrals for which the ordinary person cannot find too many fine adjectives.

MR. BLUNT'S BALLAD

THE OLD SQUIRE

To regain Crabbet. The present owner, Mr. Wilfred Scawen Blunt, poet, patriot, and breeder of Arab horses, who is a descendant of the Gales, has a long poem entitled "Worth Forest," wherein old Leonard Gale is a notable figure. Among other poems by the lord of Crabbet is the very pleasantly English ballad of

THE OLD SQUIRE.

I like the hunting of the hare
   Better than that of the fox;
I like the joyous morning air,
   And the crowing of the cocks.

I like the calm of the early fields,
   The ducks asleep by the lake,
The quiet hour which Nature yields
   Before mankind is awake.

I like the pheasants and feeding things
   Of the unsuspicious morn;
I like the flap of the wood-pigeon's wings
   As she rises from the corn.

I like the blackbird's shriek, and his rush
   From the turnips as I pass by,
And the partridge hiding her head in a bush,
   For her young ones cannot fly.

I like these things, and I like to ride
   When all the world is in bed,
To the top of the hill where the sky grows wide,
   And where the sun grows red.

The beagles at my horse heels trot,
   In silence after me;
There's Ruby, Roger, Diamond, Dot,
   Old Slut and Margery,—

A score of names well used, and dear,
   The names my childhood knew;
The horn, with which I rouse their cheer,
   Is the horn my father blew.

I like the hunting of the hare
   Better than that of the fox;
The new world still is all less fair
   Than the old world it mocks.

I covet not a wider range
   Than these dear manors give;
I take my pleasures without change,
   And as I lived I live.

I leave my neighbours to their thought;
   My choice it is, and pride,
On my own lands to find my sport,
   In my own fields to ride.

The hare herself no better loves
   The field where she was bred,

Than I the habit of these groves,
 My own inherited.

I know my quarries every one,
 The meuse where she sits low;
The road she chose to-day was run
 A hundred years ago.

The lags, the gills, the forest ways;
 The hedgerows one and all,
These are the kingdoms of my chase,
 And bounded by my wall.

Nor has the world a better thing,
 Though one should search it round,
Than thus to live one's own sole king,
 Upon one's own sole ground.

I like the hunting of the hare;
 It brings me day by day,
The memory of old days as fair,
 With dead men past away.

To these, as homeward still I ply,
 And pass the churchyard gate,
Where all are laid as I must lie,
 I stop and raise my hat.

I like the hunting of the hare;
 New sports I hold in scorn.
I like to be as my fathers were,
 n the days e'er I was born.

THE ROWFANT BOOKS

We are indeed just now in a bookish and poetical district, for a little more than a mile to the east of Crabbet, in a beautiful Tudor house in a hollow close to the station, lived Frederick Locker-Lampson, the London lyricist; and here are treasured the famous Rowfant books and manuscripts which he brought together—the subject of graceful verses by many of his friends. Not the least charming of these tributes (printed in the *Rowfant Catalogue* in 1886) are Mr. Andrew Lang's lines:

TO F. L.

I mind that Forest Shepherd's saw,
    For, when men preached of Heaven, quoth he;
"It's a' that's bricht, and a' that's braw,
    But Bourhope's guid eneuch for me!"

Beneath the green deep-bosomed hills
    That guard Saint Mary's Loch it lies,
The silence of the pasture fills
    That shepherd's homely paradise.

Enough for him his mountain lake,
    His glen the hern went singing through,
And Rowfant, when the thrushes wake,
    May well seem good enough for YOU.

For all is old, and tried, and dear,
    And all is fair, and round about
The brook that murmurs from the mere
    Is dimpled with the rising trout.

But when the skies of shorter days
   Are dark and all the "ways are mire,"
How bright upon your books the blaze
   Gleams from the cheerful study fire.

On quartos where our fathers read,
   Enthralled, the Book of Shakespeare's play,
On all that Poe could dream of dread,
   And all that Herrick sang of gay!

Fair first editions, duly prized,
   Above them all, methinks, I rate
The tome where Walton's hand revised
   His wonderful receipts for bait!

Happy, who rich in toys like these
   Forgets a weary nation's ills,
Who from his study window sees
   The circle of the Sussex hills.

THE RESOLUTE TITMICE

Rowfant was once the scene of one of the most determined struggles in history. The contestants were a series of Titmice and the G.P.O., and the account of the war may be read in the Natural History Museum at South Kensington:—"In 1888, a pair of the Great Titmouse (*Parus major*) began to build their nest in the post-box which stood in the road at Rowfant, and into which letters, &c., were posted and taken out by the door daily. One of the birds was killed by a boy, and the nest was not finished. In 1889, a pair completed the nest, laid seven eggs, and began to sit; but one day, when an unusual number of post-cards were dropped into, and nearly filled, the box, the birds deserted the nest, which was afterwards removed with the eggs. In 1890, a pair built a new nest and laid seven eggs, and reared a brood of five young, although the letters posted were often found lying on the back of the sitting bird, which never left the nest when the door of the box was opened to take out the letters. The birds went in and out by the slit."

CHAPTER XXIV

EAST GRINSTEAD

Sackville College—John Mason Neale—*Theodosius; or, The Force of Love*, at the East Grinstead Theatre—Three martyrs—Brambletye House—Forest Row—The garden of the author of *The English Flower Garden*—Diamond Jubilee clock-faces—"Big-on-Little" and the reverend and irreverend commentator.

East Grinstead, the capital of north-east Sussex, is interesting chiefly for Sackville College, that haunt of ancient peace of which John Mason Neale, poet, enthusiast, divine, historian, and romance-writer for children, was for many years the distinguished Warden. Nothing can exceed the quiet restfulness of the quadrangle. The college gives shelter to five brethren and six sisters (one of whom shows the visitor over the building), and to a warden and two assistants. Happy collegians, to have so fair a haven in which to pass the evening of life. East Grinstead otherwise has not much beauty, its commanding pinnacled church tower being more impressive from a distance, and its chief street mingling too much that is new with its few old timbered façades, charming though these are.

THE JUDGE'S HOUSES, EAST GRINSTEAD.

The town, when it would be frivolous, to-day depends upon the occasional visits of travelling entertainers; but in the eighteenth century East Grinstead had a theatre of its own, in the main street, a play-bill of which, for May, 1758, is given in Boaden's *Life of Mrs. Siddons.* It states that "Theodosius; or, the Force of Love," is to be played, for the benefit of Mrs. P. Varanes by Mr. P., "who will strive as far as possible to support the character of this fiery Persian Prince, in which he was so much admired and applauded at Hastings, Arundel, Petworth, Midhurst, Lewes, &c." The attraction of the next announcement is the precise converse: "Theodosius, by a young gentleman from the University of Oxford, who never appeared on any stage."

NOBILITY AND THE ALTAR

The play-bill continues with a delicate hint: "Nothing in Italy can exceed the altar in the first scene of the play. Nevertheless, should any of the nobility or gentry wish to see it ornamented with flowers, the bearer will bring away as many as they choose to favour him with." Finally: "N.B.—The great yard dog that made so much noise on Thursday night during the last act of King Richard the Third, will be sent to a neighbour's over the way."

The Sussex Martyrs, to whom a memorial, as we shall see, has recently been raised above Lewes, are usually associated with that town; but on July 18, 1556, Thomas Dungate, John Forman, and Anne, or Mother, Tree, were burned for conscience' sake at East Grinstead.

Between East Grinstead and Forest Row, on the east, just under the hill and close to the railway, are the remains of Brambletye House, a rather florid ruin, once the seat of the great Sussex family of Lewknor. In its heyday Brambletye must have been a very fine place. Horace Smith's romance which bears its name, and for which Horsfield, in his *History of Sussex*, predicted a career commensurable with that of the Waverley novels, is now, I fear, justly forgotten. The slopes of Forest Row, which was of old a settlement of hunting lodges belonging to the great lords who took their pleasure in Ashdown Forest, are now bright with new villas. From Forest Row, Wych Cross and Ashdown Forest are easily gained; but of this open region of dark heather more in a later *chapter.*

Between Kingscote and West Hoathly, a short distance to the south-west of East Grinstead, is another "tye"—Gravetye, a tudor mansion in a deep hollow, the home of Mr. William Robinson, the author of *The English Flower Garden*. Last April, the stonework, of which there is much, was a mass of the most wonderful purple aubretia, and the wild garden between the house and the water a paradise of daffodils.

The church of West Hoathly (called West Ho-ly), which stands high on the hill to the south, has a slender shingled spire that may be seen from long distances. The tower has, however, been injured by the very ugly new clock that has been lately fixed in a position doubtless the most convenient but doubtless also the least comely. To nail to such a delicate structure as West Hoathly church the kind of dial that one expects to see outside a railway station is a curious lapse of taste. Hever church, in Kent, has a similar blemish, probably dating from one of the recent Jubilee celebrations, which left few loyal villages the richer by a beautiful memorial. Surely it should be possible to obtain an appropriate clock-face for such churches as these.

West Hoathly has some iron tombstones, such as used to be cast in the old furnace days, which are not uncommon in these parts. Opposite the church is a building of great antiquity, which has been allowed to forget its honourable age.

"BIG-ON-LITTLE"

We are now on the fringe of the Sussex rock country, to which we come again in earnest when we reach Maresfield, and of which Tunbridge Wells is the capital. But not even Tunbridge Wells with its famous toad has anything to offer more remarkable than West Hoathly's "Big-on-Little," in the Rockhurst estate. I am tempted to quote two descriptions of the rock, from two very different points of view. An antiquary writing in the eighteenth century (quoted by Horsfield) thus begins his account:— "About half a mile west of West Hoadley church there is a high ridge covered with wood; the edge of this is a craggy cliff, composed of enormous blocks of sand stone. The soil hath been entirely washed from off them, and in many places, from the interstices by which they are divided, one perceives these crags with bare broad white foreheads, and, as it were, overlooking the wood, which clothes the valley at their feet. In going to the place, I passed across this deep valley, and was led by a narrow foot-path almost trackless up to the cliff, which seems as one advances to hang over one's head. The mind in this passage is prepared with all the suspended feelings of awe and reverence, and as one approaches this particular rock, standing with its stupendous bulk poised, seemingly in a miraculous manner and point, one is struck with amazement. The recess in which it stands hath, behind this rock, and the rocks which surround it, a withdrawn and recluse passage which the eye cannot look into but with an idea of its coming from some more secret and holy adyt. All these circumstances, in an age of tutored superstition, would give, even to the finest minds, the impressions that lead to idolatry."

COBBETT AGAIN

And this is Cobbett's description, in the *Rural Rides*:—"At the place, of which I am now speaking, that is to say, by the side of this pleasant road to Brighton, and between Turner's Hill and Lindfield, there is a rock, which they call '*Big upon Little*,' that is to say, a rock upon another, having nothing else to rest upon, and the top one being longer and wider than the top of the one it lies on. This big rock is no trifling concern, being as big, perhaps, as a not very small house. How, then, *came* this big upon little? What lifted up the big? It balances itself naturally enough; but what tossed it up? I do not like to *pay* a parson for teaching me, while I have '*God's own Word*' to teach me; but if any parson will tell me *how* big *came* upon little, I do not know that I shall grudge him a trifle. And if he cannot tell me this; if he say, All that we have to do is to *admire* and *adore*; then I tell him, that I can admire and adore without his *aid*, and that I will keep my money in my pocket." That is pure Cobbett.

WEST HOATHLY

West Hoathly is in the midst of some of the best of the inland country of Sussex and an excellent centre for the walker. Several places that we have already seen are within easy distance, such as Horsted Keynes, Worth and Worth Forest and Balcombe and Balcombe Forest.

CHAPTER XXV

HORSTED KEYNES TO LEWES

The origin of "Keynes"—The Rev. Giles Moore's expenditure—
Advice as to tithes—Lord Sheffield and cricket—The grave of Edward
Gibbon—Fletching and English History—Newick and Chailey—The
Battle of Lewes—John Dudeney and John Kimber—Leonard Mascall
and the first English carp—Advice to fruit-growers—Malling Deanery
and the assassins of Becket.

The very pretty church of Horsted Keynes, which in its lowly position
is the very antithesis of West Hoathly's hill-surmounting spire, is famous
for the small recumbent figure of a knight in armour, with a lion at his
feet, possibly a member of the Keynes family that gives its name to this
Horsted (thus distinguishing it from Little Horsted, a few miles distant in
the East): Keynes being an anglicisation of de Cahanges, a family which
sent a representative to assist in the Norman Conquest.

ANCIENT ECONOMICS

Horsted Keynes, which is situated in very pleasant country, once took
its spiritual instruction from the lips of the Rev. Giles Moore, extracts
from whose journals and account books, 1656-1679, have been printed
by the S.A.S. I quote a few passages:

"I gave my wyfe 15*s.* to lay out at St. James faire at Lindfield, all which shee spent except 2*s.* 6*d.* which she never returned mee.

"16th Sept. I bought of Edward Barrett at Lewis a clock, for which I payed £2 10, and for a new jack, at the same time, made and brought home, £1 5. For two prolongers [*i.e.* save-alls] and an extinguisher 2*d.*, and a payr of bellowes 5*s.*"

7th May, 1656.—"I bought of William Clowson, upholsterer and itinerant, living over against the Crosse at Chichester, but who comes about the country with his pack on horseback:—

A fine large coverlett with birds and bucks	£2	10	0
A sett of striped curtains and valance	1	8	0
A coarse 8 qr coverlett	1	2	0
Two middle blankets	1	4	0
One beasil or Holland tyke or bolster	1	13	6

"My mayde being sicke, I paid for opening her veine 4*d.*, to the widow Rugglesford for looking to her, I gave 1*s.*; and to Old Bess, for tending on her 3 days and 2 nights, I gave 1*s.*; in all 2*s.* 4*d.*—this I gave her.

"Lent to my brother Luxford at the Widow Newports, never more to be seene! 1*s.*"

In 1658.—"To Wm Batchelor for bleeding mee in bed 2*s.* 6*d.*, and for barbouring mee 1*s.*" A year later:—"I agreed with Mr. Batchelor of Lindfield to barbour mee, and I am to pay him 16*s.* a yeare, beginning from Lady Day."

In 1671.—"I bargained with Edward Waters that he should have 18*s.* in money for the trimming of mee by the year, and deducting 1*s.* 6*d.* for his tythes."

23rd April, 1660.—"This being King Charles II. coronation I gave my namesake Moore's daughter then marryed 10*s.* and the fiddlers 6*d.*

"I payed the Widow Potter of Hoadleigh for knitting mee one payr of worsted stockings 2*s.* 6*d.*; for spinning 2 lb of wool 14*d.*, and for carding it 2*d.*

"To the collections made at 3 several sacraments I gave 3 several sixpences."

12th May, 1673.—"I went to London, spending there, going and coming, as *alibi apparet in particularibus*, 13*s.* 8*d.*; I bought for Ann Brett a gold ring, this being the posy, 'When this you see, remember mee,' and at the same time I bought Patrick's *Pilgrim*, 5*s.*; *The Reasonableness of Scripture*, by Sir Chas. Wolseley, 2*s.* 6*d.*; and a Comedy called *Epsom Wells.*"

Mr. Moore, having suffered in his tithes, left the following "necessary caution" for his successor:—"Never compound with any parishioner till you have first viewed theire lande and seen what corne they have upon it that yeare, and may have the next."

SHEFFIELD PARK

The next station on this quiet little cross-country line to Lewes, is Sheffield Park, the seat of Lord Sheffield. The present peer, one of the patrons of modern Sussex cricket, took a famous team to Australia in 1891-2, and it was on his yacht that in 1894 cricket was played in the Ice Fiord at Spitzbergen under the midnight sun, when Alfred Shaw captured forty wickets in less than three-quarters of an hour. Australian teams visiting England used to open their season with a match at Sheffield Park, which contains one of the best private grounds in the country; but the old custom has, I fancy, lapsed. In the long winter of 1890-1 several cricket matches on the ice were played on one of the lakes in the park, with well-known Sussex players on both sides.

Sheffield Park is associated in literature with the name of Edward Gibbon, the historian, who spent much time there in the company of his friend, John Baker Holroyd, the first earl. Gibbon's remains lie in Fletching church, close by. There also lies Peter Dynot, a glover of Fletching, who assisted Jack Cade, the Sussex rebel, whom we meet later, in 1450; while (more history) it was in the woods around Fletching church that Simon de Montfort encamped before he climbed the hills, as we are about to see, and fought and won the Battle of Lewes, in 1264.

The line passes next between Newick, on the east, and Chailey on the west. Fate seems to have decided that these villages shall always be bracketed in men's minds, like Beaumont and Fletcher, or Winchelsea and Rye: one certainly more often hears of "Newick and Chailey" than of either separately. Chailey has a wide breezy common from which the line of Downs between Ditchling Beacon and Lewes can be seen perhaps to their best advantage. Immediately to the south, and just to the west of Blackcap, the hill with a crest of trees, is Plumpton Plain, six hundred feet high, where the Barons formed their ranks to meet the third Harry in the Battle of Lewes, the actual fighting being on Mount Harry, the hill on Blackcap's east. A cross to mark the struggle, cut into the turf of the Plain, is still occasionally visible. More noticeable is the "V" in spruce firs planted on the escarpment to commemorate the Jubilee of 1887.

THE SHEPHERD MATHEMATICIAN

Plumpton, which is now known chiefly for its steeplechases, has had in its day at least two interesting inhabitants. One was John Dudeney, shepherd, mathematician, and schoolmaster, born here in 1782, who, as a youth, when tending his sheep on Newmarket Hill, dug a study and library in the chalk, and there kept his books and papers. He taught himself mathematics and languages, even Hebrew, and ultimately became a schoolmaster at Lewes. In his thorough adherence to learning Dudeney was the completest contrast to John Kimber of Chailey, a wealthy farmer with a consuming but unintelligent love of books, who was once, says Horsfield, seen bringing home Macklin's Bible, a costly work in six volumes in a sack laid across the back of a cart horse. According to the excellent habit of the old Sussex farmers, Mr. Kimber's body was borne to the grave in one of his wagons, drawn by his best team.

FANTASTIC FRUITS

Plumpton Place once had a moat, in which, legend has it, the first carp swam that came into England. The house then belonged to Leonard Mascall, whom Fuller in the *Worthies* erroneously ascribes to Plumsted. In Fuller's own words, which no one could better: "Leonard Mascall, of Plumsted in this county, being much delighted in Gardening, man's Original vocation, was the first who brought over into England, from beyond the seas, *Carps* and *Pippins*; the one, well-cook'd, delicious, the other cordial and restorative. For the proof hereof, we have his own word and witness; and did it, it seems, about the Fifth year of the reign of King *Henry* the Eighth, Anno Dom. 1514. The time of his death is to me unknown." The credit of introducing carps and pippins has, however, been denied to Mascall, who died in 1589 at Farnham Royal in Buckinghamshire, where he was buried; but we know him beyond question to have been an ingenious experimentalist in horticulture. He wrote and translated several books, among them a treatise on the orchard by a monk of the Abbey of St. Vincent in France: *A Book of the Arte of and Manner howe to plant and graffe all sortes of trees, howe to set stones, and sowe Pepines to make wylde trees to graffe on*, 1572. I take a few passages from a later edition of this work:

To Colour Apples.

To have coloured Apples with what colour ye shall think good ye shall bore or slope a hole with an Auger in the biggest part of the body of the tree, unto the midst thereof, or thereabouts, and then look what colour ye will have them of. First ye shall take water and mingle your colour therewith, then stop it up again with a short pin made of the same wood or tree, then wax it round about. Ye may mingle with the said colour what spice ye list, to make them taste thereafter. Thus may ye change the colour and taste of any Apple . . . This must be done before the Spring do come . . .

To Make Apples Fall From the Tree.

If ye put fiery coles under an Apple tree, and then cast off the powder of Brimstone therein, and the fume thereof ascend up, and touch an Apple that is wet, that Apple shall fall incontinent.

To Destroy Pismiers or Ants About a Tree.

Ye shall take of the saw-dust of Oke-wood oney, and straw that al about the tree root, and the next raine that doth come, all the Pismiers or Ants shall die there. For Earewigges, shooes stopt with hay, and hanged on the tree one night, they come all in.

For to have Rath Medlars Two Months Before Others.

For to have Medlars two months sooner than others and the one shall be better far than the other, ye shall graffe them upon a gooseberry tree, and also a franke mulberry tree, and before ye do graffe them, ye shall wet them in hay, and then graffe them.

MALLING DEANERY

To return to the line, for the excursion to Plumpton has taken us far from the original route, the next station to Newick and Chailey is Barcombe Mills, a watery village on the Ouse. The river valley contracts as Lewes is reached, with Malling Hill on the east and Offham Hill on the west: both taking their names from two of the quaint little hamlets by which Lewes is surrounded. It was at Mailing Deanery that the assassins of Thomas à Becket sought shelter on their flight from Canterbury. The legend records how, when they laid their armour on the Deanery table, that noble piece of furniture rose and flung the accursed accoutrements to the ground.

On Malling Hill is the residence of a Lewes lady whose charitable impulses have taken a direction not common among those who suffer for others. She receives into her stable old and overworked horses, thus ensuring for them a sleek and peaceful dotage enlivened by sugar and carrots, and marked by the kindest consideration. The pyramidal grave (as of a Saxon chief) of one of these dependants may be seen from the road.

ON THE OUSE ABOVE LEWES.

CHAPTER XXVI

LEWES

The Museum of Sussex—The riches of Lewes—Her leisure and antiquity—A plea from *Idlehurst*—Old Lewes disabilities—The Norman Conquest—Lewes Castle—Sussex curiosities—Lewes among her hills—The Battle of Lewes—The Cluniac Priory—Repellers of the French—A comprehender of Earthquakes—The author of *The Rights of Man*—A game of bowls—"Clio" Rickman and Thomas Tipper—Famous Lewes men—The Fifth of November—The Sussex martyrs.

Apart from the circumstance that the curiosities collected by the county's Archæological Society are preserved in the castle, Lewes is the museum of Sussex; for she has managed to compress into small compass more objects of antiquarian interest than any town I know. Chichester, which is compact enough, sprawls by comparison.

The traveller arriving by train no sooner alights from his carriage than he is on the site of the kitchens of the Cluniac Priory of St. Pancras, some of the walls of which almost scrape the train on its way to Brighton. That a priory eight hundred years old must be disturbed before a railway station can be built is a melancholy circumstance; but in the present case the vandalism had its compensation in the discovery by the excavating navvies of the coffins of William de Warenne and his wife Gundrada (the Conqueror's daughter), the founders of the priory, which otherwise would probably have been lost evermore.

The castle, which dominates the oldest part of the town, is but a few minutes' stiff climb from the station; Lewes's several ancient churches are within hailing distance of each other; the field of her battle, where Simon de Montfort defeated Henry III., is in view from her north-west slopes; while the new martyrs' memorial on the turf above the precipitous escarpment of the Cliffe (once the scene of a fatal avalanche) reminds one of what horrors were possible in the name of religion in these streets less than four hundred years ago.

THE RICHES OF LEWES

Here are riches enough; yet Lewes adds to such mementoes of an historic past two gaols—one civil and one naval—a racecourse, and a river, and she is an assize town to boot. Once, indeed, Lewes was still better off, for she had a theatre, which for some years was under the management of Jack Palmer, of whom Charles Lamb wrote with such gusto. Added to these possessions, she has, in Keere Street, the narrowest and steepest thoroughfare down which a king (George IV.) ever drove a coach and four, and a row of comfortable and serene residences (on the way to St. Ann's) more luxuriantly and beautifully covered with leaves than any I ever saw. (Much of Lewes in September is scarlet with Virginia creeper.)

HIGH STREET, SOUTHOVER.

"BRIGHTHELMSTONE, NEAR LEWES"

JOHN HALSHAM'S DREAM

Although less than half an hour from Brighton by train, and an hour by road, Lewes is yet a full quarter of a century behind it. She would do well jealously to maintain this interval. Lewes was old and grey before Brighton was thought of (indeed, it was, as we have seen, a Lewes man that discovered Brighton—Dr. Russell, who lies in his grave in South Malling church); let her cling to her seniority. As a town "in the movement," as a contemporary of the "Queen of Watering Places," she would cut a poor figure. But it is amusing to think of the old address of a visitor to Brighton, "at Brighthelmstone, near Lewes," and to read the county paper, *The Sussex Weekly Advertiser; or, Lewes Journal*, of a century ago, with its columns of Lewes news and paragraphs of Brighton correspondence.

278

Lewes will cease to have charm the moment she modernises. In the words of the author of *Idlehurst*, as he looked down on the huddling little settlement from the Cliffe Hill: "Let us keep a country town or two as preserves for clean atmospheres of body and soul, for the almost lost secret of sitting still . . . I find myself tangled in half-dreams of a devolution by which, when national amity shall have become mentionable besides personal pence, London shall attract to herself all the small vice, as she does already most of the great, from the country, all the thrusters after gain, the vulgar, heavy-fingered intellects, the Progressive spouters, the Bileses, the speculating brigandage, and shall give us back from the foggy world of clubs and cab-ranks and geniuses, the poets and painters, all the nice and witty and pretty people, to make towns such as this, conserved and purified, into country-side Athenses; to form distinct schools of letters and art, individual growths, not that universal Cockney mind, smoke-ingrained, stage-ridden, convention-throttled, which now masquerades under the forms of every clime and dialect within reach of a tourist ticket."

The customs of Lewes at the end of the Saxon rule and the beginning of the Norman, as recorded in the pages of the Domesday Book, show that residence in the town in those days was not unmixed delight, except, perhaps, for murderers, for whom much seems to have been done. Thus: "If the king wished to send an armament to guard the seas, without his personal attendance, twenty shillings were collected from all the inhabitants, without exception or respect to particular tenure, and these were paid to the men-at-arms in the ships.

"The seller of a horse, within the borough, pays one penny to the mayor (sheriff?) and the purchaser another; of an ox, a half-penny; of a man, fourpence, in whatsoever place he may be brought within the rape.

"A murderer forfeits seven shillings and fourpence; a ravisher forfeits eight shillings and fourpence; an adulterer eight shillings and fourpence;

an adultress the same. The king has the adulterer, the bishop the adulteress."

THE PROVIDENT DE WARENNES

With the Conquest new life came into the town, as into South Sussex generally. The rule of the de Braoses, who dominated so much of the country through which we have been passing, is here no more, the great lord of this district being William de Warenne, who had claims upon William the Conqueror, not only for services rendered in the Conquest but as a son-in-law. When, therefore, the contest was over, some of the richest prizes fell to Earl de Warenne. Among them was the township of Lewes, whose situation so pleased the Earl that he decided to make his home there. His first action, then, was to graft upon the existing fortress a new stronghold, the remains of which still stand.

Ten years after the victory at Hastings the memory of the blood of the sturdy Saxons whom he had hacked down at Battle began so to weigh upon de Warenne's conscience that he set out with Gundrada upon an expiatory pilgrimage to Rome. Sheltering on the way in the monastery of St. Per, at Cluny, they were so hospitably received that on returning to Lewes William and Gundrada built a Priory, partly as a form of gratitude, and partly as a safeguard for the life to come. In 1078, it was formally founded on a magnificent scale. Thus Lewes obtained her castle and her priory, both now in ruins, in the one of which William de Warenne might sin with a clear mind, knowing that just below him, on the edge of the water-brooks, was (in the other) so tangible an expiation.

The date of the formation of the priory spoils the pleasant legend which tells how Harold, only badly wounded, was carried hither from Battle, and how, recovering, he lived quietly with the brothers until his natural death some years later. A variant of the same story takes the English king to a cell near St. John's-under-the-Castle, also in Lewes, and establishes him there as an anchorite. But (although, as we shall see when we come to Battle, the facts were otherwise) all true Englishmen prefer to think of Harold fighting in the midst of his army, killed by a chance arrow shot into the zenith, and lying there until the eyes of Editha of the Swan-neck lighted upon his dear corpse amid the hundreds of the slain.

THE CASTLE'S CURIOSITIES

The de Warennes held Lewes Castle until the fourteenth century; the Sussex Archæological Society now have it in their fostering care. Architecturally it is of no great interest, although it was once unique in England by the possession of two keeps; nor has it romantic associations, like Kenilworth or even Carisbrooke. The crumbling masonry was assisted in its decay by no siege or bombardment; the castle has been never the scene of human struggle. Visitors, therefore, must take pleasure chiefly in the curiosities collected in the museum and in the views from the roof. A few little rooms hold the treasures amassed by the Archæological Society; amassed, it may be said, with little difficulty, for the soil of the district is fertile in relics. From Ringmer come rusty shield bosses and the mouldering skull of an Anglo-Saxon; from the old Lewes gaol come a lock and a key strong enough to hold Jack Sheppard; and from Horsham Gaol a complete set of fetters for ankles and wrists, once used to cramp the movements of female malefactors. Here, in a case, is a tiny bronze thimble that tipped the pretty finger of a Roman seamstress—one only among scores of tokens of the Roman occupation of the county. Flint arrow heads and celts in profusion take us back to remoter times. A Pyecombe crook hangs on one wall, and relics of the Sussex ironworks are plentiful. The highest room contains rubbings of our best brasses. Outside is an early Sussex plough. In a corner is a beadle's staff that once struck terror into the hearts of Sabbath-breaking boys; and near one of the windows is a little brass crucifix from St. Pancras' Priory. But nothing, the custodian tells me, so pleases visitors to this very catholic collection as the mummied hand of a murderess.

THE BATTLE OF LEWES

Looking down and around from the roof of the keep, you are immediately struck by the wide shallow hollow in which Lewes lies. It is something the shape of a dairy basin, the gap to the north-west, between Malling Hill and Offham, serving for the lip. Nothing could be flatter than the smiling meadows, streaked with tiny streams, stretching between Lewes and the coast line to the south-east (with the exception of one symmetrical hillock just out of the town). Among them curls the lazy Ouse; just beneath you Lewes sleeps, red-roofed as an Italian town, sending up no hum of activity, listless and immovable save for a few spirals of silent smoke. The surrounding hills are very fine: Firle Beacon in the far east; Mount Caburn, a noble cone, in the near east; Mount Harry to the west, on whose slopes Henry III., assisted by the fiery Prince Edward, fought the Barons. So fiery, indeed, was this lad that he forgot all about his father, and gave chase to a small detachment of the enemy, catching them up, and hewing them down with the keenest enjoyment, while the unhappy Henry was being completely worsted by de Montfort. It was a bloody battle, made up, as old Fabian wrote, of embittered men, with hearts full of hatred, "eyther desyrous to bring the other out of lyfe." Great fun was made by the humorists of the time, after the battle, over the fact that Richard, King of the Romans, Henry's brother, was captured in a windmill in which he had taken refuge. This mill stood near the site of the Black Horse inn. In *The Barons' Wars*, by Mr. Blaauw, the Sussex antiquary, the whole story is told.

Lewes has played but a small part in history since that battle; but, as we saw when we were at Rottingdean, it was one of her Cluniac priors that repulsed the French in 1377, and her son, Sir Nicholas Pelham, who performed a similar service in 1545, at Seaford. As the verses on his monument in St. Michael's Church run:—

What time the French sought to have sackt Sea-Foord,
This Pelham did repel-em back aboord.

ANN OF CLEVES' HOUSE, SOUTHOVER.

THE CLUNIAC PRIORY

The Cluniac priory of St. Pancras was dissolved by Henry VIII. in 1537, Thomas Cromwell, that execrable vandal, not only abolishing the monks but destroying the buildings, which covered, with their gardens and fish ponds, forty acres. The ruins that remain give some idea of the extent of this wonderful priory, another relic being the adjacent mound on which the Calvary stood, probably constructed of the earth removed for the purpose from the Dripping Pan, as the hollow circular space is called where Lewes now plays cricket. One very pretty possession of the monks was allowed to stand until quite recent times—the Columbarium, which was as large as a church and contained homes for 3,228 birds. It has now vanished; but an idea of what it was may be gained from the pigeon house at Alciston, a few miles distant, which belonged to Battle Abbey.

The priory's possessions were granted to Cromwell by Henry VIII., who, tradition asserts (somewhat directly in the face of historical evidence), murdered one of his wives on a winding stair in the building, and may therefore have been glad to see its demolition. Which wife it was, is not stated, but when Cromwell went the way of all this king's favourites, the property was transferred to Ann of Cleves, who is supposed to have lived in the most picturesque of the old houses on the right hand side of Southover's street as you leave Lewes for the Ouse valley.

Southover church, in itself a beautiful structure of the grave red type, with a square ivied tower and the most delicate vane in Sussex, is rendered the more interesting by the possession of the leaden caskets of William de Warenne and Gundrada and the superb tomb removed from Isfield church and very ingeniously restored. These relics repose in a charming little chapel built in their honour.

TOM PAINE

A notable man who had association with Lewes was Tom Paine, author of *The Rights of Man*. He settled there as an exciseman in 1768, married Elizabeth Ollive of the same town at St. Michael's Church in 1771, and succeeded to her father's business as a tobacconist and grocer. Paine was more successful as a debater than a business man. As a member of the White Hart evening club he was more often than any other the winner of the Headstrong Book—an old Greek Homer despatched the next morning to the most obstinate haranguer of the preceding night. It was at Lewes that Tom Paine's thoughts were first turned to the question of government. He used thus to tell the story. One evening after playing bowls, all the party retired to drink punch; when, in the conversation that ensued, Mr. Verril (it should be Verrall) "observed, alluding to the wars of Frederick, that the King of Prussia was the best fellow in the world for a king, he had so much of the devil in him. This, striking me with great force, occasioned the reflection, that if it were necessary for a king to have so much of the devil in him, kings might very beneficially be dispensed with."

I thought of that historic game of bowls as I watched four Lewes gentlemen playing this otherwise discreetest of games in the meadow by the castle gate on a fine September evening. Surely (after the historic Plymouth Hoe) a lawn in the shadow of a Norman castle is the ideal spot for this leisurely but exciting pastime. The four Lewes gentlemen played uncommonly well, with bowls of peculiar splendour in which a setting of silver glistened as they sped over the turf. After each game one little boy bearing a cloth wiped the bowls while another registered the score. And now I feel that no one can really be said to have seen Lewes unless he has watched the progress of such a game: it remains in my mind as intimate a part of the town and the town's spirit as the ruins of the Priory, or Keere Street, or the Castle itself.

The house of Tom Paine, just off the High Street, almost opposite the circular tower of St. Michael's, has a tablet commemorating its illustrious owner. It also has a very curious red carved demon which otherwise distinguishes it. Lewes was not always proud of Tom Paine; but Cuckfield went farther. In 1793, I learn from the *Sussex Advertiser* for that year, Cuckfield emphasised its loyalty to the constitution by singing "God save the King" in the streets and burning Paine in effigy.

"CLIO" RICKMAN

Mention of Tom Paine naturally calls to mind his friend and biographer (and my thrice great uncle), Thomas "Clio" Rickman, the Citizen of the World, who was born at Lewes in 1760. Rickman began life as a Quaker, and therefore without his pagan middle name, which he first adopted as the signature to epigrams and scraps of verse in the local paper, and afterwards incorporated in his signature. Rickman's connection with Tom

Paine and his own revolutionary habits were a source of distress to his Quaker relatives at Lewes, so much so that there is a story in the family of the Citizen being refused admission to a house in the neighbourhood where he had eight impressionable nieces, and, when he would visit their father, being entertained instead at the Bear. His Bible, with sceptical marginal notes, is still preserved, with the bad pages pasted together by a subsequent owner.

After roving about in Spain and other countries he settled as a bookseller in London, and it was in his house and at his table that *The Rights of Man* was written. "This table," says an article on Rickman in the *Wonderful Museum*, "is prized by him very highly at this time; and no doubt will be deemed a rich relic by some of our irreligious connoisseurs." It was shown at the Tom Paine exhibition a few years ago. Rickman escaped prosecution, but he once had his papers seized.

TIPPER'S EPITAPH

According to his portrait Clio wore a hat like a beehive, and he invented a trumpet to increase the sound of a signal gun. His verse is exceedingly poor, his finest poetical achievement being the epitaph on Thomas Tipper in Newhaven churchyard. Tipper was the brewer of the ale that was known as "Newhaven Tipper"; but he was other things too:

Honest he was, ingenuous, blunt and kind,
And dared what few dare do, to speak his mind.
Philosophy and history well he knew,
Was versed in Physic and in surgery too,
The best old Stingo he both brewed and sold,
Nor did one knavish act to get his gold.
He played through life a varied comic part,
And knew immortal Hudibras by heart.

Charles Lamb greatly admired the end of this epitaph. Clio Rickman died in 1834.

Among other men of note who have lived in Lewes or have had association with it, was John Evelyn the diarist, who had some of his education at Southover grammar school: Mark Antony Lower, the Sussex antiquary, to whom all writers on the county are indebted; the Rev. T. W. Horsfield, the historian of Sussex, without whose work we should also often be in difficulties; and the Rev. Gideon Mantell, the Sussex geologist, whose collection of Sussex fossils is preserved in the British Museum.

In St. Ann's church on the hill lie the bones of a remarkable man who died at Lewes (in the tenth climacteric) in 1613—no less a person than Thomas Twyne, M.D. In addition to the principles of physic he "comprehended earthquakes" and wrote a book about them. He also wrote a survey of the world. I quote Horsfield's translation of the florid Latin inscription to his memory: "Hippocrates saw Twyne lifeless and his bones slightly covered with earth. Some of his sacred dust (says he) will be of use to me in removing diseases; for the dead, when converted into medicine, will expel human maladies, and ashes prevail against ashes. Now the physician is absent, disease extends itself on every side, and exults its enemy is no more. Alas! here lies our preserver Twyne; the flower and ornament of his age. Sussex deprived of her physician, languished, and is ready to sink along with him. Believe me, no future age will produce so good a physician and so renowned a man as this has. He died at Lewes in 1613, on the 1st of August, in the tenth climacteric, (viz. 70)."

DR. JOHNSON AT LEWES

Dr. Johnson was once in Lewes, on a day's visit to the Shelleys, at the house which bears their name at the south end of the town. One of the little girls becoming rather a nuisance with her questions, the Doctor lifted her into a cherry tree and walked off. At dinner, some time later, the child was missed, and a search party was about to set out when the

Doctor exclaimed, "Oh, I left her in a tree!" For many years the tree was known as "Dr. Johnson's cherry tree."

ST. ANN'S CHURCH, SOUTHOVER.

THE FIFTH

Lewes is ordinarily still and leisurely, with no bustle in her steep streets save on market days: an abode of rest and unhastening feet. But on one night of the year she lays aside her grey mantle and her quiet tones and emerges a Bacchante robed in flame. Lewes on the 5th of November is an incredible sight; probably no other town in the United Kingdom offers such a contrast to its ordinary life. I have never heard that Lewes is notably Protestant on other days in the year, that any intolerance is meted out to Roman Catholics on November 4th or November 6th; but on November 5th she appears to believe that the honour of the reformed

288

church is wholly in her hands, and that unless her voice is heard declaiming against the tyrannies and treacheries of Rome all the spiritual labours of the eighth Henry will have been in vain.

No fewer than eight Bonfire Societies flourish in the town, all in a strong financial position. Each of these has its bonfire blazing or smouldering at a street corner, from dusk to midnight, and each, at a certain stage in the evening, forms into procession, and approaching its own fire by devious routes, burns an effigy of the Pope, together with whatever miscreant most fills the public eye at the moment—such as General Booth or Mr. Kruger, both of whom I have seen incinerated amid cheers and detonations.

LEWES ROUSERS

The figures are not lightly cast upon the flames, but are conducted thither ceremoniously, the "Bishop" of the society having first passed sentence upon them in a speech bristling with local allusions. These speeches serve the function of a *revue* of the year and are sometimes quite clever, but it is not until they are printed in the next morning's paper that one can take their many points. The principal among the many distractions is the "rouser," a squib peculiar to Lewes, to which the bonfire boys (who are, by the way, in great part boys only in name, like the postboys of the past and the cowboys of the present) have given laborious nights throughout the preceding October. The rouser is much larger and heavier than the ordinary squib; it is propelled through the air like a rocket by the force of its escaping sparks; and it bursts with a terrible report. In order to protect themselves from the ravages of the rouser the people in the streets wear spectacles of wire netting, while the householders board up their windows and lay damp straw on their gratings. Ordinary squibs and crackers are also continuously ignited, while now and then one of the sky rockets discharged in flights from a procession, elects to take a horizontal course, and hurtles head-high down the crowded street.

So the carnival proceeds until midnight, when the firemen, who have been on the alert all the evening, extinguish the fires. The Bonfire Societies subsequently collect information as to any damage done and make it good: a wise course, to which they owe in part the sanction to renew the orgie next year. Other towns in Sussex keep up the glorious Fifth with some spirit, but nowhere in England is there anything to compare with the thoroughness of Lewes.

THE OUSE AT SOUTH STREET, LEWES.

THE LEWES MARTYRS

RICHARD WOODMAN

To some extent Lewes may consider that she has reason for the display, for on June 22, 1557, ten men and women were tied to the stake and burned to death in the High Street for professing a faith obnoxious to Queen Mary. Chief of these courageous enthusiasts were Richard

Woodman and Derrick Carver. Woodman, a native of Buxted, had settled at Warbleton, where he was a prosperous iron master. All went well until Mary's accession to the throne, when the rector of Warbleton, who had been a Protestant under Edward VI., turned, in Foxe's words, "head to tayle" and preached "clean contrary to that which he had before taught." Woodman's protests carried him to imprisonment and the stake. Altogether, Lewes saw the death of sixteen martyrs.

THE OUSE AT PIDDINGHOE.

CHAPTER XXVII

THE OUSE VALLEY

The two Ouses—Three round towers—Thirsty labourers—Telscombe—
The hills and the sea—Mrs. Marriott Watson's Down poem—Newhaven—
A Sussex miller—Seaford's past—A politic smuggler—Electioneering
ingenuity—Bishopstone.

The road from Lewes to the sea runs along the edge of the Ouse
levels, just under the bare hills, passing through villages that are little more
than homesteads of the sheep-farmers, albeit each has its church—Iford,
Rodmell, Southease, Piddinghoe—and so to Newhaven, the county's
only harbour of any importance since the sea silted up the Shoreham bar.
You may be as much out of the world in one of these minute villages as
anywhere twice the distance from London; and the Downs above them
are practically virgin soil. The Brighton horseman or walker takes as a rule
a line either to Lewes or to Newhaven, rarely adventuring in the direction
of Iford Hill, Highdole Hill, or Telscombe village, which nestles three
hundred feet high, over Piddinghoe. By day the waggons ply steadily
between Lewes and the port, but other travellers are few. Once evening
falls the world is your own, with nothing but the bleat of sheep and the
roar of the French boat trains to recall life and civilisation.

The air of this valley is singularly clear, producing on fine days a blue effect that is, I believe, peculiar to the district. In the sketches of a Brighton painter in water colours, Mr. Clem Lambert, who has worked much at Rodmell, the spirit of the river valleys of Sussex is reproduced with extraordinary fidelity and the minimum loss of freshness.

RODMELL.

Horsfield, rather than have no poetical blossom to deck his page at the mention of the Lewes river, quotes a passage from "The Task":

Here Ouse, slow winding through a level plain
Of spacious meads, with cattle sprinkled o'er,
Conducts the eye along his sinuous course
Delighted.

293

Dr. Johnson's remark that one green field is like another green field, might, one sees, be extended to rivers, for Cowper was, of course, describing the Ouse at Olney.

The first village out of Lewes on the Newhaven road is Kingston (one of three Sussex villages of this name), on the side of the hill, once the property of Sir Philip Sidney. Next is Iford, with straw blowing free and cows in its meadows; next Rodmell, whence Whiteway Bottom and Breaky Bottom lead to the highlands above: next Southease, where the only bridge over the Ouse between Lewes and Newhaven is to be crossed: a little village famous for a round church tower, of which Sussex knows but three, one other at St. Michael's, Lewes, and one at Piddinghoe, the next village.

SOUTHEASE THIRST

The Southease rustics were once of independent mind, as may be gathered from the following extract from the "Manorial Customs of Southease-with-Heighton, near Lewes," in 1623: "Every reaper must have allowed him, at the cost of the lord or his farmer, one drinkinge in the morninge of bread and cheese, and a dinner at noone consistinge of rostmeate and other good victualls, meete for men and women in harvest time; and two drinkinges in the afternoone, one in the middest of their afternoone's work and the other at the ende of their day's work, and drinke always duringe their work as neede shall require."

PIDD'NHOO

Telscombe, the capital of these lonely Downs and as good an objective as the walker who sets out from Brighton, Rottingdean, or Lewes to climb hills can ask, is a charming little shy hamlet which nothing can harm, snugly reposing in its combe, above Piddinghoe. Piddinghoe (pronounced Pidd'nhoo) is a compact village at the foot of the hill; but it has suffered in picturesqueness and character by its proximity to the commercial enterprise of Newhaven. Hussey, in his *Notes on the Churches of . . . Sussex*, suggests that a field north of the village was once the site of a considerable Roman villa. A local sarcasm credits Piddinghoe people with the habit of shoeing their magpies.

PIDDINGHOE.

The Downs when we saw them first, between Midhurst and Chichester, formed an inland chain parallel with the shore: here, and eastward as far as Beachy Head, where they suddenly cease, their southern slopes are washed by the Channel. This companionship of the sea lends them an additional wildness: sea mists now and then envelop them in a cloud; sea birds rise and fall above their cliffs; the roar or sigh of the waves mingles with the cries of sheep; the salt savour of the sea is borne on the wind over the crisp turf. It was, I fancy, among the Downs in this part of Sussex that Mrs. Marriott-Watson wrote the intimately understanding lines which I take the liberty of quoting:

A HILL POEM

ON THE DOWNS.

Broad and bare to the skies
The great Down-country lies,
Green in the glance of the sun,
Fresh with the clean salt air;
Screaming the gulls rise from the fresh-turned mould,
Where the round bosom of the wind-swept wold
Slopes to the valley fair.

Where the pale stubble shines with golden gleam
The silver ploughshare cleaves its hard-won way
Behind the patient team,
The slow black oxen toiling through the day
Tireless, impassive still,
From dawning dusk and chill
To twilight grey.

Far off the pearly sheep
Along the upland steep
Follow their shepherd from the wattled fold,
With tinkling bell-notes falling sweet and cold
As a stream's cadence, while a skylark sings
High in the blue, with eager outstretched wings,
Till the strong passion of his joy be told.

But when the day grows old,
And night cometh fold on fold,
Dulling the western gold,
Blackening bush and tree,

Veiling the ranks of cloud,
In their pallid pomp and proud
That hasten home from the sea,
Listen—now and again if the night be still enow,
You may hear the distant sea range to and fro
Tearing the shingly bourne of his bounden track,
Moaning with hate as he fails and falleth back;

The Downs are peopled then;
Fugitive, low-browed men
Start from the slopes around
Over the murky ground
Crouching they run with rough-wrought bow and spear,
Now seen, now hid, they rise and disappear,
Lost in the gloom again.

Soft on the dew-fall damp
Scarce sounds the measured tramp
Of bronze-mailed sentinels,
Dark on the darkened fells
Guarding the camp.

The Roman watch-fires glow
Red on the dusk; and harsh
Cries a heron flitting slow
Over the valley marsh
Where the sea-mist gathers low.

Closer, and closer yet
Draweth the night's dim net
Hiding the troubled dead:
No more to see or know

But a black waste lying below,
And a glimmering blank o'erhead.

Of Newhaven there is little to say, except that in rough weather the traveller from France is very glad to reach it, and on a fine day the traveller from England is happy to leave it behind. In the churchyard is a monument in memory of the officers and crew of the *Brazen*, which went down off the town in 1800, and lost all hands save one.

A SUSSEX MILLER

On the way to Seaford, which is nearly three miles east, sheltering under its white headland (a preliminary sketch, as one might say, for Beachy Head), we pass the Bishopstone tide mills, once the property of a sturdy and prosperous Sussex autocrat named William Catt, the grower of the best pears in the county, and the first to welcome Louis Philippe (whom he had advised on milling in France) when he landed at Newhaven in exile. A good story told of William Catt, by Mr. Lower, in his *Worthies of Sussex*, illustrates not only the character of that sagacious and kindly martinet, but also of the Sussex peasant in its mingled independence and dependence, frankness and caution. Mr. Catt, having unbent among his retainers at a harvest supper, one of them, a little emboldened perhaps by draughts of Newhaven "tipper," thus addressed his master. "Give us yer hand, sir, I love ye, I love ye," but, he added, "I'm danged if I beant afeared of ye, though."

SOUTHOVER GRANGE.

There was a hermitage on the cliff at Seaford some centuries ago. In 1372 the hermit's name was Peter, and we find him receiving letters of protection for the unusual term of five years. In the vestry of the church is an old monument bearing the riddling inscription: ". . . Also, near this place lie two mothers, three grandmothers, four aunts, four sisters, four daughters, four grand-daughters, three cousins—but VI persons." A record in the Seaford archives runs thus: "Dec. 24, 1652. Then were all accounts taken and all made even, from the beginning of ye world, of the former Bayliffes unto the present time, and there remained . . . ye sum of twelve pounds, sixteen shillings, seven pence."

THE PRICE OF TWO VOTES

Millburgh House, Seaford, was of old called Corsica Hall, having been built (originally at Wellingham, near Lewes, and then moved) by a smuggler named Whitfield, who was outlawed for illicit traffic in Corsican wine. He obtained the removal of his outlawry by presenting George II. with a selection of his choicest vintages. Another agreeable story of local corruption is told concerning Seaford's old electioneering days. It was in 1798, during the candidature of Sir Godfrey Webster of Battle Abbey. Sir Godfrey was one day addressed by Mrs. S——(nothing but Horsfield's delicacy keeps her name from fame) in the following terms: "Mr. S——, sir, will vote, of course, as he pleases—I have nothing to do or to say about him; but there is my gardener and my coachman, both of whom will, I am sure, be entirely guided by me. Now, they are both family men, Sir Godfrey, and I wish to do the best I can to serve them. Now, I know you are in great doubt, and that two sure votes are of great value: I'll tell you what you shall do. You shall give me £200; nobody will know any thing about it; there will be no danger—no bribery, Sir Godfrey, at all. I will desire the men to go and vote for you and Colonel Tarleton, and it will all be right, and no harm done. The bargain," adds Horsfield, "was struck—the money paid—the votes given as promised; and the election over, the old lady gave the two men £30 a piece, and pocketed the rest for the good of her country."

SEAFORD TO LEWES

Seaford's neighbouring village, Bishopstone, in addition to its tide mills—the only tide mills in Sussex excepting that at Sidlesham, now disused—possessed once the oldest windmill in the county. In the very charming little church is buried James Hurdis, author of *The Village Curate*, whom we shall meet again at Burwash. From Bishopstone we may return to Lewes either by the road through South Heighton, Tarring Neville, Itford Farm, and Beddingham, or cross the river again at Southease, and retrace our earlier steps through Rodmell and Iford. That is the quicker way. The road through Beddingham is longer, and interesting rather for the hills above it than for anything upon it. To these hills we come in the next chapter.

NEAR TARRING NEVILLE.

CHAPTER XXVIII

ALFRISTON

Three routes to Alfriston—West Firle—The Gages—A "Noble Dame"—
Sussex pronunciation and doggedness—The Selmeston smugglers—
Alfriston's ancient inn—The middle ages and P . . . P . . .—Alfriston
church—A miracle and a sign—An Alfriston scholar—Dr. Benbrigg—
The smallest church in Sussex—Alfriston as a centre—A digression on
walking—"A Song against Speed"—Alciston—A Berwick genius—The
Long Man of Wilmington.

Alfriston may be reached from Lewes by rail, taking train to Berwick;
by road, under the hills; or on foot or horse-back, over the hills. By road,
you pass first through Beddingham, a small village, where, it is said, was
once a monastery; then, by a southern *détour*, to West Firle, a charming
little village with a great park, which bears the same relation to Firle
Beacon that Wiston Park does to Chanctonbury Ring. The tower in the
east serves to provide a good view of the Weald for those who do not
care to climb the beacon's seven hundred feet and get a better. The little
church is rich in interesting memorials of the Gages, who have been the
lords of Firle for many a long year.

In the house is a portrait of Sir John Gage, the trusted friend of
Henry VIII., Edward VI., and Mary, and, as Constable of the Tower, the
gaoler (but a very kind one) of both Lady Jane Grey and the Princess
Elizabeth, afterwards Good Queen Bess. In Harrison Ainsworth's
romance *The Constable of the Tower* Sir John Gage is much seen. Sir John

was succeeded at Firle by his son Sir Edward, who, as High Sheriff of Sussex, was one of the judges of the Sussex martyrs, but who, even Foxe admits, exercised courtesy to them. Sir Edward's son, Sir John Gage, was the second husband of the Lady Penelope D'Arcy, Mr. Hardy's heroine, whose portrait we saw at Parham: who, being courted as a girl by Sir George Trenchard, Sir John Gage, and Sir William Hervey, promised she would marry all in turn, and did so. Sir George left her a widow at seventeen; to Sir John Gage she bore nine children.

Returning from Firle to the high road, we come next, by following for a little a left turn, to Selmeston, the village where Mr. W. D. Parish, the rector for very many years, collected most of the entertaining examples of the Sussex dialect with which I have made so free in a later *chapter*. The church is very simple and well-cared for, with some pretty south windows. The small memorial tablets of brass which have been let into the floor symmetrically among the tiles seem to me a happier means of commemoration than mural tablets,—at least for a modest building such as this.

VAGARIES OF PRONUNCIATION

In losing your way in this neighbourhood do not ask the passer-by for Selmeston, but for Simson; for Selmeston, pronounced as spelt, does not exist. Sussex men are curiously intolerant of the phonetics of orthography. Brighthelmstone was called Brighton from the first, although only in the last century was the spelling modified to agree with the sound. Chalvington (the name of a village north of Selmeston) is a pretty word, but Sussex declines to call it other than Chawton. Firle becomes Furrel; Lewes is almost Lose, but not quite; Heathfield is Hefful. It is characteristic of a Sussex man that he always knows best; though all the masters of all the colleges should assemble about him and speak reasoningly of Selmeston he would leave the congress as incorrigible and self-satisfied a Simsonian as ever.

Many years ago Selmeston churchyard possessed an empty tomb, in which the smugglers were wont to store their goods until a favourable time came to set them on the road. Any objections that those in authority might have had were silenced by an occasional tub. But of this more in the next *chapter*.

ALFRISTON

And so we come to Alfriston; but, as I said, the right way was over the hills, ascending them either at Itford (crossing the Ouse at Southease) or by that remarkable combe, one of the finest in Sussex, with an avenue leading to it, which is gained from a lane south of Beddingham. Firle Beacon's lofty summit is half-way between Beddingham and Alfriston, and from this height, with its magnificent view of the Weald, we descend steadily to the Cuckmere valley, of which Alfriston is the capital.

Alfriston, which is now only a village street, shares with Chichester the distinction of possessing a market cross. Alfriston's specimen is, however, sadly mutilated, a mere relic, whereas Chichester's is being made more splendid as I write. Alfriston also has one of the oldest inns in the county—the "Star"—(finer far in its way than any of Chichester's seventy and more); but Ainsworth was wrong in sending Charles II. thither, in *Ovingdean Grange*. It is one of the inns that the Merry Monarch never saw. The "Star" was once a sanctuary, within the jurisdiction of the Abbot of Battle, for persons flying from justice; and it is pleasant to sit in the large room upstairs, over the street, and think of fugitives pattering up the valley, with fearful backward glances, and hammering at the old door. One Birrel, in the reign of Henry VIII., having stolen a horse at Lydd, in Kent, took refuge here. The inn in those days was intended chiefly for the refreshment of mendicant friars.

In 1767 the landlord was, according to a private letter, "as great a curiosity as the house." I wish we had some information about him, for the house is quaint and curious indeed, with its red lion sentinel at the side (figure-head from a Dutch wreck in Cuckmere Haven), and its carvings inside and out. The old and the new mingled very oddly when I was lately at Alfriston. Hearing a familiar sound, as of a battledore and a ball, in one of the rooms, I opened the door and discovered the landlord and a groom from the racing stables near by in the throes of the most modern of games, amid surroundings absolutely mediæval.

THE CATHEDRAL OF THE DOWNS

The size of the grave and commanding church, which has been called the cathedral of the South Downs, alone proves that Alfriston was once a vastly more important place than it now is. Legend says that the foundations were first cut in the meadow known as Savyne Croft. There day after day the builders laid their stones, arriving each morning to find them removed to the Tye, the field where the church now stands. At last the meaning of the miracle entered their heads, and the church was erected on the new site. Its shape was determined by the slumbers of four oxen, who were observed by the architect to be sleeping in the form of a cross. Poynings church, under the Dyke Hill, near Brighton, was built, it has been conjectured, by the same architect. Within the cathedral of the South Downs, which is a fourteenth century building, is a superb east window, but it has no coloured glass. The register, beginning with 1504, is perhaps the oldest in England. Hard by the church is the simple little clergy house—unique in England, I believe—dating from pre-Reformation times. It has lately been very carefully restored.

Alfriston once had a scholar in the person of Thomas Chowne, of Frog Firle, the old house on the road to Seaford, about a mile beyond the village. Chowne, who died in 1639, and was buried at Alfriston, is thus touched off by Fuller:—"Thomas Chune, Esquire, living at Alfriston in this County, set forth a small Manuall, intituled *Collectiones Theologicarum Conclusionum.* Indeed, many have much opposed it (as what book meeteth not with opposition?); though such as dislike must commend the brevity and clearness of his Positions. For mine own part, I am glad to see a Lay-Gentleman so able and industrious." Chowne's great great grandson, an antiquary, one night left some books too near his library fire; they ignited, and Frog Firle Place was in large part destroyed. It is now only a fragment of what it was, and is known as Burnt House.

AN ALFRISTON DOCTOR

An intermediate dweller at Frog Firle was one Robert Andrews, who, when unwell, seems to have been attended by William Benbrigg. Miss Florence A. Pagden, in her agreeable little history of Alfriston, from which I have been glad to borrow, prints two of Mr. Benbrigg's letters of kindly but vague advice to his patient. Here is one:—

"MR. ANDREWS,

"I have sent you some things which you may take in the manner following, viz.:—of that in the bottle marked with a + you may take of the quantity of a spoonfull or so, now and then, and at night take some of those pills, drinking a little warm beer after it, and in the morning take 2 spoonfulls of that in—bottle fasting an hour after it, and then you may eat something, you may take also of the first, and every night a pill, and in the morning. I hope this will do you good, which is the desire of him who is your loving friend,

"WM. BENBRIGG."

Alfriston once had a race meeting of its own—the course is still to be seen on the southern slope of Firle Beacon—and it also fostered cricket in the early days. A famous single-wicket match was contested here in 1787, between four men whose united ages amounted to 297 years. History records that the game was played with "great spirit and activity." Mr. Lower records, in 1870, that the largest pear and the largest apple ever known in England were both grown at Alfriston, but possibly the record has since been broken.

The smallest church in Sussex is however still to Alfriston's credit, for Lullington church, on the hill side, just across the river and the fields to the east of Alfriston church, may be considered to belong to Alfriston without any violence to its independence. As a matter of fact, the church was once bigger, the chancel alone now standing. What Charles Lamb says of Hollington church in *Chapter XXXVI.* of this book, would be more fitting of Lullington.

HILL WALKS

We have come to Alfriston from Lewes, proposing to return there; but it might well be made a centre, so much fine hill country does it command. Alfriston to Seaford direct, over the hills and back of the cliffs and the Cuckmere valley; Alfriston to Eastbourne, crossing the Cuckmere at Litlington, and beginning the ascent of the hills at West Dean; Alfriston to Lewes over Firle Beacon; Alfriston to Newhaven direct; Alfriston to Jevington and Willingdon;—all these routes cover good Down country, making the best of primitive rambles by day and bringing one at evening back to the "Star," this mediæval inn in the best of primitive villages. Few persons, however, are left who will climb hills—even grass hills—if they can help it; hence this counsel is likely to lead to no overcrowding of Fore Down, The Camp, Five Lords Burgh, South Hill, or Firle Beacon.

I might here, perhaps, be allowed to insert some verses upon the new locomotion, since they bear upon this question of walking in remote places, and were composed to some extent in Sussex byways in the spring of 1903:—

A SONG AGAINST SPEED.

Of speed the savour and the sting,
　　None but the weak deride;
But ah, the joy of lingering
　　About the country side!
The swiftest wheel, the conquering run,
　　We count no privilege
Beside acquiring, in the sun,
　　The secret of the hedge.

Where is the poet fired to sing
　　The snail's discreet degrees,
A rhapsody of sauntering,
　　A gloria of ease;
Proclaiming their's the baser part
　　Who consciously forswear
The delicate and gentle art
　　Of never getting there?

To get there first!—'tis time to ring
　　The knell of such an aim;
To be the swiftest!—riches bring
　　So easily that fame.
To shine, a highway meteor,
　　Devourer of the map!—
A vulgar bliss to choose before
　　Repose in Nature's lap!

308

Consider too how small a thing
    The highest speed you gain:
A bee can frolic on the wing
    Around the fastest train.
Think of the swallow in the air,
    The salmon in the stream,
And cease to boast the records rare
    Of paraffin and steam.

Most, most of all when comes the Spring,
    Again to lay (as now)
Her hand benign and quickening
    On meadow, hill and bough,
Should speed's enchantment lose its power,
    For "None who would exceed
[The Mother speaks] a mile an hour.
    My heart aright can read."

The turnpike from the car to fling,
    As from a yacht the sea,
Is doubtless as inspiriting
    As aught on land can be;
I grant the glory, the romance,
    But look behind the veil—
Suppose that while the motor pants
    You miss the nightingale!

ALCISTON

To return to Alfriston, there are two brief excursions (possible in the vehicles that are glanced at in the foregoing verses) which ought to be described here: to Alciston and to Wilmington. Alciston is a little hamlet under the east slope of Firle Beacon, practically no more than a farm house, a church, and dependant cottages. It is on a road that leads only to itself and "to the Hill" (as the sign-boards say hereabout); it is perhaps as nearly forgotten as any village in the county; and yet I know of no village with more unobtrusive charm. The church, which has no vicar of its own, being served from Selmeston, a mile away, stands high amid its graves, the whole churchyard having been heaped up and ramparted much as a castle is. In the hollow to the west of the church is part of the farmyard: a pond, a vast barn with one of the noblest red roofs in these parts, and the ruins of a stone pigeon house of great age and solidity, buttressed and built as if for a siege, in curious contrast to the gentle, pretty purpose for which it was intended. Between the church and the hill, and almost adjoining it, is the farmhouse, where the church keys are kept—a relic of Alciston Grange (once the property of Battle Abbey)— with odds and ends of its past life still visible, and a flourishing fig-tree at the back, heavy with fruit when I saw it under a September sun. The front of the house looks due east, across a valley of corn, to Berwick church, on a corresponding mound, and beyond Berwick to the Downs above Wilmington. And at the foot of the garden, on the top of the grey wall above the moat, is a long, narrow terrace of turf, commanding this eastern view—a terrace meet for Benedick and Beatrice to pace, exchanging raillery.

In Berwick church, by the way, is a memorial to George Hall, a former rector, of whom it is said that his name "speaks all learning humane and divine," and that his memory is "precious both to the Muses and the Graces." The Reverend George Hall's works seem, however, to have vanished.

THE LONG MAN

Wilmington, north-east of Alfriston, occupies a corresponding position to that of Alciston in the north-west; but having a "lion" in the shape of the Long Man it has lost its virginal bloom. Wilmington is providing tea and ginger beer while Alciston nurses its unsullied inaccessibility. The Long Man is a rude figure cut in the turf by the monks of the Benedictine priory that once flourished here, the ruins of which are now incorporated (like Alciston Grange) in a farm house on the east of the village. At least, it is thought by some antiquaries that the effigy is the work of the monks; others pronounce it druidical. The most alluring of several theories, indeed, would have the figure to represent Pol or Balder, the Sun God, pushing aside the doors of darkness—Polegate (or Bolsgate) near by being brought in as evidence.

CHAPTER XXIX

SMUGGLING

The Cuckmere Valley—Alfriston smuggling foreordained—Desperado and benefactor—A witty minister—Hawker of Morwenstowe—The church and run spirits—The two smugglers, the sea smuggler and the land smuggler—The half-way house—The hollow ways of Sussex—Mr. Horace Hutchinson quoted—Burwash as a smuggler's cradle.

Alfriston's place in history was won by its smugglers. All Sussex smuggled more or less; but smuggling may be said to have been Alfriston's industry. Cuckmere Haven, close by, offered unique advantages: it was retired, the coast was unpopulated, the roadway inland started immediately from the beach, the valley was in friendly hands, the paths and contours of the hills were not easily learned by revenue men. Nature from the first clearly intended that Alfriston men should be too much for the excise; smuggling was predestined. Farmers, shepherds, ostlers, what you will that is respectable, these Alfriston men might be by day and when the moon was bright; but when the "darks" came round they were smugglers every one.

MR. BETTS'S READINESS

Chief of what was known nearly a hundred years ago as the "Alfriston Gang" was Stanton Collins, who lived at Market Cross House. Collins employed his men not only in assisting him in smuggling, but for other purposes removed from that calling by a wide gulf. Thus when Mr. Betts, the minister of the Lady Huntingdon chapel at Alfriston, was high-handedly suspended by the chief trustee of the chapel, on account of his opposition to that gentleman's proposed union with his deceased wife's sister, it was Collins's gang who invaded the chapel, ejected the new minister, replaced Mr. Betts in the pulpit, and mounted guard round it while he continued the service. Mr. Betts was equal to the occasion: he gave out the hymn "God moves in a mysterious way."

Collins terrorised the country-side for some years (except upon the score of personal bravery and humorous audacity, I doubt if his place is quite on the golden roll of smugglers) and was at length brought within the power of the law for sheep-stealing, and sentenced to seven years. The last of his gang, Bob Hall, died in the workhouse at Eastbourne in 1895, aged ninety-four.

THE CHURCH COMPLAISANT

Sussex may always be proud of her best smugglers. There were brutal scoundrels among them, such as the men that murdered Chater and were executed at Chichester in 1748 (the report may be read in Mr. H. L. Stephen's *State Trials*, vol. iv.); but the ordinary smuggler was often a fine rebellious fellow, courageous, resourceful, and gifted with a certain grim humour that led him, as we have seen, to hide his tubs as often in the belfry or the churchyard as anywhere else, and enough knowledge of character to tell him when he might secure the silence of the vicar with an oblatory keg. The Sussex clergy seemed to have needed very little encouragement to omit smuggling from the decalogue. It is, I think, the late Mr. Coker Egerton, of Burwash, who tells of a Sussex parson feigning illness a whole Sunday on hearing suddenly in the morning that a cargo, hard pressed by the revenue, had in despair been lodged among his pews. But the classical passage on this subject comes from Cornwall, from the pen of R. S. Hawker, the vicar of Morwenstowe and the author of "The Song of the Western Men." He was not himself a smuggler, but his parishioners had no scruples, and his heart was with the braver side of the business:—

It was full sea in the evening of an autumn day when a traveller arrived where the road ran along by a sandy beach just above high-water mark. The stranger, who was a native of some inland town, and utterly unacquainted with Cornwall and its ways, had reached the brink of the tide just as a "landing" was coming off. It was a scene not only to instruct a townsman, but also to dazzle and surprise. At sea, just beyond the billows, lay the vessel, well moored with anchors at stem and stern. Between the ship and the shore boats, laden to the gunwale, passed to and fro. Crowds assembled on the beach to help the cargo ashore. On the one hand a boisterous group surrounded a keg with the head knocked in, for simplicity of access to the good cognac, into which they dipped whatsoever vessel came first to hand; one man had filled his shoe. On the other side they fought and wrestled, cursed and swore. Horrified at what he saw, the stranger lost all self-command, and, oblivious of personal danger, he began to shout, "What a horrible sight! Have you no shame? Is there no magistrate at hand? Cannot any justice of the peace be found in this fearful country?"

"No; thanks be to God," answered a hoarse, gruff voice. "None within eight miles."

"Well, then," screamed the stranger, "is there no clergyman hereabout? Does no minister of the parish live among you on this coast?"

"Aye! to be sure there is," said the same deep voice.

"Well, how far off does he live? Where is he?"

"That's he, sir, yonder, with the lanthorn." And sure enough there he stood, on a rock, and poured, with pastoral diligence, 'the light of other days' on a busy congregation.

The clergy, however, did not always know how useful they were. The Rev. Webster Whistler, of Hastings, records that he was awakened one night to receive a votive cask of brandy as his share of the spoil which, to his surprise, his church tower had been harbouring. A commoner method was to leave the gift—the tithe—silently on the doorstep. Revenue officers have perhaps been placated in the same way.

Smuggling, in the old use of the word, is no more. The surreptitious introduction into this country of German cigars, eau de Cologne, and Tauchnitz novels, does not merit the term. A revised tariff having removed the necessity for smuggling, the game is over; for that is the reason of the disappearance of the smuggler rather than any increased vigilance on the part of the coastguard. The records of smuggling show that the difficulties offered to the profession by the Government were difficulties that existed merely to be overcome. Perhaps fiscal reform may restore the old pastime.

THE LAND SMUGGLER

The word smuggler arouses in the mind the figure of a bold and desperate mariner searching the coast for a signal that all is safe to land his cargo. But as a matter of fact the men who ran the greatest risks were not the marine smugglers at all, but the land smugglers who received the tubs on the shore and conveyed them to a hiding place preparatory to the journey to London, whither the major part was perilously taken. Such were the Alfriston smugglers. These were the men who fought the revenue officers and had the hair's-breadth escapes. These were the men whose houses were watched, whose every movement was suspected, who needed to be wily as the serpent and to know the country inch by inch.

Not that the sea smuggler ran no risks. On the contrary, he was continually in danger from revenue cutters and the coastguards' boats. Bloody fights in the Channel were by no means rare. He was also often in peril from the elements; his endurance was superb; he had to be a sailor of genius, ready for every kind of emergency. But the land smuggler was more vulnerable than the sea smuggler, his rewards were smaller, and his operations were less simple. There is a vast difference between a dark night at sea and a dark night on land. Once the night fell the sea was the smuggler's own: he was invisible, inaudible. But the land was not less the revenue officer's: the land smuggler had to show his signal light, he had to roll casks over the beach, he had to carry them into security. His horse's hoofs could not be stilled as oars are muffled, his wheels bit noisily into the road, he was liable to be stopped at any turn. And he ran these risks from the coast right into London. I doubt if the land smuggler has had his due of praise. Sometimes the land smuggler had to be land smuggler and sea smuggler too, for many of the ships never troubled to make a landing at all. They sailed as near the shore as might be and then sank the tubs, which were always lashed together and kept on deck in readiness to be thrown overboard in case of the approach of a cutter. The position of the mooring having been conveyed to the confederates on shore, the vessel was at liberty to return to France for another cargo, leaving the responsibility of fishing up the tubs, and getting them to shore and away, wholly with the land smuggler.

An old pamphlet, entitled, *The Trials of the Smugglers ... at the Assizes held at East Grinstead, March 13, 14, 15, and 16, 1748-9*, gives the following information about the duties and pay of the land smugglers at that day:—"Each Man is allowed Half a Guinea a Time, and his Expenses for Eating and Drinking, a Horse found him, and the Profits of a Dollop of Tea, which is about 13 Pounds Weight, being the Half of a Bag; which Profit, even from the most ordinary of their Teas, comes to 24 or 25 Shillings; and they always make one Journey, sometimes two, in a Week." But these men would be underlings. There were, I take it, land smugglers in control of the operations who shared on a more lordly scale with their brethren in the boat.

HALF-WAY HOUSES

On all the routes employed by the land smugglers were certain cottages and farm-houses where tubs might be hidden. Houses still abound supplied with unexpected recesses and vast cellars where cargoes were stored on their way to London. In many cases, in the old days, these houses were "haunted," to put forth the legend of a ghost being the simplest way not only of accounting for such nocturnal noises as might be occasioned by the arrival or departure of smugglers and tubs, but also of keeping inquisitive folks at bay. Only a little while ago, during alterations to an old cottage high on the hills near my home in Kent, corroboration was given to a legend crediting the place with being a smuggler's "half-way house," by the builders' discovery of a cavern under the garden communicating with the cellar. For the gaining of such fastnesses the hollow ways of Sussex were maintained. Parson Darby's smuggling successor, in Mr. Horace Hutchinson's Sussex romance, *A Friend of Nelson*, thus described them to the hero of Withyham:—

> "The sun strikes hot enough. Would you like to ride in the shade awhile?"
>
> "Immensely," I replied, "if I saw the shade."
>
> "Keep after me, then," said he; "but the roan will. You need not trouble!" In a moment, on his great big horse, he was forcing his way down what had looked to me no more than a rabbit-run through the roadside bushes. For a while I had noticed the road seemed flanked by a mass of boskage below it on the right-hand side. Into this, and downward, the man crammed his horse, squeezing his legs into the horse's flank. I followed closely, and in a yard or two found myself in a deep lane or cutting, very thickly overgrown, so that only occasional gleams of sunshine crept in through the leafage. We rode, as he had promised, in a most pleasant shade. The floor of this lane or passage was not of the smoothest, and we went at a foot's pace only, and in Indian file.

317

"What is the meaning of it all?" I asked him.

THE HOLLOW WAYS

"Well," said he, "you have heard, I suppose, of the 'hollow ways,' as they are called, of Sussex. This is one. They were in their origin lanes, I take it, and perhaps the only means of getting about the country. The rains, in this sandy soil, washing down, gradually deepened and deepened them. Folks grew to use the new roads as they were made, leaving the lanes unheeded, to be overgrown. Here and there certain base fellows of the lewder sort, commonly called smugglers, may have deepened them further, and improved on what Nature had begun so well, with the result that you can ride many a mile, mole-like, if you know your way, from the sea coast north'ard, never showing your face above ground at all. That is what it means," he ended.

"THE GENTLEMEN"

Smuggling was in the blood of the Sussex people. As the Cornishman said to Mr. Hawker, "Why should the King tax good liquor?" Why, indeed? Everyone sided with the smugglers, both on the coast and inland. A Burwash woman told Mr. Egerton that as a child, after saying her prayers, she was put early to bed with the strict injunction, "Now, mind, if the gentlemen come along, don't you look out of the window." The gentlemen were the smugglers, and not to look at them was a form of negative help, since he that has not seen a gentleman cannot identify him. Another Burwash character said that his grandfather had fourteen children, all of whom were "brought up to be smugglers." These would, of course, be land smugglers—Burwash being on a highway convenient for the gentlemen between the coast and the capital.

CHAPTER XXX

GLYNDE AND RINGMER

Mount Caburn—The lark's song—William Hay, the poet of Caburn—Glynde church and Glynde place—John Ellman—The South Down sheep—Arthur Young—Ringmer and William Penn—The Ringmer mud—The ballad of "The Ride to Church"—Oxen on the Hills—The old Sussex roads—Bad travelling—Ringmer and Gilbert White.

One of the pleasantest short walks from Lewes takes one over Mount Caburn to Glynde, from Glynde to Ringmer, and from Ringmer over the hills to Lewes again.

The path to Mount Caburn winds upward just beyond the turn of the road to Glynde, under the Cliffe. Caburn is not one of the highest of the Downs (a mere 490 feet, whereas Firle Beacon across the valley is upwards of 700): but it is one of the friendliest of them, for on its very summit is a deep grassy hollow (relic of ancient British fortification) where on the windiest day one may rest in that perfect peace that comes only after climbing. Caburn is not unique in this respect; there is, for example, a similar hollow in the hill above Kingly Vale; but Caburn has a deeper cavity than any other that I can recall. On the roughest day, thus cupped, one may hear, almost see, the gale go by overhead; and on such a mild spring day as that when I was last there, towards the end of April, there is no such place in which to lie and listen to the lark. If one were asked to name an employment consistent with perfect idleness it would be difficult to suggest a better than that of watching a lark melting out of sight into the sky, and then finding it again. This you may do in Caburn's hollow as nowhere else. The song of the lark thus followed by eye and ear—for song and bird become one—passes naturally into the music of the spheres: there exist in the universe only yourself and this cosmic twitter.

The Lewes golfers, of both sexes, pursue their sport some way towards Caburn, and in the valley below the volunteers fire at their butts; but I doubt if the mountain proper will ever be tamed. Picnics are held on the summit on fine summer days, but for the greater part of the year it belongs to the horseman, the shepherd and the lark.

Mount Caburn gave its title to a poem by William Hay, of Glyndebourne House, in 1730, which ends with these lines, in the manner of an epitaph, upon their author:

Here liv'd the Man, who to these fair Retreats
First drew the Muses from their ancient Seats:
Tho' low his Thought, tho' impotent his Strain,
Yet let me never of his Song complain;
For this the fruitless Labour recommends,
He lov'd his native Country, and his Friends.

William Hay (1695-1755) was author also of a curious Essay on Deformity, which Charles Lamb liked, and of several philosophical works, and was a very diligent member of Parliament.

GLYNDE.

GLYNDE

Descending Caburn's eastern slope, and passing at the foot the mellowest barn roof in the county, beautifully yellowed by weather and time, we come to Glynde, remarkable among Sussex villages for a formal Grecian church that might have been ravished from a Surrey Thames-side village and set down here, so little resemblance has it to the indigenous Sussex House of God. As a matter of fact it was built in 1765 by the Bishop of Durham—the Bishop being Richard Trevor, of the family that then owned Glynde Place; which is hard by the church, a fine Elizabethan mansion, a little sombre, and very much in the manner of the great houses in the late S. E. Waller's pictures, the very place for a clandestine interview or midnight elopement. The present owner, a descendant of the Trevors and of the famous John Hampden, enemy of the Star Chamber and ship money, is Admiral Brand.

JOHN ELLMAN

Glynde's most famous inhabitant was John Ellman (1753-1832) the breeder of sheep, who farmed here from 1780 to 1829 and was the village's kindly autocrat and a true father to his men. The last of the patriarchs, as he might be called, Ellman lodged all his unmarried labourers under his own roof, giving them when they married enough grassland for a pig and a cow, and a little more for cultivation. He built a school for the children of his men, and permitted no licensed house to exist in Glynde. Not that he objected to beer; on the contrary he considered it the true beverage for farm labourers; but he preferred that they should brew it at home. It was John Ellman who gave the South Down sheep its fame and brought it to perfection.

ARTHUR YOUNG

The most interesting account of South Down sheep is to be found in Arthur Young's *General View of the Agriculture of the County of Sussex*, which is one of those books that, beginning their lives as practical, instructive and somewhat dry manuals, mellow, as the years go by, into human documents. Taken sentence by sentence Young has no charm, but his book has in the mass quite a little of it, particularly if one loves Sussex. He studied the country carefully, with special emphasis upon the domain of the Earl of Egremont, an agricultural reformer of much influence, whom we have met as a collector of pictures and the friend of painters. For the Earl not only brought Turner into Sussex with his brushes and palette, but introduced a plough from Suffolk and devised a new light waggon. The other hero of Young's book is necessarily John Ellman, whose flock at Glynde he subjected to close examination. Thomas Ellman, of Shoreham, John's cousin, he also approved as a breeder of sheep, but it is John that stood nighest the Earl of Egremont on Young's ladder of approbation. John Ellman's sheep were considered the first of their day, equally for their meat and their wool. I will not quote from Young to any great extent, lest vegetarian readers exclaim; but the following passage from his analysis of the South Down type must be transplanted here for its pleasant carnal vigour: "The shoulders are wide; they are round and straight in the barrel; broad upon the loin and hips; shut well in the twist, which is a projection of flesh in the inner part of the thigh that gives a fulness when viewed behind, and makes a South Down leg of mutton remarkably round and short, more so than in most other breeds."

THE SOUTH DOWN SHEEP

John Ellman by no means satisfied all his fellow breeders that he was right. His neighbour at Glynde, Mr. Morris, differed from him in the matter of crossing, and his cousin Thomas had other views on many points touching the flock. In the following passage Arthur Young expresses the extent to which individuality in sheep breeding may run:—"The South Down farmers breed their sheep with faces and legs of a colour, just as suits their fancy. One likes black, another sandy, a third speckled, and one and all exclaim against white. This man concludes that legs and faces with an inclination to white are infallible signs of tenderness, and do not stand against the severity of the weather with the same hardiness as the darker breed; and they allege that these sorts will fall off in their flesh. A second will set the first right, and pronounce that, in a lot of wethers, those that are soonest and most fat, are white-faced; that they prove remarkable good milkers; but that white is an indication of a tender breed. Another is of opinion that, by breeding the lambs too black, the wool is injured, and likewise apt to be tainted with black, and spotted, especially about the neck, and not saleable. A fourth breeds with legs and faces as black as it is possible; and he too is convinced that the healthiness is in proportion to blackness; whilst another says, that if the South Down sheep were suffered to run in a wild state, they would in a very few years become absolutely black. All these are the opinions of eminent breeders: in order to reconcile them, others breed for speckled faces; and it is the prevailing colour."

It is told that when the Duke of Newcastle used to pass through Glynde, on his way from Halland House, near East Hoathly, to Bishopstone, the peal of welcome was rung on ploughshares, since there was but one bell.

Ringmer, which lies about two miles north of Glynde, is not in itself a village of much beauty. Its distinction is to have provided William Penn with a wife—Gulielma Springett, daughter of Sir William Springett, a Puritan, whose bust is in the church and who died at the siege of Arundel Castle. The great Quaker thus took to wife the daughter of a soldier. When Gulielma Penn died, at the age of fifty, her husband wrote of her: "She was a Publick, as well as Private Loss; for she was not only an excellent Wife and Mother, but an Entire and Constant Friend, of a more than common Capacity, and greater Modesty and Humility; yet most equal and undaunted in Danger. Religious as well as Ingenuous, without Affectation. An easie Mistress, and Good Neighbour, especially to the Poor. Neither lavish nor penurious, but an Example of Industry as well as of other Vertues: Therefore our great Loss tho' her own Eternal Gain."

GODLY WIVES

In Ringmer Church, I might add, is a monument to Mrs. Jeffray (*née* Mayney), wife of Francis Jeffray of South Malling, with another beautiful testimony to the character of a good wife:—

Wise, modest, more than can be marshall'd heere,
(Her many vertues would a volume fill)
For all heaven's gifts—in many single sett—
In Jeffray's *Maney* altogether mett.

324

A DETERMINED CHURCHWOMAN

Ringmer was long famous for its mud and bad roads. Defoe (or another) says in the *Tour through Great Britain*:—"I travelled through the dirtiest, but, in many respects, the richest and most profitable country in all that part of England. The timber I saw here was prodigious, as well in quantity as in bigness; and seemed in some places to be suffered to grow only because it was so far from any navigation, that it was not worth cutting down and carrying away. In dry summers, indeed, a great deal is conveyed to Maidstone and other places on the Medway; and sometimes I have seen one tree on a carriage, which they call in Sussex a tug, drawn by twenty-two oxen; and, even then, it is carried so little a way, and thrown down, and left for other tugs to take up and carry on, that sometimes it is two or three years before it gets to Chatham. For, if once the rain comes on, it stirs no more that year, and sometimes a whole summer is not dry enough to make the road passable. Here I had a sight which, indeed, I never saw in any part of England before—namely, that going to a church at a country village, not far from Lewes, I saw an ancient lady, and a lady of very good quality, I assure you, drawn to church in her coach by six oxen; nor was it done in frolick or humour, but from sheer necessity, the way being so stiff and deep that no horses could go in it." The old lady was not singular in her method of attending service, for another writer records seeing Sir Herbert Springett, father of Sir William, drawn to church by eight oxen: a determination to get to his pew at any cost that led to the composition of the following ballad, which is now printed for the first time:—

THE RIDE TO CHURCH

THE RIDE TO CHURCH.

"A true sonne of the Church of England."

Epitaph on Sir Herbert Springett, in Ringmer Church.

Let others sing the wild career
Of Turpin, Gilpin, Paul Revere.
A gentler pace is mine. But hear!

The raindrops fell, splash! thud! splash! thud!
Till half the country-side was flood,
And Ringmer was a waste of mud.

The sleepy Ouse had grown a sea,
Where here and there a drowning tree
Cast up its arms beseechingly;

And cattle that in fairer days
Beside its banks were wont to graze
Now viewed the scene in mild amaze,

And, huddled on an island mound,
Sent forth so dolorous a sound
As made the sadness more profound.

And then—at last—one Sunday broke
When villagers, delighted, woke
To find the sun had flung its cloak

Of leaden-coloured cloud aside.
All jubilant they watched him ride,
For see, the land was glorified:

The morning pulsed with youth and mirth.
It was as though upon the earth
A new and gladder age had birth.

The lark exulted in the blue,
Triumphantly the rooster crew,
The chimneys laughed, the sparks up-flew;

And rolling westward out of sight,
Like billows of majestic height,
The Downs, transfigured in the light,

Seemed such a garb of joy to wear,
So young and radiant an air,
God might but just have set them there.

* * * * *

Sir Herbert Springett, Ringmer's squire,
(No better man in all the shire)—
He too was filled with kindling fire,

Which, working in him, did incite
The worthy and capacious knight
To doughty deeds of appetite.

Sir Herbert's lady watched her lord
Range mightily about the board
Which she of her abundance stored,

(The Lady Barbara, for whom
The blossoms of the simple-room
Diffused their friendliest perfume,

Than who none quicklier heard the call
Of true distress, and left the Hall
Eager to do her gentle all,

When village patients needed aid.
And O the rich Marchpane she made!
And O the rare quince marmalade!)

Just as the squire was satisfied,
The noise of feet was heard outside;
A knock. "Come in!" Sir Herbert cried.

And lo! John Grigg in Sunday smock;
Begged pardon, pulled an oily lock;
Explained: "The mud's above the hough.

"No horse could draw 'ee sir," he said.
"Humph!" quoth the squire and scratched his head.
"Then yoke the oxen in instead."

(A lesser man would gladly turn
His chair to fire again, and learn
How fancifully logs can burn,

Grateful for such immunity
From parson. Not the squire; for see,
"True sonne of England's Church" was he.)

So, as he ordered, was it done.
The oxen came forth one by one,
Their wide horns glinting in the sun,

And to the coach were yoked. Then—dressed,
As squires should be, in glorious best,
With wonderful brocaded vest,—

Out came Sir Herbert, took his seat,
Waved "Barbara, farewell, my Sweet!"
And off they started, all complete.
Although they drew so light a load
(For them!) so heavy was the road,
John Grigg was busy with his goad.

The cottagers in high delight
Ran out to see the startling sight
And make obeisance to the knight,

While floated through the liquid air,
And o'er the sunlit meadows fair,
The throbbing belfry's call to prayer.

At last, and after many a lurch
That shook Sir Herbert in his perch,
John Grigg drew up before the church;

Moreover not a minute late.
The villagers around the gate
Were filled with wonder at his state,

And, promptly, though 'twas sabbath tide,
"Three cheers for squire—Hooray!" they cried . . .
Such was Sir Herbert Springett's ride.

* * * * *

Sad is the sequel, sad but true—
For while in sermon-time a few
Deep snores resounded from the pew

Reserved for squire, by others there
The tenth commandment (men declare)
Was being broken past repair:

For, thinking how they had to roam
Through weary wastes of sodden loam
Ere they could win to fire and home,

In spite of parson's fervid knocks
Upon his cushion orthodox,
They "coveted their neighbour's ox."

OXEN OF THE HILLS

Oxen are now rarely seen on the Sussex roads, but on the hill sides a
few of the farmers still plough with them; and may it be long before the
old custom is abandoned! There is no pleasanter or more peaceful sight
than—looking up—that of a wide-horned team of black oxen, smoking
a little in the morning air, drawing the plough through the earth, while
the ploughman whistles, and the ox-herd, goad in hand, utters his Saxon
grunts of incitement or reproof. The black oxen of the hills are of Welsh
stock, the true Sussex ox being red. The "kews," as their shoes are called,
may still be seen on the walls of a smithy here and there. Shoeing oxen

is no joke, since to protect the smith from their horns they have to be thrown down; their necks are held by a pitchfork, and their feet tied together.

Sussex roads were terrible until comparatively recent times. An old rhyme credits "Sowseks" with "dirt and myre," and Dr. Burton, the author of the *Iter Sussexiensis*, humorously found in it a reason why Sussex people and beasts had such long legs. "Come now, my friend," he wrote, in Greek, "I will set before you a sort of problem in Aristotle's fashion:— Why is it that the oxen, the swine, the women, and all other animals, are so long legged in Sussex? May it be from the difficulty of pulling the feet out of so much mud by the strength of the ankle, that the muscles get stretched, as it were, and the bones lengthened?"

ROUGH ROADS

When, in 1703, the King of Spain visited the Duke of Somerset at Petworth he had the greatest difficulty in getting here. One of his attendants has put on record the perils of the journey:—"We set out at six o'clock in the morning (at Portsmouth) to go to Petworth, and did not get out of the coaches, save only when we were overturned or stuck fast in the mire, till we arrived at our journey's end. 'Twas hard service for the prince to sit fourteen hours in the coach that day, without eating anything, and passing through the worst ways that I ever saw in my life: we were thrown but once indeed in going, but both our coach which was leading, and his highness's body coach, would have suffered very often, if the nimble boors of Sussex had not frequently poised it, or supported it with their shoulders, from Godalming almost to Petworth; and the nearer we approached the duke's, the more inaccessible it seemed to be. The last nine miles of the way cost six hours time to conquer."

To return to Ringmer, it was there that Gilbert White studied the tortoise (see Letter xiii of *The Natural History of Selborne*). The house where he stayed still stands, and the rookery still exists. "These rooks," wrote the naturalist, "retire every morning all the winter from this rookery, where they only call by the way, as they are going to roost in deep woods; at the dawn of day they always revisit their nest-trees, and are preceded a few minutes by a flight of daws, that act, as it were, as their harbingers." An intermediate owner of the house where Gilbert White resided, which then belonged to his aunt Rebecca Snooke, ordered all nightingales to be shot, on the ground that they kept him awake.

PLASHETTS

While at Ringmer, if a glimpse of very rich park land is needed, it would be worth while to walk three miles north to Plashetts, which combines a vast tract of wood with a small park notable at once for its trees, its brake fern, its lakes, and its water fowl. But if one would gain it by rail, Isfield is the station.

CHAPTER XXXI

UCKFIELD AND BUXTED

The Crowborough district—Isfield—Another model wife—Framfield—
The poet Realf—Uckfield—The Maresfield rocks—Puritan names in
Sussex—Buxted park—Heron's Ghyll—A perfect church.

Uckfield, on the line from Lewes to Tunbridge Wells, is our true starting
point for the high sandy and rocky district of Crowborough, Rotherfield
and Mayfield; but we must visit on the way Isfield, a very pretty village
on the Ouse and its Iron River tributary. Isfield is remarkable for the
remains of Isfield Place, once the home of the Shurleys (connected only
by marriage with the Shirleys of Wiston). The house can never have been
so fine as Slaugham Place, but it is evident that abundance also reigned
here, as there. Over the main door was the motto "Non minor est virtus
quam querere parta tueri," which Horsfield whimsically translates "Catch
is a good dog, but Holdfast is a better." In the Shurley chapel, one of
the sweetest spots in Sussex, are brasses and monuments to the family,
notably the canopied altar tomb to Sir John Shurley, who died in 1631,
his two wives (Jane Shirley of Wiston and Dorothy Bowyer, *née* Goring,
of Cuckfield) and nine children, who kneel prettily in a row at the foot.
Of these children it is said in the inscription that some "were called into
Heaven and the others into several marriages of good quality"; while
of Dorothy Shurley it is prettily recorded (this, as we have seen, being a
district rich in exemplary wives) that she had "a merite beyond most of her
time, . . . her pitty was the clothing of the poore . . . and all her minutes

333

were but steppes to heaven." Our county has many fine monuments, but I think that, this is the most charming of all.

FRAMFIELD

At Framfield, two miles east of Uckfield, which we may take here, we again enter the iron country, and for the first time see Sussex hops, which are grown largely to the north and east of this neighbourhood.

FRAMFIELD.

RICHARD REALF

Framfield has a Tudor church and no particular interest. In 1792 eleven out of fifteen persons in Framfield, whose united ages amounted to one thousand and thirty-four years, offered, through the county paper, to play a cricket match with an equal number of the same age from any part of Sussex; but I do not find any record of the result. Nor can I find that any one at Framfield is proud of the fact that here, in 1834, was born Richard Realf, the orator and poet, son of Sussex peasants. In England

334

his name is scarcely known; and in America, where his work was done, it is not common knowledge that he was by birth and parentage English. Realf was the friend of man, liberty and John Brown; he fought against slavery in the war, and helped the cause with some noble verses; and he died miserably by his own hand in 1878, leaving these lines beside his body:—

"De mortuis nil nisi bonum." When
  For me this end has come and I am dead,
And the little voluble, chattering daws of men
  Peck at me curiously, let it then be said
By some one brave enough to speak the truth:
  Here lies a great soul killed by cruel wrong.
Down all the balmy days of his fresh youth
  To his bleak, desolate noon, with sword and song,
And speech that rushed up hotly from the heart,
  He wrought for liberty, till his own wound
(He had been stabbed), concealed with painful art
  Through wasting years, mastered him, and he swooned,
And sank there where you see him lying now
  With the word "Failure" written on his brow.

But say that he succeeded. If he missed
  World's honors, and world's plaudits, and the wage
  Of the world's deft lacqueys, still his lips were kissed
Daily by those high angels who assuage
  The thirstings of the poets—for he was
Born unto singing—and a burthen lay
  Mightily on him, and he moaned because
He could not rightly utter to the day
  What God taught in the night. Sometimes, nathless,
Power fell upon him, and bright tongues of flame,

And blessings reached him from poor souls in stress;
And benedictions from black pits of shame,
    And little children's love, and old men's prayers,
And a Great Hand that led him unawares.

So he died rich. And if his eyes were blurred
    With big films—silence! he is in his grave.
Greatly he suffered; greatly, too, he erred
    Yet broke his heart in trying to be brave.
Nor did he wait till Freedom had become
    The popular shibboleth of courtier's lips;
He smote for her when God Himself seemed dumb
    And all His arching skies were in eclipse.
He was a-weary, but he fought his fight,
    And stood for simple manhood; and was joyed
To see the august broadening of the light
    And new earths heaving heavenward from the void.
He loved his fellows, and their love was sweet—
    Plant daisies at his head and at his feet.

Uckfield's main street is divided sharply into two periods—from the station to the road leading to the church all is new; beyond, all is old. The town is not interesting in itself, but it commands good country, and has a good inn, the Maiden's Head. It is also a good specimen of the quieter market-town of the past—with a brewery (hiding behind a wonderful tree braced with kindly iron bands), a water mill (down by the railway), and several solid comfortable houses for the doctor and the lawyer and the brewer and the parson, with ample gardens behind them.

Uckfield was once the home of Jeremiah Markland, the great classic, who acted as tutor here to Edward Clarke, son of the famous William Clarke, rector of Buxted, and father of Edward Daniel Clarke, the traveller.

It is agreeable to remember that Fanny Burney passed through the town with Mrs. Thrale in 1779, although she found nothing to interest her.

THE UCKFIELD ROCKS

Uckfield is the southern boundary of the rock district of which we saw something at West Hoathly, and it is famous for the sandstone cliffs in the grounds of High Rocks, an estate on the south of the town. The unthinking untidiness and active penknives of the holiday makers made it recently necessary for the grounds to be closed to strangers. Close by, however, just off the road from Uckfield to Maresfield, is a rocky tract that is free to all. It consists of about an acre of grey, sandy boulders, some rising to a height of twenty feet or so, which remind one a little of the *rochers* in the Forest of Fontainebleau, although on a smaller scale. All are worn with the feet of adventurous boys enjoying one of the best natural playgrounds in the county. Here blackberries come to rich perfection, the sun's ripening warmth being thrown back from the hot sand.

When I first knew Maresfield church, many years ago, its aged vicar rolled out "Thou shalt do no mur-r-r-der" with an accusing timbre that seemed to bring the sin home to all of us. He had also so peculiar a way of pronouncing "Albert," that his prayer for our rulers seemed to make an invidious distinction, and ask a blessing, not for all, but for all but Edward, Prince of Wales.

PURITAN NAMES

Some of the oddest of the composite pietistic names that broke out over England during the Puritan revolution are to be found in Sussex registers. In 1632, Master Performe-thy-vowes Seers of Maresfield married Thomasine Edwards. His full name was too much for the village, and four years later is found an entry recording the burial of "Vowes Seers" pure and simple. The searcher of parish registers from whose articles in the *Sussex Daily News* I have already quoted, has also found that Heathfield had many Puritan names, among them "Replenished," which was given to the daughter of Robert Pryor in 1600. There was also a Heathfield damsel known as "More-Fruits." Mr. Lower prints the following names from a Sussex jury list in the seventeenth century: Redeemed Compton of Battel, Stand-fast-on-high Stringer of Crowhurst, Weep-not Billing of Lewes, Called Lower of Warbleton, Elected Mitchell of Heathfield, Renewed Wisberry of Hailsham, Fly-fornication Richardson of Waldron, The-Peace-of-God Knight of Burwash, Fight-the-good-fight-of-Faith White of Ewhurst, and Kill-sin Pemble of Withyham. Also a Master More-Fruits Fowler of East Hoathly, for it seems that in such names there was no sex.

Among the curious Sussex surnames found by the student of the county archives who is quoted above are the following:—

Pitchfork	Sweetname	Lies
Devil	Slybody	Hogsflesh
Leper	Fidge	Backfield
Handshut	Beatup	Breathing
Juglery	Rougehead	Whiskey
Hollowbone	Punch	Wildgoose
Stillborne	Padge	Ann.

Almost every name here would have pleased Dickens, while some might have been invented by him, notably Fidge and Padge. One can almost see Mr. Fidge and Mr. Padge drolling it in his pages.

BUXTED DEER

From the Maresfield rocks Buxted is easily reached, about a mile due east; but a far prettier approach is through Buxted Park, which is gained by a footpath out of Uckfield's main street. The charm of Buxted is its deer. Sussex, as we have seen, is rich in parks containing deer, but I know of none other where one may be so certain of coming close to these beautiful creatures. Nor can I recall any other deer that are so exquisitely dappled; but that may be because the Buxted deer were the first I ever saw, thirty years ago, and we like to think the first the best. Certainly they are the friendliest, or least timid. The act of going to church is invested at Buxted with an almost unique attraction, since the deer lie hard by the path. Indeed, the last time I went to church at Buxted I never passed through the door at all, but sat on a gravestone throughout the service and watched the herd in its graceful restlessness. That was twelve years ago. The other day I watched them again and could see no change. Some of the stags were still as of old almost bowed beneath their antlers, although one at any rate was free, for a keeper who passed carried a pair of horns in his hand.

IN BUXTED PARK.

RALPH HOGGE

The old house at the beginning of the footpath to the church, with a hog in bas-relief on its façade, is known as the Hog House, and is said to have been the residence of Ralph Hogge. Who was Ralph Hogge? Who is Hiram Maxim? Who was Krupp? Who was Nordenfelt? It was Ralph Hogge, iron-master, who in the year 1543 made the first English metal cannon. So at any rate say tradition and Holinshed. Buxted is otherwise most pacific of villages, sleepy and undiscovered. In the early years of the last century it boasted the possession of a labourer with a memory of amazing tenacity, one George Watson, who, otherwise almost imbecile, was unable to forget anything he had once seen, or any figure repeated to him.

On the road between Maresfield and Crowborough is Heron's Ghyll, the residence of Mr. Fitzalan Hope. It stands to the east of the road, in one of those hollow sites that alone won the word "eligible" from a Tudor builder. Hard by the road is the perfect little Early English Roman Catholic church which Mr. Hope built in 1897, a miracle, in these hurried florid days, of honest work and simple modest beauty. The church being Roman Catholic one may with confidence turn aside to rest a little in its cool seclusion, relieved of the irritating search for the sexton of the national establishment, and freed from his haunting presence and suggestion that the labourer is worthy of more than his hire.

CLOSED CHURCHES

While on this subject I might remark that a county vicar describing the antiquities of his neighbourhood in one of the Sussex Archæological Society's volumes, writes magnanimously: "A debt of gratitude is certainly due to our Roman Catholic predecessors (whatever error might mix itself with their piety and charity) for erecting such noble edifices, in a style of strength to endure for a late posterity." It seems to me that a very simple way of discharging a portion of this debt would be to imitate the excellent habit of leaving the church doors wide open, as practised by those Roman Catholic predecessors. My own impulse to enter many of the Sussex churches has been principally antiquarian or æsthetic, but to rest amid their gray coolnesses is a legitimate desire which should be fostered rather than discouraged, particularly as it is under such conditions that the soul even of the stranger whose motive is curiosity is often comforted. The arguments in favour of keeping churches closed are unknown to me. Doubtless they are numerous and ingenious, but, doubtless equally, a locked church is a confession of failure; while to urge that one has but to ask for the key to be able to enter a church is no true reply, since hospitality, whether to the body or the soul, loses in sweetness and effect as it loses in spontaneity.

TO CROWBOROUGH

From Heron's Ghyll to Crowborough is a steady climb for three miles, with the heathery wastes of Ashdown Forest on the left and the hilly district around Mayfield on the right.

CHAPTER XXXII

CROWBOROUGH AND MAYFIELD

Crowborough the suburban—Rotherfield's three rivers—The extra ribs—Wild flowers and railway companies—The perfect hill—An arid district—St. Dunstan and the Devil—Why Tunbridge Wells waters are chalybeate—St. Dunstan's feats—An unencouraging *memento mori*—Mayfield church—Mayfield street—The diary of Mr. Walter Gale, schoolmaster.

In the spring of this year (1903) the walls and fences of Crowborough were covered with the placards of a firm of estate agents describing the neighbourhood (in the manner of the great George Robins) as "Scotland in Sussex." The simile may be true of the Ashdown Forest side of the Beacon (although involving an unnecessary confusion of terms), but "Hampstead in Sussex" would be a more accurate description of Crowborough proper. Never was a fine remote hill so be-villa'd. The east slope is all scaffold-poles and heaps of bricks, new churches and chapels are sprouting, and the many hoardings announce that Follies, Pierrots, or conjurors are continually imminent. Crowborough itself has shops that would not disgrace Croydon, and a hotel where a Lord Mayor might feel at home. Houses in their own grounds are commoner than cottages, and near the summit the pegs of surveyors and the name-boards of avenues yet to be built testify to the charms which our Saxon Caledonia has already exerted.

But to say this is not to say all. Crowborough may be populous and over-built; but it is still a glorious eminence, the healthiest and most bracing inland village in the county, and the key to its best moorland country. Since Crowborough's normal visitor either plays golf or is contented with a very modest radius, the more adventurous walker may quickly be in the solitudes.

In the little stone house below the forge Richard Jefferies lived for some months at the end of his life.

ROTHERFIELD

Crowborough is crowned by a red hotel which can never pass into the landscape; Rotherfield, its companion hill on the east, on the other side of the Jarvis Brook valley, is surmounted by a beautiful church with a tall shingled spire, that must have belonged to the scene from the first. This spire darts up from the edge of the forest ridge like a Pharos for the Weald of Kent. The church was dedicated to St. Denis of Paris by a Saxon chieftain who was cured of his ills by a pilgrimage to the Saint's monastery. That was in 792. In the present church, which retains the dedication, is an ancient mural painting representing the martyrdom of St. Lawrence. There is also a Burne-Jones window.

Were it not for Rotherfield both Sussex and Kent would lack some of their waterways, for the Rother and the Ouse rise here, and also the Medway. A local saying credits the women of Rotherfield with two ribs more than the men, to account for their superior height.

Under a hedge half-way between Rotherfield and Jarvis Brook grow the largest cowslips in Sussex, as large as cowslips may be without changing their sex. But this is all cowslip country—from the field of Rother to the field of Uck. And it is the land of the purple orchis too, the finest blooms of which are to be found on the road between Rotherfield and Mayfield; but you must scale a fence to get them, because (like all the best wild flowers) they belong to the railway.

Between Rotherfield and Mayfield is a little hill, trim and conical as though Miss Greenaway had designed it, and perfect in deportment, for it has (as all little conical hills should have) a white windmill on its top. Around the mill is a circular track for carts, which runs nearer the sails than any track I remember ever to have dared to walk on. Standing by this mill one opens many miles of Kent and Surrey: due north the range of chalk Downs on which is the Pilgrim's Way, between Merstham and Westerham, and in front of that Toy's Hill and Ide Hill and their sandy companions, on the north edge of the Weald.

Mayfield is a city on a hill on the skirts of the hot hop district of which Burwash is the Sussex centre. To walk about it even in April is no exhilaration; but in August one thinks of Sahara. I lived in Mayfield one August and could barely keep awake; and we used to look across at the rolling chalk Downs in the south, between Ditchling and Lewes, and long for their cool, wind-swept heights. They can be hot too, but chalk is never so hot as sand, and a steady climb to a summit, over turf odorous of wild thyme, is restful beside the eternal hills and valleys of the hop district.

SAINT DUNSTAN

Mayfield has the best street and the best architecture of any of these highland villages. Also it has the distinction of having done most for mankind, since without Mayfield there would have been no water to cure jaded London ladies and gentlemen at Tunbridge Wells. According to Eadmer, who wrote one of the lives of Dunstan, that Saint, when Archbishop of Canterbury, built a wooden church at Mayfield and lived in a cell hard by. St. Dunstan, who was an expert goldsmith, was one day making a chalice (or, as another version of the legend says, a horseshoe) when the Devil appeared before him. Instantly recognising his enemy, and being aware that with such a foe prompt measures alone are useful, St. Dunstan at once pulled his nose with the tongs, which chanced happily to be red hot. Wrenching himself free, the Devil leaped at one bound from Mayfield to Tunbridge Wells, where, plunging his nose into the spring at the foot of the Pantiles, he "imparted to the water its chalybeate qualities," and thus made the fortune of the town as a health resort. To St. Dunstan therefore, indirectly, are all drinkers of these wells indebted. For other drinkers he introduced or invented the practice of fixing pins in the sides of drinking cups, in order that a thirsty man might see how he was progressing and a bibulous man be checked.

MAYFIELD

When consecrating his little church at Mayfield St. Dunstan discovered it to be a little out of the true position, east and west. He therefore applied his shoulder and rectified the error.

The remains of Mayfield Palace, the old abode of the Archbishops of Canterbury, join the church. After it had passed into the hands of the crown—for Cranmer made a bargain with the King by which Mayfield was exchanged for other property—Sir Thomas Gresham lived here, and Queen Elizabeth has dined under its roof. The Palace is to be seen only occasionally, for it is now a convent, Mayfield being another of the county's many Roman Catholic outposts. In the great dining-room are the tongs which St. Dunstan used.

The church, dedicated to Mayfield's heroic saint, has one of the broader shingled spires of Sussex, as distinguished from the slender spires of which Rotherfield is a good example. Standing high, it may be seen from long distances. The tower is the original Early English structure. Four more of the old Sussex iron tomb slabs may be seen at Mayfield. In the churchyard, says Mr. Lower, was once an inscription with this uncomplimentary first line:—

O reader, if that thou canst read,

It continued:—

Look down upon this stone;
Death is the man, do you what you can,
    That never spareth none!

In Mayfield's street even the new houses have caught comeliness from their venerable neighbours. It undulates from gable to gable, and has two good inns. The old timbered house in the middle of the east side is that to which Richard Jefferies refers without enthusiasm in the passage which I quote in a later *chapter* from his essay on Buckhurst Park. In Louis Jennings' *Field Paths and Green Lanes* the house comes in for eulogy.

Vicar of Mayfield in 1361 and following years was John Wickliffe, who has too often been confused with his great contemporary and namesake, the reformer. And the village claims as a son Thomas May (1595-1650), playwright, translator of Lucan's "Pharsalia," secretary to Parliament and friend of Ben Jonson.

In the Sussex Archæological Collections is printed the journal of Walter Gale, schoolmaster at Mayfield in the latter half of the eighteenth century, from which a few extracts may be given:

"1750. I found the greatest part of the school in a flow, by reason of the snow and rain coming through the leads. The following extempore verse I set for a copy:—

Abandon every evil thought
For they to judgment will be brought.

In passing the Star I met with Mr. Eastwood; we went in and spent 2*d.* apiece.

PRESAGES OF DEATH

"I went to Mr. Sawyer's . . . One of his daughters said that she expected a change in the weather as she had last night dreamt of a deceased person." The editor remarks that this superstition still lingers (or did fifty years ago) in the Weald of Sussex. Walter Gale adds:—"I told them in discourse that on Thursday last the town clock was heard to strike 3 in the afternoon twice, once before the chimes went, and a 2nd time pretty nearly a ¼ of an hour after . . . The strikes at the 2nd striking seemed to sound very dull and mournfully; this, together with the crickets coming to the house at Laughton just at our coming away, I look upon to be sure presages of my sister's death."

A year later:—"My mother, to my great unhappiness, died in the 83rd year of her age, agreeable to the testimony I had of a death in our family on the 10th of May last."

"Mr. Rogers came to the school, and brought with him the four volumes of *Pamela*, for which I paed him 4*s.* 6*d.*, and bespoke Duck's *Poems* for Mr. Kine, and a *Caution to Swearers* for myself.

"Sunday. I went to church at Hothley. Text from St. Matthew 'Take no thought, saying, What shall we eat, and what shall we drink, or wherewithal shall we be clothed,' and I went to Jones', where I spent 2*d.*, and there came Thomas Cornwall, and treated me with a pint of twopenny.

"Mr. James Kine came; we smoaked a pipe together and we went and took a survey of the fair; we went to a legerdemain show, which we saw with tolerable approbation.

"May 28th. Gave attendance at a cricket-match, played between the gamesters at Burwash and Mayfield to the advantage of the latter."

OLD KENT

A series of quarrels with old Kent occupy much of the diary. Old Kent, it seems, used to enter the school house and vilify the master, not, I imagine, without cause. Thus:—"He again called me upstart, runagate, beggarly dog, clinched his fist in my face, and made a motion to strike me, and declared he would break my head. He did not strike me, but withdrew in a wonderful heat, and ended all with his general maxim, 'The greater scholler, the greater rogue!'"

Mr. Gale was removed from the school in 1771 for neglecting his duties.

CHAPTER XXXIII

HEATHFIELD AND THE "LIES."

The two Heathfields—Heathfield Park—"Hefful" Fair and the spring—The death of Jack Cade—Warbleton's martyr—Three "lies" and all true—An ecclesiastical confection—The bloodthirsty Colonel Lunsford—Halland—Tarble Down—Breeches Wood—Mr. Thomas Turner's diary—Laughton—Chiddingly's inhospitable fane—The Jefferay cheese—A devoted campanologist—Hellingly—Hailsham.

There are two Heathfields: the old village, with its pleasant Sussex church and ancient cottages close to the park gates; and the new brick and slate town that has gathered round the station and the natural gas-works. The park lies between the two, remarkable among Sussex parks for the variety of its trees and the unusual proportion of them. The spacious lawns which are characteristic of the parks in the south, here, on Heathfield's sandy undulations, give place to heather, fern and trees. I never remember to have seen a richer contrast of greens than in early spring, looking west from the house, between the masses of dark evergreens that had borne the rigours of the winter and the young leaves just breaking through. Heathfield's park is, I think, the loveliest in Sussex, lying as it does on a southern slope, with its opulence of foliage, its many rushing burns (the source of the Cuckmere), its hidden ravines and deep silent tarns, and its wonderful view of the Downs and the sea. The park once belonged to the Dacres of Hurstmonceaux, whom we are about to meet. Traces of the original house, dating probably from Henry VII.'s reign, are still to be seen in the basement. Upon this foundation was imposed a new building towards the end of the seventeenth century. The park was then known as Bailey Park. A century later, George Augustus Eliott (afterwards Lord Heathfield), the hero of Gibraltar, and earlier of Cuba, acquired it with his Havana prize money. After Lord Heathfield died, in 1790, the park became the property of Francis Newbery, son of the bookseller of St. Paul's Churchyard. The present owner, Mr. Alexander, has added greatly to the house.

GIBRALTAR TOWER

Gibraltar Tower, on the highest point of the park, was built by Newbery in honour of his predecessor. From its summit a vast prospect is visible, and forty churches, it is said, may be counted. I saw but few of these. In the east, similarly elevated, is seen the Brightling Needle. Mr. Alexander has gathered together in the tower a number of souvenirs of old English life which make it a Lewes Castle museum in little. Here are stocks, horn glasses, drinking vessels, rushlight holders, leather bottels, and one of those quaint wooden machines for teaching babies to walk. An old manuscript history of the tower, in Mr. Alexander's possession, contains at least one passage that is perhaps worth noting, as it may help to clear up any confusion that exists in connection with Lord Heathfield's marriage. "The lady to whom his lordship meant to be united," says the historian, "and who would certainly have been his wife had not death stepped in, is the sister of a lady of whom his lordship was extremely fond, but she, dying about ten years ago, he transferred his affections to the other, who is about thirty-five years of age."

A Heathfield worthy of a hundred years ago was Sylvan Harmer, chiefly a stone cutter (he cut the stone for the tower), but also the modeller in clay of some very ingenious and pretty bas-relief designs for funeral urns, notably a group known as Charity.

JACK CADE

The following scene from *The Second Part of Henry VI.* although Shakespeare places it in Kent, belongs to a little hamlet known as Cade Street, close to Heathfield:—

SCENE X.—Kent. IDEN's *Garden.*

Enter CADE.

Cade. Fie on ambition! fie on myself; that have a sword, and yet am ready to famish! These five days have I hid me in these woods, and durst not peep out, for all the country is laid for me; but now am I so hungry, that if I might have a lease of my life for a thousand years, I could stay no longer. Wherefore, on a brick-wall have I climbed into this garden, to see if I can eat grass, or pick a sallet another while, which is not amiss to cool a man's stomach this hot weather. And, I think, this word sallet was born to do me good: for, many a time, but for a sallet, my brain-pan had been cleft with a brown bill; and, many a time, when I have been dry, and bravely marching, it hath served me instead of a quart-pot to drink in; and now the word sallet must serve me to feed on.

Enter IDEN, *with Servants, behind.*

Iden. Lord! who would live turmoiléd in the court,
And may enjoy such quiet walks as these!
This small inheritance, my father left me,
Contenteth me, and worth a monarchy.
I seek not to wax great by others' waning;
Or gather wealth I care not with what envy:
Sufficeth that I have maintains my state,
And sends the poor well pleaséd from my gate.

Cade. Here's the lord of the soil come to seize me for a stray, for entering his fee-simple without leave. Ah, villain, thou wilt betray me, and get a thousand crowns of the king by carrying my head to him; but I'll make thee eat iron like an ostrich, and swallow my sword like a great pin, ere thou and I part.

> *Iden.* Why, rude companion, whatsoe'er thou be,
> I know thee not; why then should I betray thee?
> Is't not enough, to break into my garden,
> And like a thief to come to rob my grounds,
> Climbing my walls in spite of me, the owner,
> But thou wilt brave me with these saucy terms?

Cade. Brave thee? ay, by the best blood that ever was broached, and beard thee too. Look on me well: I have eat no meat these five days; yet, come thou and thy five men; and if I do not leave you all as dead as a door-nail, I pray God I may never eat grass more.

> *Iden.* Nay, it shall ne'er be said, while England stands,
> That Alexander Iden, an esquire of Kent,
> Took odds to combat a poor famished man.
> Oppose thy steadfast-gazing eyes to mine,
> See if thou canst outface me with thy looks:
> Set limb to limb, and thou art far the lesser;
> Thy hand is but a finger to my fist;
> Thy leg a stick, comparéd with this truncheon;
> My foot shall fight with all the strength thou hast;
> And if mine arm be heavéd in the air,
> Thy grave is digged already in the earth.
> As for words, whose greatness answers words,
> Let this my sword report what speech forbears.

Cade. By my valour, the most complete champion that ever I heard.—
Steel, if thou turn the edge, or cut not out the burly-boned clown
in chines of beef ere thou sleep in thy sheath, I beseech Jove on my
knees, thou mayest be turned to hobnails. [*They fight.* Cade *falls.*] O! I
am slain. Famine, and no other, hath slain me: let ten thousand devils
come against me, and give me but the ten meals I have lost, and I'd
defy them all. Wither, garden; and be henceforth a burying-place to all
that do dwell in this house, because the unconquered soul of Cade is
fled.

Iden. Is't Cade that I have slain, that monstrous traitor?
Sword, I will hallow thee for this thy deed,
And hang thee o'er my tomb, when I am dead:
Ne'er shall this blood be wipéd from thy point,
But thou shalt wear it as a herald's coat,
To emblaze the honour that thy master got.

Cade. Iden, farewell; and be proud of thy victory. Tell Kent from me, she
hath lost her best man, and exhort all the world to be cowards; for I,
that never feared any, am vanquished by famine, not by valour.
[*Dies.*

THE DEATH OF CADE

That was on July 12, 1450. Cade did not die at once, but on the way
to London, whither he was conveyed in a cart. On the 16th his body
was drawn and quartered and dragged through London on a hurdle.
One quarter was then sent to Blackheath; the other three to Norwich,
Gloucester and Salisbury. Cade's head was set up on London Bridge.
Iden was knighted. A pillar was erected at Cade Street by Newbery on
the piece of land that he possessed nearest to the probable scene of
the event. "Near this spot was slain the notorious rebel Jack Cade, by
Alexander Iden, Esq.," is the inscription.

353

Slaughter Common, near Heathfield, is said to be the scene of a more wholesale carnage, Heathfield people claiming that there Caedwalla in 635 fought the Saxons and killed Eadwine, king of Northumbria. Sylvan Harmer, in his manuscript history of Heathfield, is determined that Heathfield shall have the credit of the fray, but, as a matter of fact, if Slaughter Common really took its name from a battle it was a very different one, for Caedwalla and Eadwine met, not at Heathfield, but Hatfield Chase, near Doncaster.

HEFFUL CUCKOO FAIR

It is at Hefful Cuckoo fair on April 14—Hefful being Sussex for Heathfield—that, tradition states, the old woman lets the cuckoo out of her basket and starts him on his course through the summer months. A local story tells of a Heathfield man who had a quarrel with his wife and left for Ditchling. After some days he returned, remarking, "I've had enough of furrin parts—nothing like old England yet."

If any one, walking from Heathfield towards Burwash, is astonished to find a "Railway Inn," let him spend no time in seeking a station, for there is none within some miles. This inn was once "The Labour in Vain," with a signboard representing two men hard at work scrubbing a nigger till the white should gleam through. Then came a scheme to run a line to Eastbourne, midway between the present Heathfield line and the Burwash line, and enterprise dictated the changing of the sign to one more in keeping with the times. The railway project was abandoned but the inn retains its new style.

Warbleton, a village in the iron country, two miles south of Heathfield, is famous for its association with Richard Woodman, the Sussex martyr, who is mentioned in an earlier *chapter*. His house and foundry were hard by the churchyard. The wonderful door in the church tower, a miracle of intricate bolts and massive strength, has been attributed to Woodman's mechanical skill; and the theory has been put forward that he made this door for his own strong room, and it was afterwards moved to the church. Another story says that he was imprisoned in the church tower before being taken for trial. Warbleton has the following terse and confident epitaph upon Ann North, wife of the vicar, who died in 1780:—

Through death's rough waves her bark serenely trod,
Her pilot Jesus, and her harbour God.

From Horeham Road station, next Heathfield on the way to Hailsham, we can walk across the country to East Hoathly, and thence to Chiddingly and Hellingly, where we come to the railway again. ("East Hoathly, Chiddingly and Hellingly," says a local witticism: "three lies and all true.") East Hoathly stands high in not very interesting country, nor is it now a very interesting village. But it is remarkable for an admirably conducted inn and a church unique (in my experience of old churches) in its interior for a prettiness that is little short of aggressive. Whatever paint and mosaic can do to remove plain white surfaces has been done here, and the windows are gay with new glass. Were the building a new one, say at Surbiton, the effect would be harmonious; but in an old village in Sussex it seems a mistake.

THE CHILD-EATER

Colonel Thomas Lunsford, of Whyly (now no more), near East Hoathly, a cavalier and friend of Charles I., was notoriously a consumer of the flesh of babes. How he won such a reputation is not known, but it never left him. *Hudibras* mentions his tastes; in one ballad of the time he figures as Lunsford that "eateth of children," and in another, recording his supposed death, he is found with "a child's arm in his pocket." After a stormy but courageous career he died in 1691, innocent of cannibalism. It was this Lunsford who fired at his relative, Sir Nicholas Pelham of Halland, as he was one day entering East Hoathly church. The huge bullet, the outcome of a long feud, missed Nicholas and lodged in the church door, where it remained for many years. It cost Lunsford £8,000 and outlawry.

Halland, one of the seats of the Pelhams, about a mile from the village, was just above Terrible Down, a tract of wild land, on which, according to local tradition, a battle was once fought so fiercely that the soldiers were up to their knees in blood. In the neighbourhood it is, of course, called Tarble Down. Local tradition also states of a certain piece of woodland attached to the glebe of this parish, called Breeches Wood, that it owes its name to the circumstance that an East Hoathly lady, noticing the vicar's breeches to be in need of mending, presented to him and his successors the wood in question as an endowment to ensure the perpetual repair of those garments.

Halland House no longer exists, but in the days of the great Duke of Newcastle, who died in 1768, it was famous for its hospitality and splendour. We meet with traces of its influence in the frequent inebriation, after visits there, of Mr. Thomas Turner, a mercer and general dealer of East Hoathly, who kept a diary from 1764, recording some of his lapses and other experiences. A few passages from the extracts quoted in the Sussex Archæological Collections may be given:

> "My wife read to me that moving scene of the funeral of Miss Clarissa Harlow. Oh, may the Supreme Being give me grace to lead my life in such a manner as my exit may in some measure be like that divine creature's.
>
> "This morn my wife and I had words about her going to Lewes to-morrow. Oh, what happiness must there be in the married state, when there is a sincere regard on both sides, and each partie truly satisfied with each other's merits. But it is impossible for tongue or pen to express the uneasiness that attends the contrary.
>
> "Sunday, August 28th, 1756, Thos. Davey, at our house in the evening, to whom I read five of Tillotson's Sermons.

"Sunday, October 28th, Thos. Davey came in the evening to whom I read six of Tillotson's sermons.

"This day went to Mrs. Porter's to inform them the livery lace was not come, when I think Mrs. Porter treated me with as much imperious and scornful usage as if she had been, what I think she is, more of a Turk and Infidel than a Christian, and I an abject slave.

"I went down to Mrs. Porter's and acquainted her that I would not get her gown before Monday, who received me with all the affability, courtesy, and good humour imaginable. Oh! what a pleasure would it be to serve them was they always in such a temper; it would even induce me, almost, to forget to take a just profit.

POTATIONS

"We supped at Mr. Fuller's and spent the evening with a great deal of mirth, till between one and two. Tho. Fuller brought my wife home upon his back. I cannot say I came home sober, though I was far from being bad company.

"The curate of Laughton came to the shop in the forenoon, and he having bought some things of me (and I could wish he had paid for them) dined with me, and also staid in the afternoon till he got in liquor, and being so complaisant as to keep him company, I was quite drunk. How do I detest myself for being so foolish!

"In the even, read the twelfth and last book of Milton's *Paradise Lost*, which I have now read twice through.

"Mr. Banister having lately taken from the smugglers a freight of brandy, entertained Mr. Carman, Mr. Fuller, and myself, in the even, with a bowl of punch."

Although the Pelhams owned Halland, their principal seat was at Laughton, two or three miles to the south. Of that splendid Tudor mansion little now remains but one brick tower. In the vault of the church, which has been much restored, no fewer than forty Pelhams repose.

Chiddingly church presents the completest contrast to East Hoathly's over-decorated yet accessible fane that could be imagined. Its door is not only kept shut, but a special form of locked bar seems to have been invented for it, and on the day that I was last there the churchyard gate was padlocked too. The spire of white stone (visible for many miles)—a change from the customary oak shingling of Sussex—has been bound with iron chains that suggest the possibility of imminent dissolution, while within, the building is gloomy and time-stained. If at East Hoathly the church gives the impression of a too complacent prosperity, here we have precisely the reverse. The state of the Jefferay monument behind a row of rude railings is in keeping.

THE PROUD JEFFERAYS

In the Jefferay monument, by the way, the statues at either side stand on two circular tablets, which are not unlike the yellow cheeses of Alkmaar. It was possibly this circumstance that led to the myth that the Jefferays, too proud to walk on the ground, had on Sundays a series of cheeses ranged between their house and the church, on which to step. Their house was Chiddingly Place, built by Sir John Jefferay, who died in 1577. Remains of this great mansion are still to be seen. It was during Sir John's time that Chiddingly had a vicar, William Titelton, sufficiently flexible to retain the living under Henry VIII., Edward VI., Mary, and Elizabeth.

Here, in the eighteenth century, lived one William Elphick, a devotee of bell-ringing, who computed that altogether he had rung Chiddingly's triple bell for 8,766 hours (which is six hours more than a year), and who travelled upwards of ten thousand miles to ring the bells of other churches.

Mark Antony Lower, most interesting of the Sussex archæologists, to whom these pages have been much indebted, was born at Chiddingly in 1813.

Mr. Egerton in his *Sussex Folk and Sussex Ways* tells a story of a couple down Chiddingly way who agreed upon a very satisfactory system of danger signals when things were not quite well with either of them. Whenever the husband came home a little "contrary" he wore his hat on the back of his head, and then she never said a word; and if she came in a little cross and crooked she threw her shawl over her left shoulder, and then he never said a word.

CZAR AND QUAKER

A little to the east of Hellingly is Amberstone, the scene, in 1814, of a pretty occurrence. Alexander, the Czar of all the Russias, travelling from Brighton to Dover with his sister, the Duchess of Oldenburgh, saw Nathaniel and Mary Rickman of Amberstone standing by their gate. From their dress he knew them to be Quakers, a sect in which he was much interested. The carriage was therefore stopped, and the Czar and his sister entered the house; they were taken all over it, praised its neatness, ate some lunch, and parted with the kindest expressions of goodwill, the Czar shaking hands with the Quaker and the Duchess kissing the Quakeress.

A few minutes on the rail bring us to Hailsham, an old market town, whose church, standing on the ridge which borders Pevensey Level on the west, is capped with pinnacles like that of East Grinstead. Walking a few yards beyond the church one comes to the edge of the high ground, with nothing before one but miles and miles of the meadow-land of this Dutch region, green and moist and dotted with cattle.

Hailsham's principal value to the traveller is that it is the station for Hurstmonceux; whither, however, we are to journey by another route. Otherwise the town exists principally in order that bullocks and sheep may change hands once a week. Hailsham's cattle market covers three acres, and on market days the wayfarers in the streets need the agility of a picador.

We ought, however, to see Michelham Priory while we are here. It lies two miles to the west of Hailsham, in the Cuckmere valley—now a beautifully-placed farmhouse, but once a house of Augustinian Canons founded in the reign of Henry III. Here one may see the old monkish fish stews, so useful on Fridays, in perfection. The moat, where fish were probably also caught, is still as it was, and the fine old three-storied gateway and the mill belonging to the monks stand to this day. The priory, although much in ruins, is very interesting, and well worth seeing and exploring with a reconstructive eye.

THE TWO DICKERS

A little further west is the Dicker—or rather the two Dickers, Upper Dicker and Lower Dicker, large commons between Arlington in the south and Chiddingly in the north. Here are some of the many pottery works for which Sussex is famous.

BEACHY HEAD.

CHAPTER XXXIV

EASTBOURNE

Select Eastbourne. The "English Salvator Rosa"—Sops and Ale—Beau Chef—"The Breeze on Beachy Head"—Shakespeare and the Cliff—"To a Seamew"—The new lighthouse—Parson Darby and his cave—East Dean's bells—The Two Sisters—Friston's Selwyn monument—West Dean.

Eastbourne is the most select, or least democratic, of the Sussex watering places. Fashion does not resort thither as to Brighton in the season, but the crowds of excursionists that pour into Brighton and Hastings are comparatively unknown at Eastbourne; which is in a sense a private settlement, under the patronage of the Duke of Devonshire. Hastings is of the people; Brighton has a character almost continental; Eastbourne is select. Lawn tennis and golf are its staple products, one played on the very beautiful links behind the town hard by Compton Place, the residence of the Duke; the other in Devonshire Park. It is also an admirable town for horsemanship.

THE ENGLISH SALVATOR ROSA

Eastbourne has had small share in public affairs, but in 1741 John Hamilton Mortimer, the painter, sometimes called the Salvator Rosa of England, was born there. From a memoir of him which Horsfield prints, I take passages: "Bred on the sea-coast, and amid a daring and rugged race of hereditary smugglers, it had pleased his young imagination to walk on the shore when the sea was agitated by storms—to seek out the most sequestered places among the woods and rocks, and frequently, and not without danger, to witness the intrepidity of the contraband adventurers, who, in spite of storms and armed excisemen, pursued their precarious trade at all hazards. In this way he had, from boyhood, become familiar with what amateurs of art call 'Salvator Rosa-looking scenes'; he loved to depict the sea chafing and foaming, and fit 'to swallow navigation up'—ships in peril, and pinnaces sinking—banditti plundering, or reposing in caverns—and all such situations as are familiar to pirates on water, and outlaws on land . . .

"Of his eccentricities while labouring under the delusion that he could not well be a genius without being unsober and wild, one specimen may suffice. He was employed by Lord Melbourne to paint a ceiling at his seat of Brocket Hall, Herts; and taking advantage of permission to angle in the fish-pond, he rose from a carousal at midnight, and seeking a net, and calling on an assistant painter for help, dragged the preserve, and left the whole fish gasping on the bank in rows. Nor was this the worst; when reproved mildly, and with smiles, by Lady Melbourne, he had the audacity to declare, that her beauty had so bewitched him that he knew not what he was about. To plunder the fish-pond and be impertinent to the lady was not the way to obtain patronage. The impudent painter collected his pencils together, and returned to London to enjoy his inelegant pleasures and ignoble company."

Horsfield states that "a custom far more honoured by the breach than the observance heretofore existed in the manor of Eastbourne; in compliance with which, after any lady, or respectable farmer or tradesman's wife, was delivered of a child, certain quantities of food and of beer were placed in a room adjacent to the sacred edifice; when, after the second lesson was concluded, the whole agricultural portion of the worshippers marched out of church, and devoured what was prepared for them. This was called *Sops and Ale*."

EASTBOURNE RUG

John Taylor the water Poet, whom we saw, at Goring, the prey of fleas and the Law, made another journey into the county between August 9th and September 3rd, 1653, and as was usual with him wrote about it in doggerel verse. At Eastbourne he found a brew called Eastbourne Rug:—

No cold can ever pierce his flesh or skin
Of him who is well lin'd with Rug within;
Rug is a lord beyond the Rules of Law,
It conquers hunger in a greedy maw,
And, in a word, of all drinks potable,
Rug is most puissant, potent, notable.
Rug was the Capital Commander there,
And his Lieutenant-General was strong beer.

Possibly it was in order to contest the supremacy of Rug (which one may ask for in Eastbourne to-day in vain) that Newhaven Tipper sprang into being.

The Martello towers, which Pitt built during the Napoleonic scare at the beginning of last century, begin at Eastbourne, where the cliffs cease, and continue along the coast into Kent. They were erected probably quite as much to assist in allaying public fear by a tangible and visible symbol of defence as from any idea that they would be a real service in the event of invasion. Many of them have now disappeared.

BEACHY HEAD

Eastbourne's glory is Beachy Head, the last of the Downs, which stop dead at the town and never reappear in Sussex again. The range takes a sudden turn to the south at Folkington, whence it rolls straight for the sea, Beachy Head being the ultimate eminence. (The name Beachy has, by the way, nothing to do with the beach: it is derived probably from the Normans' description—"beau chef.") About Beachy Head one has the South Downs in perfection: the best turf, the best prospect, the best loneliness, and the best air. Richard Jefferies, in his fine essay, "The Breeze on Beachy Head," has a rapturous word to say of this air (poor Jefferies, destined to do so much for the health of others and so little for his own!).—"But the glory of these glorious Downs is the breeze. The air in the valleys immediately beneath them is pure and pleasant; but the least climb, even a hundred feet, puts you on a plane with the atmosphere itself, uninterrupted by so much as the tree-tops. It is air without admixture. If it comes from the south, the waves refine it; if inland, the wheat and flowers and grass distil it. The great headland and the whole rib of the promontory is wind-swept and washed with air; the billows of the atmosphere roll over it.

"The sun searches out every crevice amongst the grass, nor is there the smallest fragment of surface which is not sweetened by air and light. Underneath the chalk itself is pure, and the turf thus washed by wind and rain, sun-dried and dew-scented, is a couch prepared with thyme to rest on. Discover some excuse to be up there always, to search for stray mushrooms—they will be stray, for the crop is gathered extremely early in the morning—or to make a list of flowers and grasses; to do anything, and, if not, go always without any pretext. Lands of gold have been found, and lands of spices and precious merchandise: but this is the land of health."

Seated near the edge of the cliff one realises, as it is possible nowhere else to realise, except perhaps at Dover, the truth of Edgar's description of the headland in *King Lear*. It seems difficult to think of Shakespeare exploring these or any Downs, and yet the scene must have been in his own experience; nothing but actual sight could have given him the line about the crows and choughs:

Come on, sir; here's the place:—stand still.—How fearful
And dizzy 't is, to cast one's eyes so low!
The crows and choughs, that wing the midway air,
Show scarce so gross as beetles: half way down
Hangs one that gathers samphire—dreadful trade!
Methinks he seems no bigger than his head:
The fishermen, that walk upon the beach,
Appear like mice; and yond tall anchoring bark,
Diminish'd to her cock; her cock, a buoy
Almost too small for sight: the murmuring surge,
That on the unnumber'd idle pebbles chafes,
Cannot be heard so high.—I'll look no more,
Lest my brain turn, and the deficient sight
Topple down headlong.

"TO A SEAMEW"

Choughs are rare at Beachy Head, but jackdaws and gulls are in great
and noisy profusion; and this reminds me that it was on Beachy Head in
September, 1886, that the inspiration of one of the most beautiful bird-
poems in our language came to its author—the ode "To a Seamew" of
Mr. Swinburne. I quote five of its haunting stanzas:

We, sons and sires of seamen,
  Whose home is all the sea,
What place man may, we claim it;
But thine—whose thought may name it?
Free birds live higher than freemen,
  And gladlier ye than we—
We, sons and sires of seamen,
  Whose home is all the sea.

For you the storm sounds only
  More notes of more delight
Than earth's in sunniest weather:
When heaven and sea together
Join strengths against the lonely
  Lost bark borne down by night,
For you the storm sounds only
  More notes of more delight.

* * * * *

The lark knows no such rapture,
  Such joy no nightingale,
As sways the songless measure,
Wherein thy wings take pleasure:
Thy love may no man capture,
  Thy pride may no man quail;
The lark knows no such rapture,
  Such joy no nightingale.

And we, whom dreams embolden,
  We can but creep and sing
And watch through heaven's waste hollow
The flight no sight may follow
To the utter bourne beholden
  Of none that lack thy wing:
And we, whom dreams embolden,
  We can but creep and sing.

* * * * *

Ah, well were I for ever,
  Wouldst thou change lives with me,

And take my song's wild honey,
And give me back thy sunny
Wide eyes that weary never,
    And wings that search the sea;
Ah, well were I for ever,
    Wouldst thou change lives with me.

PARSON DARBY

The old lighthouse on Beachy Head, the Belle Tout, which first flung its beams abroad in 1831, has just been superseded by the new lighthouse built on the shore under the cliff. Near the new lighthouse is Parson Darby's Hole—a cavern in the cliff said to have been hewed out by the Rev. Jonathan Darby of East Dean as a refuge from the tongue of Mrs. Darby. Another account credits the parson with the wish to provide a sanctuary for shipwrecked sailors, whom he guided thither on stormy nights by torches. In a recent Sussex story by Mr. Horace Hutchinson, called *A Friend of Nelson*, we find the cave in the hands of a powerful smuggler, mysterious and accomplished as Lavengro, some years after Darby's death.

UNDER BEACHY HEAD

A pleasant walk from Eastbourne is to Birling Gap, a great smuggling centre in the old days, where the Downs dip for a moment to the level of the sea. Here at low tide one may walk under the cliffs. Richard Jefferies, in the essay from which I have already quoted, has a beautiful passage of reflections beneath the great bluff:—"The sea seems higher than the spot where I stand, its surface on a higher level—raised like a green mound—as if it could burst in and occupy the space up to the foot of the cliff in a moment. It will not do so, I know; but there is an infinite possibility about the sea; it may do what it is not recorded to have done. It is not to be ordered, it may overleap the bounds human observation has fixed for it. It has a potency unfathomable. There is still something in it not quite grasped and understood—something still to be discovered—a mystery.

"So the white spray rushes along the low broken wall of rocks, the sun gleams on the flying fragments of the wave, again it sinks, and the rhythmic motion holds the mind, as an invisible force holds back the tide. A faith of expectancy, a sense that something may drift up from the unknown, a large belief in the unseen resources of the endless space out yonder, soothes the mind with dreamy hope.

"The little rules and little experiences, all the petty ways of narrow life, are shut off behind by the ponderous and impassable cliff; as if we had dwelt in the dim light of a cave, but coming out at last to look at the sun, a great stone had fallen and closed the entrance, so that there was no return to the shadow. The impassable precipice shuts off our former selves of yesterday, forcing us to look out over the sea only, or up to the deeper heaven.

"These breadths draw out the soul; we feel that we have wider thoughts than we knew; the soul has been living, as it were, in a nutshell, all unaware of its own power, and now suddenly finds freedom in the sun and the sky. Straight, as if sawn down from turf to beach, the cliff shuts off the human world, for the sea knows no time and no era; you cannot tell what century it is from the face of the sea. A Roman trireme suddenly rounding the white edge-line of chalk, borne on wind and oar from the Isle of Wight towards the gray castle at Pevensey (already old in olden days), would not seem strange. What wonder could surprise us coming from the wonderful sea?"

BEACHY HEAD FROM THE SHORE.

EAST DEAN

The road from Birling Gap runs up the valley to East Dean and Friston, two villages among the Downs. Parson Darby's church at East Dean is small and not particularly interesting; but it gave Horsfield, the county historian, the opportunity to make one of his infrequent jokes. "There are three bells," he writes, "and 'if discord's harmony not understood,' truly harmonious ones." Horsfield does not note that one of these three bells bore a Latin motto which being translated signifies

Surely no bell beneath the sky
Can send forth better sounds than I?

The East Dean register contains a curious entry which is quoted in Grose's *Olio*, ed. 1796:—"Agnes Payne, the daughter of Edward Payne, was buried on the *first day of February*. Johan Payne, the daughter of Edward Payne, was buried on the *first day of February*.

"In the death of these two sisters last mentioned is one thing worth recording, and diligently to be noted. 'The elder sister, called Agnes, being very sicke unto death, *speechless*, and, as was thought, past hope of speakinge; after she had lyen twenty-four hours without speach, at last upon a suddayne cryed out to her sister to make herself ready and to come with her. Her sister Johan being abroad about other business, was called for, who being come to her sicke sister, demaundinge how she did, she very lowde or earnestly bade her sister make ready—she staid for her, and could not go without her. Within half an houre after, Johan was taken very sicke, which increasinge all the night uppone her, her other sister stille callinge her to come away; in the morninge they both departed this wretched world together. O the unsearchable wisdom of God! How deepe are his judgments, and his ways past fyndinge out!

"Testified by diverse oulde and honest persons yet living; which I myself have heard their father, when he was alive, report.

"Arthur Polland, Vicar; Henry Homewood, John Pupp, Churchwardens."

THE SELWYN MONUMENT

FRISTON PLACE

Friston church is interesting, for it contains one of the most beautiful monuments in Sussex, worthy to be remembered with that to the Shurleys at Isfield. The family commemorated is the Selwyns, and the monument has a very charming dado of six kneeling daughters and three babies laid neatly on a tasseled cushion, under the reading desk—a quaint conceit impossible to be carried out successfully in these days, but pretty and fitting enough then. Of the last of the Selwyns, "Ultimus Selwynorum," who died aged twenty, in 1704, it is said, with that exquisite simplicity of exaggeration of which the secret also has been lost, that for him "the very marble might weep." Friston Place, the home of the Selwyns, has some noble timbers, and a curious old donkey-well in the garden.

West Dean, which is three miles to the west, by a bleak and lonely road amid hills and valleys, is just a farm yard, with remains of very ancient architecture among the barns and ricks. The village, however, is more easily reached from Alfriston than Eastbourne.

CHAPTER XXXV

PEVENSEY AND HURSTMONCEUX

A well-behaved castle—Rail and romance—Britons, Romans, Saxons and Normans at Pevensey—William the Conqueror—A series of sieges—The first English letter—Andrew Borde, the jester, again—Pevensey gibes—A red brick castle—Hurstmonceux church—The tomb of the Dacres.—Two Hurstmonceux clerics—The de Fiennes and the de Monceux—A spacious home—The ghost—The unfortunate Lord Dacre—Horace Walpole at Hurstmonceux—The trug industry.

Pevensey Castle behaves as a castle should: it rises from the plain, the only considerable eminence for miles; it has noble grey walls of the true romantic hue and thickness; it can be seen from the sea, over which it once kept guard; it has a history rich in assailants and defenders. There is indeed nothing in its disfavour except the proximity of the railway, which has been allowed to pass nearer the ruin than dramatic fitness would dictate. Let it, however, be remembered that the railway through the St. Pancras Priory at Lewes led to the discovery of the coffins of William de Warenne and Gundrada, and also that, in Mr. Kipling's phrase, romance, so far from being at enmity with the iron horse, "brought up the 9.15."

PEVENSEY CASTLE.

Pevensey, which is now divided from the channel by marshy fields with nothing to break the flatness but Martello towers (thirteen may be counted from the walls), was, like Bramber Castle in the west, now also an inland stronghold, once washed and surrounded by the sea. The sea probably covered all the ground as far inland as Hailsham—Pevensey, Horseye, Rickney and the other "eyes" on the level, being then islands, as their termination suggests.

There is now no doubt but that Pevensey was the Anderida of the Romans, a city on the borders of the great forest of Anderida that covered the Weald of Sussex—Andreas Weald as it was called by the Saxons. But before the Romans a British stronghold existed here. This, after the Romans left, was attacked by the Saxons, who slew every Briton that they found therein. The Saxons in their turn being discomfited, the Normans built a new castle within the old walls, with Robert de Moreton, half brother of the Conqueror, for its lord. Thus the castle as it now stands is in its outer walls Roman, in its inner, Norman.

WILLIAM'S LANDING

Unlike certain other Sussex fortresses, Pevensey has seen work. Of its Roman career we know nothing, except that the inhabitants seem to have dropped a large number of coins, many of which have been dug up. The Saxons, as we have seen, massacred the Britons at Anderida very thoroughly. Later, in 1042, Swane, son of Earl Godwin, swooped on Pevensey's port in the Danish manner and carried off a number of ships. In 1049 Earl Godwin, and another son, Harold, made a second foray, carried off more ships, and fired the town. On September 28, 1066, Pevensey saw a more momentous landing, destined to be fatal to this marauding Harold; for on that day William, Duke of Normandy, soon to become William the Conqueror, alighted from his vessel, accompanied by several hundred Frenchmen in black chain armour. A representation of the landing is one of the designs in the Bayeux tapestry. The embroiderers take no count of William's fall as he stepped ashore, on ground now grazed upon by cattle, an accident deemed unlucky until his ready wit explained, as he rose with sanded fingers, "See, I have seized the land with my hands."

Pevensey's later history included sieges by William Rufus in 1088, when Odo, Bishop of Bayeux, supporter of Robert, was the defender; by Stephen in 1144, the fortress being held by Maude, who gave in eventually to famine; by Simon de Montfort and the Barons in 1265; and by the supporters of Richard of York in 1399, when Lady Pelham defended it for the Rose of Lancaster. A little later Edmund, Duke of York, was imprisoned in it, and was so satisfied with his gaoler that he bequeathed him £20. Queen Joan of Navarre, wife of Henry IV., was also a prisoner here for nine years. In the year before the Armada, Pevensey Castle was ordered to be either rebuilt as a fortress or razed to the ground; but fortunately neither instruction was carried out.

The present owner of Pevensey Castle is the Duke of Devonshire, who by virtue of the possession is entitled to call himself Dominus Aquilæ, or Lord of the Eagle.

LETTER-WRITING

Pevensey has another and gentler claim to notice. Many essayists have said pleasant and ingenious things about the art of letter-writing; but none of them mentions the part played by Pevensey in the English development of that agreeable accomplishment. Yet the earliest specimen of English letter-writing that exists was penned in Pevensey Castle. The writer was Joan Crownall, Lady Pelham, wife of Sir John Pelham, who, as I have said, defended the castle, in her Lord's absence, against the Yorkists, and this is the letter, penned (I write in 1903) five hundred and four years ago. (It has no postscript.)

My dear Lord,—I recommend me to your high Lordship, with heart and body and all my poor might. And with all this I thank you as my dear Lord, dearest and best beloved of all earthly lords. I say for me, and thank you, my dear Lord, with all this that I said before of [for] your comfortable letter that you sent me from Pontefract, that came to me on Mary Magdalen's day: for by my troth I was never so glad as when I heard by your letter that ye were strong enough with the grace of God for to keep you from the malice of your enemies. And, dear Lord, if it like to your high Lordship that as soon as ye might that I might hear of your gracious speed, which God Almighty continue and increase. And, my dear Lord, if it like you to know *my* fare, I am here laid by in manner of a siege with the county of Sussex, Surrey, and a great parcel of Kent, so that I may not [go] out nor no victuals get me, but with much hard. Wherefore, my dear, if it like you by the advice of your wise counsel for to set remedy of the salvation of your Castle and withstand the malice of the Shires aforesaid. And

376

also that ye be fully informed of the great malice-workers in these shires which have so despitefully wrought to you, and to your Castle, to your men and to your tenants; for this country have they wasted for a great while.

"Farewell, my dear Lord! the Holy Trinity keep you from your enemies, and soon send me good tidings of you. Written at Pevensey, in the Castle, on St. Jacob's day last past.

"By your own poor
"J. PELHAM."
"To my true Lord."

ANDREW BORDE AGAIN

In the town of Pevensey once lived Andrew Borde (who entered this world at Cuckfield): a thorn in the side of municipal dignity. The Dogberryish dictum "I am still but a man, although Mayor of Pevensey," remains a local joke, and tradition has kept alive the prowess of the Pevensey jury which brought a verdict of manslaughter against one who was charged with stealing breeches; both jokes of Andrew's. Borde's house, whither, it is said, Edward VI. once came on a visit to the jester, still stands. The oak room in which Andrew welcomed the youthful king is shown at a cost of threepence per head, and you may buy pictorial postcards and German wooden toys in the wit's front parlour.

Before leaving Pevensey I must say a word of Westham, the village which adjoins it. Westham and Pevensey are practically one, the castle intervening. Westham has a vicar whose interest in his office might well be imitated by some of the other vicars of the county. His noble church, one of the finest in Sussex, with a tower of superb strength and dignity, is kept open, and just within is a table on which are a number of copies of a little penny history of Westham which he has prepared, and for the payment of which he is so eccentric as to trust to the stranger's honesty.

The tower, which the vicar tells us is six hundred years old, he asks us to admire for its "utter carelessness and scorn of smoothness and finish, or any of the tricks of modern buildings." Westham church was one of the first that the Conqueror built, and remains of the original Norman structure are still serviceable. The vicar suggests that it may very possibly have stood a siege. In the jamb of the south door of the Norman wall is a sundial, without which, one might say, no church is completely perfect. In the tower dwell unmolested a colony of owls, six of whom once attended a "reading-in" service and, seated side by side on a beam, listened with unwavering attention to the Thirty-Nine Articles. They were absent on my visit, but a small starling, swift and elusive as a spirit, flitted hither and thither quite happily.

WESTHAM.

ALES CRESSEL

In the churchyard is the grave of one Ales Cressel (oddest of names), and among the epitaphs is this upon a Mr. Henty:—

Learn from this mistic sage to live or die.

Well did he love at evening's social hour
The Sacred Volume's treasure to apply.

The remembrance of his excellent character alone reconciles his afflicted widow to her irreparable loss.

The church contains a memorial to a young gentleman named Fagg who, "having lived to adorn Human Nature by his exemplary manners, was untimely snatched away, aged 24."

In the neighbourhood of Westham is a large rambling building known as Priesthaus, which, once a monastery, is now a farm. Many curious relics of its earlier state have lately been unearthed.

In Pevensey church, which has none of the interest of Westham, a little collection of curiosities relating to Pevensey—a constable's staff, old title deeds, seals, and so forth—is kept, in a glass case.

HURSTMONCEUX CASTLE.

HURSTMONCEUX CASTLE

If Pevensey is all that a castle ought to be, in shape, colour, position and past, Hurstmonceux is the reverse; for it lies low, it has no swelling contours, it is of red brick instead of grey stone, and never a fight has it seen. But any disappointment we may feel is the fault not of Hurstmonceux but of those who named it castle. Were it called Hurstmonceux House, or Place, or Manor, or Grange, all would be well. It is this use of the word castle (which in Sussex has a connotation excluding red brick) that has done Hurstmonceux an injustice, for it is a very imposing and satisfactory ruin, quite as interesting architecturally as Pevensey, or, indeed, any of the ruins that we have seen.

Hurstmonceux Castle stands on the very edge of Pevensey Level, the only considerable structure between Pevensey and the main land proper. In the intervening miles there are fields and fields, through which the Old Haven runs, plaintive plovers above them bemoaning their lot, and brown cows tugging at the rich grass. On the first hillock to the right of the castle as one fronts the south, rising like an island from this sea of pasturage, is Hurstmonceux church, whose shingled spire shoots into the sky, a beacon to travellers in the Level. It is a pretty church with an exterior of severe simplicity. Between the chancel and the chantry is the large tomb covering the remains of Thomas Fiennes, second Lord Dacre of Hurstmonceux, who died in 1534, and Sir Thomas Dacre his son, surmounted by life-size stone figures, each in full armour, with hands proudly raised, and each resting his feet against the Fiennes wolf-dog.

In the churchyard is the grave of Julius Hare, once vicar of Hurstmonceux, and the author, with his brother Augustus, of *Guesses at Truth*. Carlyle's John Sterling was Julius Hare's first curate here.

THE OLD SPACIOUSNESS

Hurstmonceux Castle was once the largest and handsomest of all the commoners' houses in the county. Sir Roger de Fiennes, a descendant of the John de Fiennes who married Maude, last of the de Monceux, in the reign of Edward II., built it in 1440. Though the Manor house of the de Monceux, on the site of the present castle, lacked the imposing qualities of Roger de Fiennes' stronghold, it was hospitable, spacious, and luxurious. Edward the First spent a night there in 1302. One of the de Monceux was on the side of de Montfort in the Battle of Lewes, and the first of them to settle in England married Edith, daughter of William de Warenne and Gundrada, of Lewes Castle.

How thorough and conscientious were the workmen employed by Roger de Fiennes, and how sound were their bricks and mortar, may be learned by the study of Hurstmonceux Castle to-day. In many parts the walls are absolutely uninjured except by tourists. The floors, however, have long since returned to nature, who has put forth her energies without stint to clothe the old apartments with greenery. Ivy of astonishing vigour grows here, populous with jackdaws, and trees and shrubs spring from the least likely spots.

The castle in its old completeness was, practically, a little town. From east to west its walls measured 206½ feet, from north to south, 214½; within them on the ground floor were larders, laundries, a brewhouse, a bakehouse, cellars, a dairy, offices, a guard room, pantries, a distillery, a confectionery room, a chapel, and, beneath, a dungeon. Between these were four open courts. Upstairs, round three sides of the Green Court, were the Bird Gallery, the Armour Gallery, and the Green Gallery, and lords' apartments and ladies' apartments "capable of quartering an army," to quote a writer on the subject. On each side of the entrance, gained by a drawbridge, was a tower—the Watch Tower and the Signal Tower.

In the reign of Elizabeth a survey of Hurstmonceux was taken, which tells us that in the park were two hundred deer, "four fair ponds" stocked with carp and tench, a "fair warren of conies," a heronry of 150 nests, and much game. The de Fiennes, or Dacres as they became, had also a private fishery in Pevensey Bay, seen from the Watch Tower as a strip of blue ribbon.

In addition Hurstmonceux had a ghost, who inhabited the Drummers' Hall, a room between the towers over the porter's lodge, and sent forth a mysterious tattoo. Sometimes he left his hall, this devilish musician, and strode along the battlements drumming and drumming, a terrible figure nine feet high. Most people were frightened, but there were those who said that the drummer was nothing more nor less than a gardener in league with the Pevensey smugglers, whose notes, rattled out on the parchment, rolled over the marsh and gave them the needful signal.

THE UNFORTUNATE LORD DACRE

Hurstmonceux once had a very real tragedy. The third Lord Dacre, one of the young noblemen who took part in the welcoming of Ann of Cleves when she landed in England preparatory to her becoming the wife of Henry VIII., was so foolish one night in 1541 as to accompany some of his roystering companions to the adjacent park of Sir Nicholas Pelham, near Hellingly, intent on a deer-stealing jest. There three gamekeepers rose up, and a bloody battle ensued in which one John Busbrig bit the dust. Pelham was furious and demanded justice, and Lord Dacre, though he had taken no part in the fray, was held responsible. Three of his friends were hanged at Tyburn, and, in spite of all the influence that was brought to bear, he also was executed. The next Dacre of importance married the Lady Ann Fitzroy, a natural daughter of Charles II., and was made Earl of Sussex. Financial losses compelling him to sell Hurstmonceux, a lawyer named George Naylor bought it in 1708, leaving it, on his death, to the Right Rev. Francis Hare, Bishop of Chichester. It remained in the family as a residence until, in 1777, an architect pronounced it unsafe, and the interior was converted into materials for the new Hurstmonceux Place in the park to the north-west. Since then nature has had her way with it.

WALPOLE AT HURSTMONCEUX

Horace Walpole's visit, as described in one of his letters, gives us an idea of Hurstmonceux in the middle of the eighteenth century, a little before it became derelict:—"The chapel is small, and mean; the Virgin and seven long lean saints, ill done, remain in the windows. There have been four more, but they seem to have been removed for light; and we actually found St. Catherine, and another gentlewoman with a church in her hand, exiled into the buttery. There remain two odd cavities, with very small wooden screens on each side the altar, which seem to have been confessionals. The outside is a mixture of grey brick and stone, that has a very venerable appearance. The draw-bridges are romantic to a degree; and there is a dungeon, that gives one a delightful idea of living in the days of soccage and under such goodly tenures. They showed us a dismal chamber which they called *Drummer's*-hall, and suppose that Mr. Addison's comedy is descended from it. In the windows of the gallery over the cloisters, which leads all round to the apartments, is the device of the Fienneses, a wolf holding a baton with a scroll, *Le roy le veut*—an unlucky motto, as I shall tell you presently, to the last peer of that line. The estate is two thousand a year, and so compact as to have but seventeen houses upon it. We walked up a brave old avenue to the church, with ships sailing on our left hand the whole way."

TRUGS

Hurstmonceux is famous not only for its castle, but for its "trugs," the wooden baskets that gardeners carry, which are associated with Hurstmonceux as crooks once were with Pyecombe, and the shepherds' vast green umbrellas, on cane frames, with Lewes.

CHAPTER XXXVI

HASTINGS

The ravening sea—Hastings and history—Titus Oates—Sir Cloudesley Shovel—A stalwart Nestor—Edward Capel—An old Sussex harvest custom—A poetical mayor—Picturesque Hastings—Hastings castle—Hollington Rural and Charles Lamb—Fairlight Glen and the Lover's Seat—Bexhill.

Brighton, as we have seen, was made by Dr. Russell. It was Dr. Baillie, some years later, who discovered the salubrious qualities of Hastings. In 1806, when the Duke of Wellington (then Major-General Wellesley) was in command of twelve thousand soldiers encamped in the neighbourhood, and was himself living at Hastings House, the population of the town was less than four thousand; to-day, with St. Leonard's and dependant suburbs, Hastings covers several square miles. With the exception of the little red and grey region known as Old Hastings, between Castle Hill and East Hill, the same charge of a lack of what is interesting can be brought against Hastings as against Brighton; but whereas Brighton has the Downs to offer, Hastings is backed by country of far less charm. Perhaps her greatest merit is her proximity to Winchelsea and Rye.

Hastings, once one of the proudest of the Cinque Ports, has no longer even a harbour, its pleasure yachts, which carry excursionists on brief Channel voyages, having to be beached just like rowing boats. The ravages of the sea, which have so transformed the coast line of Sussex, have completely changed this town; and from a stately seaport she has become a democratic watering place. Beneath the waves lie the remains of an old Priory and possibly of not a few churches.

Hastings has been very nigh to history more than once, but she has escaped the actual making of it. Even the great battle that takes its name from the town was fought seven miles away, while the Duke of Normandy, as we have seen, landed as far distant as Pevensey, ten miles in the west. But he used Hastings as a victualling centre. Again and again, in its time, Hastings has been threatened with invasion by the French, who did actually land in 1138 and burned the town. And one Sunday morning in 1643, Colonel Morley of Glynde, the Parliamentarian, marched in with his men and confiscated all arms. But considering its warlike mien, Hastings has done little.

THE ADMIRAL'S MOTHER

Nor can the seaport claim any very illustrious son. Titus Oates, it is true, was curate of All Saints church in 1674, his father being vicar; and among the inhabitants of the old town was the mother of Sir Cloudesley Shovel, the admiral. A charming account of a visit paid to her by her son is given in De la Prynne's diary: "I heard a gentleman say, who was in the ship with him about six years ago, that as they were sailing over against the town, of Hastings, in Sussex, Sir Cloudesley called out, 'Pilot, put near; I have a little business on shore.' So he put near, and Sir Cloudesley and this gentleman went to shore in a small boat, and having walked about half a mile, Sir Cloudesley came to a little house [in All Saints Street], 'Come,' says he, 'my business is here; I came on purpose to see the good woman of this house.' Upon this they knocked at the door, and out came a poor old woman, upon which Sir Cloudesley kissed her, and then falling down on his knees, begged her blessing, and calling her mother (who had removed out of Yorkshire hither). He was mightily kind to her, and she to him, and after that he had made his visit, he left her ten guineas, and took his leave with tears in his eyes and departed to his ship."

THE CHURCH MILITANT

Hastings had a famous rector at the beginning of the last century, in the person of the Rev. Webster Whistler, who combined with the eastern benefice that of Newtimber, near Hurstpierpoint, and managed to serve both to a great age. He lived to be eighty-four and died full of vigour in 1831. In 1817, following upon a quarrel with the squire, the Newtimber living was put up for auction in London. Mr. Whistler decided to be present, but anonymous. The auctioneer mentioned in his introduction the various charms of the benefice, ending with the superlative advantage that it was held by an aged and infirm clergyman with one foot in the grave. At this point the proceedings were interrupted by a large and powerful figure in clerical costume springing on the table and crying out to the company: "Now, gentlemen, do I look like a man tottering on the brink of the grave? My left leg gives me no sign of weakness, and as for the other, Mr. Auctioneer, if you repeat your remarks you will find it very much at your service." The living found no purchaser.

Mr. Whistler had a Chinese indifference to the necessary end of all things, which prompted him to use an aged yew tree in his garden, that had long given him shade but must now be felled, as material for his coffin. This coffin he placed at the foot of his bed as a chest for clothes until its proper purpose was fulfilled.

Hastings was also the home of Edward Capel, a Shakespeare-editor of the eighteenth century. Capel, who is said to have copied out in his own hand the entire works of the poet no fewer than ten times, was the designer of his own house, which seems to have been a miracle of discomfort. He was an eccentric of the most determined character, so much so that he gradually lost all friends. According to Horsfield, "The spirit of nicety and refinement prevailed in it [his house] so much during his lifetime, that when a friend (a baronet) called upon him on a tour, he was desired to leave his cane in the vestibule, lest he should either dirt the floor with it, or soil the carpet."

HARVEST HOME

One does not think naturally of old Sussex customs in connection with this town, so thoroughly urban as it now is and so largely populated by visitors, but I find in the Sussex Archæological Collections the following interesting account, by a Hastings alderman, of an old harvest ceremony in the neighbourhood:—"At the head of the table one of the men occupied the position of chairman; in front of him stood a pail—clean as wooden staves and iron hoops could be made by human labour. At his right sat four or five men who led the singing, grave as judges were they; indeed, the appearance of the whole assembly was one of the greatest solemnity, except for a moment or two when some unlucky wight failed to 'turn the cup over,' and was compelled to undergo the penalty in that case made and provided. This done, all went on as solemnly as before.

"The ceremony, if I may call it so, was this: The leader, or chairman, standing behind the pail with a tall horn cup in his hand, filled it with beer from the pail. The man next to him on the left stood up, and holding a hat with both hands by the brim, crown upwards, received the cup from the chairman, on the crown of the hat, not touching it with either hand. He then lifted the cup to his lips by raising the hat, and slowly drank off the contents. As soon as he began to drink, the chorus struck up this chant:

I've bin to Plymouth and I've bin to Dover.
I have bin rambling, boys, all the wurld over—
    Over and over and over and over,
Drink up yur liquor and turn yur cup over;
    Over and over and over and over,
The liquor's drink'd up and the cup is turned over.

"The man drinking was expected to time his draught so as to empty his cup at the end of the fourth line of the chant; he was then to return the hat to the perpendicular, still holding the hat by the brim, then to throw the cup into the air, and reversing the hat, to catch the cup in it as it fell. If he failed to perform this operation, the fellow workmen who were closely watching him, made an important alteration in the last line of their chant, which in that case ran thus:

The liquor's drink'd up and the cup *aint* turned over.

"The cup was then refilled and the unfortunate drinker was compelled to go through the same ceremony again. Every one at the table took the cup and 'turned it over' in succession, the chief shepherd keeping the pail constantly supplied with beer. The parlour guests were of course invited to turn the cup over with the guests of the kitchen, and went through the ordeal with more or less of success. For my own part, I confess that I failed to catch the cup in the hat at the first trial and had to try again; the chairman, however, mercifully gave me only a small quantity of beer the second time."

THE MAYOR'S PRETTY LAMENT

The civic life of Hastings would seem to encourage literature, for I find also in one of the Archæological Society's volumes, the following pretty lines by John Collier—Mayor of Hastings in 1719, 22, 30, 37, and 41—on his little boy's death:

Ah, my poor son! Ah my tender child,
My unblown flower and now appearing sweet,
If yet your gentle soul flys in the air
And is not fixt in doom perpetual,
Hover about me with your airy wings
And hear your Father's lamentation.

Hastings has two advantages over both Brighton and Eastbourne: it can produce a genuine piece of antiquity, and seen from the sea it has a picturesque quality that neither of those towns possesses. Indeed, under certain conditions of light, Hastings is magnificent, with the craggy Castle Hill in its midst surmounted by its imposing ruin. The smoke of the town, rising and spreading, shrouds the modernity of the sea front, and the castle on its commanding height seems to be brooding over the shores of old romance. Brighton has no such effect as this.

THE FIRST TOURNAMENT

Of the Castle little is known. It was probably built on the site of Roman fortifications, by the Comte d'Eu, who came over with the Conqueror. The first tournament in England is said to have been held there, with Adela, daughter of the Conqueror, as Queen of Beauty. After the castle had ceased to be of any use as a stronghold it was still maintained as a religious house. It is now a pleasure resort. The ordinary visitor to Hastings is, however, more interested by the caves in the hill below, originally made by diggers of sand and afterwards used by smugglers.

Before branching out from Hastings into the country proper I might mention two neighbouring points of pilgrimage. One is Hollington Rural church, on the hill behind the town, whither sooner or later every one walks. It is a small church in the midst of a crowded burial ground, and it is difficult to understand its attraction unless by the poverty of other objectives. I should not mention it, but that it is probably the church to which Charles Lamb, bored by Hastings itself, wended his way one day in 1825. He describes it, in terms more fitting to, say, Lullington church near Alfriston, or St. Olave's at Chichester, in no fewer than three of his letters. This is the best passage, revelling in a kind of inverted exaggeration, as written to John Bates Dibdin, at Hastings, in 1826:—"Let me hear that you have clamber'd up to Lover's Seat; it is as fine in that neighbourhood as Juan Fernandez, as lonely too, when the Fishing boats are not out; I have sat for hours, staring upon the shipless sea. The salt sea is never so grand as when it is left to itself. One cock-boat spoils it. A sea mew or two improves it. And go to the little church, which is a very protestant Loretto, and seems dropt by some angel for the use of a hermit, who was at once parishioner and a whole parish. It is not too big. Go in the night, bring it away in your portmanteau, and I will plant it in my garden. It must have been erected in the very infancy of British Christianity, for the two or three first converts; yet hath it all the appertances of a church of the first magnitude, its pulpit, its pews, its baptismal font; a cathedral in a nutshell. Seven people would crowd it like a Caledonian Chapel. The minister that divides the word there, must give lumping pennyworths. It is built to the text of two or three assembled in my name. It reminds me of the grain of mustard seed. If the glebe land is proportionate, it may yield two potatoes. Tythes out of it could be no more split than a hair. Its First fruits must be its Last, for 'twould never produce a couple. It is truly the strait and narrow way, and few there be (of London visitants) that find it. The still small voice is surely to be found there, if any where. A sounding board is merely there for ceremony. It is secure from earthquakes, not more from sanctity than size, for 'twould feel a mountain thrown upon it no more than a taper-worm would. Go and see, but not without your spectacles."

THE LOVER'S SEAT

The Lover's Seat, mentioned in the first sentence of the above passage, is at Fairlight, about two miles east of Hastings. The seat is very prettily situated high in a ledge in Fairlight Glen. Horsfield shall tell the story that gave the spot its fascinating name:—

"A beautiful girl at Rye gained the affections of Captain—, then in command of a cutter in that station. Her parents disapproved the connection and removed her to a farm house near the Lover's Seat, called the Warren-house. Hence she contrived to absent herself night after night, when she sought this spot, and by means of a light made known her presence to her lover, who was cruising off in expectation of her arrival. The difficulties thus thrown in their way increased the ardour of their attachment and marriage was determined upon at all hazards. Hollington Church was and is the place most sought for on these occasions in this part of the country; it has a romantic air about it which is doubtless peculiarly impressive. There are, too, some other reasons why so many matches are solemnized here; and all combined to make this the place selected by this pair. It was expected that the lady's flight would be discovered and her object suspected; but in order to prevent a rescue, the cutter's crew positively volunteered and acted as guards on the narrow paths leading through the woods to the church. However, the marriage ceremony was completed before any unwelcome visitors arrived, and reconciliation soon followed."

BEXHILL

Bexhill has now become so exceedingly accessible by conveyance from Hastings that it might perhaps be mentioned here as a contiguous place of interest; but of Bexhill, till lately a village, or Bexhill-on-Sea, watering place, with everything handsome about it, there is little to say. Both the tide of the Channel and of popularity seem to be receding. Inland there is some pretty country.

CHAPTER XXXVII

BATTLE ABBEY

Le Souvenir Normande—The Battle of Hastings—Normans and Saxons on the eve—Taillefer—The battle cries—The death of Harold—Harold's body: three stories—The field of blood—Building the Abbey—The Abbot's privileges—Royal visitors—A great feast—The suppression of the Abbey—Present-day Battle—An incredible butler—Ashburnham—The last forge—Ninfield—Crowhurst.

The principal excursion from Hastings is of course to Battle, whither a company of discreetly satisfied Normans—Le Souvenir Normande—recently travelled, to view with tactfully chastened enthusiasm the scene of the triumph of 1066; to erect a memorial; and to perplex the old ladies of Battle who provide tea. Except on one day of the week visitors to Battle must content themselves with tea (of which there is no stint) and a view of the gateway, for the rule of showing the Abbey only on Tuesdays is strictly enforced by the American gentleman who now resides on this historic site. But the gateway could hardly be finer.

BATTLE CRIES

The battle-field was half a mile south of the Abbey, on Telham hill, where in Harold's day was a hoary apple tree. We have seen William landing at Pevensey on September 28, 1066: thence he marched to Hastings "to steal food," and thence, after a delay of a fortnight (to some extent spent in fortifying Hastings, and also in burning his boats), he marched to Telham hill. That was on October 13. On the same day Harold reached the neighbourhood, with his horde of soldiers and armed rustics, and both armies encamped that night only a mile apart, waiting for the light to begin the fray. The Saxons were confident and riotous; the Normans hopeful and grave. According to Wace, "all night the Saxons might be seen carousing, gambolling, and dancing and singing: *bublie* they cried, and *wassail*, and *laticome* and *drinkheil* and *drink-to-me*!"

BATTLE ABBEY, THE GATEWAY.

At daybreak in the Norman camp Bishop Odo celebrated High Mass, and immediately after was hurried into his armour to join the fight. As the Duke was arming an incident occurred but for which Battle Abbey might never have been built. His suit of mail was offered him wrong side out. The superstitious Normans standing by looked sideways at each other with sinking misgiving. They deemed it a bad omen. But William's face betrayed no fear. "If we win," he said, "and God send we may, I will found an Abbey here for the salvation of the souls of all who fall in the engagement." Before quitting his tent, he was careful that those relics on which Harold had sworn never to oppose his efforts against England's throne should be hung around his neck.

TAILLEFER

So the two armies were ready—the mounted Normans, with their conical helmets gleaming in the hazy sunlight, with kite-shaped shields, huge spears and swords; the English, all on foot, with heavy axes and clubs. But theirs was a defensive part; the Normans had to begin. It fell to the lot of a wild troubadour named Taillefer to open the fight. He galloped from the Norman lines at full speed, singing a song of heroes; then checked his steed and tossed his lance thrice in the air, thrice catching it by the point. The opposing lines silently wondered. Then he flung it at a luckless Saxon with all the energy of a madman, spitting him as a skewer spits a lark. Taillefer had now only his sword left. This also he threw thrice into the air, and then seizing it with the grip of death he rode straight at the Saxon troops, dealing blows from left to right, and so was lost to view.

Thus the Battle of Hastings began. "On them in God's name," cried William, "and chastise these English for their misdeeds." "Dieu aidé," his men screamed, spurring to the attack. "Out, Out!" barked the English, "Holy Cross! God Almighty!" The carnage was terrific. It seemed for long that the English were prevailing; and they would, in all likelihood, have prevailed in the end had they kept their position. But William feigned a retreat, and the English crossed their vallum in pursuit. The Normans at once turned their horses and pursued and butchered the unprepared enemy singly in the open country. A complete rout followed. The false step was decisive.

THE DEATH OF HAROLD

Not till night, however, did Harold fall. He upheld his standard to the last, hedged about by a valiant bodyguard who resisted the Normans till every sign of life was battered out of them. The story of the vertically-discharged arrows is a myth. An eye-witness thus described Harold's death: "An armed man," said he, "came in the throng of the battle and struck him on the ventaille of the helmet and beat him to the ground; and as he sought to recover himself a knight beat him down again, striking him on the thick of the thigh down to the bone." So died Harold, on the exact site of the high altar of the Abbey, and so passed away the Saxon kingdom.

That night, William, who was unharmed, though three horses were killed under him, had his tent set up in the midst of the dead, and there he ate and drank. In the morning the Norman corpses were picked out and buried with due rites; the Saxons were left to rot. According to the *Carmen* William I. had Harold's body wrapped in purple linen and carried to Hastings, where it was buried on the cliff beneath a stone inscribed with the words: "By the order of the Duke, you rest here, King Harold, as the guardian of the shore and the sea." Mr. Lower was convinced of the truth of that story; but William of Malmesbury says that William sent Harold's body to his mother the Countess Gytha, who buried it at Waltham, while a third account shows us Editha of the Swan Neck, Harold's wife, wandering through the blood-stained grass, among the fallen English, until she found the body of her husband, which she craved leave to carry away. William, this version adds, could not deny her.

THE FIELD OF BLOOD

Fuller writes in the *Worthies*, concerning the wonders of Sussex:—"Expect not here I should insert what *William* of *Newbury* writeth (to be recounted rather amongst the *Untruths* than *Wonders*); viz. 'That in this County, not far from Battail-Abby, in the Place where so great a slaughter of the Englishmen was made, after any shower, presently sweateth forth very fresh blood out of the Earth, as if the evidence thereof did plainly declare the voice of Bloud there shed, and crieth still from the Earth unto the Lord.' This is as true, as that in *white* chalky Countries (about Baldock in Hertfordshire) after rain run rivolets of *Milk*; Neither being anything else than the Water discoloured, according to the *Complexion* of the Earth thereabouts."

MOUNT STREET, BATTLE.

The Conqueror was true to his vow, and the Abbey of St. Martin was quickly begun. At first there was difficulty about the stone, which was brought all the way from Caen quarries, until, according to an old writer, a pious matron dreamed that stone in large quantities was to be found near at hand. Her vision leading to the discovery of a neighbouring quarry, the work proceeded henceforward with exceeding rapidity.

ST. MARTIN'S ABBEY

Although the first Abbot was appointed in 1076, William the Conqueror did not live to see the Abbey finished. Sixty monks of the Order of St. Benedict came to Battle from the Abbey of Marmontier in Normandy, to form its nucleus. It was left to William Rufus to preside over the consecration of Battle, which was not until February, 1095, when the ceremony was performed amid much pomp. William presented to the Abbey his father's coronation robe and the sword he had wielded in the battle. Several wealthy manors were attached and the country round was exempted from tax; while the Abbots were made superior to episcopal control, and were endowed with the right to sit in Parliament and a London house to live in during the session. Indeed nothing was left undone that could minister to the pride and power of the new house of God.

The Abbey of St. Martin was quadrangular, standing in the midst of a circle nine miles round. Within this were vineyards, stew ponds and rich land. Just without was a small street of artisans' dwellings, where were manufactured all things requisite for the monks' material well-being. The church was the largest in the country, larger even than Canterbury. It was also a sanctuary, any sentenced criminal who succeeded in sheltering therein receiving absolution from the Abbot. The high altar, as I have said, was erected precisely on the spot where Harold fell: a spot on which one may now stand and think of the past.

Battle Abbey was more than once visited by kings. In 1200 John was there, shaking like a quicksand. He brought a piece of our Lord's sepulchre, which had been wrested from Palestine by Richard the Lion Heart, and laid it with tremulous hands on the altar, hoping that the magnificence of the gift might close Heaven's eyes towards sins of his own. In 1212, he was at Battle Abbey again, and for the last time in 1213, seeking, maybe, to find in these silent cloisters some forgetfulness of the mutterings of hate and scorn that everywhere followed him.

Just before the Battle of Lewes, Henry III. galloped up, attended by a body-guard of overbearing horsemen, and levied large sums of money to assist him in the struggle. After the battle he returned, a weary refugee, but still rapacious.

These visits were not welcome. It was different when Edward II. slept there on the night of August 28th, 1324. Alan de Ketbury, the Abbot, was bent on showing loyalty at all cost, while the neighbouring lords and squires were hardly less eager. The Abbot's contribution to the kitchen included twenty score and four loaves of bread, two swans, two rabbits, three fessantes, and a dozen capons; William de Echingham sent three peacocks, twelve bream, six muttons, and other delicacies; and Robert Acheland four rabbits, six swans, and three herons.

In 1331, Abbot Hamo and his monks kept at bay a body of French marauders, who had landed at Rye, until the country gentlemen could assemble and repulse them utterly.

Then followed two peaceful centuries; but afterwards came disaster, for, in 1558, Thomas Cromwell sent down two commissioners to examine into the state of the Abbey and report thereon to the zealous Defender of the Faith. The Commissioners found nineteen books in the library, and rumours of monkish debauchery without the walls. "So beggary a house," wrote one of the officers, "I never see." Battle Abbey was therefore suppressed and presented to Sir Anthony Browne, upon whom, as we saw in the first *chapter*, the "Curse of Cowdray" was pronounced by the last departing monk.

To catalogue the present features of Battle Abbey is to vulgarise it. One comes away with confused memories of grey walls embraced by white clematis and red rose; gloomy underground caverns with double rows of arches, where the Brothers might not speak; benignant cedars blessing the turf with extended hands; fragrant limes waving their delicate leaves; an old rose garden with fantastic beds; a long yew walk where the Brothers might meditatively pace—turning, perhaps, an epigram, regretting, perhaps, the world. Nothing now remains of the Refectory, where, of old, forty monks fed like one, except the walls. It once had a noble roof of Irish oak, but that was taken to Cowdray and perished in the fire there, together with the Abbey roll. One of the Abbey's first charms is the appropriateness of its gardens; they too are old. In the cloisters, for instance, there are wonderful box borders.

BATTLE ABBEY. THE REFECTORY.

TURNER'S PICTURE

Turner painted "Battle Abbey: the spot where Harold fell," with a greyhound pressing hard upon a hare in the foreground, and a Scotch fir Italianated into a golden bough.

The town of Battle has little interest. In the church is a brass to Thomas Alfraye and his wife Elizabeth—Thomas Alfraye "whose soul" according to his epitaph,

In active strength did passe
As nere was found his peere.

400

One would like to know more of this Samson. The tomb of Sir Anthony Browne is also here; but it is not so imposing as that of his son, the first Viscount Montagu, which we saw at Easebourne. In the churchyard is the grave of Isaac Ingall, the oldest butler on record, who died at the age of one hundred and twenty, after acting as butler at the Abbey for ninety-five years.

From Battle one may reach easily Normanhurst, the seat of the Brasseys, and Ashburnham Park, just to the north of it, a superb undulating domain, with lakes, an imposing mansion, an old church, brake fern, magnificent trees and a herd of deer, all within its confines. Of the church, however, I can say nothing, for I was there on a very hot day, the door was locked, and the key was at the vicarage, ten minutes' distant, at the top of a hill. Churches that are thus controlled must be neglected.

ASHBURNHAM

Ashburnham Place once contained some of the finest books in England and is still famous for its relics of Charles I.; but strangers may not see them. The best Sussex iron was smelted at Ashburnham Furnace, north of the park, near Penhurst. Ashburnham Forge was the last to remain at work in the county; its last surviving labourer of the neighbourhood died in 1883. He remembered the extinguishing of the fire in 1813 (or 1811), the casting of fire-backs being the final task. Penhurst, by the way, is one of the most curiously remote villages in east Sussex, with the oddest little church.

I walked to Ashburnham from Ninfield, a clean breezy village on the hill overlooking Pevensey Bay, with a locked church, and iron stocks by the side of the road. It is stated somewhere that at "that corner of Crouch Lane that leads to Lunford Cross, and so to Bexhill and Hastings," was buried a suicide in 1675. At how many cross roads in Sussex and elsewhere does one stand over such graves?

CROWHURST

One may return to Hastings by way of Catsfield, which has little interest, and Crowhurst, famous for the remains of a beautiful manor house and a yew tree supposed to be the oldest in Sussex. It is curious that Crowhurst in Surrey is also known for a great yew.

CHAPTER XXXVIII

WINCHELSEA AND RYE

Medieval Sussex—The suddenness of Rye—The approach by night—
Cities of the plain—Old Winchelsea—The freakish sea—New
Winchelsea—The eternal French problem—Modern Winchelsea—
The Alard tombs—Denis Duval and the Westons—John Wesley—Old
Rye—John Fletcher—The Jeakes'—An unknown poet—Rye church—
The eight bells—Rye's streets—Rye ancient and modern—A Rye
ceramist—Pett—Icklesham's accounts—A complacent epitaph—Iden
and Playden—Udimore's church—Brede Place—The Oxenbridges—
Dean Swift as a baby.

In the opinion of many good judges Sussex has nothing to offer
so fascinating as Winchelsea and Rye; and in certain reposeful moods,
when the past seems to be more than the present or future, I can agree
with them. We have seen many ancient towns in our progress through
the county—Chichester around her cathedral spire, Arundel beneath
her grey castle, Lewes among her hills—but all have modern blood in
their veins. Winchelsea and Rye seem wholly of the past. Nothing can
modernise them.

Rye approached from the east is the suddenest thing in the world.
The traveller leaves Ashford, in a South Eastern train, amid all the
circumstances of ordinary travel; he passes through the ordinary scenery
of Kent; the porters call Rye, and in a moment he is in the middle ages.

Rye is only a few yards from its station: Winchelsea, on the other hand, is a mile from the line, and one has time on the road to understand one's surroundings. It is important that the traveller who wishes to experience the right medieval thrill should come to Winchelsea either at dusk or at night. To make acquaintance with any new town by night is to double one's pleasure; for there is a first joy in the curious half-seen strangeness of the streets and houses, and a further joy in correcting by the morrow's light the distorted impressions gathered in the dark.

THE LANDGATE, RYE.

APPROACH AT DUSK

To come for the first time upon Winchelsea at dusk, whether from the station or from Rye, is to receive an impression almost if not quite unique in England; since there is no other town throned like this upon a green hill, to be gained only through massive gateways. From the station one would enter at the Pipewell Gate; from Rye, by the Strand Gate. The Strand approach is perhaps a shade finer and more romantically unreal.

THE FREAKISH SEA

Winchelsea and Rye are remarkable in being not only perched each upon a solitary hillock in a vast level or marsh, but in being hillocks in themselves. In the case of Winchelsea there are trees and green spaces to boot, but Rye and its hillock are one; every inch is given over to red brick and grey stone. They are true cities of the plain. Between them are three miles of flat meadow, where, among thousands of sheep, stands the grey rotundity of Camber Castle. All this land is *polder*, as the Dutch call it, yet not reclaimed from the sea by any feat of engineering, as about the Helder, but presented by Neptune as a free and not too welcome gift to these ancient boroughs—possibly to equalise his theft of acres of good park at Selsey. Once a Cinque Port of the first magnitude, Winchelsea is now an inland resort of the antiquary and the artist. Where fishermen once dropped their nets, shepherds now watch their sheep; where the marauding French were wont to rush in with sword and torch, tourists now toil with camera and guide-book.

The light above the sheep levels changes continually: at one hour Rye seems but a stone's throw from Winchelsea; at another she is miles distant; at a third she looms twice her size through the haze, and Camber is seen as a fortress of old romance.

Rye stands where it always stood: but the original Winchelsea is no more. It was built two miles south-south-east of Rye, on a spot since covered by the sea but now again dry land. At Old Winchelsea William the Conqueror landed in 1067 after a visit to Normandy; in 1138 Henry II. landed there, while the French landed often, sometimes disastrously and sometimes not. In those days Winchelsea had seven hundred householders and fifty inns. In 1250, however, began her downfall. Holinshed writes:—"On the first day of October (1250), the moon, upon her change, appearing exceeding red and swelled, began to show tokens of the great tempest of wind that followed, which was so huge and mightie, both by land and sea, that the like had not been lightlie knowne, and seldome, or rather never heard of by men then alive. The sea forced contrarie to his natural course, flowed twice without ebbing, yeelding such a rooring that the same was heard (not without great woonder) a farre distance from the shore. Moreover, the same sea appeared in the darke of the night to burne, as it had been on fire, and the waves to strive and fight togither after a marvellous sort, so that the mariners could not devise how to save their ships where they laie at anchor, by no cunning or shift which they could devise. At Hert-burne three tall-ships perished without recoverie, besides other smaller vessels. At Winchelsey, besides other hurte that was doone, in bridges, milles, breakes, and banks, there were 300 houses and some churches drowned with the high rising of the water course."

WINCHELSEA'S VICISSITUDES

The Winchelsea people, however, did not abandon their town. In 1264 Henry III. was there on his way to the Battle of Lewes, and later, Eleanor, wife of Henry's conqueror, de Montfort, was there too, and encouraged by her kindness to them the Winchelsea men took to active sea piracy, which de Montfort encouraged. In 1266, however, Prince Edward, who disliked piracy, descended upon the town and chastised it bloodily; while on February 4, 1287, a greater punishment came, for during another storm the town was practically drowned, all the flat land between Pett and Hythe being inundated. New Winchelsea, the Winchelsea of to-day, was forthwith begun under royal patronage on a rock near Icklesham, the north and east sides of which were washed by the sea. A castle was set there, and gates, of which three still stand—Pipewell, Strand and New—rose from the earth. The Grey Friars monastery and other religious houses were reproduced as at Old Winchelsea, and a prosperous town quickly existed.

New Winchelsea was soon busy. In 1350 a battle between the English and Spanish fleets was waged off the town, an exciting spectacle for the Court, who watched from the high ground. Edward III., the English king, when victory was his, rode to Etchingham for the night. In 1359, 3,000 Frenchmen entered Winchelsea and set fire to it; while in 1360 the Cinque Ports navy sailed from Winchelsea and burned Luce. Such were the reprisals of those days. In 1376 the French came again and were repulsed by the Abbot of Battle, but in 1378 the Abbot had to run. In 1448 the French came for the last time, the sea having become very shallow; and a little later the sea receded altogether, Henry VIII. suppressed the religious houses, and Winchelsea's heyday was over.

She is now a quiet, aloof settlement of pleasant houses and gardens, prosperous and idle. Rye might be called a city of trade, Winchelsea of repose. She spreads her hands to the sun and is content.

THE ALARD TOMBS

Winchelsea's church stands, as a church should, in the midst of its green acre, fully visible from every side—the very antipodes of Rye. Large as it now is, it was once far larger, for only the chancel and side aisles remain. The glory of the church is the canopied tomb of Gervase Alard, Admiral of the Cinque Ports, and that of his grandson Stephen Alard, also Admiral, both curiously carved with grotesque heads. The roof beams of the church, timber from wrecked or broken ships, are of an integrity so thorough that a village carpenter who recently climbed up to test them blunted all his tools in the enterprise.

SEDILIA AND TOMBS OF GERVASE AND
STEPHEN ALARD, WINCHELSEA.

THE WESTONS

All that remains of the Grey Friars monastery may now be seen (on Mondays only) in the estate called The Friars: the shell of the chapel's choir, prettily covered with ivy. Here once lived, in the odour of perfect respectability, the brothers Weston, who, country gentlemen of quiet habit at home, for several years ravaged the coach roads elsewhere as highwaymen, and were eventually hanged at Tyburn. Their place in literature is, of course, *Denis Duval*, which Thackeray wrote in a house on the north of the churchyard, and which is all of Winchelsea and Rye compact, as the author's letters to Mr. Greenwood, editor of *Cornhill*, detailing the plot (in the person of Denis himself) go to show. Thus:—

"I was born in the year 1764, at Winchelsea, where my father was a grocer and clerk of the church. Everybody in the place was a good deal connected with smuggling.

"There used to come to our house a very noble French gentleman, called the COUNT DE LA MOTTE, and with him a German, the BARON DE LÜTTERLOH. My father used to take packages to Ostend and Calais for these two gentlemen, and perhaps I went to Paris once, and saw the French Queen.

"The squire of our town was SQUIRE WESTON of the Priory, who, with his brother, kept one of the genteelest houses in the country. He was churchwarden of our church, and much respected. Yes, but if you read the *Annual Register* of 1781, you will find that on the 13th July the sheriffs attended at the TOWER OF LONDON to receive custody of a De la Motte, a prisoner charged with high treason. The fact is, this Alsatian nobleman being in difficulties in his own country (where he had commanded the Regiment Soubise), came to London, and under pretence of sending prints to France and Ostend, supplied the French Ministers with accounts of the movements of the English fleets and troops. His go-between was Lütterloh, a Brunswicker, who had been a crimping-agent, then a servant, who was a spy of France and Mr. Franklin, and who turned king's evidence on La Motte, and hanged him.

"This Lütterloh, who had been a crimping-agent for German troops during the American war, then a servant in London during the Gordon riots, then an agent for a spy, then a spy over a spy, I suspect to have been a consummate scoundrel, and doubly odious from speaking English with a German accent.

"What if he wanted to marry THAT CHARMING GIRL, who lived with Mr. Weston at Winchelsea? Ha! I see a mystery here.

"What if this scoundrel, going to receive his pay from the English Admiral, with whom he was in communication at Portsmouth, happened to go on board the *Royal George* the day she went down?

"As for George and Joseph Weston, of the Priory, I am sorry to say they were rascals too. They were tried for robbing the Bristol mail in 1780; and being acquitted for want of evidence, were tried immediately after on another indictment for forgery—Joseph was acquitted, but George was capitally convicted. But this did not help poor Joseph. Before their trials, they and some others broke out of Newgate, and Joseph fired at, and wounded, a porter who tried to stop him, on Snow Hill. For this he was tried and found guilty on the Black Act, and hung along with his brother.

"Now, if I was an innocent participator in De la Motte's treasons, and the Westons' forgeries and robberies, what pretty scrapes I must have been in.

"I married the young woman, whom the brutal Lütterloh would have had for himself, and lived happy ever after."

And again:—

DENIS DUVAL'S BOYHOOD

"My grandfather's name was Duval; he was a barber and perruquier by trade, and elder of the French Protestant church at Winchelsea. I was sent to board with his correspondent, a Methodist grocer, at Rye.

"These two kept a fishing-boat, but the fish they caught was many and many a barrel of Nantz brandy, which we landed—never mind where—at a place to us well known. In the innocence of my heart, I—a child—got leave to go out fishing. We used to go out at night and meet ships from the French coast.

"I learned to scuttle a marlinspike,
              reef a lee-scupper,
              keelhaul a bowsprit

as well as the best of them. How well I remember the jabbering of the Frenchmen the first night as they handed the kegs over to us! One night we were fired into by his Majesty's revenue cutter *Lynx*. I asked what those balls were fizzing in the water, etc.

"I wouldn't go on with the smuggling; being converted by Mr. Wesley, who came to preach to us at Rye—but that is neither here nor there . . ."

THE YPRES TOWER, RYE.

JOHN WESLEY

It was under the large tree of the west wall of the churchyard that in 1790 John Wesley preached his last outdoor sermon, afterwards walking through "that poor skeleton of ancient Winchelsea," as he called it.

411

Rye, like Winchelsea, has had a richer history than I can cope with. She was an important seaport from the earliest times; and among other of our enemies who knew her value were the Danes, two hundred and fifty of whose vessels entered the harbour in the year 893. Later the French continually menaced her, hardly less than her sister Cinque Port, but Rye bore so little malice that during the persecutions in France in the sixteenth century she received hundreds of Huguenot refugees, whose descendants still live in the town. Many monarchs have come hither, among them Queen Elizabeth, in 1573, dubbing Rye "Rye Royal" and Winchelsea "Little London."

THE THREE JEAKES

Rye has had at least one notable son, John Fletcher the dramatist, associate of Francis Beaumont and perhaps of Shakespeare, and author of "The Faithful Shepherdess." Fletcher's father was vicar of Rye. The town also gave birth to a curious father, son, and grandson, all named Samuel Jeake. The first, born in 1623, the author of "The Charters of the Cinque Ports," 1728, was a lawyer, a bold Nonconformist, a preacher, an astrologer and an alchemist, whose library contained works in fifteen languages but no copy of Shakespeare or Milton. He left a treatise on the Elixir of Life. The second, at the age of nineteen, was "somewhat acquainted with the Latin, Greek, and Hebrew, rhetoric, logic, poetry, natural philosophy, arithmetic, geometry, cosmography, astronomy, astrology, geography, theology, physics, dialling, navigation, caligraphy, stenography, drawing, heraldry and history." He also drew horoscopes, wrote treatises on astrology and other sciences, suffered, like his father, for his religion, and when he was twenty-nine married Elizabeth Hartshorne, aged thirteen and a half. They had six children. The third Samuel Jeake was famous for constructing a flying machine, which refused to fly, and nearly killed him.

Rye also possessed an unknown poet. On a blank leaf in an old book in the town's archives is written this poem, in the hand of Henry VIII.'s time:—

What greater gryffe may hape
Trew lovers to anoye,
Then absente for to sepratte them
From ther desiered joye?

What comforte reste them then
To ease them of ther smarte,
But for to thincke and myndful bee
Of them they love in harte?

And eicke that they assured bee
Etche toe another in harte,
That nothinge shall them seperate
Untylle deathe doe them parte?

And thoughe the dystance of the place
Doe severe us in twayne,
Yet shall my harte thy harte imbrace
Tyll we doe meete agayne.

THE SANGUINARY BUTCHER

The church, the largest in Sussex, dominates Rye from every point, and so tightly are the houses compressed that from the plain the spire seems to be the completion not only of the church but of the town too. The building stands in what is perhaps the quietest and quaintest church square in England, possessing beyond all question the discreetest of pawnbroker's shops, marked by three brass balls that positively have charm. The church is cool and spacious, with noble plain windows (and one very pretty little one by Burne-Jones), and some very interesting architectural features. Too little care seems, however, to have been spent upon it at some previous time. The verger shows with a pride little short of proprietary a mahogany altar said to have been taken from one of the vessels of the Armada (and therefore oddly inappropriate for a Church of England service), and the tomb of one Alan Grebell, who, happening one night in 1742 to be wearing the cloak of his brother-in-law the Mayor, was killed in mistake for him by a "sanguinary butcher" named Breeds. Breeds, who was hanged in chains for his crime, remains perhaps the most famous figure in the history of Rye.

Externally Rye church is magnificent, but the pity of it is that its encroaching square deprives one of the power to study it as a whole. Among the details, however, are two admirable flying buttresses. The clock over the beautiful north window, which is said to have been given to the town by Queen Elizabeth, is remarkable for the two golden cherubs that strike the hours, and the pendulum that swings in the central tower of the church, very nigh the preacher's head.

EIGHT BELLS

Rye's eight bells bear the following inscription:—

To honour both of God and King
Our voices shall in concert ring.

May heaven increase their bounteous store
And bless their souls for evermore.

Whilst thus we join in joyful sound
May love and loyalty abound.

Ye people all who hear me ring
Be faithful to your God and King.

Such wondrous power to music's given
It elevates the soul to heaven.

If you have a judicious ear
You'll own my voice is sweet and clear.

Our voices shall with joyful sound
Make hills and valleys echo round.

In wedlock bands all ye who join,
With hands your hearts unite;
So shall our tuneful tongues combine
To laud the nuptial rite.

Ye ringers, all who prize
Your health and happiness,
Be sober, merry, wise,
And you'll the same possess.

Hardly less interesting than the church are the by-streets of Rye, so old and simple and quiet and right; particularly perhaps Mermaid Street, with its beautiful hospital. In the High Street, which is busier, is the George Inn, the rare possessor of a large assembly room with a musicians' gallery. One only of Rye's gates is standing—the Landgate; but on the south rampart of the town is the Ypres Tower (called Wipers by the prosaic inhabitants), a relic of the twelfth century, guarding Rye once from perils by sea and now from perils by land. Standing by the tower one may hear below shipbuilders busy at work and observe all the low-pulsed life of the river. A mile or so away is Rye Harbour, and beyond it the sea; across the intervening space runs a little train with its freight of golf players. In the east stretches Romney Marsh to the hills of Folkestone.

Extremes meet in Rye. When I was last there the passage of the Landgate was made perilous by an approaching Panhard; the monastery of the Augustine friars on Conduit Hill had become a Salvation Army barracks; and in the doorway of the little fourteenth-century chapel of the Carmelites, now a private house, in the church square, a perambulator waited. Moreover, in the stately red house at the head of Mermaid Street the author of *The Awkward Age* prosecutes his fascinating analyses of twentieth-century temperaments.

RYE POTTERY

Among the industries of Rye is the production of an ingenious variety of pottery achieved by affixing to ordinary vessels of earthenware a veneer of broken pieces of china—usually fragments of cups and saucers—in definite patterns that sometimes reach a magnificence almost Persian. For the most part the result is not perhaps beautiful, but it is always gay, and the Rye potter who practises the art deserves encouragement. I saw last summer a piece of similar ware in a cottage on the banks of the Ettrick, but whether it had travelled thither from Rye, or whether Scotch artists work in the same medium, I do not know. Mr. Gasson, the artificer (the dominating name of Gasson is to Rye what that of Seiler is to Zermatt), charges a penny for the inspection of the four rooms of his house in which his pottery, his stuffed birds and other curiosities are collected. The visit must be epoch-making in any life. Never again will a broken tea-cup be to any of Mr. Gasson's patrons merely a broken tea-cup. Previously it may have been that and nothing more; henceforward it is valuable material which, having completed one stage of existence, is, like the good Buddhist, entering upon another of increased radiance. More, broken china may even become the symbol of Rye.

COURT LODGE, UDIMORE.

PETT AND ICKLESHAM

Between Hastings and Winchelsea are the villages of Guestling, Pett, and Icklesham, the last two on the edge of the Level. Of these, Icklesham is the most interesting, Guestling having recently lost its church by fire, and Pett church being new. Pett stands in a pleasant position at the end of the high ground, with nothing in the east but Pett Level, and the sea only a mile away. At very low tide the remains of a submerged forest were once discernible, and may still be.

Icklesham also stands on the ridge further north, overlooking the Level and the sea, with Winchelsea not two miles distant in the east. The church is a very fine one, with a most interesting Norman tower in its midst. The churchwardens accounts contain some quaint entries:

1732. Paid for yᵉ Stokes [stocks] £4 10s. 8¾d.

1735. January yᵉ 13 pᵈ for a pint of wine and for eight pound of mutton for Good[man] Row and Good[man] Winch and Goody Sutors for their being with Goody in her fitts 3s.

1744. Fevery yᵉ 29 paid Gudy Tayler for going to Winshelse for to give her Arthor Davy [affidavit] 1s. 6d.

1746. April 26 gave the Ringers for Rejoycing when yᵉ Rebels was beat 15s. (This refers to Culloden. There are two sides in every battle; how do Burns's lines run?—

> Drumossie moor—Drumossie day—
> A waefu' day it was to me!
> For there I lost my father dear,
> My father dear, and brethren three.)

One of the Icklesham gravestones, standing over the grave of James King, who died aged seventeen, has this complacent couplet:

> God takes the good—too good on earth to stay,
> And leaves the bad—too bad to take away.

Two miles to the west of Icklesham, at Snaylham, close to the present railway, once stood the home of the Cheyneys, a family that maintained for many years a fierce feud with the Oxenbridges of Brede, whither we soon shall come. A party of Cheyneys once succeeded in catching an Oxenbridge asleep in his bed, and killed him. Old Place farm, a little north of Icklesham, between the village and the line, marks the site of Old Place, the mansion of the Fynches, earls of Winchelsea.

PLAYDEN AND IDEN

The mainland proper begins hard by Rye, on the other side of the railway, where Rye Hill carries the London road out of sight. This way lie Playden, Iden, and Peasmarsh: Playden, with a slender spire, of a grace not excelled in a county notable, as we have seen, for graceful spires, but a little overweighted perhaps by its cross, within whose church is the tomb of a Flemish brewer, named Zoctmanns, calling for prayers for his soul; Iden, with a square tower and a stair turret, a village taking its name from that family of which Alexander Iden, slayer of Jack Cade, was a member, its home being at Mote, now non-existent; and Peasmarsh, whose long modest church, crowned by a squat spire, may be again seen, like the swan upon St. Mary's Lake, in the water at the foot of the churchyard. At Peasmarsh was born a poor artificial poet named William Pattison, in whose works I have failed to find anything of interest.

UDIMORE CHURCH.

419

The two most interesting spots in the hilly country immediately north of the Brede valley (north of Winchelsea) are Udimore and Brede. Concerning Udimore church, which externally has a family resemblance to that of Steyning, it is told that it was originally planned to rise on the other side of the little river Ree. The builders began their work, but every night saw the supernatural removal of the stones to the present site, while a mysterious voice uttered the words "O'er the mere! O'er the mere!" Hence, says the legend, the present position of the fane, and the beautiful name Udimore, or "O'er the mere," which, of course, becomes Uddymer among the villagers.

BREDE PLACE.

BREDE PLACE

From Udimore one reaches Brede by turning off the high road about two miles to the east. But it is worth while to keep to the road a little longer, and entering Gilly Wood (on the right) explore as wild and beautiful a ravine as any in the county. And, on the Brede by-road,

420

it is worth while also to turn aside again in order to see Brede Place. This house, like all the old mansions (it is of the fifteenth and sixteenth centuries), is set in a hollow, and is sufficiently gloomy in appearance and surroundings to lend colour to the rumour that would have it haunted—a rumour originally spread by the smugglers who for some years made the house their headquarters. An underground passage is said to lead from Brede Place to the church, a good part of a mile distant; but as is usual with underground passages, the legend has been held so dear that no one seems to have ventured upon the risk of disproving it. Amid these medieval surroundings the late Stephen Crane, the American writer, conceived some of his curiously modern stories.

One of the original owners (the Oxenbridges) like Col. Lunsford of East Hoathly was credited by the country people with an appetite for children. Nothing could compass his death but a wooden saw, with which after a drunken bout the villagers severed him in Stubb's Lane, by Groaning Bridge. Not all the family, however, were bloodthirsty, for at least two John Oxenbridges of the sixteenth century were divines, one a Canon of Windsor, the other a "grave and reverent preacher."

DEAN SWIFT'S CRADLE

The present vicar of Brede, the village on the hill above Brede Place, has added to the natural antiquities of his church several alien curiosities, chief among them being the cradle in which Dean Swift was rocked. It is worth a visit to Brede church to be persuaded that that matured Irishman ever was a baby.

BREDE PLACE, FROM THE SOUTH.

CHAPTER XXXIX

ROBERTSBRIDGE

Horace Walpole in difficulties—A bibliophile's threat—Salehurst—
Bodiam—Northiam—Queen Elizabeth's dinner and shoes—Brightling—
Jack Fuller—Turner in East Sussex—The Burwash country—Sussex
superstitions—*Sussex Folk and Sussex Ways*—Liberals and Conservatives—
The Sussex character—Independent bellringers—"Silly Sussex"—
Burwash at Cricket—James Hurdis—A donkey race—"A hint to great
and little men"—Henry Burwash—Etchingham—Sir John Lade and the
Prince—Ticehurst and Wadhurst.

Robertsbridge is not in itself a particularly attractive place; but it has
a good inn, and many interesting villages may be reached from it, the
little light railway that runs from the town to Tenterden, along the Rother
valley, making the exploration of this part of Sussex very simple.

Horace Walpole came to difficulties hereabout during his Sussex
journey. His sprightly and heightened account is in one of the letters: "The
roads grew bad beyond all badness, the night dark beyond all darkness,
our guide frightened beyond all frightfulness. However, without being at
all killed, we got up, or down—I forget which, it was so dark,—a famous
precipice called Silver Hill, and about ten at night arrived at a wretched
village called Rotherbridge. We had still six miles hither, but determined
to stop, as it would be a pity to break our necks before we had seen all
we had intended. But, alas! there was only one bed to be had: all the
rest were inhabited by smugglers, whom the people of the house called

mountebanks; and with one of whom the lady of the den told Mr. Chute he might lie. We did not at all take to this society, but, armed with links and lanthorns, set out again upon this impracticable journey. At two o'clock in the morning we got hither to a still worse inn, and that crammed with excise officers, one of whom had just shot a smuggler. However, as we were neutral powers, we have passed safely through both armies hitherto, and can give you a little farther history of our wandering through these mountains, where the young gentlemen are forced to drive their curricles with a pair of oxen. The only morsel of good road we have found, was what even the natives had assured us were totally impracticable; these were eight miles to Hurst Monceaux."

FOR BOOK BORROWERS

A pretty memento of the Cistercian Abbey here, of which small traces remain on the bank of the river, has wandered to the Bodleian, in the shape of an old volume containing the inscription: "This book belongs to St. Mary of Robertsbridge; whoever shall steal or sell it, let him be Anathema Maranatha!" Since no book was ever successfully protected by anything less tangible than a chain, it came into other hands, underneath being written: "I John Bishop of Exeter know not where the aforesaid house is; nor did I steal this book, but acquired it in a lawful way." On the suppression of the Abbey of Robertsbridge by Henry VIII. the lands passed to Sir William Sidney, grandfather of Sir Philip.

Salehurst, just across the river from Robertsbridge, has a noble church, standing among trees on the hill side—the hill which Walpole found so precipitous. Within, the church is not perhaps quite so impressive as without, but it has monuments appertaining probably to the Culpepers, once a far-reaching aristocratic Sussex family, which we met first at Ardingly, and which is now extinct or existent only among the peasantry.

BODIAM CASTLE.

BODIAM CASTLE

The first station on the Rother valley light railway is Bodiam, only a few steps from Bodiam Castle sitting serenely like a bird on the waters of her moat. This building in appearance and form fulfils most of the conditions of the castle, and by retaining water in its moat perhaps wins more respect than if it had stood a siege. (Local tradition indeed credits it with that mark of active merit, but history is silent.) It was built in the fourteenth century by Sir Edward Dalyngruge, a hero of Cressy and Poictiers. It is now a ruin within, but (as Mr. Griggs' drawing shows) externally in fair preservation and a very interesting and romantic spectacle.

Below Bodiam is Ewhurst, and a little farther east, close to the Kentish border, Northiam. Ewhurst has no particular interest, but Northiam is a village apart. Knowing what we do of Sussex speech we may be certain that Northiam is not pronounced by the native as it is spelt. Norgem is its local style, just as Udiham is Udgem and Bodiam Bodgem. But though he will not give Northiam its pleasant syllables, the Northiam man is proud of his village. He has a couplet:

Oh rare Northiam, thou dost far exceed
Beckley, Peasmarsh, Udimore and Brede.

Northiam's superiority to these pleasant spots is not absolute; but there are certain points in which the couplet is sound. For example, although Brede Place has no counterpart in Northiam, and although beside Udimore's lovely name Northiam has an uninspired prosaic ring, yet Northiam is alone in the possession of Queen Elizabeth's Oak, the tree beneath which that monarch, whom we have seen on a progress in West Sussex, partook in 1573 of a banquet, on her way to Rye. The fare came from the kitchen of the timbered house hard by, then the residence of Master Bishopp. During the visit her Majesty changed her shoes, and the discarded pair is still treasured at Brickwall, the neighbouring seat of the Frewens, the great family of Northiam for many generations. The shoes are of green damask silk, with heels two and a half inches high and pointed toes. The Queen was apparently so well satisfied with her repast that on her return journey three days later she dined beneath the oak once more. But she changed no more shoes.

Brickwall, which is occasionally shown, is a noble old country mansion, partly Elizabethan and partly Stuart. In the church are many Frewen memorials, the principal of which are in the Frewen mausoleum, a comparatively new erection. Accepted Frewen, Archbishop of York, was from Northiam.

A DANISH VESSEL

In a field near the Rother at Northiam was discovered, in the year 1822, a Danish vessel, which had probably sunk in the ninth century in some wide waterway now transformed to land or shrunk to the dimensions of the present stream. Her preservation was perfect. Horsfield thus describes the ship: "Her dimensions were, from head to stern, 65 feet, and her width 14 feet, with cabin and forecastle; and she appears to have originally had a whole deck. She was remarkably strongly built; her bill pieces and keels measuring 2 feet over, her cross beams, five in number, 18 inches by 8, with her other timbers in proportion; and in her caulking was a species of moss peculiar to the country in which she was built. In the cabin and other parts of the vessel were found a human skull; a pair of goat's horns attached to a part of the cranium; a dirk or poniard, about half an inch of the blade of which had wholly resisted corrosion; several glazed and ornamental tiles of a square form; some bricks which had formed the fire hearth; several parts of shoes, or rather sandals, fitting low on the foot, one of which was apparently in an unfinished state, having a last remaining in it, all of them very broad at the toes; two earthern jars and a stone mug, all of very ancient shape, a piece of board exhibiting about thirty perforations, probably designed for keeping the lunar months, or some game or amusement; with many other antique relics."

OLD JACK FULLER

Four miles west of Robertsbridge, up hill and down, is Brightling, whose Needle, standing on Brightling Down, 646 feet high, is visible from most of the eminences in this part of Sussex. The obelisk, together with the neighbouring observatory, was built on the site of an old beacon by the famous Jack Fuller—famous no longer, but in his day (he died in 1834 aged seventy-seven) a character both in London and in Sussex. He was big and bluff and wealthy and the squire of Rose Hill. He sat for Sussex from 1801 to 1812, and was once carried from the House by the Sergeant at Arms and his minions, for refusing to give way in a debate and calling the Speaker "the insignificant little fellow in a wig." His election cost him £20,000 plus £30,000 subscribed by the county. When Pitt offered him a peerage he said no: "I was born Jack Fuller and

Jack Fuller I'll die." When he travelled from Rose Hill to London Mr. Fuller's progresses were almost regal. The coach was provisioned as if for arctic exploration and coachman and footmen alike were armed with swords and pistols. ("Honest Jack," as Mr. Lower remarks, put a small value upon the honesty of others.) Mr. Fuller had two hobbies, music and science. He founded the Fullerian professorships (which he called his two children), and contributed liberally to the Royal Institution; and his musical parties in London were famous. But whether it is true that when the Brightling choir dissatisfied him he presented the church with nine bassoons, I cannot say.

TURNER IN SUSSEX

John Fuller has a better claim to be remembered in Sussex by his purchase of Bodiam Castle, when its demolition was threatened, and by his commission to Turner to make pictures in the Rape of Hastings, five of which were engraved and published in folio form, in 1819, under the title *Views in Sussex*. One of these represents the Brightling Observatory as seen from Rosehill Park. As a matter of fact, the observatory, being of no interest, is almost invisible, although Mr. Reinagle, A.R.A., who supplies the words to the pictures, calls it the "most important point in the scene." Furthermore, he says that the artist has expressed a shower proceeding "from the left corner." Another picture is the Vale of Ashburnham, with the house in the middle distance, Beachy Head beyond, and in the foreground woodcutters carrying wood in an ox waggon. "The whole," says Mr. Reinagle, A.R.A., "is happily composed, if I may use the term." He then adds: "The eye of the spectator, on looking at this beautifully painted scene, roves with an eager delight from one hill to another, and seems to play on the dappled woods till arrested by the seat of Lord Ashburnham." Other pictures in the folio are "Pevensey Bay from Crowhurst Park," a very beautiful scene, "Battle Abbey," and "The Vale of Heathfield," painted from a point above the road, with Heathfield

House on the left, the tower on the right, the church in the centre in the middle distance, and the sea on the horizon: an impressive but not strictly veracious landscape.

In Brightling church is a bust to John Fuller, with the motto: "Utile nihil quod non honestum." A rector in Fuller's early days was William Hayley, who died in 1789, a zealous antiquary. His papers relating to the history of Sussex, are now, like those of Sir William Burrell, in the British Museum.

Our next village is Burwash, three miles in the north, built, like all the villages in this switchback district, on a hill. We are now, indeed, well in the heart of the fatiguing country which we touched at Mayfield, where one eminence is painfully won only to reveal another. One can be as parched on a road in the Sussex hop country as in the Arabian desert. The eye, however, that is tired of hop poles and hills can find sweet gratification in the cottages. Sussex has charming cottages from end to end of her territory, but I think the hop district on the Kentish side has some of the prettiest. Blackberries too may be set down among the riches of the sand-hill villages.

SUPERSTITIONS

In Richard Jefferies' essay, "The Country-side: Sussex" (in *Field and Hedgerow*), describing this district of the country, is an amusing passage touching superstitions of these parts, picked up during hopping:

"In and about the kiln I learned that if you smash a frog with a stone, no matter how hard you hit him, he cannot die till sunset. You must be careful not to put on any new article of clothing for the first time on a Saturday, or some severe punishment will ensue. One person put on his new boots on a Saturday, and on Monday broke his arm. Some still believe in herbs, and gather wood-betony for herb tea, or eat dandelion leaves between slices of dry toast. There is an old man living in one of the villages who has reached the age of a hundred and sixty years, and still goes hop-picking. Ever so many people had seen him, and knew all about him; an undoubted fact, a public fact; but I could not trace him to his lair. His exact whereabouts could not be fixed. I live in hopes of finding him in some obscure 'Hole' yet (many little hamlets are 'Holes,' as Froghole, Foxhole). What an exhibit for London! Did he realise his own value, he would soon come forth. I joke, but the existence of this antique person is firmly believed in."

Burwash is one of the few Sussex villages that has been made the subject of a book. The Rev. John Coker Egerton's *Sussex Folk and Sussex Ways* (from which I have already occasionally quoted) was written here, around materials collected during the author's period as rector of Burwash. Mr. Egerton was curate of Burwash from 1857 to 1862, and from 1865 to 1867, when he became rector and remained in the living until his death in 1888. His book is a kindly collection of the shrewd and humorous sayings of his Sussex parishioners, anecdotes of characteristic incidents, records of old customs now passing or passed away—the whole fused by the rector's genial personality.

PARTY POLITICS

It is to Burwash and Mr. Egerton that we owe some characteristic scraps of Sussex philosophy. Thus, Mr. Egerton tells of an old conservative whose advice to young men was this: "Mind you don't never have nothing in no way to do with none of their new-fangled schemes." Another Sussex cynic defined party government with grim impartiality: "Politics are about like this: I've got a sow in my yard with twelve little uns, and they little uns can't all feed at once, because there isn't room enough; so I shut six on 'em out of the yard while tother six be sucking, and the six as be shut out, they just do make a hem of a noise till they be let in; and then they be just as quiet as the rest."

The capacity of the Sussex man to put his foot down and keep it there, is shown in the refusal of Burwash to ring the bells when George

IV., then Prince of Wales, passed through the village on his return to Brighton from a visit to Sir John Lade at Etchingham; the reason given being that the First Gentleman in Europe when rung in on his way to Sir John's had said nothing about beer. This must have been during one of the Prince's peculiarly needy periods, for the withholding of strong drink from his friends was never one of his failings. Another Burwash radical used to send up to the rectory with a message that he was about to gather fruit and the rector must send down for the tithe. The rector's man would go down—and receive one gooseberry from a basket of ten: all that was to be gathered that day.

Another Burwash man posed his vicar more agreeably and humorously in another manner. Finding him a little in liquor the pastor would have warned him against the habit, but the man was too quick. How was it, he asked the vicar with well affected or real concern, that whenever he had had too much to drink he felt more religious than at any other time?

The Burwash records indeed go far to redeem Sussex men from the epithet "silly," which is traditionally theirs. Concerning this old taunt, I like the rector's remarks in *Idlehurst*. The phrase, he says, "is better after all than 'canny owd Cummerlan'" or calling ourselves 'free and enlightened citizens' or 'heirs to all the ages.' But suppose Sussex as silly as you like, the country wants a large preserve of fallow brains; you can't manure the intellect for close cropping. Isn't it Renan who attributes so much to solid Breton stupidity in his ancestors?" I notice that Mr. H. G. Wells, in his very interesting book, *Mankind in the Making*, is in support of this suggestion. The *Idlehurst* rector, in contrasting Londoners with Sussex folk, continues: "The Londoner has all his strength in the front line: one can never tell what reserves the countryman may not deploy in his slow way." (Some old satirist of the county had it that the crest of the true Sussex peasant is a pig couchant, with the motto "I wunt be druv." I give this for what it is worth.)

SUSSEX RESERVES

It is to be doubted if any county has a monopoly of silliness. The fault of Sussex people rather is to lack reserves, not of wisdom but of effort. You see this in cricket, where although the Sussex men have done some of the most brilliant things in the history of the game (even before the days of their Oriental ally), they have probably made a greater number of tame attempts to cope with difficulties than any other eleven. For the "staying of a rot" Sussex has had but few qualifications. The cricket test is not everything: but character tells there just as in any other employment. Burwash, however, must be exempted from this particular charge, for, whatever its form may be now, its eleven had once a terrible reputation. I find in the county paper for 1771 an advertisement to the effect that Burwash, having "challenged all its neighbours without effect," invites a match with any parish whatsoever in all Sussex.

THE DONKEY RACE

Mr. Egerton was not the first parson to record the manners of the Burwash parishioner. The Rev. James Hurdis, curate there towards the end of the preceding century, and afterwards Professor of Poetry at Oxford (we saw his grave at Bishopstone), had written a blank verse poem in the manner of Cowper, with some of the observation of Crabbe, entitled "The Village Curate," which is a record of his thoughts and impressions in his Burwash days. One could hardly say that "The Village Curate" would bear reprinting at the present time; we have moved too far from its pensiveness, and an age that does not read "The Task" and only talks about Crabbe is hardly likely to reach out for Hurdis. But within its limits "The Village Curate" is good, alike in its description of scenery, its reflections and its satire. The Burwash donkey race is capital:—

Then comes the ass-race. Let not wisdom frown,
If the grave clerk look on, and now and then

432

Bestow a smile; for we may see, Alcanor,
In this untoward race the ways of life.
Are we not asses all? We start and run,
And eagerly we press to pass the goal,
And all to win a bauble, a lac'd hat.
Was not great Wolsey such? He ran the race,
And won the hat. What ranting politician,
What prating lawyer, what ambitious clerk,
But is an ass that gallops for a hat?
For what do Princes strive, but golden hats?
For diadems, whose bare and scanty brims
Will hardly keep the sunbeam from their eyes.
For what do Poets strive? A leafy hat,
Without or crown or brim, which hardly screens
The empty noddle from the fist of scorn,
Much less repels the critic's thund'ring arm.
And here and there intoxication too
Concludes the race. Who wins the hat, gets drunk.
Who wins a laurel, mitre, cap, or crown,
Is drunk as he. So Alexander fell,
So Haman, Cæsar, Spenser, Wolsey, James.

A STRATEGIC DUELLIST

I find in the Sussex paper for 1792 the following contribution to the history of Burwash: "A Hint to Great and Little Men.—Last Thursday morning a butcher and a shopkeeper of Burwash, in this County, went into a field near that town, with pistols, to decide a quarrel of long standing between them. The lusty Knight of the Cleaver having made it a practice to insult his antagonist, who is a very little man, the great disparity between them in size rendered this the only eligible alternative for the latter. The butcher took care to inform his wife of the intended meeting, in hopes that she would give the Constables timely notice thereof. But the good woman not having felt so deeply interested in his fate as he expected, to make sure, he sent to the Constable himself, and then marched reluctantly to the field, where the little, spirited shopkeeper was parading with a considerable reserve of ammunition, lest his first fire should not take place. Now the affrighted butcher proceeded slowly to charge his pistols, alternately looking towards the town and his impatient adversary. This man of blood, all pale and trembling, at last began to despair of any friendly interference, when the Constable very seasonably appeared and forbade the duel, to his great joy, and the disappointment of the spectators."

HENRY BURWASH

Burwash had another great man of whom it is not very proud. Fuller shall describe him:—"Henry Burwash, so named, saith my Author[3] (which is enough for my discharge) from *Burwash*, a Town in this County. He was one of *Noble Alliance*. And when this is said, *all is said* to his commendation, being otherwise neither good for Church nor State, Soveraign nor Subjects; Covetous, Ambitious, Rebellious, Injurious.

"Say not, *what makes he here then amongst the worthies*? For though neither *Ethically* nor *Theologically*, yet *Historically* he was remarkable, affording something for our *Information* though not *Imitation*.

"He was recommended by his kinsman *Bartholomew de Badilismer* (Baron of *Leeds* in *Kent*) to King *Edward* the second, who preferred him Bishop of *Lincoln*. It was not long before, falling into the King's displeasure, his *Temporalities* were seized on, and afterwards on his submission restored. Here, instead of new *Gratitude*, retayning his old *Grudge*, he was most forward to assist the Queen in the deposing of her husband. He was twice Lord Treasurer, once Chancellor, and once sent over Ambassador to the *Duke of Bavaria*. He died *Anno Domini* 1340.

"Such as mind to be merry may read the pleasant Story of his apparition, being condemned after Death to be *viridis viridarius, a green Forrester* because in his life-time he had violently inclosed other men's Grounds into his Park. Surely such Fictions keep up the *best Park of Popery (Purgatory)*, whereby their *fairest Game* and greatest Gaine is preserved."

SHOYSWELL, NEAR TICEHURST.

Etchingham, the station next Robertsbridge, is famous for its church windows, and its brasses to the Etchinghams of the past, an illustrious race of Sussex barons. Among the brasses is that of William de Etchingham, builder of the church, who died in 1345. The inscription, in French, runs:—"I was made and formed of Earth; and now I have returned to Earth. William de Etchingham was my name. God have pity on my soul; and all you who pass by, pray to Him for me." Certainly no church in Sussex has so many interesting brasses as these. A moat once surrounded the God's acre, and legend had it that at the bottom was a great bell which might never be drawn forth until six yoke of white oxen were harnessed to it. Pity that the moat was allowed to run dry and the harmless fiction exposed.

A WAGER

Sir John Lade, diminutive associate of George IV. in his young days (and afterwards, coming upon disaster, coachman to the Earl of Anglesey), once lived at Haremere Hall, near by. As we have seen, the First Gentleman in Europe visited him there, and it was there one day, that, in default of other quarry, Sir John's gamekeeper only being able to produce a solitary pheasant, the Prince and his host shot ten geese as they swam across a pond, and laid them at the feet of Lady Lade. Sir John was the hero of the following exploit, recorded in the press in October, 1795:—"A curious circumstance occurred at Brighton on Monday se'nnight. Sir John Lade, for a trifling wager, undertook to carry Lord Cholmondeley on his back, from opposite the Pavilion twice round the Steine. Several ladies attended to be spectators of this extraordinary feat of the dwarf carrying the giant. When His Lordship declared himself ready, Sir John desired him to strip. 'Strip!' exclaimed the other; 'why surely you promised to carry me in my clothes!' 'By no means,' replied the Baronet; 'I engaged to carry *you*, but not an inch of clothes. So, therefore, My Lord, make ready, and let us not disappoint the ladies.' After much laughable altercation, it was at length decided that Sir John had won his wager, the Peer declining to exhibit *in puris naturalibus.*"

THE HAWKHURST GANG

Ticehurst and Wadhurst, which may be reached either by road or rail from Robertsbridge or Etchingham, both stand high, very near the Kentish border. To the east of Hurst Green on the road thither (a hamlet disproportionate and imposing, possessing, in the George Inn, a relic of the days when the coaches came this way), is Seacox Heath, now the residence of Lord Goschen, but once the home of George Gray, a member of the terrible Hawkhurst gang of smugglers. Ticehurst has a noble church, very ingeniously restored, with a square tower, some fine windows, old glass, a vestry curiously situated over the porch, and an interesting brass.

The Bell Inn, in the village, is said to date from the fifteenth century.

At Wadhurst are many iron grave slabs and a graceful slender spire. The massive door bears the date 1682. A high village, in good accessible country, discovery seems to be upon it. London is not so near as at Crowborough; but one may almost hear the jingling of the cabs.

FOOTNOTE:

3 Weever's *Funeral Monuments.*

CHAPTER XL

TUNBRIDGE WELLS

Over the border—The beginnings of the wells—Tunbridge Wells to-day—Mr. George Meredith—The Toad and other rocks—Eridge—Trespassing in Sussex—Saxonbury—Bayham Abbey—Lamberhurst—Withyham—The Sackvilles—A domestic autocrat—"To all you ladies now on land"—Withyham church—The Sackville monument—John Waylett—Beer and bells—Parish expenses—Buckhurst and Old Buckhurst—Ashdown Forest—Hartfield and Bolebroke—A wild region.

I have made Tunbridge Wells our last centre, because it is convenient; yet as a matter of strict topography, the town is not in Sussex at all, but in Kent.

In that it is builded upon hills, Tunbridge Wells is like Rome, and in that its fashionable promenade is under the limes, like Berlin; but in other respects it is merely a provincial English inland pleasure town with a past: rather arid, and except under the bracing conditions of cold weather, very tiring in its steepnesses. No wonder the small victoria and smaller pony carriage so flourish there.

THE PANTILES, TUNBRIDGE WELLS.

The healthful properties of Tunbridge Wells were discovered, as I record a little later, in 1606; but it was not until Henrietta Maria brought her suite hither in 1630 that the success of the new cure was assured. Afterwards came Charles II. and his Court, and Tunbridge Wells was made; and thenceforward to fail to visit the town at the proper time each year (although one had the poorest hut to live in the while) was to write one's self down a boor. A more sympathetic patron was Anne, who gave the first stone basin for the spring—hence "Queen's Well"—and whose subscription of £100 led to the purchase of the pantiles that paved the walk now bearing that name. Subsequently it was called the Parade, but to the older style everyone has very sensibly reverted.

Tunbridge Wells is still a health resort, but the waters no longer constitute a part of the hygienic routine. Their companion element, air, is the new recuperative. Not that the spring at the foot of the Pantiles is wholly deserted: on the contrary, the presiding old lady does quite a business in filling and cleaning the little glasses; but those visitors that descend her steps are impelled rather by curiosity than ritual, and many never try again. Nor is the trade in Tunbridge ware, inlaid work in coloured woods, what it was. A hundred years ago there was hardly a girl of any pretensions to good form but kept her pins in a Tunbridge box.

The Pantiles are still the resort of the idle, but of the anonymous rather than famous variety. Our men of mark and great Chams of Literature, who once flourished here in the season, go elsewhere for their recreation and renovation—abroad for choice. Tunbridge Wells now draws them no more than Bath. But in the eighteenth century a large print was popular containing the portraits of all the illustrious intellectuals as they lounged on the Pantiles, with Dr. Johnson and Mr. Samuel Richardson among the chief lions.

THE DUVIDNEY LADIES

The residential districts of Tunbridge Wells—its Mounts, Pleasant, Zion and Ephraim, with their discreet and prosperous villas—suggest to me only Mr. Meredith's irreproachable Duvidney ladies. In one of these well-ordered houses must they have lived and sighed over Victor's tangled life—surrounded by laurels and laburnum; the lawn either cut yesterday or to be cut to-day; the semicircular drive a miracle of gravel unalloyed; a pan of water for Tasso beside the dazzling step. Receding a hundred years, the same author peoples Tunbridge Wells again, for it was here, in its heyday, that Chloe suffered.

ROCKS

On Rusthall Common is the famous Toad Rock, which is to Tunbridge Wells what Thorwaldsen's lion is to Lucerne, and the Leaning Tower to Pisa. Lucerne's lion emerged from the stone under the sculptor's mallet and chisel, but the Rusthall monster was evolved by natural processes, and it is a toad only by courtesy. An inland rock is, however, to most English people so rare an object that Rusthall has almost as many pilgrims as Stonehenge. The Toad is free; the High Rocks, however, which are a mile distant, cannot be inspected by the curious for less than sixpence. One must pass through a turnstile before these wonders are accessible. Rocks in themselves having insufficient drawing power, as the dramatic critics say, a maze has been added, together with swings, a seesaw, arbours, a croquet lawn, and all the proper adjuncts of a natural phenomenon. The effect is to make the rocks appear more unreal than any rocks ever seen upon the stage. Freed from their pleasure-garden surroundings they would become beautifully wild and romantic and tropically un-English; but as it is, with their notice boards and bridges, they are disappointing, except of course to children. They are no disappointment to children; indeed, they go far to make Tunbridge Wells a children's wonderland. There is no kind of dramatic game to which the High Rocks would not make the best background. Finer rocks, because more remote and free from labels and tea rooms, are those known as Penn's Rocks, three miles in the south-west, in a beautiful valley.

SAXONBURY

Eridge, whither all visitors to Tunbridge Wells must at one time or another drive, is the seat of the Marquis of Abergavenny, whose imposing A, tied, like a dressing gown, with heavy tassels, is embossed on every cottage for miles around. In character the park resembles Ashburnham, while in extent it vies with the great parks of the south-west, Arundel, Goodwood and Petworth; but it has none of their spacious coolnesses.

Yet Eridge Park has joys that these others know not of—brake fern four feet high, and the conical hill on which stands Saxonbury Tower, jealously guarded from the intruding traveller by the stern fiat of "Mr. Macbean, steward." Sussex is a paradise of notice boards (there is a little district near Forest Row where the staple industry must be the prosecuting of trespassers), and one has come ordinarily to look upon these monitions without active resentment; but when the Caledonian descends from his native heath to warn the Sussex man off Sussex ground—more, to warn the Saxon from his own bury—the situation becomes acute. By taking, however, the precaution of asking at a not too adjacent cottage for permission to ascend the hill, one may circumvent the Scottish prosecutor.

The hill is very important ground in English history, as the following passage from Sir William Burrell's MSS. in the British Museum testifies:— "In Eridge Park are the remains of a military station of the Saxon invaders of the country, which still retains the name of Saxonbury Hill. It is on the high ground to the right, as the traveller passes from Frant to Mayfield. On the summit of this hill (from whence the cliffs of Dover may be seen) are to be traced the remains of an ancient fortification; the fosse is still plainly discernible, enclosing an area of about two acres, from whence there is but one outlet. The apex of the hill within is formed of a strong compact body of stone, brought hither from a distance, on which doubtless was erected some strong military edifice. This was probably one of the stations occupied by the Saxons under Ella, their famous chief, who, at the instance of Hengist, King of Kent, invaded England towards the close of the fifth century. It is said that they settled in Sussex, whence they issued in force to attack the important British station of Anderida or Andredceaster. Antiquaries are not agreed as to the precise situation of this military station; some imagining it to have been at Newenden, on the borders of Kent; others at Pevensey, or Hastings, in Sussex. The country, from the borders of Kent to those of Hampshire, comprises what was called the Forest of Andredsweald, now commonly called the Weald, was formerly full of strong holds and fastnesses, and was consequently well calculated for the retreat of the ancient Britons from before the regular armies of the Romans, as well as for the establishment of points of attack by the succeeding invaders who coped with them on terms somewhat reversed. The attack of the Saxons on Anderida was successful, and the consequence was their permanent establishment in Sussex and Surrey, from which time they probably retained a military station on this hill.

"There is likewise within the park a place called Danes Gate. This was doubtless a part of a military way; and as it would happen that the last successful invaders would occupy the same strong posts which had been formed by their predecessors, this Danes Gate was probably the military communication between Crowborough, undoubtedly a Danish station, and Saxonbury Hill."

The view from Saxonbury extends far in each quarter, embracing both lines of Downs, North and South. The long low irregular front of Eridge Castle is two or three miles to the north-west, with its lake before it.

LORD NORTH'S DISCOVERY

Queen Elizabeth stayed at Eridge for six days in 1573, on her progress to Northiam, where we saw her dining and changing her shoes. Lord Burleigh, who accompanied her, found the country hereabouts dangerous, and "worse than in the Peak." It was another of the guests at Eridge that made Tunbridge Wells; for had not Dudley, Lord North, when recuperating there in 1606, discovered that the (Devil-flavoured) chalybeate water of the neighbourhood was beneficial, the spring would not have been enclosed nor would other of London's fatigued young bloods have drunk of it.

BAYHAM ABBEY.

BAYHAM ABBEY

Enough remains of Bayham Abbey, five miles south-east of Tunbridge Wells, to show that it was once a very considerable monastery. The founder was Sir Robert de Turneham, one of the knights of Richard Cœur de Lion, famous for cracking many crowns with his "fauchion," and the founder also of Combwell Abbey at Goudhurst, not far distant. Edward I. and Edward II. were both entertained at Bayham, while a fortunate visit from St. Richard, Bishop of Chichester, put the Abbey in possession of a bed (on which he had slept) which cured all them that afterwards lay in it. Between Bayham and Goudhurst is Lamberhurst, on the boundary. (The church and part of the street are indeed in Kent.) Lamberhurst's boast is that its furnaces were larger than any in Sussex; and that they made the biggest guns. The old iron railings around St. Paul's are said to have come from the Lamberhurst iron works—2,500 in all, each five feet six inches in height, with seven gates. The Lamberhurst

444

cannon not only served England, but some, it is whispered, found their way to French privateers and were turned against their native land.

Sweetest of spots in the neighbourhood of Tunbridge Wells is Withyham, in the west, lying to the north of Ashdown Forest, a small and retired village, with a charming church, a good inn (the Dorset Arms), Duckings, a superb piece of old Sussex architecture, Old Buckhurst, an interesting ruin, new Buckhurst's magnificent park, and some of the best country in the county. Once the South Down district is left behind I think that Withyham is the jewel of Sussex. Moreover, the proximity of the wide high spaces of Ashdown Forest seems to have cleared the air; no longer is one conscious of the fatigue that appertains to the triangular hill district between Tunbridge Wells, Robertsbridge and Uckfield.

THE SPLENDID SACKVILLES

Withyham is notable historically for its association with the great and sumptuous Sackville family, which has held Buckhurst since Henry II., and of which the principal figure is Thomas Sackville, Lord Buckhurst, first Earl of Dorset, who was born here in 1536, Queen Elizabeth's Lord Treasurer and part author of *Gorboduc*. After him came Robert Sackville, second earl, who founded Sackville College at East Grinstead; and then Richard, the third earl, famous for the luxury in which he lived at Knole in Kent and Dorset House in London. Among this nobleman's retinue was a first footman rejoicing (I hope) in the superlatively suitable name of Acton Curvette: a name to write a comedy around. Richard Sackville, the fifth earl, was a more domestic peer, of whom we have some intimate and amusing glimpses in the memorandum books and diaries which he kept at Knole. Thus:—

"Hy. Mattock for scolding to extremity on Sunday 12th October 1661 without cause   0 0 3

"Hy. Mattock for disposing of my Cast linnen without my order   0 0 3

"TO ALL YOU LADIES"

Lastly we come to Charles Sackville, sixth earl, that Admirable Crichton, the friend of Charles II. and the patron of poets, who spent the night before an engagement in the Dutch war in writing the sprightly verses, "To all you ladies now on land," wherein occurs this agreeable fancy:—

Then, if we write not by each post,
　　Think not we are unkind;
Nor yet conclude our ships are lost
　　By Dutchmen or by wind;
Our tears we'll send a speedier way:
The tide shall bring them twice a day.

The king with wonder and surprise,
　　Will swear the seas grow bold;
Because the tides will higher rise
　　Than e'er they did of old:
But let him know it is our tears
Bring floods of grief to Whitehall-stairs.

Upon the sixth Earl of Dorset's monument in Withyham Church is inscribed Pope's epitaph, beginning:—

Dorset, the grace of Courts, the Muses pride,
Patron of arts, and judge of nature dy'd!
The scourge of pride, though sanctify'd or great,
Of fops in learning, and of knaves in state:
Yet soft his nature, though severe his lay,
His anger moral, and his wisdom gay.

446

The church is very prettily situated on a steep mound, at the western foot of which is a sheet of water; at the eastern foot, the village. So hidden by trees is it that approaching Withyham from Hartfield one is unconscious of its proximity. The glory of the church is the monument, in the Sackville Chapel, to Thomas Sackville, youngest son of the fifth Earl of Dorset. There is nothing among the many tombs which we have seen more interesting than this, although for charm it is not to be compared with, say, the Shurley monument at Isfield. The young man reclines on the tomb; at one side of him is the figure of his father, and at the other, of his mother, both life-like and life-size, dressed in their ordinary style. The attitudes being extremely natural the total effect is curiously realistic. On the sides of the tomb, in bas-relief, are the figures of the six brothers and six sisters of the youth, some quite babies. The sculptor was Caius Cibber, Colley Cibber's father. Other monuments are also to be seen in the Sackville Chapel, but that which I have described is the finest.

Had Withyham church not been destroyed by fire, in 1663, in a "tempest of thunder and lightning," it would now be second to none in Sussex in interest and the richness of its tombs; for in that fire perished in the Sackville aisle, now no more, on the northern side, other and perhaps nobler Sackville monuments. The vaults, where many Sackvilles lie, were not however injured. In the Sackville Chapel is a large window recording the genealogy of the family, which is now represented by Earl De la Warr, at the foot of which are the words in Latin, "The noble family of Sackville here awaits the Resurrection."

JOHN WAYLETT, BELL-FOUNDER

Withyham has three of the bells of John Waylett, an itinerant bell-founder at the beginning of the eighteenth century. His method was to call on the vicar and ask if anything were wanted; and if a bell was cracked, or if a new one was desired, he would dig a mould in a neighbouring field, build a fire, collect his metal and perform the task on the spot. Waylett's business might be called the higher tinkering. Sussex has some forty of his bells. He cast the Steyning peal in 1724, and earlier in the same year he had made a stay at Lewes, erecting a furnace there, as Benvenuto Cellini tells us he used to do, and remedying defective peals all around. Among others he recast the old treble and made a new treble for Mayfield. It seems to have been universally thirsty work: the churchwardens' papers contain an account for beer in connection with the enterprise:

BEER

	£	s.	d.
For beer to the ringers when the Bell founder was here		2	6
When the bell was weighed		3	6
When the bell was loaded		2	0
In carrying ye bell to Lewes and back again	1	10	0
When the bell was waid and hung up		3	0
For beer to the officers and several others a hanging up ye bell		18	0
In beer to the ringers when ye bell was hung		6	6

The Withyham churchwardens also expended 3s. 6d. on beer when Waylett came to spread thirst abroad. I find also among the entries from the parish account-book, which Mr. Sutton, the vicar, prints in his *Historical Notes on Withyham*, a very interesting and informing book, the following items:

	s.	d.
1711. April ye 20, pd. to Goody Sweatman for Beere had at ye Books making	2	6
Aug. ye 19, pd. to Edward Groombridge for digging a grave and Ringing ye Nell for Goody Hammond	2	6

Aug. ye 26, pd. to Sweatman for beere at ye Writing of Boocks for ye window-tax	2	0
Aug. 15th, Pd. to Sweatman for beer at ye chusing of surveyor Dec^br ye 26	5	0
1714. Pd. to good wife Sweatman for beer when ye bells were put to be cast	2	6

Buckhurst, one of the seats of Lord De la Warr, is a splendid domain, with the most perfect golf greens I ever saw, but no deer, all of them having been exiled a few years since. The previous home of the Sackvilles was Old Buckhurst in the valley to the west, of which only the husk now remains. One can see that the mansion was of enormous extent; and the walls were so strongly built that when an attempt was recently made to destroy and utilise a portion for road mending, the project had to be abandoned on account of the hardness of the mortar. One beautiful tower (out of six) still stands. An underground passage, which is said variously to lead to the large lake in Buckhurst Park, to the church, and to Bolebroke at Hartfield, has never been explored farther than the first door that blocks the way; nor have the seven cord of gold, rumoured to be buried near the house, come to light.

OLD RURAL ARCHITECTURE

IN PRAISE OF "DUCKINGS"

It was of Duckings, the beautiful timbered farmhouse of which Withyham is justly proud, that Jefferies thus wrote, in his essay on "Buckhurst Park": "Our modern architects try to make their rooms mathematically square, a series of brick boxes, one on the other like pigeon-holes in a bureau, with flat ceilings and right angles in the corners, and are said to go through a profound education before they can produce these wonderful specimens of art. If our old English folk could not get an arched roof, then they loved to have it pointed, with polished timber beams in which the eye rested as in looking upwards through a tree. Their rooms they liked of many shapes, and not at right angles in the corners, nor all on the same dead level of flooring. You had to go up a step into one, and down a step into another, and along a winding passage into a third, so that each part of the house had its individuality. To these houses life fitted itself and grew to them; they were not mere walls, but became part of existence. A man's house was not only his castle, a man's house was himself. He could not tear himself away from his house, it was like tearing up the shrieking mandrake by the root, almost death itself. Now we walk in and out of our brick boxes unconcerned whether we live in this villa or that, here or yonder. Dark beams inlaid in the walls support the gables; heavier timber, placed horizontally, forms, as it were, the foundation of the first floor. This horizontal beam has warped a little in the course of time, the alternate heat and cold of summers and winters that make centuries. Up to this beam the lower wall is built of brick set to curve of the timber, from which circumstance it would appear to be a modern insertion. The beam, we may be sure, was straight originally, and the bricks have been fitted to the curve which it subsequently took. Time, no doubt, ate away the lower work of wood, and necessitated the insertion of new materials. The slight curve of the great beam adds, I think, to the interest of the old place, for it is a curve that has grown and was not premeditated; it has grown like the bough of a tree, not from any set human design. This, too, is the character of the house. It is not large, nor overburdened with gables, not ornamental, nor what is called striking, in any way, but simply an old English house, genuine and true. The warm sunlight falls on the old red tiles, the dark beams look the darker for the glow of light, the shapely cone of the hop-oast rises at the end; there are swallows and flowers, and ricks and horses, and so it is beautiful because it is natural and honest. It is the simplicity that makes it so touching, like the words of an old ballad. Now at Mayfield there is a timber house which is something of a show place, and people go to see it, and which certainly has many more lines in its curves and woodwork, but yet did not appeal to me, because it seemed too purposely ornamental. A house designed to look well, even age has not taken from its artificiality. Neither is there any cone nor cart-horses about. Why, even a tall chanticleer makes a home look homely. I do like to see a tall proud chanticleer strutting in the yard and barely giving way as I advance, almost ready to do battle with a stranger like a mastiff. So I prefer the simple old home by Buckhurst Park."

ASHDOWN FOREST

The forest of which Ashdown Forest was a part extended once in unbroken sombre density from Kent to Hampshire, a distance of 120 miles. It was known to the Romans as Sylva Anderida, giving its name to Anderida (or Pevensey) on the edge of it; to the Saxons it was Andreaswald. Wolves, wild boar and deer then roamed its dark recesses. Our Ashdown Forest—all that now remains of this wild track—was for long a Royal hunting ground. Edward III. granted it to John of Gaunt, who, there's no doubt, often came hither for sport. It is supposed that he built a chapel near Nutley ("Chapel Wood" marks the site) where, on one occasion at least, John Wycliffe the reformer officiated. At Forest Row, as we have seen, the later lords who hunted here built their lodges and kept their retainers. There are no longer any deer in the Forest; the modern sportsman approaches it with a cleek where his forerunner carried a bow. A hundred years ago, in the smuggling days, it was a very dangerous region.

ASHDOWN FOREST, FROM EAST GRINSTEAD.

Hartfield, the village next to Withyham in the west, is uninteresting; but it has a graceful church, and at Bolebroke, once the home of the Dalyngruges, whom we met at Bodiam, and later of the Sackvilles, are the remains of a noble brick mansion. The towered gateway still stands, and it is not difficult to reconstruct in the mind's eye the house in its best period. Of old cottage architecture Hartfield also has a pretty example in Lych-Gate Cottage, by the churchyard. "Castle field," north of the village, probably marks the site of an ancient castle, or hunting lodge, of the Barons of Pevensey. That there was good hunting in these parts the name Hartfield itself goes to prove.

OUR JOURNEY'S END

Between Withyham and Hartfield in the north, and Crowborough Beacon and Wych Cross in the south, is some of the finest open country in Sussex, where one may walk for hours and meet no human creature. Here are silent desolate woods—the Five Hundred Acre Wood, under Crowborough, chief of them—and vast wastes of undulating heath, rising here and there to great heights crowned with fir trees, as at Gill's Lap. A few enclosed estates interrupt the forest's open freedom, but nothing can tame it. Sombre dark heather gives the prevailing note, but between Old Lodge and Pippinford Park I once came upon a green and luxuriant valley that would not have been out of place in Tyrol; while there is a field near Chuck Hatch where in April one may see more dancing daffodils than ever Wordsworth did.

And here we leave the county.

CHAPTER XLI

THE SUSSEX DIALECT

French words at Hastings and Rye—Saxon on the farms—Mr. W. D. Parish's *Dictionary of the Sussex Dialect*—The rules of the game—The raciest of the words—A Sussex criticism of Disraeli—The gender of a Sussex nose—A shepherd's adventures—Sussex words in America—"The Song of Solomon" in the Sussex vernacular.

The body of the Sussex dialect is derived from the Saxon. Its accessories can be traced to the Celts, to the Norse—thus *rape*, a division of the county, is probably an adaptation of the Icelandic *hreppr*—and to the French, some hundreds of Huguenots having fled to our shores after the Edict of Nantes. The Hastings fishermen, for example, often say *boco* for plenty, and *frap* to strike; while in the Rye neighbourhood, where the Huguenots were strongest, such words as *dishabil* meaning untidy, undressed, and *peter grievous* (from *petit-grief*) meaning fretful, are still used.

But Saxon words are, of course, considerably more common. You meet them at every turn. A Sussex auctioneer's list that lies before me—a catalogue of live and dead farming stock to be sold at a homestead under the South Downs—is full of them. So blunt and sturdy they are, these ancient primitive terms of the soil: "Lot 1. Pitch prong, two half-pitch prongs, two 4-speen spuds, and a road hoe. Lot 5. Five short prongs, flint spud, dung drag, two turnip pecks, and two shovels. Lot 9. Six hay rakes, two scythes and sneaths, cross-cut saw, and a sheep hook. Lot

454

39. Corn chest, open tub, milking stool, and hog form. Lot 43. Bushel measure, shaul and strike. Lot 100. Rick borer. Lot 143. Eight knaves and seven felloes. Lot 148. Six dirt boards and pair of wood hames. Lot 152. Wheelwright's sampson. Lot 174. Set of thill harness. Lot 201. Three plough bolts, three tween sticks. Lot 204. Sundry harness and whippances. Lot 208. Tickle plough. Lot 222. Iron turnwrist [pronounced turn-riced] plough. Lot 242. 9-time scarifier. Lot 251. Clod crusher. Lot 252. Hay tedder." From another catalogue more ram=alogues, these abrupt and active little words might be called, butt at one. As "Lot 4. Flint spud, two drain scoops, bull lead and five dibbles. Lot 10. Dung rake and dung devil. Lot 11. Four juts and a zinc skip." Farm labourers are men of little speech, and it is often needful that voices should carry far. Hence this crisp and forcible reticence. The vocabulary of the country-side undergoes few changes; and the noises to-day made by the ox-herd who urges his black and smoking team along the hill-side are precisely those that Piers Plowman himself would have used.

SAXON PERSISTENT

Another survival may be noticed in objurgation. A Sussex man swearing by Job, as he often does, is not calling in the aid of the patient sufferer of Uz, but Jobe, the Anglo-Saxon Jupiter.

A few examples of Sussex speech, mainly drawn from Mr. Parish's *Dictionary of the Sussex Dialect* will help to add the true flavour to these pages. Mr. Parish's little book is one of the best of its kind; that it is more than a contribution to etymology a very few quotations will show.

THE SUSSEX RULES

Mr. Parish lays down the following general principles of the Sussex tongue:—

a before double *d* becomes *ar*; whereby ladder and adder are pronounced larder and arder.

a before double *l* is pronounced like *o*; fallow and tallow become foller and toller.

a before *t* is expanded into *ea*; rate, mate, plate, gate, are pronounced rêât, mêât, plêât, gêât.

a before *ct* becomes *e*; as satisfection, for satisfaction.

e before *ct* becomes *a*; and affection, effect and neglect are pronounced affaction, effact and neglact.

Double *e* is pronounced as *i* in such words as sheep, week, called ship and wick; and the sound of double *e* follows the same rule in fild for field.

Having pronounced *ee* as *i*, the Sussex people in the most impartial manner pronounce *i* as *ee*; and thus mice, hive, dive, become meece, heeve, and deeve.

i becomes *e* in pet for pit, spet for spit, and similar words.

io and *oi* change places respectively; and violet and violent become voilet and voilent, while boiled and spoiled are bioled and spioled.

o before *n* is expanded into *oa* in such words as pony, dont, bone; which are pronounced pôâny, dôânt, bôân.

o before *r* is pronounced as *a*; as carn and marning, for corn and morning.

o also becomes *a* in such words as rad, crass, and crap, for rod, cross, and crop.

ou is elongated into *aou* in words like hound, pound, and mound; pronounced haound, paound, and maound.

The final *ow*, as in many other counties, is pronounced er, as foller for fallow.

The peculiarities with regard to the pronunciation of consonants are not so numerous as those of the vowels, but they are very decided, and seem to admit of less variation.

Double *t* is always pronounced as *d*; as liddle for little, &c., and the *th* is invariably *d*; thus the becomes *de*; and these, them, theirs—dese, dem, deres.

456

d in its turn is occasionally changed into *th*; as in fother for fodder.

The final *sp* in such words as wasp, clasp, and hasp are reversed to wapse, clapse and hapse.

Words ending in *st* have the addition of a syllable in the possessive case and the plural, and instead of saying that "some little birds had built their nests near the posts of Mr. West's gate," a Sussex boy would say, "the birds had built their nestes near the postes of Mr. Westes' gate."

EAST AND WEST

Roughly speaking, Sussex has little or no dialect absolutely its own; for the country speech of the west is practically that also of Hampshire, and of the east, that of Kent. The dividing line between east and west, Mr. Cripps of Steyning tells me, is the Adur, once an estuary of the sea rather than the stream it now is, running far inland and separating the two Sussexes with its estranging wave.

Mr. Parish's pages supply the following words and examples of their use, chosen almost at random:—

Adone (Have done, Leave off): I am told on good authority that when a Sussex damsel says, "Oh! do adone," she means you to go on; but when she says, "Adone-do," you must leave off immediately.

Crownation (Coronation): "I was married the day the Crownation was, when there was a bullock roasted whole up at Furrel [Firle] Park. I dôân't know as ever I eat anything so purty in all my life; but I never got no further than Furrel cross-ways all night, no more didn't a good many."

Dentical (Dainty): "My Master says that this here Prooshian (query Persian) cat what you gave me is a deal too dentical for a poor man's cat; he wants one as will catch the meece and keep herself."

Dunnamany (I do not know how many): "There was a dunnamany people come to see that gurt hog of mine when she was took bad, and they all guv it in as she was took with the information. We did all as ever we could for her. There was a bottle of stuff what I had from the doctor, time my leg was so bad, and we took and mixed it in with some milk and give it to her lew warm, but naun as we could give her didn't seem to do her any good."

Foreigner (A stranger; a person who comes from any other county but Sussex): I have often heard it said of a woman in this village, who comes from Lincolnshire, that "she has got such a good notion of work that you'd never find out but what she was an Englishwoman, without you was to hear her talk."

"FRENCHYS"

Frenchy (A foreigner of any country who cannot speak English, the nationality being added or not, as the case seems to require): thus an old fisherman, giving an account of a Swedish vessel which was wrecked on the coast a year or two ago, finished by saying that he thought the French Frenchys, take 'em all in all, were better than the Swedish Frenchys, for he could make out what they were driving at, but he was all at sea with the others.

Heart (Condition; said of ground): "I've got my garden into pretty good heart at last, and if so be as there warn't quite so many sparrs and greybirds and roberts and one thing and t'other, I dunno but what I might get a tidy lot of sass. But there! 'taint no use what ye do as long as there's so much varmint about."

Hill (The Southdown country is always spoken of as "The Hill" by the people in the Weald): "He's gone to the hill, harvesting."

Ink-horn (Inkstand): "Fetch me down de inkhorn, mistus; I be g'wine to putt my harnd to dis here partition to Parliament. 'Tis agin de Romans, mistus; for if so be as de Romans gets de upper harnd an us, we shall be burnded, and bloodshedded, and have our Bibles took away from us, and dere'll be a hem set out."

Justabout (Certainly, extremely): "I justabout did enjoy myself up at the Cristial Palace on the Forresters' day, but there was a terr'ble gurt crowd; I should think there must have been two or three hundred people a-scrouging about."

Know (Used as a substantive for knowledge): "Poor fellow, he has got no know whatsumdever, but his sister's a nice knowledgeable girl."

Lamentable (Very): This word seems to admit of three degrees of comparison, which are indicated by the accentuation, thus:—

POSITIVE, COMPARATIVE, SUPERLATIVE

Positive—Lamentable (as usually pronounced).
Comparative—Larmentable.
Superlative—Larmentââble.

"'Master Chucks,' he says to me says he, "tis larmentable purty weather, Master Crockham.' 'Larmentââble!' says I."

Larder (Corruption of ladder): "Master's got a lodge down on the land yonder, and as I was going across t'other day-morning to fetch a larder we keeps there, a lawyer catched holt an me and scratched my face." (Lawyer: A long bramble full of thorns, so called because, "When once they gets a holt on ye, ye dôânt easy get shut of 'em.")

Leetle (diminutive of little): "I never see one of these here gurt men there's s'much talk about in the pêâpers, only once, and that was up at Smiffle Show adunnamany years agoo. Prime minister, they told me he was, up at Lunnon; a leetle, lear, miserable, skinny-looking chap as ever I see [Disraeli, I imagine]. 'Why,' I says, 'we dôân't count our minister to be much, but he's a deal primer-looking than what yourn be.'"

Loanst (A loan): "Will you lend mother the loanst of a little tea?"

Master (Pronounced Mass). The distinctive title of a married labourer. A single man will be called by his Christian name all his life long; but a married man, young or old, is "Master" even to his most intimate friend and fellow workmen, as long as he can earn his own livelihood; but as soon as he becomes past work he turns into "the old gentleman," leaving the bread-winner to rank as master of the household. "Master" is quite a distinct title from "Mr." which is always pronounced Mus, thus: "Mus" Smith is the employer. "Master" Smith is the man he employs. The old custom of the wife speaking of her husband as her "master" still lingers among elderly people; but both the word and the reasonableness of its use are rapidly disappearing in the present generation. It may be mentioned here that they say in Sussex that the rosemary will never blossom except where "the mistus" is master.

May be and Mayhap (Perhaps). "May be you knows Mass Pilbeam? No! dôân't ye? Well, he was a very sing'lar marn was Mass Pilbeam, a very sing'lar marn! He says to he's mistus one day, he says, 'tis a long time, says he, sence I've took a holiday—so cardenly, nex marnin' he laid abed till purty nigh seven o'clock, and then he brackfustes, and then he goos down to the shop and buys fower ounces of barca, and he sets hisself down on the maxon, and there he set, and there he smoked and smoked and smoked all the whole day long, for, says he, 'tis a long time sence I've had a holiday! Ah, he was a very sing'lar marn—a very sing'lar marn indeed."

Queer (To puzzle): "It has queered me for a long time to find out who that man is; and my mistus she's been quite in a quirk over it. He dôânt seem to be quaint with nobody, and he dôânt seem to have no business, and for all that he's always to and thro', to and thro', for everlastin'."

"MUS REYNOLDS"

Reynolds ("Mus Reynolds" is the name given to the fox): When I was first told that "Muss Reynolds come along last night" he was spoken of so intimately that I supposed he must be some old friend, and expressed a hope that he had been hospitably received. "He helped hisself," was the reply; and thereupon followed the explanation, illustrated by an exhibition of mutilated poultry.

Short (Tender): A rat-catcher once told me that he knew many people who were in the habit of eating barn-fed rats, and he added, "When they're in a pudding you could not tell them from a chick, they eat so short and purty."

Shruck (Shrieked): An old woman who was accidentally locked up in a church where she was slumbering in a high pew, said, "I shruck till I could shruck no longer, but no one comed, so I up and tolled upon the bell."

Spannel (To make dirty foot-marks about a floor, as a spaniel dog does): "I goos into the kitchen and I says to my mistus, I says ('twas of a Saddaday), 'the old sow's hem ornary,' I says. 'Well,' says she, 'there ain't no call for you to come spanneling about my clean kitchen any more for that,' she says; so I goos out and didn't say naun, for you can't never make no sense of women-folks of a Saddaday."

Surelye: There are few words more frequently used by Sussex people than this. It has no special meaning of its own, but it is added at the end of any sentence to which particular emphasis is required to be given.

Tedious (Excessive; very): "I never did see such tedious bad stuff in all my life." Mr. Parish might here be supplemented by the remark that his definition explains the use of the word by old Walker, as related by Nyren, when bowling to Lord Frederick Beauclerk, "Oh," he said, "that was tedious near you, my lord."

Unaccountable: A very favourite adjective which does duty on all occasions in Sussex. A countryman will scarcely speak three sentences without dragging in this word. A friend of mine who had been remonstrating with one of his parishioners for abusing the parish clerk beyond the bounds of neighbourly expression, received the following answer:—"You be quite right, sir; you be quite right. I'd no ought to have said what I did, but I dôânt mind telling you to your head what I've said a many times behind your back.—We've got a good shepherd, I says, an axcellent shepherd, but he's got an unaccountable bad dog!"

Valiant (Vaillant, French. Stout; well-built): "What did you think of my friend who preached last Sunday, Master Piper?" "Ha! he was a valiant man; he just did stand over the pulpit! Why you bçânt nothing at all to him! See what a noble paunch he had!"

"PAUL PODGAM"

Yarbs (Herbs): An old man in East Sussex said that many people set much store by the doctors, but for his part, he was one for the yarbs, and Paul Podgam was what he went by. It was not for some time that it was discovered that by Paul Podgam he meant the polypodium fern.

Such are some of the pleasant passages in Mr. Parish's book. In Mr. Coker Egerton's *Sussex Folk and Sussex Ways* is an amusing example of gender in Sussex. The sun, by the way, is always she or her to the Sussex peasant, as to the German savant; but it is not the only unexpected feminine in the county. Mr. Egerton gives a conversation in a village school, in which the master bids Tommy blow his nose. A little later he returns, and asks Tommy why he has not done so. "Please, sir, I did blow her, but her wouldn't bide blowed."

THE SHEPHERD'S PERILS

In the foregoing examples Mr. Parish has perhaps made the Sussex labourer a thought too epigrammatic: a natural tendency in the illustrations to such a work. The following narrative of adventure from the lips of a South Down shepherd, which is communicated to me by my friend, Mr. C. E. Clayton, of Holmbush, is nearer the normal loquacity of the type:—"I mind one day I'd been to buy some lambs, and coming home in the dark over the bostal, I gets to a field, and I knows there was a gçât, and I kep' beating the hedge with my stick to find the gçât, and at last I found 'en, and I goos to get over 'en, and 'twas one of these here gurt ponds full of foul water I'd mistook for the gçât, and so in I went, all over my head, and I tumbles out again middlin' sharp, and I slips, 'cause 'twas so slubby, and in I goos again, and I do think I should ha' been drownded if it warn't for my stick, and I was that froughtened, and there were some bullocks close by, and I froughtened them splashing about and they began to run round, and that froughtened me; and there—well, I was all wet through and grabby, and when I got home I looked like one of these here water-cress men. But I kep' my pipe in my mouth all the time. I didn't lose 'en."

SUSSEX WORDS IN AMERICA

The late Mr. F. E. Sawyer, another student of Sussex dialect, has remarked on the similarity between Sussex provincialisms and many words which we are accustomed to think peculiarly American. One cause may be the two hundred Sussex colonists taken over by William Penn, who, as we have seen, was at one time Squire of Warminghurst. "In recent years we have gathered from the works of American comic writers and others many words which at first have been termed 'vulgar Americanisms,' but which, on closer examination, have proved to be good old Anglo-Saxon and other terms which had dropped out of notice amongst us, but were retained in the *New* World! Take, for instance, two 'Southern words,' (probably Sussex) quoted by Ray (1674). *Squirm*:—Artemus Ward describes 'Brother Uriah,' of 'the Shakers,' as '*squirming* liked a speared eel,' and, curiously enough, Ray gives 'To *squirm*, to move nimbly about after the manner of an eel. It is spoken of eel.' Another word is 'sass' (for sauce), also quoted by Artemus Ward . . . Mrs. Phœbe Earl Gibbons (an American lady), in a clever and instructive article in *Harper's Magazine* on 'English Farmers' (but, in fact, describing the agriculture, &c., of Sussex in a very interesting way), considers that the peculiarities of the present Sussex dialect resemble those of New England more than of Pennsylvania. She mentions as Sussex phrases used in New England— 'You hadn't ought to do it,' and 'You shouldn't ought'; 'Be you'? for 'Are you'? 'I see him,' for 'I saw.' 'You have a *crock* on your nose,' for a smut;

nuther for neither; *pâssel* for parcel, and a *pucker* for a fuss. In addition she observes that Sussex people speak of 'the *fall*' for autumn and 'guess' and 'reckon' like genuine Yankees." So far Mr. Sawyer. Sussex people also, I might add, "disremember," as Huck Finn used to do.

I should like to close the list of examples of Sussex speech by quoting a few verses from the Sussex version of the "Song of Solomon," which Mr. Lower prepared for Prince Lucien Buonaparte some forty years ago. The experiment was extended to other southern and western dialects, the collection making a little book of curious charm and homeliness. Here is the fourth chapter:—

THE SONG OF SOLOMON

IV

1. Lookee, you be purty, my love, lookee, you be purty. You've got dove's eyes adin yer locks; yer hair is like a flock of goäts dat appear from Mount Gilead.
2. Yer teeth be lik a flock of ship just shared, dat come up from de ship-wash; every one of em bears tweens, an nare a one among em is barren.
3. Yer lips be lik a thread of scarlet, an yer speech is comely; yer temples be lik a bit of a pomgranate adin yer locks.
4. Yer nick is lik de tower of Daöved, built for an armoury, what dey heng a thousan bucklers on, all shields of mighty men.
5. Yer two brestès be lik two young roes, what be tweens, dat feed among de lilies.
6. Till de dee break, an der shadders goo away, I'll git me to de mountain of myrrh, and to de hill of frankincense.
7. You be hem purty, my love; der aünt a spot in ye.
8. Come along wud me from Lebanon, my spouse, wud me from Lebanon: look from de top of Amana, from de top of Shenir an Hermon, from de lions' dens, from de mountain of de leopards.

9. Ye've stole away my heart, my sister, my spouse. Ye've stole away my heart wud one of yer eyes, wud one chain of yer nick.

10. How fair is yer love, my sister, my spouse! how much better is yer love dan wine! an de smell of yer ïntments dan all spices.

11. Yer lips, O my spouse, drap lik de honeycomb; dere's honey an melk under yer tongue; an de smell of yer garments is lik de smell of Lebanon.

12. A fenced garn is my sister, my spouse, a spring shet up, a fountain seäled.

13. Yer plants be an archard of pomegranates wud pleasant fruits, camphire an spikenard.

14. Spikenard an saffron, calamus an cinnamon, wud all trees of frankincense, myrrh, an allers, wud all de best of spices.

15. A fountain of garns, a well of livin waters, an straims from Lebanon.

16. Wake, O north win, an come, ye south; blow upon my garn, dat de spices of it may flow out. Let my beloved come into his garn, an ait his pleasant fruits.

CHAPTER XLII

BEING A POSTSCRIPT TO THE
SECOND EDITION.

It almost necessarily follows that in a book such as this, which in brief compass attempts to take some account of every interesting or charming spot in a large tract of country, there must be certain omissions. To the stranger the survey may seem adequate; but it is a hundred to one that a reader whose home is in Sussex will detect a flippancy or a want of true insight in the treatment of his own village. Nor (rightly) does he sit silent under the conviction.

I find that, with the keenest desire to be just in criticism, I have been unfair to several villages. I have been unfair, for example, to Burpham, which lies between Arundel and Amberley and of which nothing is said; and more than one reader has discovered unfairness to East Sussex. For this the personal equation is perhaps responsible: a West Sussex man, try as he will, cannot have the same enthusiasm for the other side of his county as for his own. For me the sun has always seemed to rise over Beachy Head, the most easterly of our Downs.

The call for a second edition has however enabled me to set right a few errors in the body of the book, and in this additional chapter to amplify and fortify here and there. The result must necessarily be disconnected; but a glance at the index will point the way to what is new.

Concerning Aldworth in Tennyson's poetry (see *page 12*), there is the exquisite stanza to General Hamley:

"You came, and looked, and loved the view
　Long known and loved by me,
Green Sussex fading into blue
　With one gray glimpse of sea."

"Green Sussex fading into blue"—it is the motto for every Down summit, South or North.

SHELLEY AND TRELAWNY

With reference to Shelley and Sussex, my attention has been drawn to an interesting account of Field Place by Mr. Hale White, the author of the Mark Rutherford novels, in an old *Macmillan's Magazine*. Says Mr. White, "Denne Park [at Horsham] might easily have suggested—more easily perhaps than any part of the country near Field Place—the well-known semi-chorus in the *Prometheus* which begins

'The path through which that lovely twain
Have passed, by cedar, pine, and yew,
And each dark tree that ever grew
Is curtained out from heaven's wide blue.'

The *Prometheus*, however, was written when Horsham was well-nigh forgotten"—by its author.

Owing to a curious lapse of memory, I omitted to say that Sompting, near Worthing, should be famous as the home of Edward John Trelawny, author of *The Adventures of a Younger Son*, and the friend of Shelley and Byron. In his Sompting garden, in his old age, Trelawny grew figs, equal, he said, to those of his dear Italy, and lived again his vigorous, picturesque, notable life. Sussex thus owns not only the poet of "Adonais," but the friend who rescued his heart from the flames that consumed his body on the shores of the Gulf, and bearing it to Rome placed over its resting place in the Protestant cemetery the words from the *Tempest* (his own happy choice):—

"Nothing of him that doth fade,
But doth suffer a sea-change
Into something rich and strange."

The old man, powerful and capricious to the last, died at Sompting in 1881, within a year of ninety. His body was removed to Gotha for cremation, and his ashes lie beside Shelley's heart in Rome.

Among the wise men of Lewes I ought not to have overlooked William Durrant Cooper (1812-1875), a shrewd Sussex enthusiast and antiquary, who as long ago as 1836 printed at his own cost a little glossary of the county's provincialisms. The book, publicly printed in 1853, was, of course, superseded by Mr. Parish's admirable collection, but Mr. Cooper showed the way. One of his examples of the use of the West Sussex pronoun *en*, *un*, or *um* might be noted, especially as it involves another quaint confusion of sex. *En* and *un* stand for him, her or it; *um* for them. Thus, "a blackbird flew up and her killed 'n'"; that is to say, he killed it.

THE ANGEL'S FAN

Among the Harleian MSS. at the British Museum is the account of a supernatural visitation to Rye in 1607. The visitants were angels, their fortunate entertainer being a married woman. She, however, by a lapse in good breeding, undid whatever good was intended for her. "And after that appeared unto her 2 angells in her chamber, and one of them having a white fan in her hand did let the same fall; and she stooping to take it upp, the angell gave her a box on the eare, rebukinge her that she a mortall creature should presume to handle matters appertayninge to heavenlie creatures."

ROBERTSON OF BRIGHTON

It was an error to omit from *Chapter XVII* all reference to Frederick William Robertson—Robertson of Brighton—who from 1847 until 1853 exerted his extraordinary influence from the pulpit of Trinity Chapel, opposite the post-office, and from his home at 9, Montpellier Terrace.

Of Robertson's quickening religion I need not speak; but it is interesting to know that much of his magnetic eloquence was the result of the meditations which he indulged in his long and feverish rambles over the Downs. His favourite walk was to the Dyke (before exploitation had come upon it), and he loved also the hills above Rottingdean. Robertson, says Arnold's memoir, "would walk any man 'off his legs,' as the saying goes. He not only walked; he ran, he leaped, he bounded. He walked as fast and as incessantly as Charles Dickens, and, like Dickens, his mind was in a state of incessant activity all the time. There was not a bird of the air or a flower by the wayside that was not known to him. His knowledge of birds would have matched that of the collector of the Natural History Museum in his favourite Dyke Road."

Robertson often journeyed into Sussex on little preaching or lecturing missions (he found the auditors of Hurstpierpoint "very bucolic"), and his family were fond of the retirement of Lindfield. On one occasion Robertson brought them back himself, writing afterwards to a friend that in that village he "strongly felt the beauty and power of English country scenery and life to calm, if not to purify, the hearts of those whose lives are habitually subjected to such influences."

Mr. Arnold's book, I might add, has some pleasant pages about Sussex and Brighton in Robertson's day, with glimpses of Lady Byron, his ardent devotee, and, at Old Shoreham, of Canon Mozley.

And here I might mention that for a very charming account of a still earlier Brighton, though not the earliest, the reader should go to a little story called *Round About a Brighton Coach Office*, which was published a few years ago. It has a very fragrant old-world flavour.

To Chichester, I should have recorded, belongs a Sussex saint, Saint Richard, Bishop of Chichester in the thirteenth century, and a great man. In 1245 he found the Sussex see an Augæan stable; but he was equal to the labour of cleansing it. He deprived the corrupt clergy of their benefices with an unhesitating hand, and upon their successors and those that remained he imposed laws of comeliness and simplicity. His reforms were many and various: he restored hospitality to its high place among the duties of rectors; he punished absentees; he excommunicated usurers; while (a revolutionist indeed!) priests who spoke indistinctly or at too great a pace were suspended. Also, I doubt not, he was hostile to locked churches. Furthermore, he advocated the Crusades like another Peter the Hermit.

Richard's own life was exquisitely thoughtful and simple. An anecdote of his brother, who assisted him in the practical administration of the diocese, helps us to this side of his character. "You give away more than your income," remarked this almoner-brother one day. "Then sell my silver," said Richard, "it will never do for me to drink out of silver cups while our Lord is suffering in His poor. Our father drank heartily out of common crockery, and so can I. Sell the plate."

Richard penetrated on foot to the uttermost corners of his diocese to see that all was well. He took no holiday, but would often stay for a while at Tarring, near Worthing, with Simon, the parish priest and his great friend. Tradition would have Richard the planter of the first of the Tarring figs, and indeed, to my mind, he is more welcome to that honour than Saint Thomas à Becket, who competes for the credit—being more a Sussex man. In his will Richard left to Sir Simon de Terring (sometimes misprinted Ferring) his best palfrey and a commentary on the Psalms.

SAINT RICHARD

The Bishop died in 1253 and he was at once canonised. To visit his grave in the nave of Chichester Cathedral (it is now in the south transept) was a sure means to recovery from illness, and it quickly became a place of pilgrimage. April 3 was set apart in the calendar as Richard's day, and very pleasant must have been the observance in the Chichester streets. In 1297 we find Edward I. giving Lovel the harper 6*s*. 6*d*. for singing the Saint's praises; but Henry VIII. was to change all this. On December 14th, 1538, it being, I imagine, a fine day, the Defender of the Faith signed a paper ordering Sir William Goring and William Ernely, his Commissioners, to repair to Chichester Cathedral and remove "the bones, shrine, &c., of a certain Bishop—which they call S. Richard," to the Tower of London. That the Commissioners did their work we know from their account for the same, which came to £40. In the reformed prayer-book, however, Richard's name has been allowed to stand among the black letter saints.

BISHOP WILBERFORCE

Under Chichester I ought also to have mentioned John William Burgon (1813-1888), Dean of Chichester for the last twelve years of his life and the author of that admirable collection of half-length appreciations, *The Lives of Twelve Good Men*, one of whom, Bishop Wilberforce, lived within call at Woollavington, under the shaggy escarpment of the Downs some ten miles to the north-east. Dean Burgon thus happily touches off the Bishop in his South Down retreat:—

... "But it was on the charms of the pleasant landscape which surrounded his Sussex home that he chiefly expatiated on such occasions, leaning rather heavily on some trusty arm—(I remember how he leaned on *mine!*)—while he tapped with his stick the bole of every favourite tree which came in his way (by-the-by, *every* tree seemed a favourite), and had something to tell of its history and surpassing merits. Every farm-house, every peep at the distant landscape, every turn in the road, suggested some pleasant remark or playful anecdote. He had a word for every man, woman, and child he met,—for he knew them all. The very cattle were greeted as old acquaintances. And how he did delight in discussing the flora of the neighbourhood, the geological formations, every aspect of the natural history of the place!"

BURPHAM AND HARDHAM

A very properly indignant friend has reminded me of the claims of Burpham in the following words. "Two miles up the Arun valley from Arundel is Burpham, a pretty village on the west edge of the Downs and overhanging the river. Between South Stoke and Arundel the old course of the Arun runs in wide curves, and in modern times a straight new bed has been cut, under Arundel Park and past the Black Rabbit, making, with the old curves, the form of the letter B. Burpham lies at the head of the lower loop of the B, and while there is plenty of water in the loop to row up with the flood tide and down with the ebb, the straight main stream diverts nearly all the holiday traffic and leaves Burpham the most peaceful village within fifty miles of London. The seclusion is the more complete because the roads from the South end in the village and there is no approach by road from East or West or North. The Church contains a Lepers' window, and passengers by the railway can see, to the right of the red roofs of the village and over the line of low chalk cliffs, a white path still called the Lepers' Path, which winds away in to the lonely hollows of the Downs.

"A curious feature of Burpham is a high rampart of earth, running eastward from the cliff by the river, which according to local tradition was constructed in the days of the Danish pirates. It is said to be doubtful whether the rampart was erected by the Saxon villagers for their own protection, or by the Danes as their first stronghold on the rising ground after they had sailed up the Arun from Littlehampton. The fine name of the neighbouring Warningcamp Hill, from which there is a great outlook over the flat country past Arundel Castle to Chichester Cathedral and the cliffs of the Isle of Wight, suggests memories of the same period."

Of the little retiring church of St. Botolph, Hardham, lying among low meadows between Burpham and Pulborough, I ought also to have spoken, for it contains perhaps the earliest complete series of mural painting in England. The church dates from the eleventh century, and the paintings, says Mr. Philip Mainwaring Johnson, who has studied them with the greatest care, cannot be much less old. The subjects are the Annunciation, the Nativity, the appearance of the Star, the Magi presenting their Gifts, and so forth, with one or two less familiar themes added, such as Herod conferring with his Counsellors and the Torments of Hell. There are the remains also of a series of Moralities drawn from the parable of Dives and Lazarus, and of a series illustrating the life of St. George. The little church, which perhaps has every right to call itself the oldest picture gallery in England, should not be missed by any visitor to Pulborough.

THE TIPTEERS

At West Wittering in the Manhood Peninsula, a little village on which the sea has hostile designs, is still performed at Christmas a time-honoured play the actors of which are half a dozen boys or men known as the Tipteers. Their words are not written, but are transmitted orally from one generation of players to another. Mr. J. I. C. Boger, however, has taken them down for the S. A. C. The subject once again, as in some of the Hardham mural paintings, is the life of St. George, here called King George; and the play has the same relation to drama that the Hardham frescoes have to a picture. I quote a little:—

Third Man—Noble Captain:
      In comes I, the Noble Captain,
      Just lately come from France;

With my broad sword and jolly Turk [dirk]
I will make King George dance.

Fourth Man—King George [*i.e.*, Saint George]:
    In comes I, King George,
    That man of courage bold,
    With my broad sword and sphere [spear]
    I have won ten tons of gold.
    I fought the fiery Dragon
    And brought it to great slaughter,
    And by that means I wish to win
    The King of Egypt's daughter.
    Neither unto thee will I bow nor bend.
    Stand off! stand off!
    I will not take you to be my friend.

Noble Captain:
    Why, sir, why, have I done you any kind of wrong?

King George:
    Yes, you saucy man, so get you gone.

Noble Captain:
    You saucy man, you draw my name,
    You ought to be stabb'd, you saucy man.

King George:
    Stab or stabs, the least is my fear;
    Point me the place
    And I will meet you there.

Noble Captain:

> The place I 'point is on the ground
> And there I will lay your body down
> Across the water at the hour of five.

King George:

> Done, sir, done! I will meet you there,
> If I am alive I will cut you, I will slay you,
> All for to let you know that I am King George over Great
Britain O!
>
> [FIGHT: *King George wounds the Noble Captain.*]

Until the close is almost reached the West Wittering Tipteers preserve the illusion of mediæval mummery. But the concluding song transports us to the sentiment of the modern music hall. Its chorus runs, with some callousness:—

> "We never miss a mother till she's gone,
> Her portrait's all we have to gaze upon,
>   We can fancy see her there,
>   Sitting in an old armchair;
> We never miss a mother till she's gone."

GRANDMOTHER FOWINGTON

THE PHARISEES

Mark Antony Lower's *Contributions to Literature*, 1845, contains a pleasant essay on the South Downs which I overlooked when I was writing this book, but from which I now gladly take a few passages. It gives me, for example, a pendent to William Blake's description of a fairy's funeral on *page 64*, in the shape of a description of a fairy's revenge, from the lips of Master Fowington, a friend of Mr. Lower, who was one that believed in Pharisees (as Sussex calls fairies) as readily and unreservedly as we believe in wireless telegraphy. Mas' Fowington had, indeed, two very good reasons for his credulity. One was that the Pharisees are mentioned in the Bible and therefore must exist; the other was that his grandmother, "who was a very truthful woman," had seen them with her own eyes "time and often." "They was liddle folks not more than a foot high, and used to be uncommon fond of dancing. They jound[4] hands and formed a circle, and danced upon it till the grass came three times as green there as it was anywhere else. That's how these here rings come upon the hills. Leastways so they say; but I don't know nothing about it, in tye,[5] for I never seen none an 'em; though to be sure it's very hard to say how them rings do come, if it is'nt the Pharisees that makes 'em. Besides there's our old song that we always sing at harvest supper, where it comes in—'We'll drink and dance like Pharisees.' Now I should like to know why it's put like that 'ere in the song, if it a'nt true."

MAS' MEPPOM'S ADVENTURE

Master Fowington's story of the fairy's revenge runs thus:—

"An ol' brother of my wife's gurt gran'mother *see* some Pharisees once, and 'twould a been a power better if so be he hadn't never seen 'em, or leastways never offended 'em. I'll tell ye how it happened. Jeems Meppom—dat was his naüm—Jeems was a liddle farmer, and used to thresh his own corn. His barn stood in a very *elenge* lonesome place, a goodish bit from de house, and de Pharisees used to come dere a nights and thresh out some wheat and wuts for him, so dat de hep o' threshed corn was ginnerly bigger in de morning dan what he left it overnight. Well, ye see, Mas' Meppom thought dis a liddle odd, and didn't know rightly what to make ant. So bein' an out-and-out bold chep, dat didn't fear man nor devil, as de saying is, he made up his mind dat he'd goo over some night to see how 'twas managed. Well accordingly he went out rather airly in de evenin', and laid up behind de mow, for a long while, till he got rather tired and sleepy, and thought 'twaunt no use a watchin' no longer. It was gittin' pretty handy to midnight, and he thought how he'd goo home to bed. But jest as he was upon de move he heerd a odd sort of a soun' comin' tóe-ards the barn, and so he stopped to see what it was. He looked out of de strah, and what should he catch sight an but a couple of liddle cheps about eighteen inches high or dereaway come into de barn without uppening the doores. Dey pulled off dere jackets and begun to thresh wud two liddle frails as dey had brung wud em at de hem of a rate. Mas' Meppom would a been froughten if dey had been bigger, but as dey was such tedious liddle fellers, he couldn't hardly help bustin right out a laffin'. Howsonever he pushed a hanful of strah into his mouth and so managed to kip quiet a few minutes a lookin' at um— thump, thump; thump, thump, as riglar as a clock.

"At last dey got rather tired and left off to rest derselves, and one an um said in a liddle squeakin' voice, as it might a bin a mouse a talkin':—'I say Puck, I tweat; do you tweat?' At dat Jeems couldn't contain hisself no how, but set up a loud haw-haw; and jumpin' up from de strah hollered out, 'I'll tweat ye, ye liddle rascals; what bisness a you got in my barn?' Well upon dis, de Pharisees picked up der frails and cut away right by him, and as dey passed by him he felt sich a queer pain in de head as if somebody had gi'en him a lamentable hard thump wud a hammer, dat knocked him down as flat as a flounder. How long he laid dere he never rightly knowed, but it must a bin a goodish bit, for when he come to 'twas gittin' dee-light. He could'nt hardly contrive to doddle home, and when he did he looked so tedious bad dat his wife sent for de doctor dirackly. But bless ye, *dat* waunt no use; and old Jeems Meppom knowed it well enough. De doctor told him to kip up his sperits, beein' 'twas onny a fit he had had from bein' a most smothered wud de handful of strah and kippin his laugh down. But Jeems knowed better. 'Tâ-ünt no use, sir,' he says, says he, to de doctor; 'de cuss of de Pharisees is uppán me, and all de stuff in your shop can't do *me* no good.' And Mas' Meppom was right, for about a year ahtawuds he died, poor man! sorry enough dat he'd ever intafçred wud things dat didn't consarn him. Poor ol' feller, he lays buried in de church-aird over yender—leastways so I've heerd my wife's mother say, under de bank jest where de bed of snow-draps grows."

FAIRY RINGS AND DEW PONDS

All who know the Downs must know the fairies' or Pharisees' rings, into which one so often steps. Science gives them a fungoid origin, but Shakespeare, as well as Master Fowington's grandmother, knew that Oberon and Titania's little people alone had the secret. Further proof is to be found in the testimony of John Aubrey, the Wiltshire antiquary, who records that Mr. Hart, curate at Yatton Keynel in 1633-4, coming home over the Downs one night witnessed with his own eyes an "innumerable quantitie of pigmies" dancing round and round and singing, "making all manner of small, odd noises."

A word ought to have been said of the quiet and unexpected dew-ponds of the Downs, upon which one comes so often and always with a little surprise. Perfect rounds they are, reflecting the sky they are so near like circular mirrors set in a white frame. Gilbert White, who was interested in all interesting things, mentions the unfailing character of a little pond near Selborne, which "though never above three feet deep in the middle, and not more than thirty feet in diameter, . . . yet affords drink for three hundred or four hundred sheep, and for at least twenty head of cattle beside." He then asks, having noticed that in May, 1775, when the ponds of the valley were dry, the ponds of the hills were still "little affected," "have not these elevated pools some unnoticed recruits, which in the night-time counterbalance the waste of the day?" The answer, which White supplies, is that the hill pools are recruited by dew. "Persons," he writes, "that are much abroad, and travel early and late, such as shepherds, fishermen, &c., can tell what prodigious fogs prevail in the night on elevated downs, even in the hottest part of summer; and how much the surfaces of things are drenched by those swimming vapours, though, to the senses, all the while, little moisture seems to fall."

Kingsley has a passage on the same subject in his essay, "The Air-Mothers"—"For on the high chalk downs, you know, where farmers make a sheep pond, they never, if they are wise, make it in the valley or on a hillside, but on the bleakest top of the very highest down; and there, if they can once get it filled with snow and rain in winter, the blessed dews of night will keep some water in it all the summer thro', while ponds below are utterly dried up." There is, however, another reason why the highest points are chosen, and that is that the chalk here often has a capping of red clay which holds the water.

NICK COSSUM'S HUMOUR

To the *smuggling chapter* might have been added, again with Mr. Lower's assistance, a few words on the difficulties that confronted the London revenue officers in the Sussex humour. To be confounded by too swift a horse or too agile a "runner" was all in the night's work; but to be hoodwinked and bamboozled by the deliberate stealthy southern fun must have been eternally galling. The Sussex joker grinds slowly and exceeding small; but the flour is his. "There was Nick Cossum the blacksmith [the words are a shepherd's, talking to Mr. Lower]; he was a sad plague to them. Once he made an exciseman run several miles after him, to take away a keg of *yeast* he was a-carrying to Ditchling! Another time as he was a-going up New Bostall, an exciseman, who knew him of old, saw him a-carrying a tub of hollands. So he says, says he, 'Master Cossum, I must have that tub of yours, I reckon!' 'Worse luck, I suppose you must,' says Nick in a civil way, 'though it's rather again' the grain to be robbed like this; but, however, I am a-going your road, and we can walk together—there's no law again' that I expect.' 'Oh, certainly not,' says the other, taking of the tub upon his shoulders. So they chatted along quite friendly and *chucker*[6] like till they came to a cross road, and Nick wished the exciseman good bye. After Nick had got a little way, he turned round all of a sudden and called out: 'Oh, there's one thing I forgot; here's a little bit o' paper that belongs to the keg.' 'Paper,' says the exciseman, 'why, that's a *permit*,' says he; 'why didn't you show me that when I took the hollands?' 'Oh,' says Nick, as saucy as Hinds, 'why, if I had done that,' says he, 'you wouldn't a carried my tub for me all this way, would you?'"

ANOTHER PARISH CLERK

The story, at the end of *Chapter XIX*, of the clerk in Old Shoreham church, whose loyalty was too much for his ritualism, may be capped by that of a South Down clerk in the east of the county, whose seat in church commanded a view of the neighbourhood. During an afternoon service one Sunday a violent gale was raging which had already unroofed several barns. The time came, says Mr. Lower, for the psalm before the sermon, and the clerk rose to announce it. "Let us sing to the praise and glo—Please, sir, Mas' Cinderby's mill is blowed down!"

ANOTHER MILLER

Another word on Sussex millers. John Oliver, the Hervey of Highdown Hill, had a companion in eccentricity in William Coombs of Newhaven, who, although active as a miller to the end, was for many years a stranger to the inside of his mill owing to a rash statement one night that if what he asseverated was not true he would never enter his mill again. It was not true and henceforward, until his death, he directed his business from the top step—such is the Sussex tenacity of purpose.

Coombs was married at West Dean, but not fortunately. On the way to the church a voice from heaven called to him, "Will-yam Coombs! Will-yam Coombs! if so be that you marry Mary—you'll always be a miserable man." Coombs, who had no false shame, often told the tale, adding, "And I be a miserable man."

Coombs' inseparable companion was a horse which bore him and his merchandise to market. In order to vary the monotony of the animal's own God-given hue, he used to paint it different colours, one day yellow and the next pink, one day green and the next blue, and so on. But this cannot have perplexed the horse so much as his master's idea of mercy; for when its back was over-loaded, not only with sacks of flour, but also with Coombs, that humanitarian, experiencing a pang of sympathy, and exclaiming "The marciful man is marciful to his beast," would lift one of the sacks on to his own shoulders. His marcy, however, did not extend to dismounting. Our Sussex droll, Andrew Boorde, when he invented the wisdom of Gotham, invented also the charity of Coombs. But the story is true.

Coombs must not be considered typical of Sussex. Nor can the tricyclist of Chailey be called typical of Sussex—the weary man who was overtaken by a correspondent of mine on the acclivity called the King's Head Hill, toiling up its steepness on a very old-fashioned, solid-tyred tricycle. He had the brake hard down, and when this was pointed out to him, he replied shrewdly, "Eh master, but her might goo backards." Such whimsical excess of caution, such thorough calculation of all the chances, is not truly typical, nor is the miller's oddity truly typical; and yet if one set forth to find humorous eccentricity, humorous suspicion, and humorous cautiousness at their most flourishing, Sussex is the county for the search.

LONDON TO CHICHESTER

It ought to be known that those Londoners who would care to reach Sussex by Roman road have still Stane Street at their service. With a little difficulty here and there, a little freedom with other people's land, the walker is still able to travel from London to Chichester almost in a bee-line, as the Romans used. Stane Street, which is a southern continuation of Erming Street, pierced London's wall at Billingsgate, and that would therefore be the best starting point. The modern traveller would set forth down the Borough High Street (as the Canterbury Pilgrims did), crossing the track of Watling Street near the Elephant and Castle, and so on the present high road for several not too interesting miles; along Newington Butts, and Kennington Park Road, up Clapham Rise and Balham Hill, and so on through Tooting, Morden, North Cheam, and Ewell. So far all is simple and a little prosaic, but at Epsom difficulties begin. The road from Epsom town to the racecourse climbs to the east of the Durdans and strikes away south-west, on its true course again, exactly at the inn. The point to make for, as straight as may be (passing between Ashstead on the right and Langley Bottom farm on the left), is the Thirty-acres Barn, right on the site. Then direct to Leatherhead Down, through Birchgrove, over Mickleham Down, and so to the high road again at Juniper Hall. Part of the track on this high ground is still called Erming Street by the country folk; part is known as Pebble Lane, where the old Roman road metal has come through. The old street probably followed the present road fairly closely, with a slight deviation near the Burford Bridge Inn, as far as Boxhill Station, whence it took a bee-line to the high ground at Minnickwood by Anstiebury, four miles distant, a little to the west of Holmwood. This, if the line is to be followed, means some deliberate trespassing and a scramble through Dorking churchyard, which is partly on the site.

Hitherto the Roman engineer has wavered now and then, but from Minnickwood to Tolhurst Farm, fifteen miles to the south, the line is absolute. Two miles below Ockley (where it is called Stone Street), at Halehouse Farm, the road must be left again, but after three miles of footpath, field, and wood we hit it once more just above Dedisham, on the road between Guildford and Horsham, and keep it all the way to Pulborough, through Billingshurst, thus named, as I have said, like Billingsgate, after Belinus, Stane Street's engineer. At Pulborough we must cut across country to the camp by Hardham, over water meadows that are too often flooded, and thence, through other fields, arable and pasture, to the hostel on Bignor Hill, which once was Stane Street; passing on the right Mr. Tupper's farm and the field which contains the famous Bignor pavements, relic of the palatial residence of the Governor of the Province of Regnum in the Romans' day; or better still, pausing there, as Roman officers faring to Regnum certainly would in the hope of a cup of Falernian.

The track winding up Bignor Hill is still easily recognisable, and from the summit half Sussex is visible: the flat blue weald in the north, Blackdown's dark escarpment in the north-west, Arundel's shaggy wastes in the east, the sea and the plain in the south, and the rolling turf of the downs all around. Henceforward the road is again straight, nine unfaltering miles to Chichester, which we enter by St. Pancras and East Street. For the first four miles, however, the track is over turf and among woods, Eartham Wood on the right and North Wood on the left, and, after a very brief spell of hard road again, over the side of Halnaker Down. But from Halnaker to Chichester it is turnpike once more, with the savour of the Channel meeting one all the way, and Chichester's spire a friendly beacon and earnest of the contiguous delights of the Dolphin, where one may sup in an assembly room spacious enough to hold a Roman century.

BY ROMAN ROAD

Or one might reverse the order and walk out of Sussex into London by the Roman way, or, better still, through London, and on by Erming Street to the wall of Antoninus. Merely to walk to London and there stop is nothing; merely to walk from London is little; but to walk through London . . . there is glamour in that! To come bravely up from the sea at Bosham, through Chichester, over the Downs to the sweet domestic peaceful green weald, over the Downs again and plunge into the grey city (perhaps at night) and out again on the other side into the green again, and so to the north, *left-right*, *left-right*, just as the clanking Romans did; that would be worth doing and worth feeling.

JOHN HORNE

The best knower of Sussex of recent times has died since this book was printed: one who knew her footpaths and spinneys, her hills and farms, as a scholar knows his library. John Horne of Brighton was his name: a tall, powerful man even in his old age—he was above eighty at his death—with a wise, shrewd head stored with old Sussex memories: hunting triumphs; the savour of long, solitary shooting days accompanied by a muzzle-loader and single dog—such days as Knox describes in *Chapter V*; historic cricket matches; stories of the Sussex oddities, the long-headed country lawyers, the Quaker autocrats, the wild farmers, the eccentric squires; characters of favourite horses and dogs (such was the mobility of his countenance and his instinct for drama that he could bring before you visibly any animal he described); early railway days (he had ridden in the first train that ran between Brighton and Southwick); fierce struggles over rights-of-way; reminiscences of old Brighton before a hundredth part of its present streets were made; and all the other body of curious lore for which one must go to those whose minds dwell much in the past. Coming of Quaker stock, as he did, his memory was good and well-ordered, and his observation quick and sound. What he saw he saw, and he had the unusual gift of vivid precise narrative and a choice of words that a literary man should envy.

A favourite topic of conversation between us was the best foot route between two given points—such as Steyning and Worthing, for example, or Lewes and Shoreham. Seated in his little room, with its half-a-dozen sporting prints on the wall and a scene or two of old Brighton, he would, with infinite detail, removing all possibility of mistake, describe the itinerary, weighing the merits of alternative paths with profound solemnity, and proving the wisdom of every departure from the more obvious track. Were Sussex obliterated by a tidal wave, and were a new county to be constructed on the old lines, John Horne could have done it.

A SUSSEX ENTHUSIAST

Of his talk I found it impossible to tire, and I shall never cease to regret that circumstances latterly made visits to him very infrequent. Towards the end his faculties now and then were a little dimmed; but the occlusion carried compensation with it. To sit with an old man and, being mistaken by him for one's own grandfather, to be addressed as though half a century had rolled away, is an experience that I would not miss.

To the end John Horne dressed as the country gentlemen of his young days had dressed; he might have stepped out of one of Alken's pictures, for he possessed also the well nourished complexion, the full forehead, and the slight fringe of whiskers which distinguished Alken's merry sportsmen. His business taking him deep into the county among the farms, he was always in walking trim, with an umbrella crooked over one arm, his other hand grasping the obtuse-angled handle of a ground-ash stick. These sticks, of which he had scores, he cut himself, his eye never losing its vigilance as he passed through a copse. Under the handle, about an inch from the end, he screwed a steel peg, so that the stick, when it was not required, might hang upon his arm; while a long, stout pin, with a flat brass head, was also inserted, in case his pipe needed cleaning out. Thus furnished, with umbrella and stick, pipe and a sample of his merchandise, John Horne, in his wide collar, his ample coat with vast pockets over the hips, his tight trousers, and his early-Victorian headgear, has been, these fifty years, a familiar figure in the Weald as he passed from farm to farm at a steady gait, his interested glances falling this way and that, noting every change (and perhaps a little resenting it, for he was of the old Tory school), and his genial salutation ready for all acquaintances. But he is now no more, and Sussex is the poorer, and the historian of Sussex poorer still. I believe he would have liked this book; but how he would have shaken his wise head over its omissions!

FOOTNOTES:

4 This is the Sussex preterite of the verb "to join."
5 *In tye*—not I.
6 *Chucker*, in a cheerful, cordial manner.

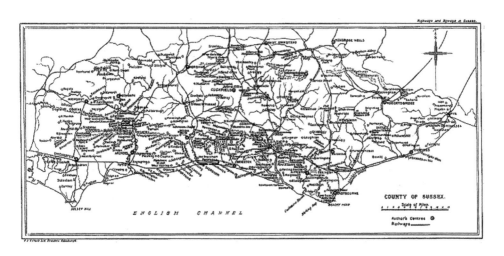

MAP OF THE COUNTY OF SUSSEX